History of Caithness

WICK ARMS

Wick
WILLIAM RAE
MDCCCLXXXVII

ACKERGILL TOWER, FROM THE SEA.

SKETCH

OF THE

CIVIL AND TRADITIONAL

HISTORY OF CAITHNESS

FROM THE TENTH CENTURY

BY

JAMES T. CALDER

AUTHOR OF " POEMS FROM JOHN O'GROAT'S," ETC., ETC.

SECOND EDITION

WITH HISTORICAL NOTES

BY

THOMAS SINCLAIR, M.A.
AUTHOR OF "HUMANITIES," ETC.

MAP AND ILLUSTRATIONS

WICK
WILLIAM RAE.
THURSO ; JOHN MALCOLM AND MISS RUSSELL.
1887.

First Published 1887
This edition reprinted 1971
for
Caithness Reprints,
Wick, Caithness

Reprinted 1973

Printed in Great Britain by
Redwood Press Limited
Trowbridge, Wiltshire

PREFACE.

I HAD long cherished a desire to draw up something like a regular history of Caithness, but on making the requisite investigation, I found that neither the public records of the county, nor yet family papers, afforded sufficient materials for the purpose. The present work, therefore, is merely a sketch or outline mostly drawn from other sources, and in some measure aided by local tradition. The writer to whom I have been chiefly indebted for information regarding what may be called the ancient history of Caithness, is Torfæus, whose authority on this point is justly entitled to credit from the following circumstance :—When the Orkney Islands, of which Caithness formed a part of the earldom for so many hundred years, had, from increase of population and proximity to Scotland, become valuable as an appendage to the crown of Norway, an historiographer was appointed to reside in the island of Flotta, and to record all transactions of any public moment that took place in the two counties. These were regularly entered into a diary or journal, entitled the "Codex Flatensis," or Book of Flotta. The work, which was one of national importance, was, for better preservation, afterwards deposited in the royal library at Copenhagen ; and from it, and the "Orkneyinga Saga"—the latter a compilation of Jonas Jonnæus, an Icelandic scholar—Torfæus drew the materials of his history. "Torfæus," says Chambers, "sustains the character of a faithful historian, and the facts which he details are probably as authentic as the early records of any portion of the British empire, while he has enabled us to correct several errors in the commonly-received accounts of Scotland." And Samuel Laing, a still higher authority on this point, says that " his history may be regarded as the only authentic record of affairs in the North for many ages." The period embraced, so far as regards Orkney and Caithness, is from 876 to 1260.

The following are a few of the leading particulars of his personal history. Thormod Torfeson (Torfæus being the Latinised name) was a native of Iceland. His father, Torfe Erlendsen, was a person of some consideration in that country. The son was born in 1636, and educated at the University of Copenhagen. While attending this seminary, he became distinguished as a student ; and his classical acquirements were such that they afterwards procured him the honourable situation of historiographer to Christian V., King of Denmark. His great work, which he composed in Latin, was published about the year 1690, under the title of " Orcades, seu rerum Orcadiensium Historiæ." He is also the author of another curious work entitled " Historia Vinlandiæ Antiquæ," which gives a description of the maritime adventures of the Norwegians and their alleged discovery of America five hundred years before Columbus. He died, according to the best accounts, in 1720 at the advanced age of 84.

With regard to the more modern history of Caithness, my information has been chiefly derived from Sir Robert Gordon's elaborate work, entitled a " Genealogical History of the Earldom of Sutherland," which contains a full account of the various feuds and conflicts which for so long a period existed between the two rival houses of Caithness and Sutherland.

Sir Robert, however, with all his industry and research, cannot be considered an impartial historian. He everywhere discovers a strong prejudice against the Sinclair family ; and his statements in regard to them, and to Caithness matters in general, must be received with large deduction. The continuator of his history, Gilbert Gordon of Sallach, in a eulogy of his many virtues and talents, candidly admits that he was a man of a passionate temper, and a " bitter enemy." Sir Robert was the second son of Alexander, Earl of Sutherland, and Lady Jane Gordon, who was divorced by Bothwell, and was born at Dunrobin 14th May, 1580. He received the best education that Scotland could afford at the time, having attended both the Universities of Edinburgh and St. Andrews. He resided much at the court of King James I. of England. James, with whom he seems to have been a favourite, conferred on him the honour of knighthood, and he also granted him a yearly pension for life of £200 stg. Sir Robert was the ancestor of the Gordonstone family, to whom he bequeathed a large estate in the county of Elgin. He died about the year 1650.

Among other works which I consulted, and which supplied me with some important facts and details, may be mentioned Mackay's " History of the House and Clan of Mackay," Henderson's " Agricultural View of Caithness," Barry's " History of Orkney," Peterkin's " Notes of Orkney," Balfour's " Odal Rights and Feudal Wrongs," Brand's " Description of Orkney, Shetland, and Caithness," " Pennant's Tour," the " Origines Parochiales Scotiæ," and a most interesting volume entitled, " An Account of the Danes and Norwegians in England, Scotland, and Ireland," by J. J. Worsaae, Royal Commissioner for the preservation of the National Monuments of Denmark.

For much interesting information connected with the rentals, roads, and pedigrees of some of the principal families in the county, I am indebted to Sir John Sinclair of Dunbeath; James Sinclair, Esquire of Forss; John Henderson, Esquire, Banker, Thurso; Mr James Mackay, Messenger-at-Arms, Thurso; and Mr George Petrie, Clerk of Supply for the county of Orkney. Mr Sinclair of Forss furnished me with the valuable paper on the Caithness roads, and Mr Mackay with the curious document entitled the " Liberties of Thurso." I would have gladly given, had they been sent me, some more pedigrees of Caithness families, as genealogical details of this kind are to many persons exceedingly interesting.

I have not, from my slight acquaintance with such subjects, touched on the geology, botany, or ornithology of the county. In this respect, however, Caithness presents a wide and varied field, and one which, in skilful hands, I have no doubt would afford materials for a highly interesting volume.

The work which I have ventured to publish is, as I have said, merely an imperfect Sketch. Such as it is, however, it may afford some interest to local readers; and with the help of additional sources of information, should any such cast up, it may prove useful to some future writer in supplying materials for a fuller and more connected history of the county.

J. T. CALDER.

1861.

PREFACE TO SECOND EDITION.

THE first edition of my work on Caithness having been received by the public with a degree of favour exceeding my most sanguine hopes, it is with great pleasure that I now publish a second impression, in which the reader will find a good deal of new and curious information bearing on the civil and traditional history of the county. This has been derived from various sources. To John Henderson, Esq., W.S., in Thurso, I have once more to express my obligations. That gentleman, besides furnishing me with additional notices of his own, very kindly favoured me with the perusal of a manuscript entitled "The past and present state of Caithness," by his brother, the late Patrick Brodie Henderson, M.D., which displays great research on the part of the writer, and is particularly valuable as embodying the statistics of the county from about the year 1700 down to 1837. Dr. Henderson was the eldest son of the late William Henderson, Esquire, Sheriff-Substitute of Caithness, and appears to have been a man of more than ordinary talent and accomplishment. He died at Dingwall, in 1840, of fever caught in the discharge of professional duty.

I might have considerably enlarged my book by giving more of the antiquities and statistics of the county from Dr. Henderson's compilation; but details of this kind, though interesting to a few, appear dry and uninviting to the majority of readers, who relish most the events and incidents of local history when they are related in anything like a readable style. A work chiefly intended for the public must contain somewhat of the element of popularity.

Before concluding, I would here express my obligation also to Mr Alexander Gunn, Braehour Cottage, in the parish of Halkirk, for the striking tradition respecting the capture of Sutherland of Dirlot by Mackay, his uncle, and for several new and authentic particulars connected with the famous duel which was fought by Sinclair of Olrig and Innes of Sandside.

To those conductors of the press who honoured me with favourable notices of the first edition of my book, I have to return my best thanks. The only critical objection of any moment I have seen, is the numerous details of barbarous clan fights, and still more barbarous assassinations, in the olden time, which it has been said have a tendency to shock the feelings of the reader. There is no doubt some truth in this; but if I had purposely omitted all mention of atrocities of this nature, I would not have acted the part of a faithful annalist. I may observe, further, that, so far as regards ancient criminal statistics, Caithness does not present a darker moral picture than any other county in Scotland. Outrages fully as revolting and cruel as any I have described will be found in the local records of them all. Human nature in its progress from barbarism to civilisation is everywhere the same; and to the Christian philanthropist the present condition of Caithness, compared with what it was in former times, will afford a pleasing and happy contrast.

I have only further to add that I have carefully revised the text, and corrected several inaccuracies which had crept into

the former edition, so that it is hoped the work as now published will be found still more worthy of the public approba-
tion.   No doubt errors will be found in this new edition also ;
for it would be ridiculous presumption in a mere annalist to
claim exemption from the common frailty.

J. T. CALDER

1863.

PUBLISHER'S PREFACE.

THIS work was first published in 1861, and having been rapidly sold off, has now been long out of print. The author had prepared a second edition, containing a considerable body of new, interesting, and valuable matter, and was contemplating its early publication, having even written the preface for it, when his lamented death occurred in 1864. The present publisher, having purchased the copyright of the work, at length issues this second edition exactly as it was prepared for publication by the author. A great deal of new matter appears in the text, and a great deal more in the appendix, but both text and appendix stand here precisely as they left Mr Calder's own hands. But these twenty-three years have seen fresh light cast on some portions of Caithness history, and have themselves brought changes with them that require to be recorded, and accordingly a number of supplementary notes have been added, with the view of bringing the information contained in the work in both these respects down to the present date. These supplementary notes have been written in part by Mr Thomas Sinclair, M.A., the best living authority on Caithness history, and in part by various local gentlemen well known in the county for their stores of Caithness lore, among whom we must select for special acknowledgments Mr Charles Bruce, J.P. of Caithness, F.S.A. Scot., who supplies the article on the Hill of Wick case, Mr George Miller Sutherland, solicitor, and Mr

James Grant, teacher, Forres, who contributes the communication on plants lately found in the county. A Map of Caithness has been inserted, reduced from the Ordnance Survey Map, which, it is hoped, will still further enhance the value of the work. The few illustrations given of well-known places in the county will, perhaps, be appreciated by natives at a distance, at least, as they call up thoughts of former days.

February, 1887.

MEMOIR OF THE AUTHOR.

JAMES TRAILL CALDER, author of this work, was the son of
George Calder and Janet Reid, and was born on the 18th
October, 1794, at Stangergill, near the village of Castletown,
in Caithness. His father was at that time gardener to James
Traill, Esq. of Ratter, but was afterwards for many years
farmer and innkeeper in Castletown. When a boy of four,
Calder lost in a fever the use of one of his limbs, and never
recovered it. He received his education first at the parish
school of Olrig under Mr John Abernethy, afterwards minister of Bolton, and then at the parish school of Dunnet,
which was at that time very ably conducted by Mr John Dunn,
afterwards minister of Kirkwall. On leaving school, Calder
was for a short time tutor in the family of Mr Gunn, Dale,
and a little later in that of Mr Mackid, Watten, and then
entered the University of Edinburgh as a student of arts in
November, 1814. His academical course was interrupted by
his appointment to the parochial school of Canisbay in 1815,
and though he eventually completed the usual four years'
curriculum of the student of arts, he did not do so till 1832.
His career at college was one of distinction, more especially
in the department of mental philosophy. In 1820 he took
the fourth prize in the logic class, and in 1832 the second
in the moral philosophy, then taught by the celebrated
Professor Wilson.

After settling in Canisbay, Calder began occasionally to

contribute poetical pieces to the *Inverness Courier*, which
had been but lately started by Mr Robert Carruthers, and
this connection brought him into correspondence with a
fellow-contributor who was afterwards to make an honoured
name in literature, Hugh Miller. They used to send their
writings each to the other, and exchange criticisms upon
them, and Calder prophesied even at that early stage that
his correspondent, whatever might be said of his poetry, was
certainly destined to shine among writers of English prose.
They never met, however, either then or in after life, though
Miller, when once in Caithness, called at the Canisbay school-
house in the hope of seeing his old correspondent.

In 1825 Calder caused some sensation in Caithness by the
publication — through a friend, without the author's own
knowledge — of his poem "Macroary," a satire on a local
probationer, which touched on some phases of religious life
in the north ; and during the years 1826 and 1827 he carried
on a controversy with Mr Alexander Ewing, Independent
minister of Thurso, defending the Established Church against
Mr Ewing's attacks in a series of vigorous pamphlets. When
the *John O'Groat Journal* was established at Wick in 1836,
Calder became one of its principal contributors, and he
collected a number of his contributions—chiefly poems and
tales—in a volume, entitled "Sketches from John O'Groat's,"
which was published by subscription in 1842. In that same
year he visited Edinburgh, and saw a good deal of the poets,
Robert Gilfillan and David Vedder. In 1846 he published,
at Edinburgh, "The Soldier's Bride," and in 1849, "St.
Mary's Fair, and other Poems."

Calder was now beginning to feel the effects of advancing
years, and finding that his health was unequal to the work

of his school, he engaged, in 1850, a permanent substitute, and finally, in 1856, retired altogether from the school on the petty pension of £25 a year. With this income he removed to Dunnet, and lived with his step-mother, coming occasionally to Wick or Thurso to deliver a popular lecture or visit an old friend. One of his lectures was on National Education; and it shows the liberality of his mind that so early as 1853 he advocated the opening of parochial schools to qualified teachers of all denominations, though he incurred blame from his friends in the Established Church for doing so. In 1856 he collected greater part of his best poems in a single volume, which was published under the title of "Poems from John O'Groat's;" and about the year 1858 he began gathering materials for the present work, which was published in Glasgow in 1861. While in Glasgow in connection with its publication, he was entertained by the Glasgow Caithness Association and presented with a testimonial. The next winter he spent in Orkney with his brother, Mr Peter Calder, at Stronsay, and on his way back to Caithness in June, 1863, was taken ill in Kirkwall, and removed to Elwick Bank, the residence of his brother Marcus, where he died on the 14th of January, 1864.

CONTENTS.

CHAPTER I.

CHAPTER V.

CHAPTER VI.

CHAPTER VII.

CHAPTER VIII.

CHAPTER IX.

CHAPTER X.

CHAPTER XI.

CHAPTER XII.

CHAPTER XIII.

CHAPTER XIV.

CHAPTER XV.

APPENDIX.

POSTSCRIPT.

NOTES TO SECOND EDITION.

By T. Sinclair, M.A.

MISCELLANEOUS.

CAITHNESS IN 1887.

ILLUSTRATIONS.

CIVIL AND TRADITIONAL

HISTORY OF CAITHNESS.

CHAPTER I.

CAITHNESS is the most northern county on the mainland of
Scotland. It bore originally, with Sutherland, the Gaelic
name of Cattey or Cattadh. The present name is of Scandinavian origin. In the old Norse the county was called
Katanes, which means the naze *(Anglice,* the nose) of Cattey;
and this corresponds exactly with the appearance of the
district, which forms a real naze, shooting out in a north-
eastern direction at Duncansbay-head. Caithness extends from
south to north about forty miles, and from east to west about
thirty. It is divided from the Orkneys by the Pentland Firth,
and from the county of Sutherland by a picturesque mountain
range, stretching from the celebrated headland of the Ord to
Drumholisten on the north Atlantic. The greater part of
Caithness is what geologists term a secondary formation,
consisting chiefly of flagstone with more or less calcareous
matter. With the exception of the Ord, which is a mass of
granite, all the other headlands and rocks around the sea-coast
are mostly composed of sandstone. The general aspect of the
county, which measures in area about 712 square miles, is flat;
and this peculiarity is rendered still more striking by the
almost total absence of wood. There are a few plantations,
as at Castlehill, Berriedale, and one or two other places, but

it requires much nursing and shelter to get them to attain to any height. The only tree that indicates congeniality with the soil is the common "bourtree," or elder, which thrives everywhere, and without any protection from the northern blast. This is the more remarkable, as the county would seem, at one period, to have been almost a complete forest. It contains a vast deal of moor or peat-moss, the well-known product of decayed vegetable matter; and, in cutting for fuel, trunks of birch, pine, hazel, and other trees have been very frequently found with the bark quite entire. Some of the roots seem charred with fire, an appearance which gives countenance to the tradition that the woods were burnt down for the purpose of expelling the wolves and other wild animals with which the county was anciently infested.

There is another tradition, that the Danes wantonly set fire to the old forests, and thus caused that lack of wood which acts so injuriously on the climate. But M. Worsaae, the learned Danish archæologist, satisfactorily, we think, disposes of this charge against his countrymen. "Similar discoveries," says he, "are very common in other countries, as, for instance, in Denmark itself, where trunks of trees, especially firs, have been dug up as in the Scotch Highlands. They are the produce of vegetative processes in the pre-historical times; and the apparent scorching has been produced either by accidental fires, or more probably by the simple mode of felling trees in use among the aboriginal inhabitants of Europe, who, like certain savage tribes of the present day, were obliged to burn the trunks of trees which they wished to fell."

"But the most remarkable evidence of ancient woods in Caithness," says the author of the New Statistical Account of Wick, "is found in the Bay of Keiss. Between the links and the sand, and running down under the sea, are found the remains of a submarine forest. These are, like peat-moss, entirely composed of decayed wood. The barks of various kinds of trees are quite discernible, and even the seeds of the birch and ash are so well preserved as to appear but lately taken from the tree." But if Caithness is destitute of trees, nature has liberally supplied it with plants and flowers ; and, in this respect, it offers a highly interesting field to the botanist. The native flowering plants and ferns enumerated amount to about 420. In the moors, and along the hill-sides, which are covered with the finest heather, you find, in their proper season, the bilberry, the cranberry, and the barberry. The Scotch myrtle, thyme, woodbine, and juniper, are also to be met with in several places. White and red clovers are indigenous. The different species of wild flowers are innumerable. Amongst these may be particularised the bird's-eye primrose, the Scotch primrose, the blue-bell, the fox-glove, and the beautiful gem called the white flower of Parnassus. The following, with their Linnaean names, are some of the more rare and interesting plants hitherto not regarded as natives of the county :—Draba incana, Pyrus aria, Saxifraga stellaris, S. tridactylites, Valeriana dioica, Hieracium boreale, H. prenanthoides, Arctostaphylos Alpina, Anchusa semper virens, Veronica polita, Rumex sanguineus, Juncus Balticus, Carex limosa, Osmunda regalis, Isoetes lacustris, Lycopodium annotinum, etc.

Within the last forty years the appearance of the county has, by means of excellent roads* and an improved system of agriculture, undergone a mighty change for the better. Indeed, no county in Scotland, or in England, considering its local disadvantages, has made such remarkable progress as Caithness. In proof of this may be adduced the following statement, drawn up by an eminent statistician : — " It is," says Dr Cleland of Glasgow, " perhaps the most extraordinary circumstance recorded in the history of political economy, that the remotest and most northern county of Great Britain should, on an accurate comparison between the two last enumerations, surpass all the other 85 districts of the kingdom in regard to that great criterion of national prosperity, when it is

* Since 1806 no less a sum than £97,000 has been expended on roads alone. See Appendix, No. 2.

properly regulated and employed, increased population. It proves what would have been the prosperous state of the other districts in Great Britain, had the same zeal for improvement by which this remote county was actuated been extended with equal judgment over the other districts of the kingdom. This increased rate of population is certainly much owing to the establishment of a valuable herring fishery, to the erection of villages for carrying it on, and to the number of persons employed in it. But, the improvement of agriculture, and the cultivation of waste lands, have gone on progressively with the fisheries; and hence it is that, notwithstanding the great addition to the population of Caithness, there has been no occasion for importing grain from other districts at home, and far less from foreign countries. The formation of roads, accompanied by the establishment of a mail-coach to Thurso,* have likewise greatly contributed to the prosperity of the county." Compare this highly-improved condition of Caithness with the state in which it was when visited by Pennant, the celebrated tourist, in 1769. At that time there was not a single cart, nor a mile of road, properly so called, in the county. Pennant describes the whole district as little better than an " immense morass," with here and there some fruitful spots of oats and bere, and much coarse grass, almost all natural, there being as yet very little artificial. "Here," says he, " are neither barns nor granaries; the corn is thrashed out and preserved in the chaff in bykes, which are stacks in the shape of bee-hives, thatched quite round." And he adds, " the tender sex (I blush for the Caithnessians) are the only animals of burden; they turn their patient backs to the dunghills and receive in their cassies or straw baskets as much as their lords and masters think fit to fling in with their pitchforks, and then trudge to the fields in droves. The common people are kept in great servitude, and most of their time is given to their lairds, an invincible impediment to the prosperity of the

* The mail-coach was established in 1818.

county." Such is Pennant's picture of the county in 1769. Could he have seen it at the present day, he would have been struck with the extraordinary change which has taken place since then.

I have alluded to the want of wood in Caithness. Wood, unquestionably, adds much to the warmth and beauty of a country. It is, poetically speaking, the finest feature of a landscape. There is, however, a difference of opinion, or I should rather say of taste, in this matter as in everything else. An anecdote is told of an American tourist who visited John O'Groat's some years ago. In his progress through Caithness, he continually ejaculated, "Beautiful county! very beautiful county!" Some one remarked to him that it could hardly be called a beautiful county from its want of trees. "Trees!" cried the Yankee, "all stuff; Caithness, I calculate, is the finest clearance I ever saw in my life!" Notwithstanding its nakedness in this respect, when the corn-fields and pastures are all green and smiling in the genial summer sunshine, the scene is in the highest degree interesting, and may even be pronounced beautiful. The richness of the scene makes up, in a great measure, for its tameness. Nor is the county destitute of interest to the lover of the "wild and wonderful." The sea-coast, which is generally lofty and rugged, presents scenery of the grandest description. The iron-bound precipices are cleft by innumerable "goes," or fissures, whose steep sides, in the breeding season, are covered with thousands of wild-fowl. At their base, gloomy caves open out : and here and there shoot up tall isolated pillars of rock called stacks, which impart a peculiar and striking feature to the scene, and have been, poetically, likened to so many "advanced pickets of the land standing out amid the ceaseless turmoil of the breakers." Some of them are hollowed into arches by the restless surge, which, when agitated by a gale, is ever and anon seen pouring through them with a rush of foam. One of the most remarkable of these stacks is situated at the mouth of a small haven at Hempriggs, to the south of

Wick. This immense conical rock is perforated from top to bottom, and from side to side, and exhibits two large pillars so regularly formed as almost to appear artificial. The passage is so wide that a boat can easily pass through it.

There are several lofty headlands along the coast, but the four most celebrated are the Ord of Caithness, Holborn-head, and the promontories of Dunnet and Duncansbay. The Ord, so well known as a formidable pass between Sutherland and Caithness, is situated at the eastern boundary of the two counties. According to Jamieson, the derivation of the term Ord is either from the Gaelic "ard" or the Icelandic "urd," both of which signify a steep hill or eminence. I am inclined to think it is from the Icelandic, more especially as the names of most places along the Caithness coast are Norwegian. Besides, in Shetland, where the names of the places are all purely Scandinavian, there is a promontory near Lerwick called the Ord of Bressay. The Ord is the "Verubium promontorium" of Ptolemy; and in a curious geographical fragment, entitled, "De Situ Albaniæ,"* and generally ascribed to Andrew, Bishop of Caithness, who died in 1185, it is called "Mons Mound." The Ord forms the termination of a long mountain ridge, and is, strictly speaking, the brow of a steep hill overhanging the sea, whose strand, at the lowest state of the tide, is the perpendicular face of the rock. On the Sutherland side, the headland is cleft into a huge ravine or gorge of great depth, running a long way up into the interior among the hills. The old road, the only practicable route without making a circuit of some twelve or fourteen miles, was a mere path, or rather shelf, along the outer edge of the promontory, and without any protection from the precipice, so that it could not be passed with any safety in stormy weather. This terrific path, which never failed to inspire travellers with dread, was about a mile in length. Its dangers have been alluded to by several tourists. Pennant, who was accustomed to such passes, describes it as

---

* By some archæologists this work is ascribed to Geraldus Cambrensis, an ancient British author.

"infinitely more high and horrible than Penmaen Mawr, in Wales." The Rev. John Brand, in his "Description of Orkney, Shetland, and Caithness," in the year 1701, quaintly says, "The Ord, which divideth Caithness from Sutherland, is a high mountain down which our way from Caithness to Sutherland doth lie. The road is but narrow and the descent steep, and if any stumble thereupon they are in danger of falling down a precipice into the sea, at the bottom of the rock, which is very terrible to behold." Travellers in carriage or on horseback, when they came to the Ord, always alighted and crossed it on foot, leading their horses, or having them led by servants. In 1802 a Government survey of the Ord was made by Mr Charles Abercrombie, an eminent engineer, who suggested a new plan of a road, by which all danger would be avoided ; and the ascent, instead of being so uncommonly steep, would not exceed one foot in thirty in any part of it. It was not, however, till 1811 that the new road was constructed, and a bridge thrown across the wild yawning chasm, by which means the entrance from the one county to the other is now rendered perfectly safe and easy at any time. By the traveller from Helmsdale the old path may still be seen like a sheep track winding up the steep brow of the hill, some three or four hundred feet above the rolling surge. The scene altogether is one of that wild and savage character which would have afforded a fit subject for the pencil of Salvator Rosa.

Holborn-head, which lies about three miles from Thurso, is a magnificent promontory. It runs out along the west side of the roadstead of Scrabster ; and, with its bold precipitous ridge, forms, as it were, a gigantic wall to protect it from the fury of the Atlantic. At the extremity of the headland there is an immense insulated rock called the "Clett," fully 400 feet high, which adds considerably to its picturesque and striking appearance. The roadstead of Scrabster, which may be termed the "portus salutis" of Caithness, has been long famous as an anchorage. The most violent gales from the west or north-

west leave it comparatively unruffled. A local writer, speaking of its natural advantages as a resort for shipping, says :—
"It is large enough to contain from 200 to 300 sail at a time, is well sheltered on all sides, especially towards the south and west, has good holding ground, with no tide-way, with from eight to ten fathoms water, and sufficient room to work out with any wind that blows." This account must be received with some little deduction. It is exposed to the north-east, and a storm from this quarter raises a very heavy sea in Thurso Bay, which renders the anchorage somewhat unsafe ; and vessels have, not unfrequently, been driven from their moorings, and gone ashore on the sands. Of late an excellent harbour has been erected at Scrabster, of sufficient extent and depth of water to accommodate steamers. Passengers, goods, and stock can, with the greatest facility, be transferred to and from the vessel at the quay ;' and in this respect, Thurso has greatly the advantage of Wick. Formerly iron rings were kept fixed in the rocks at Scrabster, to which vessels, when it was found necessary, were attached. Every vessel that put a hawser ashore for this purpose was charged by the proprietor of Holborn-head a merk Scots of ring dues ; and from this circumstance, the roadstead was frequently called the "Rings." A lighthouse was erected on the headland in 1862. It is a flashing light, showing a flash every ten seconds, white towards the Pentland Firth and Dunnet Bay, and red towards the anchorage ground at Scrabster. It is elevated 75 feet above spring tides, and may be seen at the distance of 13 miles in clear weather.

Dunnet-head, supposed to be the Cape Orcas of Diodorus Siculus,* forms a peninsula containing about three thousand acres of uncultivated moor, with no fewer than ten small lochs, and is protected by a huge wall of precipices, averaging two hundred feet in height. This immense rampart of "nature's

---

* Diodorus Siculus, the geographer, lived in the time of Julius Cæsar, about 53 years before Christ ; and Pinkerton says, "this (meaning Cape Orcas) is the first mention of any place in Scotland by any writer."

masonry," with its numerous wild " goes " and caves, runs
along the northern side of the Bay of Dunnet, and then following the direction of the Pentland Firth, bends towards what is
called Easter-head, on which the lighthouse is erected. The
entire extent of rock encompassing the neck of land from
Dwarwick round to the village of Brough, is nearly eight
miles. Easter-head, which is the highest point of the whole,
and the most northerly on the mainland of Scotland, being
situated in latitude 58° 40′ N., and longitude 3° 21′ W., is
fully 300 feet above the level of the sea. From the summit
of the contiguous eminence, of which it forms a part, the height
above the sea is more than 500 feet. The scene is horribly
grand ; and, in looking down from the verge of the promontory
on the toiling ocean beneath, one is forcibly reminded of
Shakspeare's description of Dover cliff—

> " How fearful and dizzy 'tis to cast one's eyes so low !
> .   .   .   .   .   The murmuring surge,
> That on the unnumbered idle pebbles chafes
> Cannot be heard so high.   I'll look no more,
> Lest my brain turn, and the deficient sight
> Topple down headlong."

On a green spot near what is called " The Head of Man,"
there was anciently a small chapel, the trace of which is still
to be seen. It is called by an old writer " templum Donati,"
and is supposed to have been a sanctuary or place of penance,
and to have been dedicated to St Donatus, one of the multitude
of saints in the Romish calendar. The tradition of the place
says that a hermit once lived in it. M. Worsaae in his
account of Ireland mentions a Norwegian, named Donat, who
was bishop of Dublin in the eleventh century. It is probable
that Dunnet is a corruption of this term, and was originally
pronounced Donat.

The lighthouse, which was erected in 1832, is, at one part,
not much more than fifty feet from the edge of the precipice.
During a heavy storm from the west, the enormous billows,
as they dash against the rugged face of the cliff, throw up the

spray as high as the lights of the building, often mingled with stones, which occasionally break the glass. And such is the prodigious force of the wind and the sea united upon the headland, that the very rock itself seems to tremble; while the lighthouse shakes from top to bottom, as if it were affected by an earthquake. The light, which is fixed, is seen at the distance of twenty-three miles. The height of the lantern above the highest spring tides is 346 feet. Easter-head and the Berry, in the opposite island of Walls, in Orkney, form the western entrance of the Pentland Firth. They nearly correspond in their geological properties; and, as is remarked by a statistical writer, various circumstances contribute to render the conjecture probable, that at a remote period the Orkneys were, by some convulsion of nature, torn from Scotland. Dunnet-head is altogether composed of freestone, and the strata dip or incline to the north-east at an angle of 45°.

The point of Dwarwick which I have mentioned forms partly the scene of the following curious legends:—It happened that a young lad on one occasion caught a mermaid bathing, or rather amusing herself, in a sandy pool betwixt Murkle and Castlehill. By some means or other he got into conversation with her, and rendered himself so agreeable that a regular meeting at the same spot took place between them. This continued for some time. The young man grew exceedingly wealthy, and no one could tell how he became possessed of such riches. He began to cut a dash amongst the lasses, making them presents of strings of diamonds of vast value, the gifts of the fair sea nymph. By and by he began to forget the day of his appointment; and when he did come to see her money and jewels were his constant request. The mermaid lectured him pretty sharply on his love of gold; and exasperated at his perfidy in bestowing her presents on his earthly fair ones, enticed him one evening rather farther than usual, and at length showed him a beautiful boat, in which she said she would convey him to a cave in Dwarwick Head, where she had all the wealth of all the ships that ever were lost in the

Pentland Firth and on the sands of Dunnet. He hesitated at first, but the love of gold prevailed, and off they set to the cave in question. And here, says the legend, he is confined with a chain of gold, sufficiently long to admit of his walking at times on a small piece of sand under the western side of the Head ; and here, too, the fair siren laves herself in the tiny waves on fine summer evenings, but no consideration will induce her to loose his fetters of gold, or trust him one hour out of her sight. Dr Hibbert, in his work on the superstitions of the Shetlanders, mentions that connubial attachments were occasionally formed between the merwomen and the natives, but that these strange helpmates generally in the end betook themselves to their native element.

But by far the most beautiful promontory on the coast of Caithness is Duncansbay-head. It is a small headland compared with that of Dunnet, but it possesses several features of greater interest. It is of a semicircular shape, and about two miles in extent, the greater part of which is surrounded by the sea, and forms a continued precipice, remarkable for its stupendous boldness, and the wild and striking appearance of the few chasms and goes by which it is indented. On the land side the surface is composed of a beautiful green, which slopes gently down towards a small rivulet which bounds it on that quarter. From the summit of the rock there is a magnificent view of the German Ocean, of the Pentland Firth, with the Skerry lighthouse, and of several of the Orkney islands. A little to the south of the head, in the direction of Freswick, are seen the Stacks of Duncansbay, two immense pillars of rock of an oval form, standing out in the sea, wholly detached from the adjacent precipices, and shooting up their fantastic summits to a great height. They are situated in a sort of recess, where in certain directions of the wind during bad weather boats, and even vessels, can lie with safety. On the top of the highest stack the eagle has for ages sat in " undisturbed royalty " and taken out her young. There is a tradition, however, that about eighty or ninety years ago a

tailor, of the name of Hogston, one day climbed up to the
eyrie for the purpose of appropriating to himself a young
eaglet or two. No sooner, however, had he got to the top
than the old eagle, a majestic bird of the golden species, came
flying forward for the protection of her young. It was a
perilous moment for the poor tailor. One flap of her wings
was sufficient to hurl him headlong three hundred feet to the
bottom. Fortunately he had his large scissors in his pocket,
with one stroke of which he managed to fell the bird. Still
he was not out of danger. The coming down was greatly
more difficult than the going up ; and he afterwards declared
that he would not perform such a hazardous feat again if he
were to get the whole of Caithness. The term Duncansbay
is from the Norse, and was originally written Dungalsbae.
Near the top of the promontory stood the ancient fort of
Dungalsbae, the earliest stronghold of the Scandinavian Earls
of Orkney and Caithness. It was generally held by a prefect
or captain under the Earl. Not a vestige of the building,
which would seem to have been of a circular form, now
remains.

About a mile and a-half to the west of Duncansbay-head lies
the celebrated locality of John O'Groat's, situated close by the
sea, and near the middle of a long strip of " links," or downs.
The stranger who visits the spot is naturally disappointed,
when instead of the house which his imagination had pictured,
he sees nothing but a small green mound which is pointed out
as the site on which it stood. The sea view, however, is
good ; and the visitor, if he be a conchologist, will have an
opportunity of enjoying his favourite study, and of picking up
in his walk along the beach, among others, some of those
beautiful little shells called " John O'Groat's buckies."   Speci-
mens of this shell, the " cyprea Europea " of the naturalist,
have occasionally been found with the animal alive, from which
it would appear to be a native of our seas. The following is
the tradition respecting the far-famed John and his banqueting-
house. In the reign of James IV. of Scotland, three brothers,

SWAIN'S 'NATURE'.

JOHN O'GROAT'S HOUSE.

Malcolm, Gavin, and John de Groat, natives of Holland, came to the county, carrying with them a letter in Latin from that monarch, recommending them to the protection and countenance of his loving subjects in Caithness. They purchased, or obtained by royal charter, the lands of Wares and Duncansbay, in the parish of Canisbay ; and in process of time, by the increase of their families, and the subdivision of the property, there came to be eight different proprietors of the name of Groat.* An annual festive meeting having been established to commemorate the anniversary of their arrival in Caithness, a dispute arose on one of these occasions respecting the right of taking the door, the head of the table, etc., which increased to such a height as threatened to be attended with very disagreeable consequences, when John, who was now considerably advanced in years, happily interposed. He expatiated on the comforts which they had hitherto enjoyed in the land of their adoption, and conjured them, by the ties of blood and their mutual safety, to return quietly home, pledging himself that he would satisfy them on all points of precedency at their next meeting. They acquiesced and departed in peace. In due time, to fulfil his engagement, John built a house, distinct by itself, of an octagonal form, with eight doors and windows ; and having placed a table of oak, of the same shape, in the middle, when the next meeting took place, he desired each of his friends to enter at his own door, and sit at the head of the table. By this happy contrivance any dispute in regard to rank was prevented, and the former harmony and good humour of the party were restored. Such was the origin of John O'Groat's House. The above interesting tradition, which furnishes an excellent moral, first appeared in the Old Statistical Account of Canisbay, drawn up by the late ingenious Dr Morison, minister of the parish. It is added in a note that John

* Dr Henderson says, "The first John O'Groat was most probably a Fleming. He held the ferry ; and there is reason to believe that it was to take charge of it he was sent into the county, as the ferry appears to have belonged at one time to the Crown."

Sutherland of Wester, in the parish of Wick, had the particulars from his father, who was then advanced in life, and who had seen the letter written by James IV. in the possession of George Groat of Warse. The story, however, notwithstanding the imprimatur of Dr Morison, has been regarded by many as merely a beautiful myth. Certain it is that Mr Pennant, in his tour, says nothing about it ; nor does Mr Pope of Reay, who was well acquainted with the ancient history of the county, make any mention of it in his appendix to that work. The latter merely says that " the town of Duncansbay and the ferry of old belonged to a gentleman of the name of Groat." It is a pity that the letter said to have been written by the king—if there ever was any such missive —was not religiously preserved. It would not only have been an object of great antiquarian interest, but it would have completely removed all doubts as to the authenticity of the story.* But whether the tradition be true or false, there can be no question that a family of the name of Groat possessed for many ages the lands of Wares and Duncansbay. About the end of the fifteenth century, the proprietors of the latter township appear to have been the Earl of Caithness, and Oliphant of Oldwick. In 1496,† John Groat, son of Hugh, obtained by charter from William, Earl of Caithness, a portion of land in Duncansbay called One Penny land, paying yearly " tres modios Brasii " (three measures of malt) ; and in 1507, his son William Groat had a charter from William Oliphant, and Christian Sutherland, his spouse, of some Halfpenny land

* Robert Mackay, in his History of the House of Mackay, gives the following origin, purporting to be from tradition, of the name Groat :—" It is said that the ancestor of the Groats was a ferryman betwixt Caithness and Orkney, and had frequent disputes with passengers about his fares, till at length the magistrates interfered, and fixed the rates at fourpence, or a *groat*, for each passenger ; and that the ferryman, whose name was John, was thenceforward termed Johnny Groat." There is no doubt that one of the family was proprietor of the ferry-boat that plied betwixt Caithness and Orkney ; but the writer of this sketch, who lived many years near John O'Groat's, never heard the origin of the name ascribed to any such circumstance as that mentioned by Mackay.

† See Appendix, No. 3.

in the same locality, paying yearly 5 shillings Scots. One of the Groats became proprietor of Brabsterdorran, which in 1567 was given in tack to Andrew Calder of Lynegar. Previous to 1496 and 1507, the family of Groat is not mentioned in any of our local records. The name afterwards frequently occurs in the parochial records of Canisbay, and other public documents. In 1609 Donald Groat of Warse was killed in a fray in Kirkwall ; and in the Scottish parliament of 1702, John Groat, portioner of Duncansbay, was commissioner of supply for the county. Next to the celebrated site of John O'Groat's, and the wild and beautiful scenery about Duncansbay-head, the most interesting object to a stranger, historically speaking, is the Pentland Firth, which, in the old Norse was called " Petland Fiord."* It forms a communication between the German and Atlantic Oceans, and is about fourteen miles long, and, at an average, eleven broad. It is calculated that about 10,000 vessels pass through it annually. The tide often runs in it at the rate of ten miles an hour ; and when a vessel is met by this impetuous current, she may be seen, even with a favourable breeze, and under a press of canvas, drifting rapidly backward after the stern. The passage through the Pentland Firth has long been accounted a dangerous one ; and, although its perils have been somewhat magnified, it requires mariners who are well acquainted with its numerous eddies and currents to navigate it with safety. At St John's Head, in the district of Mey, and at Duncansbay-head, near the eastern entrance of the firth, there arises a violent agitation of the waves, locally called the " Men of Mey," and the " Boars of Duncansbay." They appear only alternately ; the former with the ebb, and

---

* The derivation of the term Pentland is uncertain. Blaeu, in his Geographical Atlas, gives the following tradition respecting the origin of the name. The Picts, on being defeated by the Scots, fled to Duncansbay, whence they crossed over to Orkney, but meeting with opposition from the natives, they were forced to retire ; and on their way back to Caithness they all perished in the Firth, from which catastrophe it was ever after called the Pictland or Pentland Firth. Buchanan calls it " Fretum Penthlandicum." It owes its name most probably to some circumstance connected with the Picts.

the latter with the flood-tide ; and the roughness, which is at times much greater than at others, is produced by the collision of currents running in opposite directions. The huge breakers jet up as from a boiling cauldron, and foam, and dance, and tumble over each other in the most frantic manner. Sometimes they spread to a considerable distance from the shore, and at other times they confine themselves to a certain spot, and may be seen raging furiously, even when the surrounding firth is as smooth as a mirror. It is a fearful sight to see a vessel, especially in a storm, labouring in one of these dangerous pieces of sea—the Scylla and Charybdis of the Canisbay shore—now whirling round like a ball, and now plunging down half buried amidst the white breakers. Captain Lyon, in the narrative of his expedition to the Arctic regions in 1824, mentions that the Griper, the ship in which he sailed, was twice whirled round in an eddy in the Pentland Firth, and with some difficulty got out of it. Generally, however, when the tide is with them, vessels are not long in passing through the " Men " or the " Boars."

Situated half way between Duncansbay-head and the head of Mey, and about a league from the opposite shore of Canisbay, to which it belongs, lies the small picturesque-looking island of Stroma. Its name in the old Norse was " Straumsey," which means the island in the current. It is two miles long, and a mile in breadth, and contains about two hundred inhabitants. They are evidently of pure Norwegian descent, and like their ancestors, the male part of the population are all excellent boatmen. On its west and north-west sides the island is surrounded with very high rocks, which rise up like an iron rampart to protect it from the fury of the Atlantic surge. In a winter storm from the west, the spray is tossed up over the loftiest precipices, and drifted in showers a long way into the interior. There is no rivulet or burn in the island ; and the salt water carried inland by the storm was at one time collected in a " dam," or reservoir, and with the rain supplied from the clouds, made to turn the wheel of a small meal mill. In the west corner of Stroma there is a large round open chasm, shaped like a bowl, and about thirty yards from the precipice, to which the sea has access by an opening at the bottom. The natives call it the "glupe." It is about 100 feet in diameter, and as many in depth. The subterranean opening between it and the sea is about 30 feet high and 12 feet wide; and the waves growl and thunder through it in their constant ebb and flow. When illicit distillation was carried on in Stroma (which it was to a great extent some years ago), the smugglers used to hide in this cavern their brewing apparatus, etc., from the officers of the revenue; but these lynx-eyed gentlemen found out all their places of concealment here, and in other parts of the island, and finally put a stop to the demoralising traffic. The officer who really suppressed smuggling in Stroma, and indeed through Caithness generally, was a Mr Terence Macmahon, a native of Ireland. So active and successful was he in the discharge of his duty, that his very name spread terror over the whole country, from the Ord to Duncansbay-head. Mr Macmahon was an excellent specimen of the better class of his countrymen; and, notwithstanding the terror inspired by his name, those who were acquainted with him, found him to possess a well-cultivated mind and a fine taste for literature. On receiving his retiring allowance he resided for a short time in Edinburgh, and afterwards emigrated to the Cape of Good Hope. Stroma, or at least certain portions of it, would seem to have belonged to different proprietors at different times. The Sinclairs, soon after their accession to the earldom of Caithness, obtained by royal grant the property of the island. In 1574, George Sinclair of Mey, youngest son of George, Earl of Caithness, was, in addition to other lands belonging to the family in Canisbay, served heir of entail to his brother William in the lands of Stroma.*

In 1726 all the arable land in Stroma was delved with the

* Origines Parochiales Scotiæ, vol. ii., p. 813.

spade, and it paid, says a writer of the period, "in victual and money 1300 merks in yearly rent."*

The present proprietors of Stroma are the Earl of Caithness and Mrs Thomson Sinclair of Freswick. The former draws about one-third, and the latter two-thirds of the rental of the island, which amounts to about £200 per annum. There is some excellent land in Stroma, particularly in the northern part of it, but the inhabitants may be said to depend for their livelihood chiefly upon the sea. The finest cod in the north is to be got in the Pentland Firth; and, at certain seasons of the year, the shores of the island teem with cod fish, and the young fry, provincially called sillocks. Large and excellent lobsters are also caught around the island. Accordingly the time that is not employed in the cultivation of their little crofts, the male portion of the inhabitants devote to fishing; and many among them earn a good deal in the course of the year by piloting vessels through the firth.

The island rises to a considerable altitude above the neighbouring shore of Canisbay. It is entirely destitute of anything in the shape of a tree; and as Trinculo says in the "Tempest," "Here's neither bush nor shrub to bear off any weather at all." There is a school, but no church, in the island; and when the weather is suitable, the inhabitants cross over to attend divine service in Canisbay. George Gibson, a near relative of Mr Gibson, minister of Canisbay, was the first schoolmaster of Stroma on the foundation of the Society for Propagating Christian Knowledge. His appointment took place in 1723. He married a daughter of Bailie Roreson of Thurso, whose maiden name was Catherine. When a young woman, she had been the sweetheart of Gow, who afterwards turned out a noted pirate. Gow was, according to the tradition of the place, a native of Scrabster, near Thurso, and was ultimately executed for the many crimes and robberies which he had committed on the high seas. Near the south-west corner of the island, and

* Macfarlane's Geog. Collection.

in what is called Stroma Sound, an outlying reef of rock, partly visible at ebb-tide, but entirely covered with the flood, has occasioned frequent accidents to vessels. Of late a beacon has been erected on it. It consists of six strong iron columns, thoroughly joined together with tie-beams or arms, and dove-tailed into the solid rock. In height it is 45 feet, and in weight about 43 tons. At the top is a cage which can be reached by a cast-iron ladder in the centre of the construction. Opposite the north corner of the island there is a remarkable eddy or whirlpool, called the "Swelchie of Stroma," which is particularly dangerous in a storm ; and instances have occurred in which boats, and even vessels, have been sucked down into it and lost. Pennant and Pope of Reay both mention a singular natural curiosity which was to be seen in their time in Stroma. In this island, says the latter, "there is a vault built by one Kennedy of Carmunks. The coffins are laid on stools above ground ; but the vault being on the sea-edge, and the rapid tides of the Pentland running by it, there is such a saltish air continually as has converted the bodies into mummies— insomuch that Murdo Kennedy, son of Carmunks, is said to beat the drum on his father's belly !" A family of the name of Kennedy at one time possessed a part of Stroma. They belonged originally, it is said, to Fifeshire ; and the amiable young gentleman, who amused himself in the way mentioned by Mr Pope, was the last of his race who were lairds of Stroma. Accounts differ as to how they lost their property ; but the general belief is that it was forcibly seized upon—a mode of acquiring land very common in the north at a period when might and not right was the leading rule of conduct. From a note in Henry Glassford Bell's "Life of Queen Mary," I am led to think that the Kennedys of Stroma, who were also called the Kennedys of Carmunks, were the descendants of the family of that name in Fife, connected by marriage with an ancestor of the Traills of Orkney. It is mentioned in the note that George Traill, son of the laird of Blebo in Fife, married Jean Kennedy of Carmunks. She was a relative of Lady Jean Kennedy, daughter of the Earl of Casillis, and wife of Robert Stewart, Earl of Orkney. Traill accompanied the Earl to Orkney in capacity of factor, and became proprietor of some lands in the island of Rousay. Thus it is highly probable that from their connection with the Traills and the Earl's family, the Kennedys came first to Orkney, and afterwards obtained property in the island of Stroma. The name of Kennedy of Stroma appears in the list of Caithness proprietors in 1687. The house in which the Kennedys dwelt still exists in the northern part of the island, and, what is more remarkable, it is still inhabited. There is an amusing legend, in an old topographical work on Scotland, which says that a dispute once arose between the Earls of Orkney and Caithness as to which county Stroma belonged. Instead of deciding the quarrel by the sword, the chiefs on both sides ultimately agreed to refer the decision of the matter to an experiment in natural history. Some venomous animals—of what kind we are not told—lived in Stroma. A certain number of them were shipped, at the same time, as colonists to Orkney and Caithness. Those that were brought to Caithness took kindly to the soil as to a congenial habitat; while those that were sent to Orkney, from the unfavourable effects of the climate on their constitution, sickened and died. By this singular fact Stroma was adjudged to belong to Caithness!

During the Norwegian rule in Caithness Stroma, from its proximity to the mainland, and other natural advantages, was regarded as a place of much importance, and a sub-deputy or governor usually resided in it. This official also acted in the capacity of what might be termed special reporter for the district, and forwarded to his superior in Orkney intelligence of every event affecting the interests of the earldom in that quarter. An instance of this is mentioned as occurring about the end of the tenth century. At this time two Highland chiefs having invaded Caithness with a large band of followers, plundered the county as far as Canisbay; and, among other acts of atrocity, killed a Norwegian nobleman who lived at

Freswick. Arnilot, the governor of Stroma, as soon as he heard of it, despatched a boat to Orkney with the news of the invasion. The Earl lost no time in transporting across the firth a sufficient body of troops, attacked the two chiefs near Duncansbay-head, routed them with great slaughter, and retook all the booty which they had collected in Caithness.

In the eastern entrance of the firth, and nearly half-way between Orkney and Caithness, lie the Pentland Skerries, called in the Old Norse " Pentlandsker," and in the Danish " Petland Skjaere." They are three in number. On the largest, which is about a quarter of a mile in length, and situated 4½ miles east-north-east from Duncansbay-head, a lighthouse was erected in 1794. It consists of two towers— the one considerably higher than the other—with a fixed light on each. This double beacon, with the one now on Dunnet-head, have rendered the navigation of the firth, in the night-time, much safer than it was before.

The " Stormy Pentland," as it has been well named, has proved a watery grave to thousands. The old sagas point out in strong terms its manifold dangers. On the return of Haco, king of Norway, after his disaster at Largs, one of his ships was lost in the Pentland Firth, and another escaped only with the greatest difficulty. From the account given in Haco's Journal, the vessel would seem to have foundered in what are called the " Wells of Swana," a series of whirlpools at the south end of that island. They are most dangerous with an ebb-tide and a strong breeze from the west. Even in modern times, with all the advantages afforded by science, many melancholy shipwrecks have occurred on its wild shores. A few years ago a fine schooner belonging to the West of England was, on her way home from the Baltic, caught in a severe gale on entering the firth, and literally swallowed up in the Boars of Duncansbay. The catastrophe, which happened during the middle of the day, was witnessed by numerous spectators on shore, who could render the hapless crew no assistance. So frightful, indeed, was the surge that all the lifeboats in Britain could not have saved them at the time.

The three largest bays on the coast are Wick Bay, Sinclair's Bay, and Dunnet Bay. The two first are completely exposed. Sinclair's Bay, under which designation are included the bays of Keiss and Ackergill, is a magnificent inlet about six miles wide at the entrance. The shore, which everywhere else is bold and rocky, here subsides into low, level, benty links, and sweeps round in the form of a semi-circle ; while along the whole head of the bay extends a sand of some four miles in length. The river of Wester, issuing from the loch of the same name, intersects the links nearly in the middle, and then flows into the bay. At one spot near the beach there are two mounds covered with sand, which indicate the ruins of two old castles, named Castles Linglas, and which are supposed to have been Danish or Norwegian strongholds. Tradition says they were surprised and burned down by the natives, and this seems to be confirmed by the calcined state of such stones as have been dug from the ruins. Owing to the want of a light-house on Nosshead, frequent shipwrecks formerly took place in Sinclair's Bay. There is now a very fine one, with a tower 70 feet high, erected on that promontory. The light, which is revolving, was first opened in the summer of 1849. It is seen 15 miles off, and flashes out once every half minute— alternately exhibiting a coloured red light, and one of the usual appearance, each within a certain range of the compass. A tourist from the south draws the following vivid picture of this lighthouse :—" It is one of the strongest and best in the kingdom, and will well repay inspection. It commands a magnificent and far-stretching view of land and sea. Seen through its red-stained windows, the surf breaks along the shore of Ackergill Bay in flickering flame. The coast seems one mass of still red fire, and the white gulls, wavering o'er the billows, are transformed into winged splendours." As the principal Skerry light is apt to be obscured in thick or stormy weather, and at such times cannot be seen at a distance, the light on Nosshead is of great benefit to stranger vessels, and especially to those from the south that are shaping their course for the Pentland Firth.

On the south-east side of Sinclair's Bay, and about a mile to the west of Nosshead, on a bold peninsular neck of land, are seen the picturesque ruins of the castles Sinclair and Girnigoe, the chief baronial strongholds of the ancient Earls of Caithness of the Sinclair family. The length of the rock on which they are situated is fully three hundred feet, with a main breadth of thirty-four, and fenced on the side towards the land by a long deep creek or "goe" running up to the neck of the isthmus. Of Castle Sinclair, which was erected about the year 1606, as an appendage to Girnigoe, no part is standing except one tall chimney-stalk of the main tower. The rest of the superstructure, owing to some defect in the foundation has fallen down, and being strongly cemented with lime, is seen lying in one solid mass in the hollow between the castle and the mainland. The sides of several of the prostrate arches are of such durable masonry, that they present to the hammer a surface nearly as hard as granite. The date of the erection of Girnigoe, apparently so named from the adjacent goe, is not known. It is, however, notwithstanding its great antiquity, comparatively entire. The main tower, which is about fifty feet in height, consists of five stories, three of which, including the ground floor, are vaulted. Its thick massy walls are solid as iron ; while that part of the edifice fronting the sea is built to the very edge of the precipice, and rises up perpendicular with it. On the land side the court was protected by a high screen wall pierced with seven loopholes. Immediately opposite, on the side facing the bay, ran a range of low rooms, supposed to have been used as barracks for the retainers and domestics of the establishment. There were two stairs inside, both of which are now gone. The great dining-hall would seem to have been a spacious apartment, being about thirty feet long and twenty broad, with a large bow-window in the west end. At the extremity of the tongue of land, towards the east, a stair consisting of a flight of narrow steps cut out of the solid rock, with an arch at the top, leads to the sea. There is another archway at the west corner, betwixt the two castles, evidently for the same purpose ; but there being no trace of a stair here in the rock, it is not easy to say whether the descent was through a subterranean passage, or by a portable trap or ladder. At the foot of the precipice at this point is a small goe capable of admitting an ordinary-sized boat. There can be no doubt that the object in getting to the sea in both places was to secure to the inmates of the castle a communication with the mainland, in case of a siege, when all other means of ingress and egress were cut off.

In going over the ruins, two striking objects present themselves. The one is a large stump of wood projecting from a part of the wall in the tower, which is said to be a portion of the gibbet used in the execution of criminals, or of such unhappy wretches as had incurred the Earl's displeasure. The other is the subterranean cell in which prisoners were confined. This horrid dungeon, partly formed in the rock, had but one small aperture opening on the bay, but beyond the reach of the captive, which afforded just light enough to reveal the gloom that pervaded the interior. The view of it forcibly suggests to the mind an idea of the oppressive tyranny and cruelty of former times. No situation can be conceived more miserable than that of the unfortunate beings who were shut up, it might be said, without light or air, many of them for years, in this damp and noisome pit, where, in the words of Byron's prisoner of Chillon—

> " A double dungeon wall and wave
> Did make—and like a living grave."

A drawbridge over a natural chasm in the rock connected the two castles, the new and the old, together. Hence, in the case of an attack, if the one stronghold was in danger of being taken, the besieged could easily retire into the other. On the land side, in addition to this goe, both were protected by a deep and broad artificial ditch, cut across the neck of the peninsula, over which was the main or principal drawbridge, which afforded access through an arched passage to the court of Castle Sinclair. The situation of this double fortress was naturally strong; and before the invention of artillery, it might with its well-constructed defences, be considered impregnable.

The castles seem to have been inhabited till about the year 1690. As the country became more settled and civilised, the principal gentry began to desert their wild abodes on inaccessible rocks and precipices overhanging the sea, and to erect comfortable houses of modern construction in more agreeable situations. Sinclair and Girnigoe shared the fate of similar strongholds along the coast. After being abandoned, they gradually went to decay; and time and tempest did their work upon them, until they have become the striking ruins which they now exhibit, conveying a moral more impressive than a thousand homilies on the perishable nature of all earthly grandeur. The ivy which proverbially clings to decay, and with its green mantling foliage imparts even to the hoary ruin a pleasing look, is here totally wanting; and the bare delapidated walls, where nothing is seen but the rank weed, and no sounds are heard but the scream of the sea-fowl and the moan of the weltering billow, present one of the gloomiest of pictures, and fill the mind with feelings of a melancholy kind.

On the north side of the bay, opposite Sinclair and Girnigoe, stand the ruins of the castle of Keiss, anciently called the "fortalice of Raddar." It belonged also to the Earls, and was the favourite residence of the second Earl George. The castle and lands connected with it became latterly the patrimony of George Sinclair, who disputed the titles with Glenorchy.

Dunnet Bay may be said to commence between Holbornhead and the opposite headland of Dunnet. It forms a deep indentation, somewhat in the shape of an oblong, and runs down towards the south-east for the space of nearly four miles. Its breadth across is about two miles and a half, and it is completely land-locked on the south side by the low rocky shore of Castlehill and Murkle, and on the north or Dunnet side by the lofty wall of precipices formerly mentioned, amongst which the bluff bold brow of Dwarwick rises up conspicuously. It is a beautiful inlet, but still a very dangerous one, when the wind blows right down from the north-west. A gale from this quarter throws in a heavy sea from the Atlantic; and, if a vessel should unfortunately get embayed, her destruction, from the great difficulty of working out again, is almost certain. Before the erection of the present lighthouse, scarce a winter passed without one or two shipwrecks. In the darkness vessels frequently mistook the bay for the Pentland Firth, and before they were aware, they struck either on the rocks or on the sand at the bottom of the inlet. In 1811, a very melancholy case of this kind occurred. A large barque, called the Fingal, of London, with a cargo of wood from America, shaped her course by mistake down the bay. The night was dark and stormy, in the month of November, and the vessel, being heavily laden, struck far out in the sands in deep water, and went almost instantly to pieces. The crew—sixteen in number—all perished, several of them being crushed to death by the logs which were set loose and floated around when the vessel broke up.

When roused by a heavy westerly gale the bay, from the tumultuous agitation and magnitude of the breakers, presents a sublime spectacle. The huge, long, white-crested billows, lashed into fury by the storm, seem to chase each other; and as they hurry on towards the beach, burst with astounding force—the broken surge churned into foam rushing up along the sand with the speed of a race-horse, and then rushing back again as rapidly, as if sucked down by the raging flood. Here and there a few gulls, perhaps in quest of prey, may be seen vainly struggling with the blast, while from all sides of the bay is heard one continued roar like that of the loudest thunder.

Caithness contains a multitude of small lakes. In the parish of Halkirk alone, there are no fewer than twenty-four. The three largest in the county are the loch of Watten, the loch of Calder, and Lochmore. The first is about three miles in length, and about a mile in breadth. But the most celebrated loch in the county is that of Dunnet, or St John's, which lies a few hundred yards to the north of the church, and is little more than half a mile long, and one-fourth of a mile broad. In the olden time it was greatly famed for its supposed virtues in curing all kinds of chronic and lingering disorders; and, in consequence, people resorted to it from all parts of the county, and even from Sutherland and the Orkneys. There were particular times for visiting it, viz., the first Monday of each quarter of the year. The summer quarter was on many accounts considered the best. The patient had to walk round the loch early in the morning; and if his strength did not permit him to do so, he was carried round it. The ceremony which he had to go through consisted in washing his face and hands in the lake, and throwing a piece of money, commonly a halfpenny, into it; and, if he would derive any permanent benefit to his health, it was absolutely necessary that he should be out of sight of it before sunrise. It is difficult to account for the origin of this superstition, for superstition it undoubtedly was. The waters of the loch do not seem to possess any healing or medicinal qualities. There was anciently on the east end a Catholic chapel dedicated to St John, and it is extremely probable that the alleged virtues of the loch may have been conferred on it by the priests, and converted by them into a source of pecuniary emolument. After the subversion of the Popish religion in the district, the practice still maintained its ground; and the money which was formerly given to the church was now thrown into the consecrated waters of St John. At present it is seldom visited except by a few valetudinarians of the lowest class from the more remote parts of the county. The people living in its immediate neighbourhood have no faith whatever in its healing virtues, and only laugh at the superstition. It is quite possible, however, that from the united influence of

imagination, change of air, and exercise, several of the patients
may have been not a little benefited by their jaunt to the
"halie loch."*

The only hilly parish in Caithness is Latheron, especially
that part of it immediately bordering on Sutherland, where
majestically tower up the long alpine ridge of Scaraben, and
the lofty peaks of Morven and Maiden Pap. At the foot of
these mountains lies Braemore, a solitary and romantic glen,
shut out, like the valley of Rasselas, from the rest of the
world. For wild picturesque grandeur, nothing can exceed
the scene which here meets the eye. The Pap, in particular,
a spur of the Scaraben range, has a striking appearance,
standing up grey and weather-beaten, and looking exactly like
a stupendous cone split near the top into two round eminences.
Morven, which is rather more than a mile farther off, is much
higher than the Pap, being upwards of 2000 feet above the
level of the sea. The view from the summit is magnificent,
embracing in a clear atmosphere, it is said, a great part of
twelve different counties, besides a vast range of the Atlantic
and German oceans. There are two circumstances connected
with this mountain deserving of notice. In the case of a
vessel entering the Moray Firth on her way northward, the
first land descried is Morven, which appears emerging like a
vast pyramid from the deep, at a distance of about fifty miles.
Next, from the infallible indications which it gives of dry or
wet weather, it may be called the great weather-glass of the
county. When mist settles round its base, rain is sure to
follow ; but when it ascends to the top and disperses, leaving
the majestic outline of the mountain clear and exposed to
view, there will be drought. "During harvest especially,"

* There is a loch in Strathnaver called Lochmonar, which the common
people believed to possess the same wonderful healing qualities as the one at
Dunnet ; and what is curious enough, the ceremonies which the patients had
to go through were the very same at both lochs. There is an old tradition
(evidently a monkish invention) which says that on St Stephen's day its basin
was occupied by a pleasant meadow and that on St John's day the meadow was
covered with water. This story of its origin, so akin to the marvellous,
would, among a simple and credulous people, very naturally heighten their
belief in its supposed curative powers.

says a local writer, "all eyes are directed towards it, and it never deceives." Thus Morven serves the double purpose of a landmark to the sailor, and a barometer to the husbandman.

From Braemore to Berriedale the character of the scenery partakes more of the mountainous feature of Sutherland than of the generally tame level aspect of Caithness. Berriedale is, beyond all comparison, the sweetest spot in the county. It is the Tempe of Caithness, and has been likened to a beautiful Swiss scene in miniature. The unique and charming appearance of the romantic dell, with its steep and richly-wooded banks, together with the air of profound seclusion that reigns around it, would at first sight almost make one think that he was gazing not on an actual spot of earth, but on a scene in fairy land.

> "So sweet a spot of earth, you might, I ween,
> Have guessed some congregation of the elves
> To sport by summer moons, had shaped it for themselves."

The two rivers of Langwell and Berriedale, the one rising in the heights beyond Braemore, and the other in the wilds of Kildonan, meet immediately below the inn, and soon after discharge their united current into the small haven, which is about a hundred yards or so from the head of the glen. This feature of the scene reminds one of Moore's beautiful poem, "The Meeting of the Waters." On a rock jutting into the sea are the ruins of the old castle of Berriedale, the original stronghold of the Sutherlands of Langwell and Berriedale, who were related to the Dunrobin family. The late ingenious Dr Macnish, who practised some time as a surgeon in the parish of Latheron, was a great admirer of the scenery in this quarter, and has even celebrated it in verse. His farewell address to this "romantic wilderness of vales and mountains," as he happily terms it, is exceedingly graphic, and at the same time full of beauty and feeling. He says :—

> " Of early reminiscence full to me
> Are thy grey summits, bald with countless years,
> Thy glens hung o'er with strange tranquillity,
> Thy streams unruly bubbling to the sea,

And even the wild heath that thy bosom bears.
In vision I behold tall Morven stand,
And see the morning mist distilling tears
Around his shoulders, desolate and grand.
And Scaraben, that girdles round the land
With his broad giant-belt, arises up ;
And Berriedale and Langwell, thy twin fountains ;
And Corriechoich's glen, like to a cup,
Reposing in the bosom of its mountains.
O ! ever dear unto my memory
Shall thy romantic hills and fountains be.
How often have I seen the morning star
Warning the shepherd to his native dell ;
And seen the thunder-cloud, opaque and far,
Lower heavily on Morven's citadel,
Awing the hearts that in thy valleys dwell
With the divinity of nature's God ! "

The only towns in the county are Wick and Thurso. Wick, which may be considered the capital, is situated close by the sea, at the mouth of the river which bears its name. The term Wick, which is of pure Scandinavian origin, and signifies an opening, or bay, is quite descriptive of the situation of the town. In ancient times the place was much frequented by the Northmen ; and a colony of those daring adventurers would seem to have formed an early settlement in it and the neighbourhood. Indeed, with the exception of, perhaps, Canisbay, there is no parish in Caithness that indicates more clearly the impress of the Norwegian colonisation than that of Wick. The town was erected into a royal burgh by James VI. of Scotland, in the year 1589 ; and the set, as it is termed, consists of a provost, two bailies, a dean of guild, a treasurer, and seven councillors. This municipal honour, with its accompanying privileges, was conferred on it at the request of the then Earl of Caithness. Although at this period it could have been only a mean-looking village, consisting of a few thatched houses, it would appear to have been a place of some little trade ; for in an inroad of the Sutherland men in 1588, it is said, that among other acts of spoliation, they plundered the ship and carried away the goods of one Andrew Wardlaw, a

merchant in the town. From the date of its charter to the
Union in 1707, Wick sent a commissioner to the Scottish
Parliament. At the Union it was associated with Kirkwall,
Dornoch, Tain, and Dingwall, in the return of one member to
the British House of Commons. In 1832, when the Reform
Act was passed, Cromarty was added to this batch; and Wick,
comprehending within its parliamentary bounds the suburban
village of Louisburgh, and Pulteneytown, was constituted the
returning burgh. The Earls of Caithness held the superiority
till 1672, when Glenorchy purchased it. He afterwards sold
the superiority to the Ulbster family; and in 1821 Sir John
Sinclair disposed of it to the Duke of Sutherland for £3500.
This municipal privilege, which formerly gave the superior so
much political influence in the burgh, has now become of little
value. Of late years, the appearance of the town has been very
much improved by the erection of a number of excellent new
houses and shops. The Town and County Hall, and the Commercial Bank are two very handsome public buildings. The
latter is built entirely of freestone, and ornamented in front
with Ionic pillars. Dr Sinclair, of Wick, who has directed much
attention to the natural history of the county, has a very fine
museum, which will well repay a visit. This valuable and
interesting collection of curiosities is particularly rich in the
department of ornithology. It contains upwards of 200 birds
indigenous to the county, besides a great variety of quadrupeds, insects, and fishes, all beautifully prepared and
arranged by this ingenious gentleman himself. It includes
also a number of rare coins, and medals of different countries,
many of them of great antiquity. Amongst other objects of
interest, there are two deserving of special notice. The one is
the petrified tongue of an animal found some years ago at
John O'Groat's, and differing in form from that of any qua-
druped which at present is known to exist. The other is the
key of the old castle of Girnigoe, handed down through the
descendants of the last warden, whose name was John
Sinclair. It measures nearly one foot in length, and about

two inches in circumference. The bole, which is elaborately carved, is about three and a half inches in diameter ; and the ward, which displays much ingenuity in the construction, is about three inches on the square. Altogether, the museum is a most interesting one ; and strangers visiting Wick are frankly admitted to see it on calling at the doctor's residence, Montpellier House, in the suburbs of the town. Pulteneytown, on the south side of the bay and river, consists of two parts, the upper and lower. In the latter is the harbour. Upper Pulteneytown stretches eastward on an elevated terrace along the sea bank, and occupies a fine airy situation. It is regularly laid out in streets with a square near the centre. The houses are built of the blue Caithness flagstone which, it must be confessed, gives to the whole a somewhat sombre appearance. The principal public building is the Academy, near the upper end of Sinclair Terrace. It stands conspicuously on a high brae looking down on Lower Pulteneytown. It was erected in 1838 by the British Fishery Society at an expense of about £1600. It has had several eminent teachers, and among others, Mr Andrew Scott, the present professor of oriental languages in King's College, Aberdeen, was a short time rector of the institution. Pulteneytown and Wick proper are connected by a bridge of three arches flung across the river not many yards from where it runs into the bay. Before the erection of this bridge about the year 1800, the principal access to the town from the south side of the river was by a foot bridge which consisted of eleven pillars of stone connected by planks. In 1665 a complaint is made against the shoemakers and glovers of the burgh for breaking down the bridge by dressing skins and leather on it. The population, including that of Pulteneytown and Louisburgh, is about 7475. There are two newspapers published in Wick—the *John O'Groat Journal*, and the *Northern Ensign*. The former was started in 1836, and the latter in 1850. Both advocate Liberal views in politics ; both are conducted with much spirit and ability, and have each a respectable circulation. Wick derives its chief importance from being the great emporium of the herring fishery in Scotland ; and a brief account of its rise and progress may not be uninteresting.   Its founders were John Sutherland, of Wester, John Anderson, of Wick, and Alexander Miller, of Staxigoe.   They fitted out two small sloops, on the bounty, and began to fish in 1767 ; but, from various causes, the speculation was not very encouraging, and comparatively little was done till 1786, when the British Fishery Society was incorporated by Act of Parliament. The first fishing station was at Staxigoe, a pretty large creek, not far from Nosshead—there being then no harbour at Wick except the mouth of the river.   In 1790 there were thirty-two small sloops fishing on the bounty.   The bounty allowed was fifty shillings per ton.   Afterwards boats began to be used ; and in 1795 no fewer than 200 small boats were fishing at Wick, but great inconvenience was suffered from the want of a harbour.

In 1808 the British Fishery Society commenced their establishment of Pulteneytown by making a harbour and granting feus in perpetuity, for building, on liberal terms.   The ground on which the town is situated was purchased by the British Fishery Society from Lord Duffus, and it was called Pulteney in honour of Sir William Pulteney, who was chief director or governor of the Society at the time of the purchase. In 1810 the inner harbour was completed, at an expense of £16,000, of which £7500 were defrayed by Government. Owing to the great increase of trade, an outer harbour was planned in 1824, and in 1831 completed, at an expense of £22,000.   The quantity of herrings caught, and the number of persons engaged, vary each year considerably.   " On an average," says a writer on the subject, " it may be stated that the quantity caught during the season may be from 100,000 to 120,000 barrels or crans, and the number of people partially or wholly employed, including fishermen, coopers, packers, etc., about 12,000."   Numbers of fishermen come from the western isles—from Orkney and Shetland, and from the counties of Sutherland, Ross, Moray, Banff, etc. The number of boats is generally about 1000, each with a crew of five or six hands. Sometimes they have amounted to 1100 ; and, on a fine evening in July or August, the scene presented by this large fleet of boats leaving the harbour, and spreading over the bay in full sail, is truly magnificent. The cost of each boat, with nets and appurtenances, is about £150 ; and the netting of the whole fleet, if lineally extended, would stretch, it is said, from the Pentland Firth to the English Channel ! For the export of fish, shipping resort to the port of Wick alone to the extent of 60,000 tons a-year. The annual value of herrings exported may be estimated at £150,000.

According to the report of Tucker, one of the commissioners appointed by Cromwell to arrange the customs and excise in Scotland, Wick in 1654 did not possess a single vessel of any description. Thurso had just one small craft of 30 tons, and a Custom House officer was stationed in the county for looking after that town and Wick. " From these two ports," says Tucker, " a good store of beef, hides, and tallow is usually sent coastwise." But, he adds, " The officer's work is rather for preventing these commodities from being sent into foreign parts than from anything he is likely to recover here." The number of vessels at present belonging to Wick and Pulteney-town is 56, fitted to carry 3386 tons. The harbour accommodation is still greatly inadequate, and it is, moreover, unfortunately exposed to a heavy swell from the bay when the wind blows from the east, which renders the entrance to the port extremely dangerous. Both harbours, too, have sanded up to a great extent ; and there is not sufficient depth of water for the Aberdeen steamer to enter at any time. In the fall of the season, the coast is frequently visited by great and sudden outbursts of storm. The morning of the 19th August, 1848, will long be remembered in Wick. The sky on the preceding evening had a very unfavourable appearance about sunset, especially towards the east, where a mass of dark lurid cloud, streaked with fiery red, hung around the horizon, like a warning signal of the coming gale. The barometer, too, was observed to have fallen considerably. Notwithstanding these ominous prognostics, a number of boats left the harbour, and proceeded to the fishing ground. Early in the morning the threatened storm burst forth with all the suddenness and fury of a tropical hurricane. The wind blew from the south-east with the utmost vehemence. Houses shook, and windows rattled, and families were roused from their slumbers by the unusual noise. Hundreds in the first moments of alarm ran to the harbour. The bay was fearfully agitated ; and the heavy surge ever and anon broke over the bar, sweeping everything before it. Consternation was painted in every countenance. It was an appalling scene, deepened into tenfold intensity by the distress and agony of those who had relatives in the tiny craft that were dimly seen at times tossing on the crests of the foaming billows, and making for the shore, which was surrounded with a tremendous surf. Destruction was imminent, and no power of man could avert it. On that fatal morning forty-one boats were lost, and no fewer than thirty-seven men perished, many of them within a few yards of the harbour.

Next to Wick, the most important fishing station in the county is Lybster, which contains a population of about 800. The number of boats in the fishing season is upwards of 200. The village, which is near the sea, is provided with an excellent harbour, and the inhabitants are distinguished for their public spirit and enterprise.

About two miles to the south of Wick, on a tongue of land having a steep goe on each side, stand the remains of the Castle of Auldwick. This huge unshapely ruin forms an excellent landmark to vessels approaching the coast, and is by seamen called the " Auld Man of Wick." It consists of a grim-looking tower or keep of rudest masonry, perforated here and there with small arrow-slits, and rising to the height of three storeys. It is entirely roofless, and open within from top to bottom. A deep and broad moat defended it on the land side. Behind, or rather in front of the tower—for the only door looked towards the sea in the direction of the north-east—there were two ranges of lower buildings for domestic purposes, and a small space, near the extremity of the peninsula, would seem to have been used as a garden. Traces of a wall which surrounded it are still discernible. At this point the rocks shelve down in the form of rugged terraces ; and, in front of the entrance, in dangerous position, lie large black isolated lumps of rock, waiting, as it were, to destroy any boat that, without a proper knowledge of the place, might venture to enter either of the goes. The whole aspect of the scene is peculiarly wild and repulsive, without a single redeeming feature of beauty. With a gale from the east or north-east, the sea-breach is horrible, reminding one of the poet's epithet of a "hell of waters." The maddened breakers roar, and foam, and dash in fiend-like fury against the iron cliffs, while the old keep, gray and weather-beaten, scowls amid the storm, like an angry demon.

The date of the erection of Auldwick, which is believed to be one of the oldest buildings of the kind in Caithness, is not known. It was, at an early period, a stronghold of the Cheynes, a race of early chieftains who held great sway in the county, and of whom further notice will be taken in a subsequent part of this work. About the end of the fifteenth century it was inhabited by the Oliphants. In 1497, James IV. conferred by charter on George Oliphant and his spouse, Lady Duffus, the lands of Auldwick and Berriedale. A deadly feud, originating in a dispute about some property, is said to have arisen between this George, styled Lord Oliphant, and the Earl of Caithness. Oliphant, it appears, was fond of the chase ; and, as he happened to be out one day hunting, in the vicinity of the hill of Yarrows, he was attacked by the Earl and some of his retainers. Oliphant was without any attendants ; but, fortunately for him, he had a fleet horse. He immediately set spurs to the animal, and galloped home towards Auldwick, hotly pursued by the Earl and his dependants.

On approaching the castle he found that the drawbridge was not lowered. His pursuers were close behind him, and he had not even time to wind his hunting-horn, and warn the inmates of his return. It was a critical moment, and the noble animal on which he rode seemed fully to understand the danger. No application of spur or whip was needed. Exerting his full power, the horse leaped across the terrific chasm— clearing at one bound twenty-five feet—and landed his rider safe on the other side ! Lord Oliphant's leap was long talked of in Caithness, and was a familiar saying among the people.*

Between this old tower and Wick some geological appearances of a curious and rather puzzling kind present themselves. The cliffs in this quarter are about thirty feet in height, and their upper strata would appear to have been deranged by some extraordinary convulsion. Enormous masses of rock have been broken off from their beds, and thrown upon one another in most terrific confusion. One vast mass, apparently more than two hundred tons in weight, has been reft from its original bed, and tossed up on a similar layer immediately above it. Between the masses is a smaller rock, on which the one that has been hurled up rests in a most perilous position, looking as if "an infant's touch could urge its headlong passage down the verge." Theorists keenly differ as to the cause of this singular disruption. Some ascribe it to the force of the sea during some more than usually heavy tempest from the German Ocean ; others, who are advocates of what is called the glacial theory, maintain that it is the result of ice action at one of those infinitely remote eras in the geological history of the globe, which ingenious men, by the aid of a lively imagination, have described so eloquently. Icebergs driven against the cliffs with prodigious fury, in their estimation, sufficiently account for the entire phenomena.

Thurso, which lies about twenty-one miles to the west of

* The Oliphants were an ancient family, and possessed of considerable property in the county. They were superiors, it is said, of one-fourth part of Caithness. In 1606, the last Lord Oliphant sold all the lands he had in it to the Earl of Caithness. The family is now quite extinct.

Wick, is also situated at the mouth of a river, close by the sea. Etymologists differ about the origin of the name. Some suppose that it is so called from Horsa, a Saxon general, who, it is said, landed there some time in the fifth century, and plundered the county. Others, and among them Mr Worsaae, derive the name from the Icelandic term Thorsaa. In the pagan mythology of the Scandinavians, Thor was the title of one of their principle deities; and in the old Norse, *aa* signifies a river. Hence Thorsaa, or Thor's river. This latter derivation seems the more probable. The name of the river was afterwards extended to the town and the surrounding district. Thurso was a place of great note in ancient times, and there is frequent mention of it by Torfæus. In one place he calls it "*oppidum Cathnesiae*," the town of Caithness. It has been the scene of some remarkable events, and its environs afford a number of Norwegian memorials. At Ormlie, on a rising ground closely adjoining the new town, stood the Castle of Thurso—the "castrum de Thorsa" of Torfæus—in which the old Scandinavian earls of the county used frequently to reside. Of this once famous stronghold not a vestige is now to be seen. In clearing away the foundations of the ruins, some years ago, the workmen discovered the well, which was about twenty feet deep. The modern house, named Castle-green, stands nearly on the site of the ancient structure. Thurso was, by royal charter of Charles I., constituted a free burgh of barony in 1633, in favour of John, Master of Berriedale, who frequently resided in it. The seal of the burgh represents the figure of St Peter and the keys, with a tall staff crossed at the top, having the motto, "Sigillum Burgi de Thurso in Caithnes." In 1726, according to the M'Farlane Manuscript, it was four times as populous as Wick. The population by the last census was 3426. For nearly two centuries Thurso was the chief seat of the Sheriff Court of Caithness, and the residence of the several legal functionaries. But at length the superior and magistrates of Wick, considering this an usurpation of the just rights of the burgh, brought the case before the Court of

Session, when a decision was given in their favour, and the Sheriff Court was in 1828 removed to Wick.*   Thurso was, in consequence, shorn of much of its public importance; but it has survived the heavy blow and great discouragement, and is now progressing rapidly, both as respects internal improvements and increase of commerce.

In point of situation, Thurso has greatly the advantage of Wick; and the surrounding landscape has been much admired by strangers.   The view, as you approach it from the eastward, is particularly striking.   Immediately before you, stretching along the west side of the river, over which there is an excellent bridge of three arches, lies the town.   About two miles further west you see the celebrated roadstead of Scrabster, with a long ridge of Holborn-head; and, immediately opposite, about two leagues to the north-east, Dunnet-head, at the western entrance of the Pentland Firth.   On the hill of Clairdon, some two miles from the town, in an easterly direction, appears Harold's Tower, a monument erected over the grave of Harold, Earl of Orkney and Caithness, who was slain there in battle in the twelfth century.   From the point of Clairdon, near this monument, all along the shore to Holborn-head, swells in the beautiful Bay of Thurso.   To the north, in the back-ground, tower up the lofty summits of the Hoy hills in Orkney.   Near the mouth of the river, on the east side, is Thurso-east, the seat of Sir George Sinclair of Ulbster.   The edifice, though of late considerably modernised, is said to have been erected about the year 1660, by George, the sixth Earl of Caithness of the Sinclair family.   Miss Sinclair, speaking of the old castle, says:—"In stormy weather, the sea spray

* The transference of the courts from Thurso to Wick took place in terms of the decree of the Court of Session in an action at the instance of Earl Gower and the magistrates of Wick against G. Douglas and others.   Wick being the royal burgh, and there being, moreover, several statutes ordaining the Sheriff to hold his courts there, the Court of Session found that the Sheriff was bound to hold his regular stated courts at Wick, without prejudice to holding courts at other places, in terms of the 20th Geo. II., c. 43.   And further, that the Sheriff-clerk's office must be situated at Wick.   For a particular account of this case, vide Shaw and Dunlop's Decisions, vol. vi., pp. 650-657.

has sometimes passed over the roof. Fish have been caught with a line from the drawing-room window ; and vessels have been wrecked so close under the turrets that the cries of the drowning sailors could be heard." Thurso contains some handsome new streets and houses ; but the finest building of the whole is the new parish church, which is in a superior style of architecture, with a lofty tower and clock, and cost about £6000. In a square, opposite the east end of the church, is a statue, by Chantry, of Sir John Sinclair, in his uniform as colonel of the Rothesay and Caithness Fencibles. Among the recent buildings is an academy, to be named the " Miller Institution," after its founder, Mr Alexander Miller, of Thurso, a benevolent gentleman who has been at the sole expense of the erection, and has set apart a fund, we believe, for the maintenance of the teachers. There is also a female school, in which young girls of the poorer class are taught gratis. This Institution, which has been productive of immense good, was, much to their honour, originally got up by the ladies of Thurso by means of voluntary contributions, and is chiefly, if not altogether, supported in this way.

It was not till the year 1800 that a bridge was thrown across the river at Thurso. Before then, people going to and coming from the town were ferried over in a small coble. The passage, although short, was in stormy weather, and especially during a " spate," not unattended with danger ; and the small skiff, if crowded, as was sometimes the case on market-days, was liable to be upset. Some melancholy accidents of this nature are recorded, when all on board were swept down by the current, and lost. In 1749, no fewer than seventeen persons were drowned in this way. There were several instances, too, of persons having perished in rashly attempting to ford the stream after a heavy fall of rain, and when the tide was in. In the year 1756, a Mr Richard Sinclair, a merchant in Thurso, was drowned in crossing the water. The accident is remarkable from its having been accompanied or foreshadowed by one of those mysterious appearances, or as they would now be called, illusions of the imagination, which entered so largely into the popular creed of old, and the belief in which modern science and philosophy have not yet been able wholly to remove. The story is told in a curious old work, entitled, "A Treatise on the Second Sight, &c., by Theophilus Insulanus,"* and is as follows :— "Mr Richard Sinclair returning home late at night with his servant, as they came to the river close by the town, they found it swelled by a fall of rain, and much increased by the tide, which was in. The latter seemed averse to ford, which his master observing, alighted and gave him his own horse, and mounted his servant's horse, with which having entered the river, he was soon carried by the flood out of his saddle, and drowned. His wife knowing nothing then of the matter, as she was going from one room to another in her own house, saw Mr Sinclair go up the stair to his own room, and called to the servant to bring him a candle and make up a fire ; but after the servant had brought the light in great haste, she found no person within. In less than an hour the report was through the town that the gentleman was drowned. This account," adds the writer, "I had from a person that came to the town next day, when the accident of the preceding night was the common subject of conversation."

The river of Thurso, which is the largest in the county, is valuable as a salmon-fishing stream, and has been long cele-brated for the abundance and the excellent quality of the fish caught in it. In the month of July, 1743, no fewer than 2560 salmon were taken in this river at one sweep of the net. The circumstance, though it looks somewhat incredible, is confirmed by the written attestation of the chief magistrate and other two respectable inhabitants of the town, who were present at the time. In this document, which still exists, it is stated that this extraordinary draught took place in the cruive pool above the town ; that the net containing the salmon was carried

* Printed by Ruddiman & Co. in 1763.

down the water by from eighteen to twenty men, with long poles in their hands keeping down the ground rope, and that the fish were afterwards taken ashore by degrees in a smaller net. About the end of the last century, the shore dues at the river mouth, then the principal harbour, were only one shilling and sixpence, but from this charge vessels belonging to the port were exempted.

The river of Thurso has its rise in a small brook among the hills on the confines of Sutherland. At the distance of eight miles from its source it enters Lochmore. Issuing from the outlet at the north corner of this lake, it proceeds onwards through a pretty wide extent of country. Some of the localities through which it passes, especially in the upper parts of the parish of Halkirk, possess features of no ordinary beauty. The scene at Dirlet is particularly romantic. Here the banks on each side are steep, and richly clothed with brushwood ; and on the summit of a precipitous, rock, said at one time to have been surrounded by the river, and accessible only by a drawbridge, may be seen the ruins of a castle which, about the end of the fifteenth century, was inhabited by a chief of the name of Sutherland. After a winding course of nearly thirty miles, during which it is fed by many smaller tributaries, the river finally flows into the Bay of Thurso.

I have already noticed the greatly improved condition of Caithness. This is abundantly shown by the large increase in rent,* and the extraordinary rise in the value of landed property in the county since the beginning of the century. One striking instance of the increased value of land may be mentioned. About the year 1788, the late Sir John Sinclair of Ulbster purchased the estate of Langwell for £7000. He sold it in 1813 to the late Mr James Horne, writer in Edinburgh, for £42,000 ; and Mr Donald Horne, who succeeded to the property on the death of his uncle, lately sold it to the Duke of Portland for £90,000. In other departments, such

* See Appendix No 4.

as the rearing of stock, the pavement trade,* etc., Caithness is making the same remarkable progress ; and, indeed, it may be said the material resources of the county are only beginning to be developed. The present proprietors who have most distinguished themselves for their agricultural and other improvements are the Earl of Caithness, Sir George Dunbar of Hempriggs, Sir John Sinclair of Dunbeath, Mr Sinclair of Forss, Mr Traill of Ratter, and Mr Henderson of Stemster. And here it is but proper to mention two gentlemen to whom the county of Caithness is largely indebted, namely, Mr William Darling and Mr James Purves. Mr Darling was, for a considerable time, manager at Stirkoke for the late Mr Horne, Sheriff of Haddington ; and Mr Purves was for several years also factor for the late James Traill, Esq. of Ratter. Possessed of great intelligence, and thoroughly acquainted with the best mode of husbandry in the south, of which they are natives, they introduced the system, as far as it was practicable, on the estates under their management, and showed in a very satisfactory manner what great improvements, superior skill, combined with a judicious outlay of capital, could effect on a soil not naturally rich, and in a changeable climate like that of Caithness. In the agricultural annals of the county their names will have a permanent place.

Caithness is divided into ten parishes, *quoad civilia*, and composed of highlands and lowlands. In the former the Gaelic language is spoken, and in the latter the English, or rather a dialect of the Scotch, with some provincial peculiarities. The Gaelic, which is said to be not of the purest school, is fast disappearing before the march of education ; and Caithness may in truth be called a lowland county. In 1801 the population was only 22,609. By the last census in 1861 it amounts to 41,216.

The natives are an intermixture or incorporation of two originally distinct races—the Celts and Scandinavians ; and in

* In the Memoir of the late James Traill, Esq. of Rattar, some account is given of the pavement trade of Caithness.

personal qualities they yield to the inhabitants of no county in
Scotland.   The men are hardy, active, and well made, and the
women are in general exceedingly good-looking.   Finer figures
and more attractive countenances than are to be seen among
the latter will not be found anywhere.   As a people, the Caithnessians are acute, shrewd, and practical, with a decided turn
for business.   Their imagination seldom gets the upper hand of
their judgment; and they are, consequently, not very apt to
indulge in matters of speculation, or to suffer themselves to be
carried away with any untried or fanciful theories.   There
is also a strong clannish feeling among Caithness men, and
wherever any number of them are located they usually form
themselves into clubs and societies.   There are four distinguished societies of this kind—one in Glasgow, one in Edinburgh, one in London, and one in Australia.   Of the first and
oldest of these, the Glasgow Caithness Association, I shall
here give a brief account.   This excellent society was instituted
in the month of January, 1837.   The objects contemplated by
its founders were the promotion of friendly intercourse among
the natives of Caithness residing in Glasgow, and the relief of
any of them who might be in necessitous circumstances.   At
its first meeting, the late Mr Alexander Coghill was elected
chairman, Mr Daniel Macadie was appointed treasurer, and
Mr William Levack, secretary.   James Traill, Esq. of Ratter,
was chosen patron, and laid the foundation of the society by a
donation of ten guineas.   After his death, his son, George
Traill, Esq. of Ratter, the present M.P. for the county, became
patron, and with the same liberality continued for many years
to assist the society.   The succeeding patrons have also contributed liberally, among whom may be mentioned Alexander
Miller, Esq., a native of Thurso.   The amount of money
expended by the society in its legitimate sphere is about
fifteen pounds per annum; but various sums, amounting to
about one hundred pounds, have been sent to Caithness to
relieve destitution there.   The number of members is about
sixty, and the principal source of revenue arises from a small

sum payable by each of them at the quarterly meetings. The present office-bearers are five, with twelve directors.*

Formerly Caithness was particularly distinguished for its military spirit. At the time of the Irish rebellion the county furnished no fewer than three battalions of fencibles, two of which did duty in Ireland for several years. At a later period it had its volunteer and local militia corps stationed within the bounds, and ready to defend life and property in the event of a hostile invasion. During the Peninsular War, about ten recruits a month were sent south from the Thurso district alone. They commonly enlisted into the Highland regiments; and at one time, it is said, nearly one-tenth of the 79th regiment was composed of Caithness men. Soldiering was then a recognised and ordinary profession, to which young men took as naturally as they did to the plough. All this, however, has changed; and the great reason why the youth do not enlist for the regular service as formerly is the increased value of labour, and the more comfortable position of the labourer. I may observe, however, that in coming forward to aid the recent grand embodiment of a national volunteer force, Caithness was not behind the rest of Scotland. The old martial spirit of the county was seen once more to revive; and, stirred by the patriotic movement that was everywhere going on throughout the length and breadth of the land, the young men of Wick and Thurso speedily enrolled themselves as volunteers; and, in point of appearance and proficiency in drill, they can stand a comparison with any of their brethren in the south.

Within the last few years the county has been very much infested by tinkers, and their number seems to be greatly on the increase. There are, between young and old, it is said, nearly a hundred and forty of them in Caithness, composed of different bands or tribes, named the Macfees, the Newlands, the Johnstones, and the Williamsons. They have no particular place of abode, but roam about through the several parishes,

* In chapter xiii. will be found some account of the origin and progress of the Edinburgh Caithness Association.

following the profession of tinsmiths, but subsisting in a great measure by begging and stealing. They lie out all the year round, even in the roughest weather. A frequent haunt of theirs in the winter season is the Links of Dunnet, which abounds with sand hillocks covered with long bent. Another place to which they betake themselves for shelter from the storm is a cave near the village of Brough, in the same parish. What money they acquire by the disposal of their tinware they commonly spend in drink; and their orgies never terminate without a quarrel and a regular fight by both sexes. In this respect, when inflamed by liquor, they very much resemble the lower orders of the Irish. From their personal appearance, they would seem to be of a mixed race. Some of them have all the characteristics of the genuine gipsy, viz., very brown complexions, dark hair and eyes; while others have fair complexions, with red hair and blue eyes, indicative of a Saxon or Gothic origin. They have a patois of their own, which they use when they find it convenient to do so, but they all speak the English with a whining tone, which is particularly marked when they beg, and so importunate are they as beggars that they will not leave any house they enter until they get either food or money. They are a regular pest and scourge to the community; and what with begging, thieving, and occasional maintenance in prison, they cost the county a very considerable sum annually. About two years ago a benevolent scheme was set on foot to impart some religious instruction to these pariahs of society, and, if possible, to reclaim them from their wandering habits and dishonest practices. For this purpose a missionary was sent among them, but his labours were fruitless, and the scheme, which promised no success, was ultimately given up. Hugh Miller makes a striking remark that he never knew a gipsy that seemed to possess a moral sense. The Caithness gipsies apparently possess nothing of the kind, and, humanly speaking, it would seem as hopeless a task to civilize them as it is to convert the Jews.

Besides the tinkers, there is during the herring fishing at

Wick an influx of the very worst characters of both sexes from the south—some pretending to be shipwrecked sailors, some going about with baskets in the guise of hawkers, but all expert thieves and beggars. To check this enormous evil a stringent Vagrancy Act of the legislature is imperatively required. At present the police have no powers to suppress it. Charles Lamb, in a paper entitled "Complaint of the Decay of Beggars," whimsically argues that charitable people suffer deeply from the paucity of such objects of benevolence. Caithness would afford them an ample field for the exercise of this virtue.

Chambers, in his "Gazetteer of Scotland" (published, we believe, in 1831), draws a dismal picture of the county. "To the eyes of a Lowlander," says he, "or one accustomed to see fertile enclosed fields, or warm woody valleys, the appearance of Caithness is frightful, and productive of melancholy feelings. When this is enhanced by the consideration that the climate is of a very unfavourable kind, ideas of all that is comfortless are conveyed. Wood there is none, and the few enclosures are of a very rude quality. It may sound like a reproach, but it is a well-known fact, that the improvements and modern comforts of Caithness have been brought about entirely by wealth drawn from the sea."

If Chambers, otherwise an excellent and popular writer, visited Caithness at the period in question, and in the summer season, he must have surveyed the county with a jaundiced eye. It is true, it has no wood, properly speaking; but though wood adds vastly to the beauty of a landscape, there is a difference of opinion as to its advantages in a purely agri-cultural district. *There*, as our transatlantic friends would say, "a good clearance" is the main desideratum. I once heard a Berwickshire farmer affirm that trees were a "positive nuisance, and served only to collect vermin!" But did Cham-bers see no beauty in the rich corn-fields of Caithness? There is a Scotch song which says the "corn rigs are bonny," and they are so to the vulgar as well as to the poetical eye, independently of their affording us the "staff of life." Caithness has, from the earliest period of which we have any record, been celebrated as a corn-producing county, and now, so far as grain, stock, and several other commodities are concerned, it can compete with any county in Scotland. "At this moment," says the *Northern Ensign* (March 15, 1860), "we are exporting large quantities of superior oats; our cattle and sheep are carrying off the top price in the southern markets, and our wool frequently fetches the highest price at the public sales of Leith and Edinburgh." Moreover, if it were the case, which it is not, that "the improvements and modern comforts of Caithness have been brought about almost entirely by wealth drawn from the sea," this, instead of "sounding like a reproach," says very much for the intelligence, public spirit, and industry of the inhabitants. Let Mr Chambers visit Caithness now, in the month of July or August, and we can assure him that the aspect of the county will not inspire him with any "melancholy feelings."

Previous to the Union, Caithness had the right of sending to the Scottish Parliament three representatives or commissioners—two for the county, and one for the burgh of Wick. They were paid for their attendance, and had an additional allowance besides, for sixteen days, to perform the journey out and home. In 1707, when the union of the two kingdoms came to be discussed, the measure was opposed by the Earl of Caithness, and supported by Mr Dunbar, younger of Hempriggs, member for the burgh. Caithness was then reduced to one county member, and was allowed only an alternate representation with Bute. This most absurd arrangement continued until the passing of the Reform Act, when the county became entitled to a separate representative, and was put on a similar political footing with the other counties in Scotland.

CHAPTER II.

WITH respect to the history of Caithness for the first five or six hundred years of the Christian era, nothing with certainty is known. Tradition, as well as history, is silent on the matter; and the whole subject is involved in impenetrable darkness. It is probable that for a great part of that time the county was a mere desert, uninhabited except by wild beasts. The aboriginal inhabitants would appear to have been the Picts,* a people, from the best antiquarian authority, not of Scandinavian, but of Celtic descent. There are still to be seen here and there in the county the remains of what are called Picts' houses. These, however, were not the ordinary dwellings of that people, but strongholds or places of defence. "Their houses," says Scott, "were constructed of wattles; or in more dangerous times they burrowed under ground in long, narrow, tortuous excavations, which still exist, and the idea of which seems to have been suggested by a rabbit warren." About the year 920, Caithness would appear to have been partially peopled, for at that period it was subdued by Sigurd,† Earl of Orkney. Sigurd's immediate predecessor was his brother, Ronald, the first Norwegian Earl of Orkney, on whom the administration of the islands was conferred by the celebrated Harold Harfager. This Ronald was the father of the famous Rollo, the invader of Normandy, and paternal ancestor of William the Conqueror. Caithness continued subject to Norwegian rule for nearly four hundred years.

---

* The first writer who mentions the Picts is Eumenius, the orator, who was a professor at Autun, in Burgundy. In the year 297, and again in 308, he speaks of the Caledonians and Picts as the same people—"Caledones aliiqui Picti." (Brown His. High., chap. 1, p. 33.)

† He conquered also Ross, Sutherland, and Moray; and from Helgy, his principal officer, the name of Elgin is supposed to be derived.

From time to time after its annexation to Orkney, numerous bands of Norsemen landed in the county, and, driving the natives into the interior, gradually established themselves around the whole sea-coast. On the Latheron side, they extended their settlements as far as Berriedale. This, however, was not effected without some severe struggles with the inhabitants, who felt grievously annoyed at being thus expelled from their usual abodes, and winced not a little under the Scandinavian yoke. Most of the names of places, and not a few of the surnames in the lowland parts of the county, are Norwegian. It is a remarkable circumstance, however, that the Norsemen never succeeded in establishing their language, or any of their peculiar laws or usages, in Caithness. All that we can trace to them are a few superstitions which still linger in some parts of the county, but are soon destined to disappear before the increasing light of knowledge. The case was very different in Orkney. Some of their udal institutions exist there even to this day, or, at all events, were but very recently abolished. The language spoken by the natives of that county, while under the sway of the sea-kings, was the old Icelandic, or Norse; and it continued in general use till near the end of the sixteenth century. Their language is now the English, with a peculiar "singing accent."

Orkney, while it was the chief seat of the earldom, formed, with its fine natural harbours, the great rendezvous of the war galleys of the Norsemen, whence they issued out on their various piratical expeditions. These vessels, from their peculiar construction and equipment, were admirably adapted for the service in which they were employed. They were generally long, narrow, and low in the water. They were protected with a parapet or breastwork of shields, and many of them were of great size, containing from twenty to thirty banks of oars. The largest of them carried a crew of from 80 to 100 fighting men, whose arms consisted of swords, bows, arrows, and pikes, besides which they had on board a quantity of stones to throw into the vessels of the enemy. On their prows were usually carved figure-heads of dragons, which added not a little to their formidable appearance. This most probably suggested to the picturesque fancy of Scott the striking figure which he uses when describing the Scandinavian rovers and their ships in the "Lay of the Last Minstrel:"—

> "Kings of the main, their leaders brave,
> Their barks the *dragons of the wave*."

These sea-kings, as they were called, made descents upon most of the maritime countries of Europe, and carried home with them silks, armour, golden vases, jewels, embroidered carpets and tapestry, wines, and various other articles of luxury from the several castles, churches, and palaces which they plundered.

Sigurd, who was, strictly speaking, the first Norwegian Earl of Orkney and Caithness, died, and was buried at Burghead, in Morayshire. The circumstances connected with his death are not a little extraordinary. "He gained," says Mr Worsaae, "the victory in a foray over the Scotch jarl Melbrigd, and cut off his head, which, in the overweening pride of his triumph, he hung at his saddle; but a sharp tooth that projected from the head chafed his leg, and caused a wound which proved his death." Sigurd having left no issue, the earldom reverted to the family of his brother Ronald.* About the middle of the tenth century, two brothers, Liot and Skuli, lineal descendants of that family, contended for the earldom. The former was supported in his claim by the King of Norway, and the latter, so far as Caithness was concerned, by the King of Scotland. Arms, the usual mode of deciding disputes at the time, were resorted to. Skuli was assisted by a Sutherland chieftain, to whom Torfæus gives the high-sounding title of "Comes Magbragdus." In a battle which was fought at Dale, in the parish of Halkirk, Skuli was defeated and slain,

---

* Einar, one of Ronald's sons who succeeded to the earldom, was the first who taught the natives of Orkney and Caithness to use turf for fuel. From this circumstance, he acquired the additional appellation of Torf Einar. He was the natural brother of Rollo, afterwards Duke of Normandy.

on which Liot seized the whole of Caithness, and kept forcible possession of it. Not long after, the Sutherland chief, burning with a desire to be revenged for the affair at Dale, collected as many followers as he could, and invaded the county. Liot, with a nearly equal force, met him at Toftingall, near the hill of Spittal, where a desperate engagement took place. Victory at length declared for Liot, but he received a severe wound, of which, in the course of a few days, he died.

It is supposed that the tall standing stone near Brabster-dorran, in the parish of Bower, was erected in memory of Liot, and that it indicates the spot where he was buried. This supposition derives some confirmation from the circumstance that the stone was anciently called " stone Lud," which would seem to be a corruption of stone Liot or Liot's stone. There can be no doubt, however, that it is a sepulchral monument commemorative of some great man. The doctrine of Odin commanded it as a sacred duty to erect stones of this description in memory of the brave. "The large stones," says the late Mr Pope, of Reay, " erected at Rangag and along the burn of Latheron, are all sepulchral monuments." This is confirmed by the testimony of Mr Worsaae. " Tall bauta* stones," says that writer, " are to be seen in several places in Caithness, to which some legend about the Danes is generally attached; they now stand in a leaning posture, as if mourning over the departed times of the heroic age. A monument of a Danish princess who, according to tradition, suffered shipwreck on the coast, was formerly to be found in a churchyard at Ulbster." The story is that Gunn of Clyth, having paid a visit to Denmark, married a young princess of that country. On his way home with his bride the vessel was wrecked near Ulbster, and the lady unfortunately perished. The accident, which hap-

* The learned Danish antiquary has here fallen into a slight error. A bauta stone is a tomb stone inscribed with runics ; but so far as we know, there are no such sepulchral monuments in the county. The monoliths, which are still standing, are all plain and unhewn, without any written characters or figures whatever, with the exception of the one in the burying ground at Ulbster, on which there are rudely sculptured a cross and a half moon, together with the forms of various uncouth animals, including the serpent.

pened at night, was said to be owing to the pilot, who mistook a light at Ulbster for one at Clyth.

While noticing these strange relics of a former age, I may here mention that one of the most curious monuments of antiquity in the county is to be seen on the south side of the loch of Stemster, in the parish of Latheron. It consists of a number of standing stones ranged in the form of an elongated horse shoe, with the opening to the south, and the convex end next the loch. The distance between the two points that form the opening is 85½ feet, and the depth from the centre of the opening to the centre of the concave is 226 feet. Several of the stones have fallen, but there are still about thirty-three standing. Eight feet seems to have been the regular distance between each. This remarkable structure is said by the writer of the statistical account of Latheron to have been a Druidical temple ; but it is extremely doubtful if Druidism ever penetrated into Caithness, and it is more likely that the monument in question was erected by the Scandinavians, and used by them as a place of meeting both for judicial and religious purposes. We learn from the Eyrbiggja Saga, and from the works of Bartholin, Wormius, and others, that the northern nations, while in a state of heathenism, held courts of justice, and offered up sacrifices to their deities in circles of standing stones.

But to proceed with our narrative. Ragnhilde, the widow of Liot, and daughter of the famous Erik, King of Norway, surnamed the bloody, lived for some time at Murkle.* She was a woman of a most infamous character, and had been thrice married. She caused her two former husbands, who were brothers of Liot, to be murdered—the one at Murkle, and the other at Stennis, in Orkney ; and yet, with incredible effrontery, affecting entire innocence of the heavy crimes laid to her

* Murkle was a place of great note in ancient times. It was the seat of a famous nunnery ; and here, John, one of the old Earls of Caithness, signed a document binding himself and his followers to support Edward I. of England in his war with Scotland. The seal, which was affixed to the writ, bore the Earl's coat of arms, which was a ship with a tressure of flower de luce around it.

charge, she offered Liot her hand, and being a beautiful woman, and of an insinuating address, he was induced to marry her.

In the year 1014, Sigurd, the second of that name, Earl of Orkney and Caithness, embarked with a large body of troops for Ireland to assist one of the Norwegian chiefs in a war with the Irish King Brian. A celebrated battle took place at Clontarf,* about three miles to the north-east of Dublin, in which both Brian and the Earl were slain. The Norwegian annalists, like most ancient writers, appear to have been fond of the màrvellous, and in some cases without any nice discrimination or sifting of materials, to have mingled fact and fable together. A short time before setting out on his expedition to Ireland, Audna, Sigurd's mother,† presented him with a standard made by her own hand, in which was woven, with exquisite art, the image of the raven, a bird sacred to Odin, the Scandinavian god of war. The raven was represented with outspread wings, and in the act of soaring upwards. On receiving the banner the Earl was assured by his mother that

* In the old traditional records of Ireland, the battle of Clontarf holds a prominent place, and the issue is described as the greatest and most decisive victory which the Irish ever had over the Danes. During the famous repeal agitation, O'Connell, with consummate tact and knowledge of the Irish character, turned the circumstance to account in arousing the so-called patriotism of his countrymen. King Brian, from whom he gave out that he was descended, was extolled to the skies as a martyr for the deliverance of his country from the yoke of the oppressors. Fancied prints of the battle and of Brian were largely distributed among the deluded peasantry; and the battle was further celebrated in songs and speeches as having completely annihilated the Danish power in Ireland, and saved her independence and freedom. In this matter, however, O'Connell and his partisans did not adhere to strict historical truth; for the battle of Clontarf did not annihilate the Danish power in Ireland; and the northern adventurers, under their respective chiefs, maintained their sway in some parts of that country for a long time afterwards. But agitation, and not veracity, was the object of O'Connell. At length, when he had sufficiently raised the excitable feelings of his followers, he concluded one of his seditious harangues with a notice that he would hold a great repeal meeting on the celebrated plain of Clontarf. "Everybody knew beforehand," says an able writer, "that the real meaning of this was, that just as the Irish, with Brian at their head, had formerly defeated the Danes on that very place, so should they now, in like manner, follow O'Connell, and make every sacrifice to wrest back their lost independence from English or Saxon ascendancy; but Government forbade the meeting, and indicted O'Connell."

† This ingenious lady was the daughter of an Irish chief. Her husband, Ludovic (Sigurd's father), died in Caithness, and was buried at a place called Stenhone in the parish of Watten.

it had this remarkable property, that whoever had it carried before him would be victorious, but that the standard-bearer himself was doomed to fall. In the battle of Clontarf, accordingly, two of Sigurd's standard-bearers were killed. After this, none of his officers would take up the fatal colours, on which the Earl wrapped them round his body, and gallantly fought until he fell, pierced with innumerable wounds. It was only after a long and desperate struggle that the Irish obtained the victory.

Torfæus gives an account of a remarkable prodigy which was seen at the time in Caithness. On Good Friday (the day of the battle) a man named Daraddus, saw a number of persons on horseback ride at full speed towards a small hill, near which he dwelt, and seemingly enter into it. He was led by curiosity to approach the spot, when, looking through an opening in the side of the hillock, he observed twelve gigantic figures, resembling women, employed in weaving a web. As they wove, they sang a mournful song or dirge descriptive of the battle in Ireland, in which they foretold the death of King Brian, and that of the Earl of Orkney. When they had finished their task, they tore the web into twelve pieces. Each took her own portion, and once more mounting their horses, six galloped to the south, and six to the north. This singular legend derives a peculiar interest from the circumstance that it forms the subject of Gray's celebrated ode, the "Fatal Sisters." The sisters mentioned by the poet were the Valkyries, or choosers of the slain in the Gothic mythology, and the special ministers of Odin. They were mounted on swift horses, with drawn swords in their hands ; and, in the throng of battle, selected such as were destined to slaughter, and conducted them to Valhalla (the hall of Odin, or paradise of the brave), where they attended the banquet, and served the departed heroes with horns of mead and ale. Gray's ode purports to be the song sung by the unearthly ladies. The following are some of its more striking stanzas :—

> " Now the storm begins to lower,
>   (Haste the loom of hell prepare,)

Iron sleet of arrowy shower
  Hurtles in the darkened air.
See ! the grisly texture grow—
  'Tis of human entrails made ;
And the weights that play below,
  Each a gasping warrior's head.
Shafts for shuttles, dipt in gore,
  Shoot the trembling chords along ;
Sword, that once a monarch bore,
  Keep the tissue close and strong.

*   *   *   *   *

Low the dauntless Earl is laid,
  Gor'd with many a gaping wound ;
Fate demands a nobler head.
  Soon a King shall bite the ground.

*   *   *   *   *

Horror covers all the heath,
  Clouds of carnage blot the sun ;
Sisters ! weave the web of death,
  Sisters ! cease—the work is done.
Mortal ! thou that hear'st the tale,
  Learn the tenor of our song ;
Scotland ! through each winding vale
  Far and wide the notes prolong.
Sisters ! hence with spurs of speed
  Each her thundering falchion wield,
Each bestride her sable steed,
  Hurry, hurry to the field."*

The scene of this extraordinary legend is supposed to be a knoll or hillock in the parish of Olrig, called Sysa, which has been particularly celebrated, from time immemorial, as a favourite haunt of witches and fairies. Of late years its appearance has been somewhat altered by the agricultural improvements which have taken place in the common in which it is situated. Sysa, originally, notwithstanding its bad name, possessed some features of interest. On gaining the top from the north, you saw the side fronting the south shaped into a

* Torfaeus gives the song from the original Norse with a Latin translation. North Ronaldshay is said to have been the last place in Orkney where the Norse was spoken. Some time after Gray's ode was published, the clergyman of that island read it to some of the oldest inhabitants, who assured him that they were quite familiar with it in the original, and had often heard it sung in their younger days.

beautiful green hollow, having a gentle slope downwards. This hollow contained a spring of delicious water, clear as crystal; and, in the summer season, the sward around it was of the richest green, thickly sprinkled with wild-flowers, and contrasting strongly with the brown and stunted herbage of the surrounding moor. It was, on the whole, a rather pretty spot, and, situated as it was, it came upon the eye like an oasis in the desert.

Among the local legends of a supernatural kind connected with Sysa, is the following, which may, not inappropriately, be appended to that from Torfæus.

THE PIPER OF THE WINDY HA'.

Many years ago a young man, named Peter Waters, after driving his cattle to the then undivided common, halted about noon, on his way home, at the well of Sysa, in order to quench his thirst with a draught from that refreshing spring. It was a warm and beautiful day in the "leafy month of June"—one of nature's holidays—and the sun shone out with unclouded brilliancy. The spot had a peculiarly sweet and tranquil air about it that invited to repose. Not a living thing seemed to intrude within the fairy hollow, save the golden honey-bee that came humming along, lighted for a moment on a flower to sip its nectared sweets, and then flew away with its glad murmuring note as before. Having quenched his thirst, Peter resolved, before proceeding farther, to indulge himself with half an hour's rest; and, accordingly, he lay down and stretched himself at full length on his back. For a minute or two he continued to follow with his eye a lark that rose a few yards from him, and carolled like a "musical cherub" as it mounted higher and higher in the air; but an irresistible drowsiness, like that produced by mesmerism, stole over him, and he finally fell fast asleep. He slept till near sunset, when he was awakened by a gentle shake on the shoulder. Starting in a moment from his recumbent position, and rubbing his eyes, our hero beheld, to his astonishment, a most beautiful young lady, dressed in green, with golden ringlets, blue eyes, and the sweetest countenance in the world, standing beside him. Though a great admirer of the sex, Peter had not been accustomed to the society of ladies, and he, therefore, very naturally, felt not a little nervous and confused in the presence of his fair visitant. A blush overspread his countenance, and his heart throbbed violently. His first impulse was to take to his heels; but the lady bestowed on him such a bewitching smile, that he became rivetted to the spot, and could not move a single step. By degrees his timidity wore away, and he recovered his self-possession so far as to be able, without much stammering, to converse with the beautiful stranger.

"Don't be afraid of me, Peter," said the lady, with one of her most captivating smiles, and in a voice soft and clear as a silver bell. "I feel a great interest in you, and I am come to make a man of you."

"I am much obliged to you, indeed," stammered Peter; "the greatest nobleman in the kingdom might be proud of your fair hand, but I have no desire as yet to enter into the silken cord; and, besides, I would require to be better acquainted with you before I took such a step. People commonly court a little before they marry."

"You mistake me altogether, Peter," said the lady, giving way to a hearty laugh. "Though you appear a very nice young man, I make no offer of my hand; what I mean is, that I will put you in the way of rising in the world and making your fortune. Here are two things, a book and a pipe. Make your choice of the one or the other. If you take the book, you will become the most popular preacher in the North; and if you take the pipe, you will be the best performer on that martial instrument in Scotland. I shall give you five minutes to consider," added she, drawing from her bosom a small golden time-piece about the size of a sovereign.

The book was a splendidly-bound copy of the Bible, richly embossed with gold, with a golden clasp; the pipe a most

beautiful instrument of its kind, with a green silken bag of
gold and silver tissue, and superbly furnished with a number
of silver keys. Peter gazed with admiration on the two
articles, and was greatly puzzled which of the two to choose.
It would be a grand thing, he thought with himself, to be a
popular preacher, to have a good glebe and manse, to be
company for the laird and his lady, and to be cried up as a
" fine man," and worshipped by the crowd. On the other
hand, he was a great enthusiast for music, and he should like,
above all things, to be able to play the bagpipe. Should he
once become famed as the best piper in Scotland, he had no
doubt that he would get plenty of employment, and the money
would flow like shells into his pocket. After thus considering
the matter in his own mind, Peter at length came to a determination, and said to the lady, " Since you are so kind, I
think I will choose the pipe ; but as I never fingered a chanter
in my life, I fear it will be a long time before I learn to play
on such a difficult instrument."

" No. fear of that," rejoined the lady, " blow up, and
you'll find that the pipe of its own accord will discourse the
most eloquent music."

Peter did as he was desired, and to his great surprise
and delight he played " Maggie Lauder" in a stlye that Rob
the Ranter himself could not have surpassed. Some cattle
that were grazing hard by lifted their heads from the ground
the moment they heard the first notes of the tune, and
kept flinging and capering about in the most extraordinary
manner.

" This is perfectly wonderful," exclaimed Peter, delighted
beyond measure with his own performance ; " there must
surely be some glamour about this instrument."

Then thanking the lady for the invaluable present, he was
about to take his departure, when she said—

" Stop a moment ; there is one condition attached to the
gift : this day seven years, at the very same hour of the
evening, you will have to meet me by moonlight at the

well of Sysa. Swear by its enchanted spring that you will
do so."

Peter rashly swore by the fairy well, and promised, if alive,
to keep the appointment ; then thanking the fair donor for her
gift, he retraced his way over the hill of Olrig to his paternal
residence, which was called the " Windy Ha'."

On reaching home, Peter, with an air of triumph, produced
his pipe, which excited much curiosity and wonder, and was
greatly admired ; but when he related how he came by it, the
old people were not a little staggered, and began to regard the
gift with suspicion.

"It's no canny," said his father, shaking his head ; "and I
would advise you, Peter, to have nothing to do with it."

"The Best protect us !" exclaimed his mother ; "my bairn
is lost. He must have got it from none other than the queen
of the fairies."

"Nonsense," said Peter ; "it was not the queen of the
fairies, but a real lady—and a kind and beautiful lady she
was—that gave me the pipe."

"But of what use can it be to you," said his father, "when
ye canna play on it."

"Can I not ?" returned Peter. "I'll let you see that
directly ;" and, putting the wind-pipe to his mouth and
inflating the bag, he struck up the "Fairy Dance" in a style
that electrified the household. The whole family, including
the grandmother—ninety years of age—started at once to their
feet and danced heartily, overturning stools, and scattering
the fire, which was in the middle of the floor, with their
fantastic movements. The piper continued to play as if he
would never stop.

At length his father, panting for breath, and with the per-
spiration trickling down his cheeks, cried out, "For mercy's
sake, Peter, gie ower, or you'll be the death of me and yir
mither, as well as poor old grannie."

"I think," said Peter, laying aside his pipe out of compassion
for their limbs, "I think you'll no longer say that I can't play."

From this time our hero's fame as a musician spread rapidly
over the country, and as he was sent for to perform at every
wedding and merry-making that took place for miles around,
he began to realise a little fortune. But "no man can tether
time and tide." The seven years soon rolled away, and the day
big with destiny arrived, when he must keep his appointment
with the strange lady. He accordingly set off with rather
uneasy feelings, for he did not know what might be the result,
whether for good or evil, of this interview. Rover, the house
dog, attempted to follow him, but when he was chid back, the
affectionate animal gazed after his master as long as he could
see him, then raised his head and howled long and pitifully.
The evening was just such another as that on which he first
met the mysterious stranger. The sun — near its setting —
poured a flood of yellow radiance over the brown moor ; and
in the succeeding moonlight, Sysa seemed to glow with more
than earthly lustre. The lark had ceased to sing, and the
plover's note alone was heard wailing like the voice of a spirit
over the desert waste. As to what happened at this second
and final interview the legend is silent ; but poor Peter never
returned again to the Windy Ha', and the general belief was
that he was carried away to Fairyland.

To resume the thread of our narrative. Sigurd, who was
killed in Ireland, left four sons, Summorlid, Brusi, Einar,
and Thorfin. He was twice married. His second wife was a
daughter of King Malcolm, the second of Scotland. Thorfin
was the son of this lady, and is said to have been brought up
in the Scottish court. The three eldest sons divided the
sovereignty of Orkney and Shetland between them, and Thorfin
was, by his maternal grandfather, created Earl of Caithness.
Having refused to pay tribute to his successor on the Scottish
throne, he was supplanted in the earldom of Caithness by
one Moddan, who, with a body of troops, had fixed his head-
quarters in Thurso. Highly resenting the indignity, Thorfin
was determined to maintain his rights by either fair means or

foul. With this view he came to the town, and surprising his rival in the night-time, he set fire to his house, and slew him as he attempted to escape by a window from the flames. For a number of years Thorfin pursued the profession of a regular viking, and in that capacity performed many daring achievements along the coasts of Scotland and Ireland. He made an incursion even into England, fought three successive pitched battles with the bravest troops of Hardicanute,* and returned home laden with plunder. When in Caithness, he frequently resided in Canisbay,† from the advantage of its proximity to Orkney. Some years before his death, he was seized with remorse for the many crimes and outrages of which he had been guilty ; and, as was customary at the period, he set out on a pious pilgrimage to Rome, and was there absolved by the Pope of all his sins. On his return home, he retired to Birsa, in the mainland of Orkney, where he founded and dedicated a church to Christ, and lived afterwards a devout life. He died about the year 1064, and was buried in the church which himself had built. " Thorfin," says Mr Worsaae, " was the last of the Earls in whom the old Scandinavian viking's spirit lived and stirred. His power was greater than that of any of his predecessors ; for, according to the Sagas, he ruled over no fewer than eleven earldoms in Scotland, over all the Hebrides, and a large kingdom in Ireland." This statement of the Sagas in regard to Thorfin's ruling over eleven counties in Scotland is very questionable. That he may have plundered and devastated eleven counties is highly probable ; but that he held them under his sway, there is no ground whatever for believing. There is not the least hint of such a thing in any of our Scotch or English annals. At the time of his death Thorfin was about 80 years of age. Torfæus describes his personal appearance and character in nearly the following terms. He was a thin, tall man, with dark hair, large shaggy

---

* Abercrombie, Mar. Ach. Scots Nation.
† Torfæus calls the place of his residence " Gadgedlis," which is supposed to be the present township of Gills in that parish.

eyebrows, and a visage frightfully ugly ; but he possessed a bold and resolute spirit, and was every inch a warrior. His widow, Ingibing, was the daughter of Finn Arnason, a Norwegian grandee. The Norse writers say, that after the the death of Thorfin she was married to Malcolm Canmore ; but this is evidently a pure fiction, for, as the translator of Torfæus justly remarks, "neither the Scotch nor English historians mention anything of this union, which they could not omit had it been a fact. Indeed, they state a much more suitable match, to wit, good Queen Margaret, and none else, so it is clear the Sagas are not to be depended upon in this matter."

CHAPTER III.

WHILE the Earls of Orkney possessed Caithness they chiefly managed the affairs of the county by deputies. These deputies or governors resided at Duncansbay, in the parish of Canisbay, under the title of "Prefecturæ de Dungaldsbeis." About the beginning of the twelfth century the name of the resident governor was Olaus Rolfi. He belonged to the island of Gairsay, in Orkney, and from his bravery and other estimable qualities, was a chief in high estimation with the Earl, who had selected him particularly for that office. His wife, whose maiden name was Asleif, was descended of a noble Norwegian family. Frakirk, the relict of a powerful chieftain in Sutherland, had, it would appear, conceived a mortal grudge against Olaus, and she determined to destroy him. For this purpose she sent her grandson, Aulver Rosti, with a party of men, to Duncansbay about Christmas, a season which the Norsemen—from whom the festival of Yule has its origin—particularly devoted to festivity. On their arrival there they surrounded the governor's house at midnight, and after plundering it of everything that was valuable, they barbarously set fire to the building, and burnt him with the most of his attendants. His wife, with her two sons, Sweyn and Gunn, happened to be from home that evening on a visit at a friend's house in the neighbourhood, and thus fortunately escaped the fate that befell her husband. As soon as she heard of the shocking event she took boat and hurried across with her sons to Orkney.

Frakirk, the instigator of this atrocious outrage, was a singularly daring and wicked woman; and her history, as related in the Norse chronicle, of which we can give only a few particulars, is a strange one. She was the daughter of Maddan, a Norwegian nobleman, who resided in that part of the parish of Bower which is supposed to be named after himself—Bowermadden. This chief had another daughter, Helga, who in wickedness, at least, perfectly resembled her sister, and was married to Haco, Earl of Orkney. Frakirk at this time was living with them at Orphir. The Earl had by Helga a son called Harold, and by a former marriage a son whose name was Paul. The two brothers were of opposite dispositions ; and, it might be said, never agreed from their boyhood. On the death of their father, the earldom (a thing quite customary at the period) was partitioned between them. But this served only to embitter their animosity. From the moment that the government and property of the islands, etc., came into their hands, they began to quarrel about their respective plans and interests. Helga, an ambitious woman and a genuine stepdame, did all she could—in which she was seconded by her sister—to widen the breach between them. She naturally wished her own son to have the whole earldom, and she never ceased urging him to use every means in his power to wrest his brother's half from him. To avert the pernicious consequences to be apprehended from an open rupture between the two brothers, their best and most judicious friends on both sides strongly advised them to drop all their differences, and to live on terms of amity befitting such near relations. They both acknowledged the salutariness of the advice, and with the view to confirm a bond of mutual reconciliation, Harold agreed to give a splendid entertainment to his brother at the approaching Christmas. Accordingly, at the time appointed, a sumptuous banquet was got up in his palace at Orphir, and everything seemed to betoken the dawn of an era of much future concord and happiness. But these brilliant anticipations were destined to be clouded by an occurrence of an extraordinary and tragical character. About the conclusion of the feast, Harold having entered his mother's apartment, found his aunt Frakirk in the act of finishing an exquisitely embroidered shirt of fine linen, spangled with gold thread. He was greatly struck with its beauty, and on inquiring for whom this splendid article of dress was intended, Helga, his mother, with some reluctance told him that it was for his brother Paul. Harold, who was naturally hasty, and now flushed with wine, keenly upbraided his mother for her supposed partiality, and demanded to have the shirt for himself. Helga on her bended knees implored him not to touch it, assuring him that if he did so it would cost him his life. But all her entreaties and tears were to no purpose. Harold forcibly wrested it from her hands, and put it on. No sooner, however, did the fatal garment—for it was impregnated with the most deadly poison—come into contact with his body, than he was seized with a trembling fit, which was succeeded by the most excruciating pain. He was carried to bed, and soon after died in extreme agony. This story, which is entitled the "Tale of the Poisoned Shirt," and which reminds one of the classical fable of Hercules and the poisoned tunic, when divested of the marvellous, simply resolves itself into the fact, that Harold was unintentionally poisoned by his mother and aunt. Paul, who saw that his own death was intended, immediately banished them from Orkney. They went over to Caithness, and thence to Kildonan, in Sutherlandshire, where Frakirk's castle and property were situated. After the death of Harold, the earldom of Orkney and Caithness was jointly ruled over by his half-brother Paul, and by Ronald, nephew of Magnus, who was assassinated in the isle of Eaglesay in 1110.

I have mentioned that on the death of Olaus Rolfi, the late governor at Duncansbay, his widow, with her two sons Sweyn and Gunn, who were both born, it is believed, in Canisbay, had retired to Orkney. Sweyn took his mother's name, and was afterwards called Sweyn Asleifson. He turned out a celebrated pirate, and was, altogether, one of the most extraordinary characters of the time in which he lived. He had two castles—one in the island of Gairsay, lying about four miles to the north of Kirkwall, and the other in Freswick, in the county of Caithness. A part of the ruins of his castle at Freswick, consisting of a small dilapidated tower, grey and ghastly-looking with age, is still to be seen on a wild peninsular rock rising abruptly from the sea, about fifty or sixty yards from the main line of precipices which runs along the shore. A more gloomy and solitary place to have lived in it is hardly possible to conceive, with nothing but the bare rugged rocks on the one hand, and the monotonous prospect of a seemingly interminable ocean on the other. In the winter season, and particularly during a storm from the east, when the winds and the waves battled in tremendous fury around it, it must have been a frightful residence. Mrs Radcliffe herself could not have imagined anything wilder. Torfæus gives it the strange name of "Lambaburgum," and says that the building was strong and well executed, and from its peculiar situation could not be easily taken. It was, in fact, a regular pirate's keep; and there is little doubt that it was originally built by Sweyn,* or some one who followed his unhallowed profession. Sweyn spent the winter sometimes in it, and sometimes in his other castle in the island of Gairsay, with a retinue of about eighty followers, during which time there was nothing but one continued round of revelry and wassail. As soon, however, as spring arrived, he equipped his galleys and set out on his marauding expeditions. At the period in question, piracy among the Norsemen was quite a common and fashionable employment. "The occupation of a pirate," says Crichton in his history of Scandinavia, "like that of a robber among the Arabs, was not only lawful, but honourable. As the mechanical arts were despised, and the learned professions unknown, the practice of sea-roving became the favourite pursuit. It possessed the interest of romance, and was surrounded with all the lustre of chivalry, so that it might be said to form not only the most lucrative, but the most graceful accomplishment of the princes and chieftains of that

* Many of the old castles along the coast, and in the interior of the county are supposed to have been constructed at first by the Norsemen.

heroic age." Haco, the Earl of Orkney's son, used to accompany Sweyn as an amateur in his piratical expeditions, and the young nobleman could not have been placed under an abler and more skilful leader. To a thorough knowledge of his business, Sweyn added a most daring and adventurous spirit. He not only exercised his calling along the coast of Scotland, but he went in quest of plunder as far as Cornwall, the Isle of Man,* and even Ireland. Sweyn was on intimate and friendly terms with Earl Paul; but having slain in a drunken quarrel at Christmas one of his favourite retainers, he fled for safety to Perthshire, where he remained for some time with the Earl and Countess of Athole. Margaret, the countess— a half-sister of Paul—was a beautiful woman, but notorious for her inordinate ambition, want of principle, and profligacy. At her instigation a plot was hatched to seize Paul, and convey him to Athole. Her object in this was to put him out of the way, and get her own son made Earl of Orkney in his stead. Sweyn, who was ready for any plot, however mischievous or perilous, whether against friend or foe, at once agreed to execute her intention. Accordingly, being furnished with a large galley and a crew of thirty desperate vagabonds, he set sail for Orkney, and landing on the island of Rousay, where the Earl was at the time amusing himself with catching seals, he instantly seized him and carried him off to the residence of his sister in Perthshire. There he was closely confined, and forced to convey to young Harold, his nephew, all his rights and titles to the earldom of Orkney. Paul never returned to that county; and it is believed that he was put to death by the orders of his wicked and unnatural sister. The place in Rousay from which Sweyn kidnapped Earl Paul is still called Sweyndroog. He was at the time the guest of Sigurd of Westness. It was not, however, without a severe struggle, in the course of which nineteen of his attendants and six of Sweyn's party were killed, that the Earl was abducted.

Young Harold, the protegé of Sweyn, was brought to

* His devastations in the Isle of Man are confirmed by the Manx Chronicle.

Orkney, where, under the superintendence of Ronald, he received a suitable education, and as soon as he became of age, was admitted to a share of the earldom. Not long after this, Ronald set out on a pious pilgrimage to Jerusalem ; and being left to his own guidance, Harold discovered all those bad qualities of his nature which afterwards procured him the appellation of Harold the Wicked. During the absence of his colleague he ruled like an independent sovereign, and oppressed the people to such a degree, that Eistein, King of Norway, set sail for Orkney with the determination to bring down his lofty pretensions, and put a check to his tyranny. As soon as Harold heard of his arrival in St Margaret's Hope, he fled to Thurso in a war galley of forty oars with eighty men. Eistein crossed over in pursuit of him with three smaller vessels, captured his war galley in Scrabster* Roads, seized Harold himself in the town and threw him into prison. When he had enjoyed the pleasures of solitude for a few days, the king ordered the delinquent to appear before him, and after obliging him to pay a fine of seven marks of gold, and to declare upon oath that he held Orkney as a fief of Norway, and would continue so to hold it, he set him at liberty. There was no alternative for Harold but to submit to these stringent measures. It is possible, however, that if he had had at this juncture the able counsel and assistance òf his friend Sweyn, he might have escaped this humiliation. But that ingenious gentleman was absent at the time on a piratical excursion.

Torfæus gives a long and minute account of the different adventures of this famous pirate. As illustrative of the singular and daring character of the man, I will briefly glance at one or two of his more notable exploits, subsequent to his kidnapping the Earl of Orkney. Not long after this he inflicted a summary vengeance on Frakirk for the part which she had in the death of his father at Duncansbay. Having

*The term Scrabster, like the names of most of the places in the neighbourhood, is of Icelandic derivation. By the old Norse writers it was called Skarabolstad.

landed in Sutherlandshire with a select band of associates, he first plundered her house, then set it on fire, and burnt her, with her sister Helga and all their domestics. This is said to have been done with the concurrence of Margaret, Countess of Athole, who furnished Sweyn with guides to the particular locality in Sutherland where Frakirk resided. History is full of crime; but there are few instances of such unnatural and shocking barbarity as that of which this woman appears to have been guilty—namely, first putting her brother, Earl Paul, to death, and next consenting to make an *auto da fe* of her mother and aunt.

Sweyn was not very steady in his friendships; and it happened that he and Earl Harold had a temporary difference. While this misunderstanding lasted, he one day sallied out from his castle at Freswick, attacked and robbed, in the Pentland Firth, a vessel with the Earl's rents from Shetland. The vessel was on her way to Wick, where Harold was sojourning at the time.

On another occasion, while cruising in the Irish Channel, he attacked two merchant ships bound for the Isle of Man, having on board a large quantity of scarlet cloth and other commodities of great value, the whole of which he seized. On his way home he played off a singular freak. " When near the Orkney Islands with his fleet," says Torfæus, " he caused sew some of the cloth on the sails, so that they appeared like sails of scarlet, for which reason that expedition was called the 'scarlet cruise.' "

To great courage and presence of mind, Sweyn united all the instinctive cunning of the fox, of which the following story affords an amusing instance. Along the east side of Elwick Bay, in the island of Shapinshay, lies an uninhabited islet called Elgarholm, forming a natural breakwater to it in that direction. It happened that while the parties were on bad terms, the Earl of Orkney, one forenoon, with a large and well-manned galley, gave chase to Sweyn, who at the time was cruising about Shapinshay in a small boat with only two or three of his followers. As soon as he saw that he was pursued, the oars were plied with the utmost vigour; and on his side it might be said to be a run for personal liberty, if not for life. Fortunately for him he was near Elgarholm, and turning one of the points of the islet, he ran his skiff into a cave. On rounding the same point a few minutes afterwards, the Earl was amazed to see nothing of Sweyn or his boat, and he could not imagine in the wide world what had become of the vaga-bond. The Earl and his men, it would seem, were but slightly acquainted with the natural features of the spot; and the full tide had so effectually concealed the entrance of the cave, that its existence was not suspected by them. The wily pirate enjoyed their perplexity, and lay secure in his hiding-place until the coast was clear. The following characteristic anec-dote of Sweyn is given in the Orkneyinga Saga. A Norseman named Arne had obtained some goods from a tenant of Sweyn's, and when the man afterwards demanded payment Arne beat him, and bade him go and seek aid of the pirate of whose prowess he boasted so much. The peasant went straight to his master and told him how he had been treated. Sweyn thereupon seized an axe with a short handle, and taking four men with him crossed over in an eight-oared boat to the island where Arne resided. On reaching the landing place, he ordered the crew to remain there and take charge of the boat till his return. He then proceeded to Arne's residence, where he found him in his store-room with four of his companions. After exchanging the customary salutation, Sweyn desired Arne to make immediate payment of the sum due his tenant, and on his refusing to do so he drove his axe into his skull, so that, as the Saga says, " the iron was buried therein," and in the hurry of the moment, losing hold of the weapon, he leaped out of the room, and ran for the shore followed by the four com-panions of Arne. One of the men, who was swifter of foot than the others had nearly overtaken him, when Sweyn lifted a lump of sea-weed mixed with mud and dashed it in the face of his pursuer. The man, who was completely blinded by the mud, stopt to cleanse his eyes, and by this dexterous manœuvre Sweyn was enabled to reach the boat, into which he flung himself and immediately set off for the island of Gairsay.

As the pirate was seldom at home, especially in the summer season, he had appointed one Margad Grimson, a native of Swana, manager over some property which belonged to him in Duncansbay. Margad was a regular tyrant, and his usage of the people was so harsh and oppressive that they complained to Roald, a Norwegian of some note in Wick, who promised that he would lay their grievances before Earl Ronald, an upright and compassionate nobleman, and endeavour to procure them some redress. The factor was incensed at Roald's inter-ference in a matter with which he thought he had no concern. He went to Wick with a party of ruffians, managed to get access to Roald, and killed him, with several of his attendants, in his own house. Sweyn, who was absent at the time, instead of dismissing his factor for the atrocious act, with characteristic inconsistency and laxity of principle, approved of his conduct. Roald's son repaired to the Earl, complained of the horrible outrage committed in Wick, and prayed that he would avenge his father's death. On this Ronald collected a body of troops, marched to Freswick and attacked the castle to which Sweyn and Margad had betaken themselves with sixty retainers, and which they resolved to defend to the last extremity. Finding that he could not take it by force, the Earl determined to cut of all supplies, and accomplish his purpose by famine. The garrison was, in consequence, soon reduced to great straits and began to exhibit symptoms of discontent and insubordination. In this unpleasant dilemma, when their provisions were nearly spent, Sweyn assembled his retainers, and in a short speech advised them to surrender at once, and throw themselves on the generosity of the Earl, who, he was confident, would do them no injury. It was only himself and his agent that the Earl wished to seize, but that he would disappoint him in this, and devise for themselves some means of escape. He then ordered a long rope to be got, and by means of it he and Margad were let down from the brow of the rock on which the castle stands, into the sea ; and though they were both clad in armour, they swam safely ashore.   They then pursued their way southward until they came to Banff, where they found an Orkney pirate boat with ten men on board. Sweyn engaged the crew and set sail on a piratical expedition. He landed on the Isle of May, in which there was at that time a monastery, presided over by an abbot whose name was Baldwin. Sweyn at first pretended that he was an ambassador from the Earl of Orkney and Caithness to the King, and was in consequence entertained with all due respect and hospitality by the holy brotherhood. He professed, too, to be an ardent devotee of the Church ; but somehow he manifested a much greater predilection for good cheer and the wine-cup than for the religious exercises and vigils prescribed by the rules of the order. After he had been a week in the island, the monks began to suspect that the pretended ambassador and his attendants were but a band of pirates, and despatched a boat to the mainland for men to protect them. As soon as Sweyn understood this, he robbed the monastery of everything valuable it contained, and set sail on another cruise.

Sweyn at length terminated his worldly career in Dublin, which he had surprised and plundered. Having carried off to his ships some of the principal men of the city, they agreed to purchase their ransom at a high price. Next day, when he went ashore to receive his money, or "Danegelt," as it was called, he fell into an ambuscade which the inhabitants had laid for him ; and he and the whole party that accompanied him were slain. This event happened in the autumn of the year 1160.*

Much about the same time, Earl Ronald was basely mur- dered at North Calder, in the parish of Halkirk, by a villain of the name of Thiorbiorn Klairke, whom he had banished for his misdeeds from Orkney. He and Harold, his colleague in

* Ware, in his History of Ireland, confirms the account from Irish records.

the earldom, had come over, as was their usual practice, on a
hunting excursion to Caithness. It was this Ronald who, in
conjunction with his father Koll, founded the cathedral of
Kirkwall. He was a nobleman of many excellent qualities;
and on account of his eminent piety, and the share which he
had in erecting that splendid edifice, was canonized by the
Pope. Klairke, the assassin of Ronald, did not escape with
impunity. After committing the murder, he fled to a place in
the neighbourhood called Assary, where he was overtaken and
put to death by some of the Earl's retainers. The body of the
Earl was conveyed from Thurso to Orkney, and buried in the
church of the holy virgin in South Ronaldshay. His remains
were afterwards transferred to the cathedral of Kirkwall, and
were among the first that found a resting place in that celebrated northern minster.

CHAPTER IV.

IN the year 1196, a famous battle was fought on the hill of Clairdon, about two miles to the east of Thurso, between Earl Harold, son of the infamous Countess of Athole, and Harold, grandson of that Earl Ronald who was assassinated in Caithness. By way of distinction they are called Harold the Elder and Harold the Younger. The former, who, from his extraordinary cruelty and tyranny, has acquired the cognomen of Wicked Earl Harold, was a perfect scourge to Caithness, and his memory is handed down by tradition in it even to this day, confirming the truth of the poet's remark, that "the evil that men do lives after them." This bold bad man had violently dispossessed Harold the Younger of one-half of the county, which belonged to him by inheritance from his grandfather, Earl Ronald; and it was to recover his share of the earldom and his hereditary rights that the latter took the field. Each mustered a large force. The army of Harold the Younger was mostly all natives of Caithness; that of Harold the Elder was chiefly composed of Orkneymen or Norwegians. Murt and Lifolf, two brave and experienced officers, led on the Caithnessmen. The battle commenced with a furious attack on both sides, and raged for some time without any decided advantage to either. At length, notwithstanding their superiority in numbers, the Norwegians were on the point of being completely routed — and were, in fact, pursued with great slaughter to a hollow near the head of Murkle Bay—when the leaders of Harold the Younger's army were both unfortunately slain. Harold himself had fallen in the early part of the engagement; and the Caithnessmen, having none now to lead them, got into confusion, and fled from the field with the utmost precipitation. Harold was buried near the spot where he fell, and a small temple or chapel was erected over his grave, which was afterwards resorted to as a shrine by the inhabitants of the neighbourhood. The author of the "Book of Flota" says that "the many miracles by which God was pleased to honour his remains certified to those that then lived that he was a good man, and had a just cause." The chapel, in process of time, fell into decay, and the late Sir John Sinclair, in memory of the event, erected a monument over the spot, which bears the name of Harold's Tower. Some of the weapons used in this battle were found in a peat moss near the old castle of Haymer. They were ugly-looking machines, resembling a ploughshare, and were all of solid iron.

After this victory Harold easily subdued the whole of Caithness, and then returned in triumph to Orkney. When William the Lion, who was then king of Scotland, heard of the state of matters in Caithness, he despatched a message to Reginald,* Lord of the Isles, with whom he was on terms of amity, asking him to give his assistance in recovering that county from the tyranny of Harold. Reginald readily undertook the task, and having transported a body of troops into Caithness, he defeated and put to flight the Norwegians that opposed him, and soon placed the whole county under the authority of its legitimate sovereign. He next appointed three governors to administer the civil affairs of the district, and then set sail for the isles. As soon as Reginald departed, Harold, who was biding his time, sent over a confidential emissary to Caithness with private instructions to assassinate the deputies, one of whom the miscreant succeeded in putting to death. Harold soon after followed himself with a large army, fully determined to reconquer the county. He disembarked his troops at Scrabster Roads, where the fleet which conveyed them found a safe and commodious anchorage. The inhabitants of Thurso,

---

* By the Norse writers this Hebridean chief is named Rognvald Gudrodson. He was of Norwegian extraction, being the son of Ingeborg, daughter of Earl Hacon Paulson.

who had sided with the king's party in the recent contest, were thrown into the utmost consternation when they heard of Harold's arrival; and, anticipating nothing but the severest punishment, they applied to John, bishop of the county, and begged of him to intercede with the tyrant in their behalf. The bishop, who lived near Scrabster, agreed to do so, and having met Harold on his way into the town, strongly pleaded for mercy to the poor people, but the savage Earl only laughed at his request, and ordered one of his attendants, named Lomberd, to seize the prelate, and cut out his tongue, and put out both his eyes!"* He then proceeded to the town, where he scourged and imprisoned all of the inhabitants who could not pay the heavy fine which he imposed, and hanged such of the principal men in it as he knew were not favourable to his rule. In this way, he overran the whole of Caithness, and forced the terrified natives everywhere to submit to his despotic authority. In the meantime, messengers were despatched to the Scottish Court to inform King William of the atrocious outrage on the bishop, and of the cruel and tyrannical proceedings of Harold in the county. William forthwith collected a large body of troops, and marched with all speed to Caithness, for the purpose of chastising Harold and putting a check to his wicked and barbarous measures in the north. After crossing the Ord of Caithness, he encamped at Ausdale, a solitary valley about four miles from Berriedale. Harold mustered an army to oppose him, but finding that he had much fewer troops than the king, he proposed terms of accommodation, and sued for peace.† The king, with ill-judged

* This crime would appear to have been very common in ancient times. In Hume's "History of England" there occurs the following passage:—"By an Act of the fifth of this reign (Henry IV.) it is made felony to cut out any person's tongue or put out his eyes;" crimes which the Act says were very frequent. "This savage spirit of revenge," he adds, "denotes a barbarous people."

† Sir Robert Gordon, on the authority of Boethius, says that King William chased Harold to Duncansbay, where, by way of retaliation, he first put out his eyes, etc., and then hanged him. But this story is not entitled to the slightest credit. Boethius, as Robertson justly observes, is a credulous writer; and Torfæus' account of the matter, as given in the text, is, beyond a doubt, the correct one.

lenity, granted him a pardon for the outrages he had committed, and, only mulcting him in a heavy fine, re-instated him in the earldom. This fine, which Fordan says, amounted to two thousand pounds of silver, Harold forced the inhabitants to pay. The Pope ordered Lomberd to undergo a long and mortifying penance for the cruel and unchristian manner in which he had used the bishop. The missive of his Holiness,* which we have slightly condensed, is addressed to the Bishop of Orkney, and enjoins as follows :—" Lomberd, bare-footed and naked, except breeches and a short woollen vest without sleeves, having his tongue tied by a string and drawn out so as to project beyond his lips, and the ends of the string bound round his neck, with rods in his hand, in sight of all men, shall walk for fifteen days successively through his own native district, etc.; he shall go to the door of the church without entering, and there, prostrate on the earth, be scourged with the rods he is to carry; he is to spend each day in fasting and silence, and to be fed in the evening on bread and water only. After these fifteen days are passed, he shall prepare within a month to set out for Jerusalem, and there labour in the service of the cross for three years ; and for two years he shall fast every Friday on bread and water, unless by the indulgence of some discreet bishop, on account of bodily infirmity, this abstinence be mitigated." It does not appear that Harold, the author of the barbarity, was made to undergo any penitentiary discipline.† He died in the year 1206, aged 73. He was a man of large stature, and his face was remarkable for its ferocity of expression. He was succeeded by his son John.

After this, few events of any local or historical importance

* Cosmo Innes' Sket. Early Scotch His., pp. 74-75.

† In the former edition, the author fell into an error in stating that it was Harold, and not Lomberd, who was ordered by the Pope to do penance for the mutilation of John, Bishop of Caithness. The account of this barbarous deed was transmitted to the Pope by the Bishop of Orkney ; and that dignitary, most probably from fear of Harold's resentment, would seem to have withheld the truth, and thrown the whole blame on Lomberd, who was merely an instrument in the hands of the more guilty chief.

occurred till the year 1222. At this time, Adam, Bishop of Caithness, was barbarously put to death in his own palace at Halkirk by the people, on account of the rigour with which he exacted his tithes. He excommunicated, it is said, several of them for not paying their allotted portion of tiend—a terrible infliction in those days, when it was believed that no person who died under that curse could escape eternal punishment. The blame of much of this undue severity was imputed to a monk of Newbottle, named Serlo, who lived with him as a companion, and was known to be his confidential friend and adviser. A part of the bishop's revenue consisted of a tax on butter ; and it was the established usage in Caithness, that for every score of cows, a span of butter should be paid to that dignitary. Adam at first exacted a span (about a stone of Scots measure) from fifteen cows, then from twelve, and at length demanded a span for every ten cows. This the people considered an intolerable imposition to which they would not submit, and waxed exceedingly wroth against the bishop and the monk. There was an annual fair held on a hill, near the Castle of Brawl,* where John, Earl of Caithness, at this time usually resided. At this fair, the inhabitants of the district, to the number of about 300, collected, and led on by two sons of one Simon Harbister, in Harpsdale, they went in a body to the Earl, complained bitterly of the hardship and injustice of the impost, and demanded redress. The Earl at first refused to interfere in the matter, as being one with which he had no concern ; but feeling annoyed at their importunity,

*The Castle of Brawl (the ruins of which still exist) was anciently called Brathwell. In Scottish record mention of it is made as far back as the year 1375. Like the castle of Girnigoe, it comprehended two buildings belonging to different eras of architecture. The part of the tower which remains of the older building is 35 feet in height ; and the walls, which are 9 feet thick, are pierced with numerous loopholes. There are several recesses in the walls, about the size of small rooms, which were evidently used as such by the inmates, and which would appear to have communicated with passages and staircases similarly placed. The front of the newer castle, which seems not to have been completed, is from 12 to 15 feet high, with a ground floor measuring 100 feet long and 50 broad, and divided into 6 vaults. The ruins are situated on a beautiful spot close by the river of Halkirk ; and the old tower, or keep, from its being the occasional residence of the Scandinavin Earls of Orkney and Caithness, was in all probability erected by one of them.

and disapproving at the same time of the conduct of the bishop, he hastily ejaculated, "The devil take the bishop and his butter; you may roast him if you please !" The people took this remark in its literal sense, as an order to burn the prelate, and off they set to the palace to put it into execution. The bishop and the logmadr, or lawman of the place, whose name was Rafn, were at the time in an upper room of the mansion, discussing the subject of the tithes, and solacing themselves with a glass of ale. The lawman seriously advised Adam to depart from his last demand, and not to exasperate the people, but the latter was obstinate and refused to listen to the salutary advice. In the meantime, the disorderly mob drew near, shouting out, "Roast him alive !" and when the bishop and the sheriff saw that matters were beginning to assume a serious aspect, Serlo, the monk, was sent out to pacify them ; but no sooner did he make his appearance, than he was felled to the ground by the stroke of a heavy bludgeon, and trampelled to death by the crowd. The sheriff now came forward and tried to mollify their rage. He assured them that Bishop Adam was disposed to lighten the exaction, and that he was coming out to speak with them on the subject. He beseeched them to listen to reason, and not to commit any further outrage, having already done what was sufficient to bring down upon them the heaviest punishment of the law. But his address had little or no effect on the infuriated rabble ; and when the prelate, clad in the robes of his office, and with a small crucifix hanging from his breast, advanced to offer terms, they dragged him forcibly to his own kitchen, heaped on the fire additional fuel, and there burned him to death !* The sheriff, who saw that his own life would be in jeopardy if he attempted to interfere, was obliged to remain a passive spectator of the horrid deed.

When King Alexander II. heard of the barbarous murder

---

* The common tradition in the county is that the bishop was boiled to death in his own brewing kettle, but the account given in the text is the one which history authenticates.

of the bishop, he came all the way from Jedburgh to Caithness, and inflicted on the perpetrators thereof as barbarous a punishment.* The greater part of them were, by the king's orders, hanged, and the rest had their feet and hands cut off, and were otherwise mutilated in a manner too shocking for description. Pope Celestine the Fourth issued a bull, still extant, in which he highly commends the king for his praiseworthy conduct on this occasion. All the ancient writers, who treat of the North, relate this story, and though they differ in a few particulars, they agree in the main fact as to the burning of the bishop. Boethius lays the whole blame of the crime upon the Earl. He says—" Adam, Bishop of Caithness, because he piously maintained the rights and dignities of the church, was thrown into a glowing furnace by the Earl of that county, and burnt to ashes, and thus took his flight to heaven." Wyntoun, in his quaint, old rhyming chronicle, thus describes the murder of the Bishop—

> " Himself bindyn and woundyt, syne
> Thai put him in his awyn kychyne, (kitchen)
> In thair felony and thair ire,
> Thare thai brynt him in a fyre."

This unfortunate prelate was a native of the south of Scotland, and had been for some time Abbot of Melrose. He was consecrated Bishop of Caithness in 1214. The ceremony is thus stated in the chronicle of Melrose :—" Anno MCCXIIII. consecratus est Adam, Abbas Melrosenensis in Episcop. de Cathanesiæ." The newly-elected Bishop seems to have been a man of a proud and unbending disposition ; and coming as

---

* The writer of the old statistical account of Halkirk says—"The Bishop of Caithness was assassinated by a set of ruffians from Harpsdale, a place belonging to the chaplainry. These savages were the sons of John of Harpsdale, whom the Earl of Caithness suborned as instruments very fit for the execution of that horrid deed, in revenge of the bishop having assessed his lands in the chaplainry with an addition to the chaplain's living." This account, which the writer says he had from tradition, differs materially from that given in the text from Torfæus, but I am inclined to think that the Norse chronicler's version of the story is the true one, more especially as it agrees in most particulars with the accounts found in the "Monastic Annals of Tweedale," and other ancient records.

he did from Melrose, it is not improbable also that he was a
bon vivant ; for, according to the popular rhyme,—

> " The monks of Melrose they made gude kail
>   On Fridays, when they fasted ;
> They never wanted beef or ale
>   As lang's their neighbour's lasted." *

It would appear, however, that he was a scholar, and possessed
of considerable literary talent.   Among other works, he is said
to have been the author of a history of Scotland in three
books.†   By the clergy he was regarded as a martyr, who had
died in defence of the rights and privileges of the order ; and
his body not having been altogether consumed by the flames,
the remains were afterwards disinterred from the common
burying ground in Halkirk, and removed to a more honourable
sepulture in the cathedral church of the diocese at Dornoch.

Nothing can more forcibly show the barbarous—or I might
rather say savage—condition of the natives of Caithness at the
period in question than this murder.   The Church of Rome
was then in the full zenith of her power.   The whole of
Christendom yielded to her the most implicit obedience.   The
priestly office was held in the utmost veneration, and the
person of an ecclesiastic was hedged round with a divinity
which rendered him sacred in the eyes of the multitude.
Such being the almost idolatrous reverence paid to the clergy,
it is evident that the people of Caithness, barbarous as they
were, must have been very harshly dealt with in the matter of
tithes, and wrought up to a desperate pitch of frenzy before

---

* The monks of old, both in England and Scotland, would appear to have
kept a first-rate table.   Hume, in his history of England, gives the following
amusing anecdote in proof of this from an ancient writer :—The monks and
prior of St Swithin threw themselves one day prostrate on the ground before
Henry II. complaining, with many tears and much doleful lamentation, that
the Bishop of Winchester, who was also their abbot, had cut off three dishes
from their table.   "How many has he left you ?" said the king.   "*Ten*
only," replied the disconsolate monks.   "I myself," exclaimed the king,
never have more than three ; and I enjoin your bishop to reduce you to the
same number."

† In a long list of authors whom Sir Robert Gordon consulted, when writing
his History of the House of Sutherland, the first mentioned is " Adamus,
Episcopus Cateynensis," Adam, Bishop of Caithness.

they could have committed such a heinous crime as that of putting to death a churchman, and that churchman, too, the highest dignitary in the county. Although there is no sufficient reason to believe that the Earl really instigated the people to burn the bishop, yet he was justly reprehensible for the rash and indiscreet expression which they construed into an order for committing the deed. He absconded for some time; but afterwards took courage, and resolved to justify himself in person before the king. "With this view," says a Scotch chronicler, "he made his application upon the day of the Epiphany, when, conform to custom, the court was all in mirth, and the king, with wine and music, more than usually exhilarated." These circumstances were favourable to the Earl, who attested his innocence with oaths, and was therefore pardoned. Not many years after he was murdered himself in Thurso by a set of ruffians from Orkney. The house in which he resided when in town being attacked, he ran down to a cellar under-ground to conceal himself, but being found out by the assassins, he was dragged from his hiding-place, and cruelly stabbed to death. They then, according to the usual practice, set fire to the house. The two principal actors in this tragedy were Haneff, the collector of the King of Norway's revenue in Orkney, and Svekoll, a descendant of Earl Ronald. The latter had some time before quarrelled with Earl John about some property in Caithness which the Earl refused to give up, and on this account Svekoll, in particular, cherished towards him a violent animosity. The party sallied out from a tavern where they had been carousing to perpetrate the crime.

Adam, the late bishop, was succeeded in the diocese of Caithness by the celebrated archdeacon, Gilbert Murray, who is said to have been one of the most pious, learned, and accomplished prelates of his time. He was a native of Duffus, in Morayshire, of highly-respectable parentage, and was chiefly educated abroad. When he had finished his studies, he travelled through the greater part of Germany, France, and Italy, in order to enlarge his knowledge of the world, and observe in person the political, social, and religious condition of the people in the different places through which he passed. On his return to his native country, he entered the Church, and by his eminent talents, learning, and qualifications for the ministerial office, soon rose to be Archdeacon of Moray. He particularly distinguished himself as a strenuous supporter of the rights and liberties of the Scottish Church; and when yet a young man, was sent by William, King of Scotland, to attend a convocation of the clergy at Northampton,* in order to prevent any measure being adopted there which might be prejudicial to her interests. "At this convocation," says Sir Robert Gordon, "the Pope's legate was present, and went about to persuade the Scots to receive the Archbishop of York for their metropolitan; which motion this Gilbert, then Archdeacon of Moray, did altogether cross and hinder as a novation and encroachment upon the Scottish liberties, and did argue so eagerly and eloquently to the contrary, and with so great admiration, that the legate was obliged to leave his pursuit and break up the convocation, whereat the English clergy were much grieved."

Murray was also in high favour with Alexander II., who made him treasurer for the North of Scotland, and committed to his safe keeping the Bulls which were issued by sundry popes concerning the rights and liberties of the Scottish Church. He was, unquestionably, an able and patriotic prelate; and, when circumstances demanded it, he could lay aside the crosier and take up the sword—a thing quite common with churchmen of spirit in those days. On one remarkable occasion he is said to have greatly distinguished himself in this military capacity. A large band of Danish pirates had landed at the Little Ferry; and as they were on their way to

---

* Cosmo Innes, a learned and able writer on antiquities, discredits altogether this account of Sir Robert and others, touching Murray's presence at the convocation, and it must be admitted that his remark carries much force with it. "The story," says he, "of his having distinguished himself at the council of Northampton in 1176, and thereby winning a rapid promotion to his bishopric, when the election to the see of Caithness happened forty-seven years after that council, needs no refutation. He had better titles to respect. He had a large share in civilising his rude province," etc.

plunder Dornoch, they were attacked by a body of Highlanders under William, Earl of Sutherland, assisted by the bishop and his brother, Richard Murray, at a place called Embo, not far from the town. After a severe conflict the Danes were completely routed, and their leader was slain. A number of them were cut down by the Sutherland men as they chased them to the ferry ; while the few that escaped the sword immediately took to their galleys and left the coast. At the commencement of the action, Bishop Murray's armour-bearer, it is said, took to his heels and fled, carrying his master's shield along with him ; and being deprived of this important safeguard, the worthy prelate was obliged to fight without it. His brother, Richard, was killed in the course of the engagement.

In the time of Bishop Gilbert Murray, Sutherland and Caithness formed one diocese. His residence when in Caithness was the Castle of Burnside,* near Thurso, a part of the ruins of which still remains. It stood, like most of the other castles of the period, close by the sea, on the margin of the crescent-shaped bank overlooking Scrabster Roads, and on the land side was protected by a drawbridge. A terrace formed in the bank, and extending to about half a mile from the castle, was called the Bishop's Walk. Here Murray died in the year 1245, and his remains were carried all the way to Dornoch, and interred in the cathedral there which himself had founded. He was an excellent prelate, and did much to instruct and civilise the inhabitants. He translated, it is said, for the benefit of the people composing his see, the Psalms and the Gospels into the Gaelic language, from which it may be inferred that in his time the Gaelic was the common dialect of both Sutherland and Caithness. Indeed, it is now generally allowed by antiquarians that it was the common language of all Scotland, with the exception of the Lothians, down till the

* This castle of Burnside was in 1568 the residence of Bishop Robert Stewart, who dates from it a charter of some property in the town of Thurso, of which, as well as of the adjoining lands of Ormlie, the bishops were superiors. He was brother of Mathew Stewart, Earl of Lennox, and uncle of Darnley. He afterwards renounced Popery, and became an intimate friend of the great Reformer. He died in 1586.

reign of Malcolm Canmore, in the eleventh century. The deceased prelate was, on account of his many eminent virtues, duly canonised. His festival was celebrated on the first day of April, and St. Gilbert was among the Scotch saints restored to the kalendar of the Scotch church in the ill-starred Service Book of Charles the First.

1263.—After a lapse of some eighteen years from the death of Murray, the only matter of any public interest connected with the county refers to the celebrated expedition of Haco, King of Norway, to Largs. On his way thither Haco called at Orkney, where he remained for about three weeks, providing his fleet with additional stores and other necessaries for his expedition. The first place to which he came was Elwick bay, in Shapinshay. He afterwards, accompanied by Magnus, Earl of Orkney, who had joined him with all his available force, removed to St. Margaret's Hope, in the island of South Ronaldshay. During the time he was there he despatched agents to Caithness for the purpose of exacting tribute from the natives. These officials were instructed to acquaint the people that if they refused to pay the tax the King of Norway would punish them by laying waste the country with fire and sword, and rather than incur the threatened infliction they paid the impost. At length, early in the month of August, Haco set sail with his fleet from St. Margaret's Hope, and nearing the Caithness coast, passed through the Pentland Firth. His own ship, the royal galley, is described as being of large dimensions, and constructed wholly of oak. " Its dragon head glowed with burnished gold ; the banner of Norway was displayed at the stern, and the warrior champions were ranged along the deck in proud array." In the meantime, to repel the threatened invasion, of which he had timely notice, the Scottish King, Alexander III., had collected about two thousand horse and a numerous host of foot soldiers, which were commanded by Alexander Stewart, grandfather of the first monarch of that name who sat on the Scottish throne. In this army, Abercromby, in his " Martial Achieve-

ments," says there was a body of Caithnessmen.   The natives
of the county never became thoroughly reconciled to the
Norwegian yoke; and it is probable that the body of men
in question went to assist the Scottish king on this occasion
chiefly out of revenge for the impost which had been levied
on them by Haco, and the despotic manner in which they
were in general used by their Scandinavian governors.   Tytler,
the historian, mentions a curious precautionary measure which
was adopted by Alexander in order to secure the allegiance of
the petty chiefs of the Hebrides, namely, the seizing of a
number of their children as hostages.   Similar hostages were
also taken from Caithness, who were allowed each a penny
a-day for their support.

The result of Haco's expedition is well known.   In the
battle of Largs he lost 16,000 of his men, and the greater
part of his vast fleet, which consisted of more than 100 ships,
was destroyed by a tempest.   Haco himself, on his way home,
died of a broken heart in the bishop's palace at Kirkwall; and
his remains, which were at first laid in the cathedral, were
afterwards brought over to Norway, and buried, with all the
funeral pomp befitting royalty, in Bergen.   Torfæus mentions
that a few days before the battle an annular eclipse of the sun
happened.   "Nonis Augusti tenebræ solem obfuscabant, circulo
tantum lucido sidus ambienti."

CHAPTER V.

ABOUT the beginning of the fourteenth century, Reginald or Ronald Cheyne, a celebrated chieftain, held great sway in Caithness. The Cheynes were, it appears, of Norman extraction, and came to Scotland in quest of better fortune, with the Sinclairs and other chiefs who had followed the standard of William the Conqueror. The principal residence of the Cheynes was the old castle of Inverugie, in the parish of St. Fergus, Aberdeenshire. They became proprietors of the whole of that parish, as well as of other landed estates in the counties of Banff and Moray. In the old statistical account of St. Fergus, mention is made of a Sir Reginald Cheyne, who married a daughter of Cumming of Badenoch. By her he had two sons, Reginald Cheyne, who in 1267 was promoted to the office of Lord Chamberlain of Scotland, and Henry Cheyne, who was elected Bishop of Aberdeen in 1281. In the battle of Harlaw, in 1411, was one of the Cheynes, on the side of the Earl of Mar. The leader of the men-at-arms is represented in a ballad as asking counsel at him when they came in sight of the Celtic army under the Lord of the Isles :—

> " Noo, what wad ye do, Ronald Cheyne,
> War ye Strathallan's Earl ? "
> " War I Strathallan's Earl this day,
> And thou wert Ronald Cheyne,
> My spurs wad be in my horse's side,
> And the bridle upon his mane.
>
> " Tho' they are twenty thousand men,
> And we twice ten times ten,
> Yet ha'e they but their tartan plaids,
> And we are mail-clad men.

THE OLD MAN OF HOY, 1818. L.W.W.

" My horse wad ride through ranks sae rude,
    And through the muirlan' fern ;
Let it ne'er be said that the Norman blood
    Ran cauld for Highland kern."

A branch of this family would seem to have early settled in
Caithness.* Reginald Cheyne, the subject of our notice, had
a very extensive property in it, comprehending, it is said,
nearly a third of the county. He inherited also from his
mother, who was the only daughter and co-heiress of Freskyn
de Moray, the manor and castle of Duffus, with other lands in
Morayshire. Among other possessions in Caithness, the castle
and lands of Auldwick belonged to him. But being extremely
fond of the chase, he frequently resided in the upper part of
the parish of Halkirk, in a castle, or rather hunting lodge,
situated at the north corner of Lochmore, just at the point
where the river of Thurso issues from it. In the old statistical
account of Halkirk, it is said that he had "a chest, or some
kind of a machine fixed in the mouth of the stream below the
castle for catching salmon in their ingress into the loch or
their egress out of it ; and that immediately on the fish being
entangled in the machine, the capture was announced to the
whole family by the ringing of a bell, which the motions and
struggles of the fish set agoing by means of a cord fixed at one
end to the bell in the middle of an upper room, and at the
other end to the machine in the stream below." In this
stronghold, Morar-na-Shean, or the great Cheyne, as he was
styled by the Celtic inhabitants of the district, kept about him
a number of retainers, lived in great feudal pomp, and chiefly
employed his time in hunting, for which he had ample room
and verge enough in the highlands of Caithness. Cheyne was
altogether a remarkable man in his day. He was one of the
Scottish chiefs and barons who, in the Parliament held at

* The lands in Caithness seem to have been conferred on the Cheynes by
charter from David II. The name, as originally spelt in Norman French,
was Du Chesyne. Henry Cheyne, the Bishop, built at his own expense,
about the year 1320, the old bridge over the Don, called the "brig o'
Balgownie," and celebrated by Byron as a favourite haunt of his in his
boyhood.

Arbroath in 1320, drew up the spirited remonstrance to the
Pope on the national independence of Scotland in church and
State. He was also present at the disastrous battle of Halidon
Hill in 1333, with Kenneth, Earl of Sutherland. The Earl
was slain, and Cheyne was taken prisoner by the English, but,
after a short captivity, he was released, when he returned to
Caithness and soon after married a young lady of considerable
talent and beauty, a descendant of one of the old Scandinavian
prefects or governors of the district. Tradition has handed
down many strange anecdotes of this Nimrod of the North.
The following, which is believed to be strictly founded in
truth, is one of the most remarkable and interesting. Being
the last representative of his family in the male line, he was
extremely anxious to have an heir to inherit his large property.
The first child which his lady had was a daughter. This dis-
appointment exasperated him so much that he gave imperative
orders to drown the infant. Lady Cheyne, however, by
means of a faithful domestic, managed to convey the child
away to a nurse. The second child, which was also a daughter,
was preserved in the same manner. After this, she bore no
more children. The circumstance was a source of bitter disap-
pointment to Cheyne, who could not help viewing it as a
punishment inflicted upon him for the crime of which he had
been guilty; and he began to have some compunctions of
remorse, which neither the sophistry of his confessor nor yet
the riot of the festive board could allay. In the meantime, the
two female children grew up and prospered, and received the
best education that the county at the time could afford. After
a lapse of eighteen years, Lady Cheyne, with the concurrence
of her husband, got up a grand entertainment at Christmas, to
which all their friends and acquaintances throughout the
county were invited. Among the female guests on this occasion were two young ladies, whose extraordinary beauty and
elegance of manners excited the admiration of the company.
Reginald, in particular, was greatly struck with their appearance, and as he had never seen them before, he asked his wife

whose daughters they were ?   After some little hesitation, she said they were his own.   This unexpected announcement affected him so much that, for a minute or two, he could not articulate a word.   When he had recovered, he embraced his two daughters with the most affectionate tenderness, and finally gave way to his pent-up feelings in a flood of tears. Cheyne died about the year 1350, and was buried in the chapel of Olgrimbeg.   Tradition says he was so attached to Lochmore that he made it his dying request that his grave should be filled up with sand taken from the margin of that lake.

Having no male heir, Cheyne, some years before his death, divided his estate between his two daughters, whose names were Marjory and Mary.   In 1337, Nicholas, second son of the Earl of Sutherland, and ancestor of the Barons of Duffus, married Marjory, and thus became proprietor of the lands of Auldwick in this county.   The property was afterwards successively occupied by the Oliphants, by the Earls of Caithness, and by Lord Glenorchy.   Glenorchy sold the castle and lands to Dunbar of Hempriggs, and finally, by the marriage of Sir James Sutherland, second son of Lord Duffus, with Elizabeth, daughter of Sir William Dunbar of Hempriggs, they became the property of the present Sir George Dunbar, the lineal male representative of Nicholas Sutherland and Marjory Cheyne. Mary, the other daughter, was married to John, second son of Edward Keith, the Marischal, and her son, Andrew, in right of his mother, became possessed of the lands of Ackergill. By the same right he also obtained the castle of Inverugie and the estate connected with it.   The family of the Keiths were among the most powerful in Scotland.   They had extensive property in the south ; and their residence, when in this county, was the Tower of Ackergill.*   It is not known when

* Sir George Dunbar, the proprietor, has lately erected a splendid new mansion, with which the old tower is finely incorporated.   He has made many other admirable improvements about the place ; and Ackergill Tower, which name it still retains, is now one of the finest gentlemen's seats in the north.

this formidable stronghold was erected, but it cannot be less than from four to five hundred years old. In the "Origines Parochiales Scotiæ," * it is mentioned that in 1538 the castle was granted by James V., with half of the lands of Ackergill, to William, Earl Marischal, and Lady Margaret Keith, his wife. And the same authority also states that in 1547 the Queen Regent granted a remission to George, Earl of Caithness, and others, "for their treasonable taking and holding of the castle belonging to William Earl Marischal, and for their treasonable taking of Alexander Keith, captain of the castle, and of John Scarlet, his servitor, and detaining them against their will in Girnigoe, Brawl, and other places." The tower— the only part of the old building which remains—stands on a level plain, close by the sea, and is of a rectangular form, measuring about eighty-two feet in height; and in breadth, at each of the angles, forty-five feet. It consists of four storeys, two of which are arched; and the massive walls are from ten to eleven feet in thickness. In the centre of these are arched passages, from three to four feet wide, with slits in the walls for the discharge of arrows and other warlike missiles. On the land side, the castle was defended by a deep and broad moat. The winding stair in the inside is so narrow, that even should an enemy have forced the external defences, a resolute retainer or two could have kept a whole host at bay, and prevented them from getting access to the upper storeys. The ground, too, in the vicinity of the castle is low, and before the invention of artillery, it might be considered impregnable. There was, moreover, a draw-well within the tower, twenty-four feet deep, which afforded the inmates a constant supply of water, and nothing but sheer famine could have forced the garrison to surrender. I may here notice a tradition connected with the well. One of the domestics, a black man, is said to have fallen into it, and was drowned. After this accident, the water was never used, and the well was shut up.

The Keiths and Gunns occupy a prominent place in the

* Vol. ii., part ii.

ancient history of Caithness. The latter are of Norwegian
origin. Their progenitor was Gunnius or Gunn, brother of
Sweyn, the celebrated Freswick pirate.* This promising
youth was banished from Orkney by Wicked Earl Harold for
a criminal intrigue with his mother, the infamous Countess of
Athole, who, on the death of her husband, had removed to
that county. She afterwards eloped with one named Erlend
to the castle of Mousa, in Shetland. Harold followed with
an army, but finding that he could not take the place by
assault or reduce it by famine, he listened to a treaty of
accommodation, and agreed that the parties should be married.
Gunn, her former paramour, came over to Caithness, and fixed
his residence in Ulbster, in the parish of Wick, where, by
turning over a new leaf, he increased so much in wealth and
power that he was called the Great Gunn of Ulbster. His
descendants, in process of time, became a numerous race, and
assumed the distinctive appellation of the Clan Gunn. They
and the Keiths bore a mutual hatred to each other, and were
continually at feud. The original quarrel is said to have been
caused by the following unhappy occurence :—Lachlan Gunn,
a small proprietor in Braemore, had an only daughter, named
Helen, who was particularly distinguished for her good looks,
and was called the "Beauty of Braemore." The fame of her
personal charms had spread through the whole of Sutherland
and Caithness. A long and ardent attachment, commencing,
it might be said, from childhood, had subsisted between her
and her cousin, Alexander Gunn ; and the day of their marriage was fixed. About this time, Dugald Keith, a retainer of
Keith of Ackergill, and who acted as factor on his property in
Caithness, having seen Helen Gunn, was greatly struck with

* In the statistical account of Kildonan, in the county of Sutherland, a different origin is assigned to the Clan Gunn. It is therein stated that they
were descended from the Norwegian Kings of Man, and that Guin or Gunn,
their progenitor, was the eldest son of Olave, king of that island, by his third
wife, Christina, daughter of Farquhar, Earl of Ross. On this point, however,
we are disposed to place more reliance on the authority of Torfæus than on
that of the Chronicle of Man, from which the Sutherland account of the
origin of the race purports to be taken.

her beauty, and made a dishonourable proposal, which she indignantly rejected. Mortified with this repulse, the proud and unprincipled villain resolved to gratify his passion at all hazards. Accordingly, having mustered a strong party of Keiths, he set out for Braemore, and on the wedding eve surrounded the house of Lachlan, where a few of the relations had met to partake of the festivity usual on such an occasion. The Gunns, who were quite unprepared for such an attack, were, after a brave resistance, mostly all killed; and the young bride was forcibly seized and carried away to Ackergill Tower, where she was kept a prisoner, and became the victim of the brutal and licentious Keith. The unfortunate young woman could not endure the disgrace and misery of her situation. Like another Lucretia, she resolved on self-destruction ; and, having found an opportunity one evening when the keepers were off their guard, she ascended to the top of the tower, and threw herself headlong from the battlements. This tragical affair inspired the whole clan with implacable resentment against the Keiths, and was the cause of much future strife and bloodshed. As the property of the Gunns lay chiefly in the highlands of the county, they were also frequently at feud with the Mackays of Strathnaver, who were, every now and then, dashing across the borders and harassing them with their predatory incursions.

1426.—During one of those raids, a desperate battle took place between the two clans at Harpsdale, in the parish of Halkirk, about eight miles south of Thurso. Angus Dhu Mackay, or Black Angus, as he was called, a powerful chieftain, and brother-in-law of Alexander, Lord of the Isles, accompanied by his son, Neil, led on the Strathnaver men. The contest was long and obstinate, and attended with much slaughter on both sides, but the result was not decisive.

At this time, the whole of Scotland, and particularly the Highlands, was in a fearful state of insubordination. Rapine, robbery, murder, and an utter contempt of the law, prevailed to an alarming extent. A contemporary monkish writer thus describes the state of the country in his rude Latin :—"In diebus illis non erat lex in Scotia, sed quilibet potentiorum juniorem oppressit; et totum regnum fuit unum latrocinium; homicidia depredationes, incendia, et cætera maleficia remanserunt impunita; et justitia relegata extra terminos exulavit." (In those days, there was no law in Scotland, but everywhere the strong oppressed the weak. The whole kingdom was one scene of plunder. Murders, robberies, burnings, and other outrages remained unpunished, and justice in fetters was banished out of the country.)   James I., who had been released from his captivity in England in 1423, saw with regret and mortification the distracted condition of the country in which he found himself merely a king in name, with hardly any of the power belonging to the regal office. He determined, therefore, to punish the refractory chiefs, and put a check to these disorders. Accordingly, in the year 1427, he set out for Inverness, and, on his arrival there, summoned the principal northern chiefs to appear before him, including Angus Dhu Mackay, who had so recently distinguished himself in the affair at Harpsdale. The greater part of them obeyed the royal mandate, and repaired to Inverness. Those who were most conspicuous for their crimes, and defiance of lawful authority, were executed. Angus Dhu Mackay was imprisoned, but shortly afterwards liberated, on agreeing to give up his son, Neil Mackay, as a hostage for his future good behaviour. Neil was accordingly sent to the Bass,* in the mouth of the Firth of Forth, even then a sort of State prison; and from that circumstance was called Neil Bass Mackay. Neil was detained there in durance till the year 1437, when he acquired his freedom, chiefly through the influence of Sir Robert Lauder, governor of the prison, who was married to a

---

* "This singular rock," says Sir W. Scott, "rises perpendicularly out of the sea. The surface is pasture land, sloping to the brink of a tremendous precipice, which, on all sides, sinks sheer down into the stormy ocean. There is no anchorage ground on any point near the rock; and the ascent to the table land, on the summit, is not without danger. It was, during the reigns of Charles II. and James II., converted into a State prison, and was often the melancholy abode of the Nonconformists who were prisoners to Government."

relation of his. But no sooner did Neil set foot in Strathnaver
than he assembled his followers, entered Caithness, and spoiled
the county. The Mackays were met by the Caithness men at
Sandside, in the parish of Reay. After a fierce encounter, the
latter were defeated, and pursued to Downreay. This conflict
was called, *par excellence*, the " Chase of Sandside."

The warfare was still carried on between the two rival clans
—the Keiths and the Gunns ; and in the year 1438, they had
an engagement on a larger scale than usual. Having heard
that the Gunns had got a number of the other inhabitants of
Caithness to join them, and were preparing for an immediate
attack, Keith of Ackergill, mistrustful of his own strength,
applied for aid to Angus Mackay, son of the famous Neil Bass
Mackay, who readily complied with the request, and having
assembled all the able-bodied of his followers, made a hurried
march of about thirty miles through Caithness to assist his
friend. The hostile armies met on the moor of Tannach,
about three miles from Wick, where a furious conflict ensued,
attended with great slaughter on both sides. In the end, the
Keiths obtained the victory, chiefly through the extraordinary
prowess of a herculean Highlander, who rejoiced in the
euphonious appellation of John More-Macean-Reawich-Mackay.
This battle, however, did not terminate hostilities between the
two contending parties. The feud continued for a long time
after, during which they strove to harass and inflict as much
injury on each other as possible.

About the middle of the fifteenth century the chief of the
Clan Gunn was George Gunn, who lived in great feudal pomp
in his castle of Haberry, at Clyth, in the parish of Latheron.
This George was a man of commanding influence in the county
at the time, and exercised the office of Crowner, from which
circumstance he was commonly known by the title of Crowner
or Cruner Gunn. * By the Highlanders he was called " N'm

* According to Jamieson, the Crowner in Scotland was an officer to whom it
belonged to attach all persons against whom there was an accusation in matters
pertaining to the Crown. He had also the charge of the troops raised in the
county. Proof of the existence of the office occurs in the reign of David II.

Braistach-more," from a great silver brooch which he wore as the badge or cognizance of his office.

Wearied out at length with the long-continued sanguinary strife, the Crowner and the chief of the Keiths agreed to meet with twelve horsemen on each side, and settle all their differences amicably in a conference; or, if they could not effect a reconciliation in that way, to decide the quarrel at once on the spot in fair and equal combat. To invest the matter with more solemnity, the meeting was appointed to take place at the Chapel of St. Tears, or, as it was vulgarly called, St. Tayre. This religious edifice, of which not a vestige now remains, was situated half way between Castles Sinclair and Girnigoe and the Tower of Ackergill. It was dedicated to the holy tears shed by the mothers at Bethlehem over their children that were slain by the command of Herod, and was held in great veneration by the inhabitants of the district. Nor did this veneration cease for a long time even after the Protestant religion was fully established in the county. "It was customary for people," says the writer of the new statistical account of Wick, "to visit the Chapel of St. Tears on Innocents' Day, and leave in it bread and cheese as an offering to the souls of the children slain by Herod, but which the dog-keeper of a neighbouring gentleman used to take out and give to the hounds."

Another of these chapels stood close by the present house of Freswick, in the parish of Canisbay. It was dedicated to St. Moddan, and even so late as the beginning of the present century devotees were in the habit of resorting to it on Candlemas day and exhibiting proof of the most abject superstition. They first crept round the walls of the chapel on their bare knees, each muttering some petition to the saint, and then going to the neighbouring burn, threw handfuls of water over their heads. After performing this latter part of the ceremony, they adjourned to the nearest ale-house and got drunk!

1464.—On the day appointed for the meeting, the party of the Crowner, numbering exactly twelve horsemen, arrived first at the chapel, and entered it to perform their devotions. Soon after the Keiths came up, also on horseback, but on each of the horses were two men, making their number twenty-four instead of twelve. They hastily dismounted, rushed into the chapel with drawn swords, and attacked the Gunns while they were yet kneeling in the attitude of prayer. The latter saw that they were basely betrayed, but resolved to sell their lives as dearly as possible. A fierce and bloody struggle ensued. The unfortunate Gunns fought with all the desperate courage of men who expect no quarter; but in the end they were over-powered by the superiority in numbers of their enemy, and the whole party, including their chief, were massacred, it might be said, at the foot of the altar. The Crowner's helmet, shirt of mail, sword, and brooch of office were all stripped off his dead body, and seized on as a spoil by the dastardly foe. But the Keiths did not retire from the scene of blood scathless. The greater part of them also fell mortally wounded—thus deservedly paying the penalty of an act of the basest treachery and sacrilege on record. Sir Robert Gordon, who gives a brief account of this shocking tragedy, says that the blood of the combatants was to be seen on the walls of the chapel in his time, nearly a century and a half after the occurrence. George Gunn, the Crowner,* who had been twice married, had a number of grown-up sons, two of whom were killed on this occasion along with himself. Five of them that were left at home escaped this direful calamity, and among the number was James, his eldest son, who succeeded his father as chief of the clan. There is a Highland version of the tradition which says that this treacherous affair happened in Strathmore, on the confines of the county. According to this account, the two chiefs had first a private conference in the Chapel of St. Tayre, when a solemn compact

* Hugh Macdonald of Sleat, third son of Alexander, Earl of Ross, married a lady of the clan Gunn, who is supposed to have been the Crowner's daughter. By her he had a son, Donald, who afterwards became heir of the family, and from whom the present Lord Macdonald is descended.—Stat. Acct. Kildonan.

was entered into at the altar, that a meeting for finally deciding their differences should take place in a solitary part of the county, where no interruption would occur ; and the escort of each leader was fixed at twelve armed horsemen.   They met at a burn called Altnagawn, below the "glut" of Strathmore. The Gunns, notwithstanding the great odds against them, scorned to retreat before their perfidious enemies, and, dismounting from their horses, fought with the most determined bravery.   The weapon chiefly used on the occasion was the huge double-handed sword.   After a long and deadly struggle, the survivors on both sides were so much exhausted that the combat was mutually dropt.   The Crowner, and seven of his party, including his two sons, Robert and John, were killed, and the remaining five, who were also sons of his, were severely wounded.   After the fight, the Keiths proceeded to the castle of Dirlet—then occupied by a chief of the name of Sutherland, by whom they were hospitably entertained.   Henry Gunn, the youngest of the surviving brothers, proposed that they should follow the Keiths, and endeavour to obtain some revenge.   Two of them, who were the least wounded, agreed to accompany him, and, setting out, they arrived at the castle after nightfall.   Henry stole softly to an open window in the lowest apartment of the castle, from which a light issued. Here, seated around a large fire, the Keiths were quaffing bumpers of ale, and boasting how they had done for the Gunns.   The chief, not apprehensive of any danger, accidentally approached the window, when Henry instantly drew his bow and discharged an arrow, which pierced him to the heart, exclaiming, as he did so, in Gaelic, "Iomach gar n' Guinach gu Kaigh ;" that is, "The Gunns' compliments to Keith."   The chief dropped down dead.   On this, the Keiths made a sudden rush to the door.   The Gunns slew one or two of the first persons who came out ; but finding that they could not retain their position long, they hastily fled from the castle, and escaped under cover of the darkness of the night.   Alexander Sutherland, the proprietor of the castle, styled, in Gaelic, "Ruder Dearg," or, the red knight, was a near relative of the Dunrobin family, and a man noted for his rude and lawless conduct. Having in a quarrel slain Sir Alexander Dunbar of Cumnock, he was apprehended by his uncle, Mackay of Strathnaver, and brought to Stirling, where he was executed, along with some half-dozen of his accomplices, in the year 1499. In reward of his services, James the fourth conferred on Mackay the castle of Dirlet,* and the whole estate belonging to his nephew, which was very considerable. Among the lands specified in this charter, mention is made of two-tenths of the island of Stroma, in the Pentland Firth. The seizure of Sutherland, as reported by tradition, affords another instance of the most revolting cruelty and treachery. Mackay, accompanied by ten followers of his clan, came to Dirlet ostensibly to pay a friendly visit to his nephew. Having not the least suspicion of his design, Sutherland gave him a cordial welcome, and had a sumptuous entertainment prepared for him and his attendants. There were about twenty retainers in the castle, and they and the party belonging to Mackay, as was the feudal custom of the time, sat down to dinner in the great hall along with their masters. By some adroit management on the part of the Strathnaver chief, it was so arranged that each of the Mackays had one of Sutherland's men on his right hand and another on his left. Everything seemed to go on with the utmost harmony and good humour. The guests partook heartily of the viands set before them, and the wassail cup had circulated pretty freely round the board, when all at once, by a preconcerted signal, the Mackays drew their dirks, which they had concealed under their clothes, and stabbing right and left on each side of them, put to death in less than a minute the whole of Sutherland's retainers. Having now none to support him, Sutherland himself was easily seized, and immediately conveyed away under a strong guard to Edinburgh. After the tragical death of his father, James Gunn, now the head of the

---

* The castle of Dirlet was one of the residences of the famous Ronald Cheyne, and is believed to have been originally built by him.

clan, with his two brothers, William and Henry, and a number of followers, removed to Sutherlandshire.   The dwelling-house of the chief was at Killernan, in the parish of Kildonan.   It was destroyed accidentally by fire about the year 1690.   From Henry Gunn are descended the Hendersons of Caithness. The great body of the Gunns, notwithstanding the removal of their chief to Sutherland, still continued to inhabit the highlands of the county.   They were chiefly located in the upper parts of the parishes of Latheron and Halkirk.   But the horrid treachery of the Keiths was not forgotten by the clan.   The memory of it still rankled in their breasts; and many years afterwards William Gunn, son of James, and grandson of the Crowner, intercepted in Sutherland George Keith of Ackergill and his son, with twelve domestics, on their way from Inverugie to Caithness, and in revenge of the massacre at St. Tayre, cut off the whole party. *

* Sir R. Gordon, His. p. 92.

CHAPTER VI.

THE rule of the Norwegian Earls in Caithness terminated in 1331. At this time, Magnus the Fifth,* the last of those Earls, died without leaving a successor in the male line, when Henry St. Clair or Sinclair, son of the Baron of Roslin, who was allied to the family by marriage, claimed the earldom, and received investiture of it from Haco the Sixth, King of Norway. The Sinclairs of Roslin, from whom all the other chief families of that name are sprung, were originally of French or Norman extraction, and came over with William the Conqueror in 1066.† But not meeting in England with those rewards to which they considered their talents and services entitled them, they withdrew to Scotland during the reign of Malcolm Canmore. At the Scottish Court they were received with much distinction, and, in process of time, acquired high rank and extensive possessions. The first of the family who is said to have settled in Scotland, was William de St. Clair, second son of Walderne de St. Clair, and Margaret, daughter of Richard, Duke of Normandy. He obtained from Malcolm large grants of land in Mid-Lothian. These were increased by the liberality of succeeding monarchs, and comprehended, among others, the baronies of Roslin and Pentland. Roslin Castle is said to have been erected by Henry Sinclair, second of the name, Earl of Orkney, about the year 1400.‡ It stands on an almost insulated rock overlooking the romantic vale of the Esk, and from the size and appearance of the ruins—for it has partly

---

* This Magnus, who is styled "Comis Cathaniæ et Orcadiæ," seems to have been a chief of a noble and patriotic spirit; and in 1320, along with the other Scottish barons, signed the famous letter to the Pope upholding the national independence.
† They are mentioned among the leading chiefs in the roll of Battle Abbey.
‡ Hay's Memoirs of the House of Roslin, MS.

fallen into decay—it must originally have been a large and massive structure. To the lovers of song, it possesses a special interest, from its being associated with the fine old air named " Roslin Castle."   Roslin Chapel, the most exquisitely beautiful edifice of its kind in Britain, was founded in 1446 by William St. Clair, great grandson, by the female line, of Robert II., and the third of his name, Earl of Orkney and Caithness.   He was also Chancellor of Scotland, and had the foreign title of Duke of Oldenburgh.   The principal residence of this illustrious family was at Roslin, one of the loveliest spots in the south ; and the family burying vault was within the abbey, where the old barons were all deposited in their armour.   A superstitious belief prevailed that on the night before the death of any of the barons, the chapel was supernaturally lighted up.   Sir Walter Scott makes a fine poetical use of this superstition in the dirge of Rosabelle, in the "Lay of the Last Minstrel : "—

> " Seemed all on fire that chapel proud,
>   Where Roslin's chiefs uncoffined lie ;
>   Each baron for a sable shroud
>   Sheathed in his iron panoply.
>   Blazed battlement and pinnet high,
>   Blazed every rose-carved buttress fair ;
>   So still they blaze when fate is nigh,
>   The lordly line of high St Clair."

In the ancient history of Scotland, not a few of the Sinclairs are celebrated for their great gallantry in the field.   One of these distinguished chiefs was Sir William Sinclair of Hermandston.   In the battle of Bannockburn, says Abercrombie in his martial achievements, Sir William behaved so well that King Robert the Bruce was afterwards pleased to present him with a sword, on the broad side of which these words were engraved :—" La Roi me donne, St. Clair me poste," the king gifts me, the Sinclair carries me.   He was afterwards killed in a battle with the Moors in Spain, while accompanying James Earl of Douglas to the Holy Land with the heart of Bruce.

After the failure of the Norwegian line of Earls, there is not a little confusion in the history of the earldom, from the circumstance that there were at times two Earls of Caithness, the one appointed by the King of Denmark and the other by the King of Scotland. Of this we have an instance in the case of William Sinclair, chancellor, and Allan Stewart, styled Earl of Caithness, who, with sixteen of his personal retinue, was killed at the battle of Inverlochy in 1431, fighting against Donald Balloch,* brother of Alexander, Lord of the Isles. Although Caithness had been long annexed, as a conquered province, to the Norwegian rule in Orkney, it was never acknowledged as such by the Scottish monarchs; and nothing but its extreme distance from the seat of Government, the divided state of the kingdom, and the difficulty of sending troops so far north and maintaining them there, forced them to tolerate the usurpation. The county was, both geographically and politically, a part of the kingdom of Scotland. The author of the " History of the House of Mackay," who appears to have directed his attention to the state of matters in the north at the time, has the following remarks on the subject :—" During the period in which the Sinclairs held Orkney, they were under the sovereignty of Denmark, to whom these islands belonged ;† and as the Sinclairs also claimed titles and lands in Scotland, the Kings of Denmark were jealous of them, and on that account admitted their claims to Orkney under strict and severe conditions and burdens. On the other hand, because of their subordination to Denmark, and the exorbitancy of their power should they hold both Orkney and Caithness, the Kings of

* This Donald Balloch is the hero of the gathering in Sir W. Scott's " Pibroch of Donald Dhu." Donald was afterwards killed in Ireland, and his head was sent to the king, James I. of Scotland.

† The Orkney and Zetland Islands were disjoined from the crown of Norway and Denmark and annexed to Scotland in 1468. They were pledged by Christian I. of Denmark for 58,000 Rhenish florins, being part of the dowry of 60,000 promised with his daughter Margaret on her marriage with James III. of Scotland. Of this sum, only 2000 florins were ever paid. Orkney and Zetland remained impignorated for the balance, amounting to about £24,166 13s 4d sterling; and one object of Torfæus in compiling the " Orcades " was to vindicate the right of Christian V. to redeem the mortgage of the sovereignty of these islands, by re-paying the money for which they were pledged.

Scotland never admitted their claim to the latter while they held the former, but to which claim they, notwithstanding, adhered as part of their titles." At length, William, the chancellor, obtained from King James II. a confirmation by charter of the earldom of Caithness in 1455.* Being dissatisfied with certain political changes which took place in Orkney after it was ceded to Scotland in 1468, he resigned to the Crown the earldom of that county, in compensation for which he received the castle of Ravenscraig and sundry adjacent lands in the county of Fife, with an annuity of forty marks secured on the customs of Edinburgh. He was twice married. By his first wife, a daughter of Archibald, fourth Earl of Douglas, he had a son called William, who was ancestor of the Lords Sinclair. This nobleman was distinguished by the princeliness of his mode of living. "He kept," said one who was attached to the household, "a great court in his castle of Roslin, and was royally served at his own table in vessels of gold and silver. He had his halls and other apartments richly adorned with embroidery hangings. His princess, Elizabeth Douglas, was served by seventy-five gentlewomen, whereof fifty-three were daughters of noblemen, all clothed in velvets and silks, with their chains of gold and other ornaments, and was attended by two hundred riding gentlemen in all her journeys; and if it happened to be dark when she went to Edinburgh, where her lodgings were at the foot of Blackfriars' Wynd, eighty lighted torches were carried before her." By his second wife, Marjory, daughter of Alexander Sutherland of Dunbeath,† he had a son, also named William, in whose favour he resigned the earldom of Caithness. His son's title was recognised and confirmed by James III. in 1476. William, now second Earl of Caithness of the Sinclair family, married a daughter of Keith of Ackergill. He was a gallant and high-spirited nobleman, and the few notices that we have

* In Appendix, No. 5, see genealogical list of the Earls of Caithness of the Sinclair family.
† For a very curious document, "The Testament of Alexander Sutherland of Dunbeath," see Appendix, No. 6.

of him are extremely interesting. In 1481 he joined the confederacy of the nobles who hanged Cochran * and the other favourites of James III. at the bridge of Lauder. On the second rebellion of the barons, headed by the king's own son, he appears to have allied himself to the royal cause, as well as Huntly, Crawford, and many others who had leagued for the destruction of the favourites. Huntly and Crawford fought at Sauchie burn on the king's side, but Caithness appears not to have arrived in time for the battle, although Abercrombie and Holinshed distinctly state that he and others were on their way to his assistance. He sat in Parliament in 1505. This derives some interest from the circumstance that it was referred to in the case of William Sinclair of Ratter, when he was a claimant for the title of Earl of Caithness. When James IV. made his unfortunate expedition to Flodden, William readily obeyed the royal summons issued for the feudal array of the kingdom, and evinced his loyalty by raising a body of about 300 men, with which he hastened off to his assistance. Among the leaders on this occasion his name is not particularly mentioned by our principal historians, but it appears from Sir Robert Gordon's history that he took a distinguished part in the battle of Flodden. The Earl of Huntly, who led the right wing of the Scottish army, was supported by Adam Gordon, Earl of Sutherland, William Gordon of Gight, and by the Earl of Caithness. Huntly charged with impetuosity the left wing of the English, and after a desperate encounter drove them off the field; but on returning from the pursuit of the enemy he found that matters were not going on so satisfactorily in the other parts of the field. It is unnecessary, and besides it is foreign to our purpose, to describe a battle the details of which are so well known to the general reader. Suffice it to say that the

* Cochran was an ancestor of the Dundonald family. The late Earl of Dundonald, in his Autobiography, says:—"Cochran possessed a landed estate, which he resigned in favour of his son, and devoted himself wholly to architecture. He became a great favourite with the king, who had also a taste for that science, and thereby incurred the hatred and jealousy of the proud nobles, who contemptuously called him the 'mason chiel.'"

Scottish army, after fighting for several hours with the most determined bravery, got at length into complete disorder. The Earls of Huntly and Sutherland saved themselves by flight, but Gordon of Gight and the Earl of Caithness stood their ground, and at the head of their men gallantly yielded up their lives. There fell also on this unhappy occasion Andrew Stewart, Bishop of Caithness. He was a churchman of high standing, and enjoyed a plurality of offices, being at the same time Abbot of Fearn, in Ross, and Lord Treasurer of Scotland. In a list of the killed, which is given in a contemporary gazette written in French, he and the Earl are thus mentioned by their titles :—" L'Evesque de Katnes" (the Bishop of Caithness); "Le Conte de Katnes" (the Earl of Caithness).*

There is an interesting tradition current in the county connected with this battle, so disastrous to Caithness as well as to the rest of Scotland. It is said that the Earl of Caithness was at the time under attainder, and when, an evening or two before the engagement, the king saw a fresh body of troops coming up all clad in green, he was much struck with their appearance, and eagerly inquired of those who stood next him whose men they were. They replied that they thought they were the men of Caithness, and that the Earl himself was at the head of them. The king mused a little, and then said, " Well, if that be William Sinclair, I will pardon him." There being no parchment in the camp, James ordered the deed of removal of forfeiture, etc., to be extended on a drum-head. When the document had received the royal signature, it was cut out and handed to the Earl, who forthwith despatched one of his men with it to Caithness, strictly enjoining him to deliver the same into the hands of his lady, so that in the event of his falling in battle the family might be secured in their titles and lands.† The bearer of it was the only one of

---

* Pinkerton, Hist. Scot., vol. ii., p. 456.

† The above romantic tradition, which tells so honourably to both parties, would appear to be unsupported by any proper basis of historical evidence. On calling at the Register House, Edinburgh, to see if there were in its

the Caithness corps that ever returned, the rest having been all killed in the engagement. The Earl on his way south had crossed the Ord of Caithness on a Monday, and for a long time after no Sinclair would cross it on that day of the week, or wear anything approaching the colour of green.*

The disaster at Flodden, so serious to Caithness, was the greatest that ever befell Scotland. Tradition, legend, song, and history have all told the melancholy tale. It has given birth to one of the sweetest and most plaintive of our Scottish airs, the "Flowers of the Forest," and it afforded a theme of inspiration to Scott, who, in his "Marmion," has described the battle in a strain of poetry that for splendour and animation has never been surpassed.

William Sinclair, who fell at Flodden, was succeeded in the earldom by his son John, who married Mary Sutherland, daughter of the Laird of Duffus. In the month of May, 1529, John invaded Orkney with a body of 500 men. Various causes are assigned for this invasion, which seems to have been rash and ill-judged. Some say that he went to assist Lord Sinclair of Ravenscraig, with the object of recovering certain lands which belonged to the latter in that county; others, that he went to support his relative in enforcing his right to the governorship of the castle of Kirkwall, to which he had been appointed, but which Sir James Sinclair, natural

archives a copy of the deed said to have been drawn out at Flodden, Mr Joseph Robertson, a gentleman profoundly versed in Scotch antiquities, assured the writer that the House contained no such document, and that he had no reason to think that the Earl of Caithness was at the time under forfeiture. There are two writers, however, whose statements would seem to give some countenance to the tradition. Pitcairn, in his "Tales of the Scottish Wars," alludes to the story of the "drum-head charter;" and Sir James Balfour, in his "Annals," expressly says that "William, Earl of Caithness, was forfaulted by King James III.," but he does not mention the year when the forfeiture took place, nor the crime which subjected him to the royal displeasure.

* This superstition does not seem to have been confined to the Sinclairs. Brown, in his History of the Highlands, says:—"Green was the colour of the dress which the fairies always wore, and they were supposed to take offence when any of the mortal race presumed to wear their favourite colour. The Highlanders ascribe the disastrous result of the battle of Killiecrankie to the circumstance of the Viscount of Dundee having been dressed in green on that ill-fated day.

son of Sir William Sinclair of Wassalter, in Sanday, who then held the situation, refused to give up. Mr Worsaae, in referring to this matter, says :—" The islanders took up arms under the command of their governor, Sir James Sinclair, to oppose the appointment of a crown vassal over the islands." Mr Balfour, the latest writer on Orkney, gives the clearest and most satisfactory account of the circumstances which led to this unfortunate affair. Lady Sinclair, widow of Henry, Lord Sinclair, who fell at Flodden, held at the time the tack of the crown lands in Orkney and Shetland. The Udallers, headed by Sir James Sinclair of Sanday, resisted payment of her rents for the space of three years. They also forced her son, William, Lord Sinclair, to surrender the castle of Kirkwall, and escape to Caithness, in 1528, and then elected Sir James their leader and virtual governor. In these circumstances she applied to John, Earl of Caithness, for assistance ; and he and her son, Lord William, fitted out the expedition, which, it further appears, was sanctioned by royal authority. In the meantime, Sir James Sinclair mustered a large body of Orkneymen to repel the invasion. The hostile parties met, and a sanguinary battle was fought at a place called Summerdale, about four miles north-east from Stromness, in which the Earl of Caithness and all his men were slain, and Sinclair of Ravenscraig was taken prisoner. Many of the Caithnessmen were killed, not in the heat of battle, but in their retreat from the field. The ferocious islanders gave no quarter, and the unhappy fugitives were butchered in cold blood among the rocks and caves to which they had fled for shelter. The body of the Earl of Caithness was buried in Orkney ; but tradition says that his savage enemies cut off his head, and sent it over in way of mockery to Caithness. Such a terrible calamity, occurring so soon after that at Flodden, filled the whole county with mourning and lamentation. It was then but thinly peopled, and the two fatal expeditions nearly drained it of all its young and able-bodied men. Among those who accompanied the Earl of Caithness to Orkney was William

Sutherland of Berriedale,* a young man of gigantic stature. Sutherland, who had some presentiment that he would never return, stretched himself on the ground in the old churchyard of Berriedale before setting out, and caused two stones to be fixed, the one at his head and the other at his feet, which were to be seen for ages after. The distance between the stones is said to be eight feet three inches. It fell out as he but too truly anticipated : he was slain in Orkney.

The following tradition in Orkney of the battle of Summerdale, which was communicated to the author by a gentleman residing in that county, will be found not a little curious and interesting. It presents a striking picture of the superstition and savage barbarity of the people of the north at the period in question :—

"When the Earl of Caithness and his men landed at Orphir, in Orkney, a witch preceded them on their march, unwinding two balls of thread as she walked before them. One was blue and the other red, and the thread of the latter having first become exhausted, the witch assured the Earl that the side on which blood was first drawn would certainly be defeated. Placing implicit faith on this prognostication, the Earl resolved to slay the first Orkneyman that crossed his path, and so insure victory to himself and his followers in the coming conflict. Soon afterwards a boy was descried herding cattle, so, thinking that if it was Orkney blood, it was no great matter whether it was of man or boy, the Earl and his men, with eager haste, caught the boy, and mercilessly slew him without

---

* This William Sutherland was proprietor of Langwell, and ancestor of the Brabster family. Of the castle of Berriedale, which the Sutherlands long inhabited, very little now remains. An old writer, speaking of it, says :—"Upon a rock at the mouth of the water stands the castle, to which they entered by a drawbridge, and the entry to the bridge was so sloping from the top of a high brae that only two could go abreast. The entry was very dangerous, the sea being on the right hand, and the water to the left, and the rock very high on both sides, especially to the north." As to Sutherland's reported stature, there seems no reason to doubt the truth of the traditional account. Two instances of extraordinary height have occurred in Scotland, and in times not very remote from our own. Samuel Macdonald, commonly called "Big Sam," a native of Sutherland, was upwards of seven feet high ; and a Mr Bookless, schoolmaster of Hutton, in Berwickshire, is said to have measured seven feet four inches.

a moment's warning. But they had reckoned without their host, for the boy was then recognised by some of them to be a native of Caithness, who had for some time been a fugitive in Orkney; and it speedily occurred to them that if the words of the witch were worth anything, they had, by the cruel murder of a poor helpless boy, now lying a bleeding corpse at their feet, rendered certain their own discomfiture. Prone to superstition as the Earl and his men seem to have been, this untoward circumstance must have had a strong tendency to depress their spirits and unnerve their arm; and this is probably the key to the issue of the subsequent battle at Summerdale, where they were met and completely routed by the Orkneymen.

"The battle, says the tradition, was fought on a piece of smooth grass, where no stones were to be seen previous to the morning of the encounter, but then they were found in such abundance that the Orkneymen threw down the pitchforks with which they were armed, and plied their Caithness foes so effectually with stones that they were unable to get near enough to use their weapons. The incessant and murderous showers of those primitive missiles soon told with effect on the ranks of the Caithness men, who were at last compelled to betake themselves to an ignominious flight. Throwing their arms into the Loch of Kisbister, they fled pell-mell over the broken ground towards their landing-place; but they were closely pursued, and in a short time only a few survived to continue the hopeless race for life. Amongst these was the Earl of Caithness, who reached the farm of Oback in Orphir, and dashing through the 'close' between the dwelling-house and the offices, in the hope of escaping his merciless pursuers who were close at his heels, rushed unwittingly into the arms of another party of his foes, who slew him on the spot. Not one of the Caithness men escaped to carry home the tale of their discomfiture. The Earl was amongst the last that fell, and his head, sent back in proud defiance, was the sole relique of the fated band that reached the shores of Caithness.

" Only one Orkneyman fell on that day, which proved so fatal to their adversaries, and his death was a very tragic one. He had dressed himself in the clothes of one of the slaughtered Caithness men, and was coming towards his own house in the evening, when he was met by his mother, who, not recognising him, but believing him to be one of the enemy that had escaped the general carnage, struck him a fatal blow on the forehead with a stone which she had put into the foot of one of his own stockings, and was carrying in her hand.

" The motive which led to the Earl's hostile visit to Orkney is involved in considerable obscurity, but the relentless spirit of the contending parties, as displayed in the murder of the boy, and in the complete slaughter of the invaders, and in the fiendish thirst for vengeance exhibited by the woman, who, in the blindness of her fury, murdered her own son, sufficiently proves that a bitter animosity existed between the inhabitants of Orkney and Caithness, which it has taken upwards of three centuries to extinguish."

Regarding the ultimate fate of Sir James Sinclair, the tradition in Orkney is, that he drowned himself at a place called the " Glupe " of Linkness, about eight miles from Kirkwall. But in the records of the Privy Seal it is particularly stated that he committed suicide at Stirling on the 18th April, 1539. One account says that a fear of being prosecuted for the slaughter of the Earl of Caithness, and a sense of the King's displeasure whom he had offended by obtaining on a false representation that they were holms, a life-lease of the islands of Eday and Sanday, drove him to the act of self-destruction.

Mr Balfour gives a different account of this matter. He says that the King not only pardoned Sir James Sinclair, the principal rebel, but gave him a feudal grant of the islands, containing all the usual rights, with a clause of single primogeniture, the infraction of Odal succession. This grant, he adds, " was the purchase of the independence of the Odal leader, begged and accepted with a selfish inconsistency mournfully explained by his madness and suicide within a year." It appears also from a complaint of Lord William Sinclair that Sir James had been guilty of excessive cruelty. Previous to the fight at Summerdale he slew several of his lordship's friends and attendants in the Castle of Kirkwall; and a week or two after the battle, among other atrocities, he put to death in cold blood thirty men who had fled for sanctuary to the Cathedral of St. Magnus and other places of worship in the country. It is stated in the complaint that he dragged them by force out of the church, stript them naked, and then cruelly killed them " in his contemption of God and halikirk, and breaking of the privilege of the Girth." The great mystery in the case is that the King should not only have pardoned such a man but have given him a grant of the islands. The King afterwards restored to Barbara Stewart, the relict of Sir James, the whole of his goods, moveable and immoveable, which had been forfeited to the Crown by his suicide.

In the course of this same year (1529) Sutherland of Duffus, a descendant of the old Dunrobin family, and a chief possessed of landed property in Moray, Sutherland, and Caithness, was basely assassinated by some of the clan Gunn in Thurso. The perpetrators of the crime, says Sir R. Gordon, were instigated to it by Andrew Stewart, Bishop of Caithness, " on account of some conceived displeasure which he had received from Duffus." It is strongly suspected, however, that Adam, Earl of Sutherland, the first of the Gordon line, and who had obtained the earldom by not very justifiable means, was at the bottom of the affair, and that, through the agency of the bishop, he had bribed the Gunns to commit the horrid deed. His lordship, it was well known, entertained a mortal grudge against Duffus for thwarting some of his favourite schemes, and doing what he could to have the earldom restored to the rightful heir. In the meantime, young Duffus, whose uncle, Alexander Sutherland, was Dean of Caithness, prosecuted the bishop for the murder of his father. Caithness was in a state of much excitement, and, for better security, the prelate left the county and retired to Athole. The case was brought before the proper tribunal at Edinburgh, but, on one pretence or another, it was put off from time to time and never thoroughly investigated. The accused had many powerful friends at head-quarters, and through their influence the young Laird of Duffus was finally induced to abandon the charge, and the bishop returned white-washed to his diocese.

It would appear from " Pitcairn's Criminal Trials," that Bishop Andrew Stewart was not the only churchman in the county implicated in the crime. In that curious collection of Scottish *causes célèbres*, it is mentioned that Thomas Stewart, treasurer of Caithness, Andrew Petre, vicar of Wick, John Thomson, rector of Olrig, and William Murray, David Reid, and Hugh Groat, chaplains, were obliged to find caution for their appearing in court, to answer for being art and part in the slaughter of the Laird of Duffus.

CHAPTER VII.

JOHN SINCLAIR, who was slain in Orkney, was succeeded by his son George, who married Elizabeth Graham, daughter of the Earl of Montrose.* This George was distinguished for talent and political intrigue, and became possessed of greater influence in the north than any of his predecessors. All his authority, however, was inadequate to suppress the intestine feuds that from time to time broke out in the county. In the autumn of 1561, William and Angus Sutherland, of Berriedale, committed some gross outrages in Caithness, and killed several of the inhabitants of the name of Clyne, against whom they had a grudge. For these acts the Earl of Caithness banished them from the county, and took possession of their castle of Berriedale. But they soon returned again; and being assisted by Hugh Murray of Aberscross, in Sutherland, they retook the castle, and by the admission of Sir Robert Gordon, "brunt and wasted all the country next adjacent, and molested Catteyness with divers incursions." John, Earl of Sutherland, it was believed, countenanced these proceedings. At all events, he threw his protecting shield over the aggressors; and by his interest at Court obtained from Queen Mary, then newly arrived in Scotland, a pardon for William and Angus Sutherland and their accomplices. This interference on the part of the Earl of Sutherland greatly exasperated Earl George, and laid the foundation of that hatred which the two houses

* In Barrogill Castle, the seat of the present Earl of Caithness, there is a wood carving of Caithness and Montrose. At the upper side are the initials G. S. and E. G. One supporter is a crane, the other a griffin, with the mottoes "Commit thy wish to God," and "Ne oublie" (Don't forget), and the arms of Montrose are impaled on the escutcheon with those of Caithness. These arms are no doubt those of George, fourth Earl of Caithness of the Sinclair family, and of his Countess, Elizabeth Graham, daughter of William, Earl of Montrose. Barrogill Castle was built about the year 1606.

of Sutherland and Caithness for a long period after bore to each other.

In the year 1556, the Earl of Caithness obtained an hereditary grant of the office of Justiciary, with full power of life and death over Caithness and Sutherland. " The charter conferring these rights," says Sir Robert Gordon, " was obtained by credit and means of the Earl of Bothwell, because the Earl of Caithness was then a plotter with him of King Henry's death, and was thereafter a partner with him in the execution of that enterprise with the Earl of Bothwell, whose sister* the Earl of Caithness' eldest son married."

Sir Robert loudly accuses Buchanan of prejudice and partiality in his History of Scotland ; and there is no doubt of the truth of the charge. But, unfortunately, the worthy baronet is guilty of the very same fault which he imputes to that historian. He evidently bears no good feeling to the Caithness family, and throughout he makes the most of their misdeeds, and paints them in the very blackest colours. The first George, Earl of Caithness, was certainly not over-burdened with principle ; but it does not appear from the history of the period that he had any participation in the murder of Darnley. It is true that at the trial of Bothwell he was chancellor of the jury that acquitted him ; but although there can be no doubt of the guilt of Bothwell, the jury, under the circumstances, could not have given any other verdict. Robertson, the historian allows this, and says that " the Earl of Caithness protested in their name that no crime should be imputed to them on that account, because no accuser had appeared, and no proof was brought of the indictment." It is also true that after the mock trial—for it was nothing else—the Earl of Caithness, along with the other Popish and Protestant lords

* The lady that John, the Earl's eldest son, married is by other writers said to have been Jean Hepburn, the niece, and not the sister of Bothwell. But Laing, in his dissertation on the murder of Darnley, states explicitly that she was Bothwell's sister. She had been first married to John Stewart, Prior of Coldingham. On the acquittal of Bothwell, she came to reside at Holyrood, and when Mary was carried off to the castle of Dunbar she accompanied her thither.

present subscribed the bond* acquitting Bothwell of the crime with which he was charged, and recommending him as a fit husband for the Queen ; but so did John, Earl of Sutherland. Both were members of the Privy Council, and both were equally friendly to Bothwell. It further appears, that immediately after the murder of Darnley, the Earl of Sutherland, as well as the Earl of Caithness, signed the letter† written by the Privy Council (1567) to the queen-mother of France, in which a delusive account is given of this shocking tragedy. Sir Robert Gordon, however, while he would fain fasten on the Earl of Caithness the serious charge of aiding and abetting Bothwell in the murder of the King, is discreetly silent with regard to the conduct of the Sutherland chieftain throughout the whole of this affair.

Sir Robert's statement that the justiciaryship was conferred on the Earl of Caithness for plotting against the King's life is manifestly false as well as malicious. The grant was bestowed for a very different service. On this point we have received the following communication, founded on the authority of Miss Strickland and Mignet the French writer, from a gentleman well versed in the history of the period :—" On the night of the murder of Rizzio, whilst Mary was confined by the brutal ruffians in the private cabinet, and whilst the Earl of Morton, with 500 men, occupied the court-yard of Holyrood Palace and secured the gates, a noise was heard below, caused by the arrival of the Earls of Huntly, Bothwell, Caithness, Sutherland and others, whose followers were fighting with those of Morton and attempting to rescue the Queen. Ruthven went out to parley with the Lords, and assured them that the plot had been concocted by the King, and they, finding

* There is a copy of this bond in the State paper office. It was signed by the Earls of Argyle, Morton, Caithness, Huntly, Sutherland, Cassillis, and Rothes ; by Lords Boyd, Seton, Sinclair, Sempill, Oliphant, Ogilvy, Ross, Carlyle, Home, and Innermeath ; and by the Archbishop of St. Andrews and the Bishops of Ross, Dunblane, Aberdeen, Brechin, Galloway, Orkney, and the Isles.

† See a duplicate of this letter in the Appendix No. 5 to Laing's History of Scotland.

themselves outnumbered, retired from the contest for that night. Two days afterwards the Queen and Darnley (to whom she had become reconciled) contrived to escape to Dunbar Castle, and were joined there by several of their friends, amongst whom was the Earl of Caithness with his followers. Bothwell and Caithness, who had been active in support of the Queen, were both liberally rewarded, the former being made Lieutenant-General of the kingdom, and the latter receiving the appointment of Justiciary of the North of Scotland—his jurisdiction to include the whole of Sutherland and Caithness. This commission included a power to banish and kill, and to pardon any crime except treason. It is dated 17th April, 1556, and ratified by Parliament 19th April, 1567. Sir Robert Gordon is thus quite in error in stating that Caithness obtained the grant by Bothwell's influence in consequence of his complicity in Darnley's murder." But the truth is, the grant in question was merely the confirmation of an ancient right. "The Earls of Caithness," says Dr Henderson, "from an early date enjoyed the heritable jurisdiction of Caithness and Sutherland under repeated grants from the Crown. In 1455 James II. gave a charter to William Sinclair, Earl of Caithness, of the justiciary and sheriffdom of Caithness, and in 1470 he obtained a Crown charter confirming all gifts and concessions regarding the offices of justiciary, chamberlain, and sheriff of Caithness. On the resignation of his father, his son William obtained a charter, dated 7th Dec., 1476, of the earldom with offices of justiciary, chancellor, and sheriff within the bounds, from Portnaculter (now the Meikle Ferry) to the Pentland Firth. This was followed by another charter of the jurisdiction in 1480.

In the month of July this same year, the Earl of Sutherland and his lady were both poisoned at Helmsdale, at the instigation, says Sir Robert Gordon, of the Earl of Caithness. The Earl and Countess, with their son Alexander, were at the time passing a few days at a hunting lodge near the river of Helmsdale, the ruins of which are still to be seen. The poison

was administered to them at supper by Isobel Sinclair, wife of
Gilbert Gordon of Garty, and daughter of William Sinclair of
Dunbeath.   Alexander, for whom the deadly draught was
chiefly intended, had not returned in time from a hunting
excursion in Kildonan to join them at supper, and thus had a
very narrow escape.   When he arrived at the lodge, his father,
fully sensible of the danger of his situation, would not allow
him to taste anything, and sent him home that very same evening to Dunrobin.   By a singular retribution, Isobel Sinclair's
own eldest son, John Gordon, became the victim instead of
Alexander.   Happening to call at the lodge, he complained of
thirst, when one of the domestics, not aware of the deadly
nature of the preparation, handed him some of the poisoned
liquid, which he drank.   He died in the course of two days
after ; and the appearance of the body, along with other circumstances, afforded a clue to the discovery of his mother's
guilt.   The Earl and his lady, after a lingering illness of eight
days, expired at Dunrobin.   Isobel Sinclair was apprehended
and sent to Edinburgh, where, after being tried and condemned,
she died, or as it was generally believed, committed suicide on
the morning of the day appointed for her execution.   Although
she accused, it is said, her relative, the Earl of Caithness, of
having instigated her to commit the horrid crime, her mere
assertion in this case is no proof, and cannot be credited.   The
ambitious and cruel woman had a sufficient motive of her own.
Her eldest son was the next male heir to the earldom, and had
she succeeded in her diabolical scheme, he would have become
Earl of Sutherland.*

Influenced no doubt partly by political motives, the Earl of
Caithness managed to become curator or guardian of the young
Earl of Sutherland, then only fifteen years of age.   He brought
his ward to Girnigoe, where the latter remained for some time,
and married his lordship's eldest daughter, Lady Barbara
Sinclair, a woman past thirty years of age.   The young Earl

* Isobel Sinclair's husband, Gilbert Gordon of Garty, was the fourth son of
Adam Gordon, the late Earl.

and his bride then removed to the castle of Dunrobin, where his father-in-law also took up his temporary residence. By this family alliance and his office of Justiciary of Sutherland, the Earl of Caithness acquired immense power in that county, which he exercised, it is alleged, in a very oppressive and tyrannical manner. He was cordially detested by the inhabitants and by some of the principal families, who took every method of thwarting his schemes and resisting his authority. The Murrays of Dornoch, in particular, were his inveterate enemies. By representing to the young Earl, who was still a minor, that his father-in-law had a design upon his life, and intended to make his son William Earl of Sutherland, they made him hurriedly quit Dunrobin, and fly to Strathbogie, that he might be under the protection of his relative, the Earl of Huntly. His escape is said to have been effected thus. One, Alexander Gordon of Sidoray, came to Dunrobin in the evening disguised as a pedlar, and drawing the young Earl aside, whispered in his ear that a party of his friends would be waiting for him next morning at a certain spot near the burn of Golspie, for the purpose of conveying him away out of the county. Accordingly the Earl rose betimes, and telling the servants, in order to lull suspicion, that he was to take a short stroll before breakfast, he went direct to the place the party lay concealed; and on his coming up, they immediately set off with their charge, and stopped not until they had lodged the young nobleman in safety with his friends in Aberdeenshire. When Earl George heard of the flight of his ward, and how it was caused by the malicious counsel and insinuations of the Murrays, his rage knew no bounds, and he resolved to inflict a signal chastisement on them and their adherents. With this view he solicited assistance from Mackay of Strathnaver, which that chieftain readily agreed to give. The Earl's eldest son, John, commonly called the Master of Caithness, was forthwith despatched from Wick with a strong body of men. He and Mackay joined their respective forces on the borders of the county, and then marched to Dornoch, where the Murrays and their confederates had assembled. After some hard fighting, the assailants set fire to the town, when the Murrays betook themselves for safety, some of them to the castle, and others to the steeple of the Cathedral. After holding out in both places for nearly a week, the besieged at length agreed to surrender on certain conditions, for the due performance of which they delivered up three of their principal young men as pledges. Earl George, however, refused to ratify the agreement, and because the Murrays would not yield to his terms, he ordered the three hostages to be put to death. The Laird of Duffus, his son-in-law, whose lands the Murrays had lately ravaged, superintended the execution. The Master of Caithness and Mackay, with a humanity of spirit not very common at the period, would have nothing to do with such a cruel affair. This highly incensed the Earl of Caithness, and from that time he contracted a deep-rooted prejudice against his son, who, in order to avoid his father's displeasure, went with Mackay to Strathnaver, where he continued to reside. At length certain rumours reached the Earl, that his son and Mackay were in conspiracy against him, and were devising schemes to put an end to his tyranny and oppression. Nay, it was even hinted that his life was in danger from them. Suspicion and jealousy were now added to anger, and he secretly resolved to inveigle them to Girnigoe, and if they could not clear themselves of the alleged conspiracy, to punish them by imprisonment. In order to accomplish his purpose, he sent repeated messages to Mackay, to come to the castle with the Master, and visit him, professing the utmost anxiety to be reconciled to his son, and to be on the usual friendly terms with Mackay himself. They at last, after some hesitation, agreed to pay him a visit, and accordingly set off on horseback without any escort. On their arrival at Girnigoe, they were met by the Earl himself, who saluted them with a show of much kindness. On passing the draw-bridge, however, Mackay observed—what struck him as somewhat singular—a more than usual number of armed men about the castle.   Suspecting treachery, he immediately turned round, set spurs to his horse, dashed across the bridge, which was still down, and galloped away as fast as the animal could carry him.   In the meantime the Master was seized—though not without a severe struggle, being a man of great bodily strength—fettered, and cast into a dark and noisome dungeon, where he lay for several years.   There were three keepers appointed over him, namely, Murdoch Roy, and two brothers, Ingram and David Sinclair.   Roy was the person who regularly attended him, and did all the menial services connected with the office.   The other two, who were kinsmen of the Earl, and had a bend sinister in their escutcheon, might be said to be inspectors or head jailers.   Roy, it would appear, was not altogether a hardened miscreant and steeled against the ordinary feelings of humanity.   His heart was touched with pity for the unfortunate nobleman, and at the earnest and oft-repeated solicitations of the latter, he agreed to endeavour to set him at liberty.   Unfortunately, the scheme was discovered by John's brother, William, who bore him no good will, and who informed his father of the meditated escape.   The Earl immediately ordered Roy to be executed ; and the poor wretch was accordingly brought out and hanged on the common gibbet of the castle, without a moment being allowed him to prepare for his final account.   Soon after, in revenge of Roy's death, and of his brother William's unnatural enmity towards himself, the Master, whose mind was affected by the long confinement and the bad usage which he had received, managed to seize William on the occasion of a visit to the dungeon, and strangled him.   This deepened the father's antipathy towards his unhappy son.   He had now been nearly six years in confinement ; and his keepers, tired of watching him so long, resolved, with the concurrence, it is said, of his inhuman parent, to hasten his death.   The plan adopted was such as could have entered only into the imagination of fiends.   They withheld food from the poor man for the space of five days.   They then set before him a piece of salt beef, of which

SWAIN'S 'NATURE'

CASTLES SINCLAIR AND GIRNIGOE,

he ate voraciously. Soon after, when he called for water, they refused to give him any, and he died of raging thirst. Another account says that they gave him brandy, of which he drank so copiously that he died raving mad. There can be no doubt, however, that he was barbarously murdered.* His remains were interred in the "Sinclair aisle," in the churchyard of Wick, which his father had built some years before. The inscription on the stone over his grave is still legible. It says, "Here lies entombed ane noble and worthie man, John, Master of Caithness, who departed this life, the 15th day of March, 1576." By his lady he had three sons, namely, George, who succeeded to the earldom, James Sinclair of Murkle, and John Sinclair of Greenland and Rattar.

The tragic event which we have just described was not the only misfortune which about this period befell the family of the Earl of Caithness. The marriage of his daughter, Lady Barbara, with the young Earl of Sutherland, as might have been anticipated from their great disparity of age, turned out unhappily. Independently of this, the conduct of the Countess herself was far from being correct. On the flight of her husband to Strathbogie, she carried on an improper intercourse with Mackay of Strathnaver, and indeed for some time openly lived with him. Accordingly, when Earl Alexander came to his majority, he divorced her, and curiously enough, afterwards married Lady Jean Gordon,† the sister of the Earl of Huntly, whom Bothwell had divorced to pave the way for his marriage

---

* The history of Scotland records an instance of similar atrocity, even still more revolting, in the case of the Duke of Rothsay, son of Robert III., who was starved to death in the castle of Falkland in 1402. He was fifteen days without food; and Tytler says that in the extremities of hunger "he had gnawed and torn his own flesh."

† She is said to have been a beautiful and altogether a very superior woman. She was one of the heroines of the fine old ballad (admired by Burns) called "The Lord of Gordon's Daughters," and commencing thus :—

"The Lord of Gordon had three daughters—
    Elizabeth, Margaret, and Jean.
They would not stay at bonny Castle Huntly,
    But they would go to bonny Aberdeen."

After the death of the Earl of Sutherland, she married Sir George Ogilvie of Boyne, in Banffshire. Her father, George, fourth Earl of Huntly, was killed at the battle of Corichie in 1562.

with Queen Mary. It is not a little remarkable that his father, Patrick Earl of Bothwell, also divorced his wife, Agnes Sinclair, daughter of Henry, Lord Sinclair, in order to attempt a marriage with the Queen Dowager, Mary of Guise. Inordinate ambition and want of moral principle would thus seem to have been hereditary in the family.

George, Earl of Caithness, died at Edinburgh in 1582, and was buried in the Chapel of Roslin, where there is a monument to his memory, with the following inscription, in Latin :—
" Hic jacet nobilis ac potens Dominus Georgius quondam Comes Cathanensis, Dominus Sinclair, Justiciarius hereditarius, Diocesis Cathanensis, qui obit Edinburgi, 9 die mensis Septembris, anno Domini 1582." (Here lies a noble and potent lord, George, formerly Earl of Caithness, Lord Sinclair, hereditary justiciary of the diocese of Caithness, who died at Edinburgh the 9th day of September, 1582.) His heart, which was extracted and put in a casket of lead, was sent to Caithness, and deposited in the church of Wick. This was done at his own dying request. He had been fifty-four years Earl of Caithness, and being of an avaricious and grasping turn, had amassed much wealth, and greatly enlarged his hereditary property. The whole of his money he bequeathed to his youngest son, George Sinclair of Mey.*

The deceased earl was undoubtedly a nobleman of high standing and influence in his rank, and possessed of very considerable talents. He was a member of the Privy Council, and one of the Lords of Articles, and was much at Court, especially during the brief and troubled reign of the unfortunate Mary. Tytler says—and its truth cannot be denied— that " he was of accommodating principles both in politics and

* The Earl's second son, William, who was slain by the Master of Caithness in Girnigoe, was first Laird of Mey, and ancestor of the Ulbster family. He was succeeded in the property by his brother George, the founder of the family of Mey. George's son William (afterwards Sir William Sinclair of Mey) acquired some notoriety by shooting an Edinburgh bailie in a mutiny of the boys of the High School in the month of September, 1595. For a particular detail of this affair, taken from Robert Chambers's "Domestic Annals of Scotland," see Appendix No. 7, in which the pedigree of the Mey family, and of one or two other collateral branches, is also given.

religion." There were, indeed, few intrigues of the day in which he did not bear more or less a part—at one time supporting the Reformers, and at another the abettors of popery—but in this respect his conduct was not worse than that of many of his brother peers. At heart, however, he seems to have been attached to the Church of Rome, and in 1560 he dissented, along with the Earls of Athole, Borthwick, Somerville, and Cassillis, from the confession of the Reformers, when it was laid before Parliament. One league into which he entered does credit to his memory. In 1567 he joined the lords who had banded together and taken up arms for the young prince against Bothwell, and he was thus so far instrumental in driving out of the kingdom a man who had disgraced Scotland, and rendered himself odious to all parties by the enormity of his crimes. In 1581, the year before his death, he was one of the principal leaders in the confederacy against Morton.

The great object of this Earl had been to aggrandise his house ; but with all his policy and intrigue, he was not successful in some of his most ambitious schemes. The heaviest charge against him is the long imprisonment and death of his son, the Master of Caithness, in the Castle of Girnigoe. I have given the account of this shocking crime, as it is handed down by tradition, and recorded in the history of Sir Robert Gordon. But atrocious and unjustifiable as was the deed, there would appear to have been some extenuating circumstances in the case. It is contrary to human nature that the Earl, unless he was a perfect monster of wickedness, totally devoid of the usual parental feeling, could have been guilty of such barbarous cruelty towards his son, without having what he at least considered a sufficient cause. Now, it appears that while the Master of Caithness resided with Mackay, information, which the Earl believed to be correct, reached him that they were plotting against his life. Nor can this alleged conspiracy be considered at all improbable. Mackay was, from every account, a most unprincipled man. He had been guilty of two crimes of the deepest dye—murder and adultery. Having conceived a violent passion for the wife of a neighbouring chief, named Mac Ian More, he seduced her and slew her husband. An improper intimacy, as has been already mentioned, existed between him and the Countess of Sutherland ; and the better to carry on the criminal intercourse he repudiated his own wife, Christina Sinclair, daughter of the Laird of Dunn. Now, we think, that a man who could unblushingly do all this was capable of anything ; and, therefore, it is not at all unlikely that he might have counselled the son to take away the life of his father, whereby he would rid the county of a tyrant, and thus become earl himself. There is, indeed, every reason to conclude that it was not so much the disobedience of orders in the affair at Dornoch, as the apprehension of a conspiracy against his life, which he regarded as an unpardonable offence, that made Earl George visit his son with such a cruel and barbarous punishment.

CHAPTER VIII.

THE late George, Earl of Caithness, was succeeded by his grandson, George, son of the Master of Caithness, who died in prison at Girnigoe. This George inherited much of the talents of his grandfather, with, if possible, greater cruelty of disposition. In the traditional history of the county, he is called by way of distinction the "Wicked Earl George;" and his conduct in many respects shows that the appellation was no misnomer. He signalised his accession to the earldom by deliberately killing, in broad day, David and Ingram Sinclair, the two principal keepers of his late father. David lived at Keiss, and Ingram at Wester. Ingram's daughter was to be married, and a large party, including his lordship, was invited to the wedding. On the forenoon of the day fixed for the marriage, as the Earl was taking an airing on horseback, he met David on the Links of Keiss, on his way to Wester, and ran him through with his sword. Immediately on doing so, he galloped over to Wester, and calling Ingram aside—who was at the time amusing himself with some friends at foot-ball —he drew out a pistol and shot him dead on the spot. He then coolly turned his horse's head towards Girnigoe, and rode off with as little concern as if he had merely killed a brace of moor-fowl. There was, strictly speaking, no law in the county at the time; and being a great nobleman, and possessed of ample power of "pit and gallows," he escaped with impunity. The crime seems to have been winked at; and, doubtless, from dread of a similar fate, never made the subject of complaint by the relatives of the murdered parties. Sir Robert Gordon's version of the story differs a good deal from the preceding account, which is derived from the Caithness tradition. He says that "the Earl, after dinner, without any other preamble," slew the two brothers while they were amusing themselves at foot-ball, having previously secreted their weapons, so that they might have nothing wherewith to defend themselves. "And the reason," he adds, "that moved Earl George to kill them, was because they favoured the Earl of Sutherland." This is not at all likely. The true reason, beyond a doubt, was revenge for their having been instrumental in the murder of his father, the late Master of Caithness. This, in his opinion, justified the deed; and it certainly must be allowed to plead as an extenuating circumstance in the commission of a crime otherwise the most atrocious and cold-blooded that can be conceived. Tradition adds that during the alarm and confusion caused by this shocking affair, the company dispersed, and the wedding ring was lost. Not many years since, a finger ring of a curious construction— supposed to be the identical wedding ring—was found at Wester. It was of pure gold, twisted so as to represent a serpent coiled, with his tail in his mouth, an emblem of eternity.

To strengthen and extend his influence in the north, George married Lady Jane Gordon, sister of the Earl of Huntly. But all the power he gained by this alliance was more than needed. From the day that he succeeded to the earldom, his restless and turbulent disposition involved him in continual strife and conten-tion. He and the Earl of Sutherland were almost constantly at war. Nothing but mutual foray, rapine, and plunder prevailed in both counties; while the Mackays of Strathnaver, with a trimming and sefish policy, now joined the one side, and now the other, according as they saw hope of acquiring booty, and advancing their own interests. Of the savage ferocity displayed on these occasions, the following traditional anecdote affords a striking instance. In one of those barbarous fights between the natives of Sutherland and Caithness, the Sutherland men were on the point of being routed, when a party of the clan Mackay very opportunely came to their assistance, and the poor

Caithnessians, all but one man, were literally butchered. The greatest havoc was committed by a powerful Highlander belonging to the aforesaid clan, who wielded a huge Lochaber axe. He took up his position in a narrow pass through which the fugitives endeavoured to escape, and cut down every one of them as they came up, with the exception of this one individual, who some way or other evaded his merciless weapon and got safe home, like one of Job's messengers, to tell the mournful tale. Many years after this, when the Strathnaver warrior was on his death-bed, he was visited by the parish priest, who earnestly advised him to confess his sins, and "make a clean breast," now that he was about to leave the world and appear in the presence of the great Judge. "Is there anything, Donald," inquired the priest, "that lies peculiarly heavy on your conscience?" "No," said the dying Celt, raising himself up with a great effort from the pillow, and striking the bed with his clenched fist, "No, nothing, but that I allowed that vagabond of a Caithnessman to escape!"

1586.—A temporary reconciliation having been patched up between the two potentates of Sutherland and Caithness, they at this time secretly laid a plan to attack the Gunns, and drive them out of both counties. The Gunns fortunately got timely notice of the plot. They prepared for resistance; and being assisted by William Mackay, brother of Hugh Mackay of Strathnaver, they attacked the Caithness men before they could be joined by their allies, at a place called Auldgown, on the borders of Sutherland, and completely routed them. Henry Sinclair, brother of the Laird of Dunn, and cousin of the Earl of Caithness, and about one hundred and forty men, were left dead on the field. The Earl was so enraged when he heard of this affair, that he immediately hanged John Gunn, a leading man among the clan, whom he had some time before got hold of, and who was then a prisoner in Girnigoe.

The hollow friendship between the two Earls lasted for about a year, when a contest, or rather a series of contests, arose, from what in legal phrase would be termed a piece of "malicious mischief." It happened that as Earl George's servants were journeying on horseback through Sutherland, on their way to Edinburgh, one George Gordon, a relative of the Earl of Sutherland, and a man of very indifferent character, in order to show his disrespect for his lordship, waylaid the servants and cut off the tails of the horses, desiring them at the same time to tell their master that he had done so! The Earl highly resented this indignity, and on his return to Caithness, finding that he was not likely to get any redress from the Earl of Sutherland, he resolved to take it at his own hands, and to visit the offender with condign punishment. For this purpose he set out with a picked body of men to Helmsdale, near to which Gordon lived, and arriving in the night-time, surrounded his house with the party. Gordon, after a desperate resistance, took to flight and was pursued by Sinclair of Mey and some half-dozen followers. He then flung himself into the river of Helmsdale, hard by, and tried to make his escape by swimming across, but a shower of arrows was discharged upon him, and he was slain in the water. The Earl of Sutherland sent a threatening message to Earl George, demanding satisfaction for the slaughter of his kinsman, and insisting on his immediately delivering up the principal actors in that affair. But George, who had Norman blood in his veins, was not to be daunted by any menace of the kind. He desired the messenger to tell his brother of Sutherland that he held him at defiance, and he advised the messenger himself, if he had any regard for his neck, to make home as fast as he could. Sutherland felt highly indignant at this additional provocation and insult to himself in the person of his ambassador, and as a *dernier resort*, determined to obtain satisfaction by force of arms. His first movement was to despatch two hundred men into Caithness on a predatory incursion. The party, which was commanded by two leaders of the name of Gordon, ravaged and plundered the whole of the parish of Latheron, and then returned home with a large booty in cattle, which was divided among them. This foray was called "Creach Iarn," that is, the "harship" or harrying of Latheron. In the meantime, having obtained a commission from the Privy Council against the Earl of Caithness for killing George Gordon, the Earl of Sutherland himself, accompanied by Mackay of Strathnaver, the Laird of Assynt, and other chiefs, next entered Caithness with all the forces he could muster, fully resolved to carry everything before him with fire and sword. His great object, however, was, if possible, to get hold of the Earl of Caithness (1588), and thus force him to agree to whatever terms he thought proper to propose; but the Earl very prudently on this occasion shut himself up within the iron walls of the castle of Girnigoe. Sutherland's first exploit was burning the town of Wick, an achievement of no great difficulty, as the place at that time merely consisted of a few mean straggling houses thatched with straw. The only building which was spared was the church. While the town was in flames, a Highlander named John Mac-gilli-calum Rasay, intent on plunder, entered the church, when his eye lighted on the leaden case enclosing the heart of the late Earl of Caithness. He broke it open, but finding that it contained no treasure as he expected, he flung it away in disgust, and thus scattered the ashes to the winds. Such was the singular fate which befell the heart of that proud and cruel nobleman. The Earl of Sutherland then sat down before the castle of Girnigoe, but not being able to take it after a siege of twelve days, he proceeded to wreak his vengeance on the unoffending inhabitants of Caithness. He ravaged the county as far as Duncansbay, killed several of the peasantry, and then returned home with a great "spoil of cattle," which was equally divided among his followers. This affair was called "La na creach-more" or the great spoil.

The two Earls now entered into a truce, which, however, was soon broken. The Earl of Caithness, who was burning to be revenged for the injuries done to the county, retaliated by a succession of inroads into Sutherland. His brother, Sir James Sinclair of Murkle, conducted one of those expeditions,

and coming unexpectedly on the sentinels or warders appointed
by the Earl of Sutherland to watch the borders, he set fire to
the watch-house in which they were carelessly amusing themselves, instead of keeping a good outlook. Three of them
were killed, and the fourth, escaping with great difficulty,
announced to his countrymen the arrival of the enemy. Sinclair pushed on to the heights of Strathbrora, and began to
drive away the cattle which he had collected towards Caithness.
Hugh Mackay, the chief of Strathnaver, who was at this time
on terms of amity with the Earl of Sutherland, and happened
to be on a visit at Dunrobin, set off from the castle with 500
men in pursuit of Sinclair. He quickly crossed the river of
Brora, and joining his force with that of John Gordon of
Kilcolmkil, attacked the army of Sinclair, which they defeated
after a long and arduous contest. The Caithness men were
forced to retreat with the loss of their booty, and were pursued by a body of the enemy for nearly sixteen miles.
Flushed with the advantage gained in this affair, the Earl of
Sutherland now assembled in person a large body of men, and
entered Caithness with the intention of laying it waste. He
advanced as far as Corriechoich, in Braemore, where he
encamped. The Earl of Caithness lost no time in mustering
his forces, and marched to the hill of Spittal,* where he
resolved to wait the approach of the enemy. The Earl of
Huntly, the friend of both, on hearing of these warlike pre-
parations, sent with all speed his relative Sir Patrick Gordon
to mediate between the two hostile Earls. He arrived at the
head-quarters of the Earl of Sutherland about the very time he

* In the olden time, Spittalhill, as being in the centre of the county, was
the usual rendezvous on occasions of this kind. At the foot of the hill,
fronting the west, was the hospital of St Magnus, which is supposed to have
been founded by that eminent Orcadian saint. Magnus was Earl of Orkney
and Caithness in 1103. In 1476, King James III. granted to William Sinclair,
the son of William Sinclair, Earl of Caithness, by his Countess, Marjory
Sutherland, the advowson of the hospital. Its revenues were confiscated at
the Reformation. The real nature of the institution is not known; but it is
believed to have partaken somewhat of the double character of a modern
hospital and poorhouse, in which religious instruction was at the same time
imparted to the inmates. Closely adjoining was the cemetery of the famous
Clan Gunn.

was getting ready to march for Spittal. By his mediation, an armistice was concluded, and the two Earls agreed to meet at Elgin, in presence of the Earl of Huntly, and refer all their differences to him. A meeting accordingly took place, and the two Earls subscribed a deed, by which Huntly and his successors were appointed hereditary judges and arbiters of all disputes and differences that might thenceforth arise between the two houses. This written agreement was no better than so much waste paper. The whole affair was a farce, and only a few weeks elapsed before the two Earls were again at war.

1589.—The severest battle which was fought during this campaign was at Clyne, in Sutherland. In this engagement the Caithness men were ably supported by a number of archers under the command of Donald Balloch Mackay of Scourie. The Sutherland men were led on by Patrick Gordon of Garty, and John Gordon of Embo ; and although numerically inferior to the invaders, they advanced resolutely to the attack. As they came up they were met with a thick shower of arrows ; but nothing daunted, they pushed on in true Highland fashion, and drawing their bows, gave their opponents in return a volley that staggered them. The combat raged with great fury for a considerable time. Thrice were the Caithness archers driven back, and thrice did they return to the conflict, cheered on and encouraged by their intrepid leader. At length night put an end to the fight. The loss in killed and wounded on both sides was nearly equal. The principal persons killed in the Caithness army were Nicholas Sutherland, brother of the Laird of Forse,* and one Angus Macangus, who, on account of his extraordinary activity and swiftness, was com-

* Ancestor of the present Mr Sutherland of Forse, who is lineally descended from an elder branch of the house of Dunrobin. The family, it is said, have been in possession of the estate of Forse since about the year 1400. In 1767, after the death of William, Earl of Sutherland, Robert Gordon of Gordonstone, great-grandson of the family historian, and George Sutherland of Forse, presented separate petitions to the House of Lords anent their respective claims to the earldom of Sutherland. These applications were opposed by the guardians of Lady Elizabeth, daughter of the deceased Earl ; and the House (21st March, 1771) decided that the succession of right belonged to her as the lineal descendant of Earl William who died in 1275.

monly known by the strange appellation of "Birlig." During the temporary absence of the Caithness forces in Sutherland, Hugh Mackay, brother of Donald, invaded the county on the Reay side, and having, as Sir Robert says, "brunt and spoiled much of that countrie, even to the gates of Thurso, brought home a great booty, which he divided amongst his countriemen after their custome." One is surprised to find the two brothers on this occasion espousing opposite sides; but the reason for their doing so may be easily explained. Donald Mackay having been banished by his brother from Strathnaver and Sutherland for some misdemeanors, had retired to Caithness, where he found protection from the Earl; and in these circumstances it was natural that he should offer him his services. On the other hand, Hugh Mackay's first wife was Elizabeth Sinclair, aunt of the Earl; and he had incurred his lordship's displeasure by divorcing her, and marrying Lady Jane Gordon, daughter of Alexander, Earl of Sutherland.

1591.—This year an occurrence took place in the county, which, from its connection with a well-known historical personage, possesses some little interest. Francis Stewart, Earl of Bothwell, had, by his factious and turbulent conduct, rendered himself peculiarly obnoxious to James VI. of Scotland. To avoid being punished for audaciously entering the palace of Holyrood at night with a party of armed men, for the purpose of coercing the King and securing the person of Maitland the Chancellor, against whom he bore a mortal enmity, he fled to the north. Sir Robert Gordon says that he came to Caithness, where he remained for some time in the castle of Girnigoe, under the protection of the Earl of Caithness, who was his half-brother. Some dispute having arisen between the parties, Earl George meditated a plot to deliver him up to the King. In this critical situation, he owed his safety to Sir James Sinclair of Murkle, who informed him of his brother's design, on which Bothwell immediately made his escape out of the county. Not long after, he was obliged, on account of his treasonable practices, to quit the kingdom altogether. He fled to the Continent, and after wandering about for some years in France and Spain, he ultimately took up his residence at Naples, where he died a miserable exile. He was nephew, by his mother, to the noted Bothwell, murderer of Darnley. The Earl of Caithness was so offended at his brother, Sir James, for befriending Bothwell in the way he did, that he banished him, it is said, for some time out of the county. On the 6th of December this year (1594), Alexander, Earl of Sutherland, who had been so formidable an enemy to the house of Caithness, died at Dunrobin, and was buried at Dornoch. His son, Sir Robert, passes a high eulogium on his character. Among other things, he says, "he was verie upright in all his actions, unfit for these our dayes, when integritie lyeth speechless, and upright dealing is readie to give up the ghost."

After the battle of Clyne, hostilities between the two rival houses ceased for several years. But Earl George could not be idle; and among other strange doings, he was guilty of a mischevious practical joke, which Sir Robert, like a faithful historian, relates with all due circumstantiality. It happened that a boat, with some of the Earl of Orkney's servants on board, being overtaken with a severe gale while crossing (1608) the Pentland Firth, ran for refuge to Sinclair's Bay. As soon as they landed, the Earl, who had a pique at Earl Patrick Stewart, a man very similar in disposition to himself, ordered the servants to be brought to Girnigoe. After making them drink a good deal of liquor, he then caused the one side of their heads and the one side of the beards to be shaved, and in this condition forced them to take boat, and go to sea before the storm had abated! They fortunately reached Orkney in safety, and told their master how they had been treated. The Earl very naturally highly resented the barbarous usage which his domestics had received at the hands of the Earl of Caithness, and complained thereof to the King. His Majesty ordered the Privy Council to summon before them the two Earls, and have the matter duly investigated. Both parties appeared at Edinburgh, but by the mediation of friends the case was not brought before the Council, and a reconciliation was effected between them. The historian of Sutherland quaintly remarks—" Only one example of this crime I do remember. The servants of David, King of Israel, were so entreated by Hannum, King of the children of Ammon. The Earl of Caithness thus far exceeded Hannum, that not satisfied with what himself had done, he forced the Earl of Orkney his servants to take the sea in such a tempest, and exposed them to the extremity of the raging waves; whereas Hannum suffered King David his servants to depart home quietly after he had abused them."

The Earl of Caithness at this time possessed an extensive and valuable landed property in the county, including nearly the whole of the parish of Wick. By his reckless and extravagant habits, however, he had become deeply involved in debt, and was obliged to mortgage several portions of his estate to satisfy his creditors. To recruit his exhausted finances, he fell, it is alleged, on a desperate expedient, and employed an ingenious vagabond of the name of Arthur Smith to coin money for him. The history of this man is not a little singular. He was bred a blacksmith, and for some time prosecuted his calling in the town of Banff. Being detected there in the act of making counterfeit coin, he fled with an accomplice to Sutherlandshire, but they were not long in that county when they were both apprehended, and sent to Edinburgh (1549) to be tried. The accomplice was condemned and executed, but Smith himself, for some reason or other, was remitted back to prison and kept for further trial. During his confinement, he managed to procure the necessary materials, and made a lock of such an ingenious construction, that it excited the admiration of every one who saw it. It was exhibited to the King, who was so struck with the remarkable ingenuity displayed in the workmanship, that he granted him a respite. · At length he was set at full liberty, chiefly through the recommendation of Lord Elphinstone, the

Secretary of State, who thought it a pity that such an ingenious and skilful workman should be lost to society. Smith then went north and offered his services to the Earl of Caithness, by whom they were gladly accepted. He was accommodated with a workshop or smithy in a retired apartment of Castle Sinclair, which the Earl had lately built close by the castle of Girnigoe. Sir Robert Gordon says that the workshop was under the rock of Castle Sinclair in a place called the "Gote," to which there was a secret passage through the Earl's own bed-chamber and to which none had access but himself. Here Smith diligently plied his vocation for seven or eight years. At length he removed to Thurso, where he ostensibly prosecuted his calling as a blacksmith. In the meantime, Caithness, Sutherland, and Orkney were inundated with base coin; and the outcry against the iniquitous fraud practised on the public became loud and universal. Smith, whose antecedents were well known, was very generally suspected as guilty of the crime. The case was laid before the King by Sir Robert Gordon; and a commission was granted to him conjointly with Donald Mackay and John Gordon of Embo to apprehend Smith, and bring him once more for trial to Edinburgh. Mackay and Gordon, to whom the business was subsequently entrusted, forthwith proceeded with a sufficient body of men to Thurso, to execute their commission. After a brief search they found Smith, and on examining his house, they also found in it a quantity of bad money, with all the necessary apparatus for coining. He was immediately put under a strong guard, and conveyed some little distance out of the town. In the meantime the alarm-bell was rung to assemble the inhabitants, who, although satisfied with the guilt of Smith, were yet, from recollection of the past, jealous of the Sutherland authorities, and regarded the commission pretty much in the light of a hostile invasion. They accordingly rushed to the street; and shortly after, John Sinclair, younger of Stirkoke, James Sinclair of Durran, James Sinclair, brother of the Laird of Dunn, and other relatives of Lord Caithness who

happened to be in town on a visit to Lady Berriedale, made
their appearance. Mackay and Gordon showed their commission and endeavoured to satisfy them that they were acting
under the King's authority; but Sinclair of Stirkoke, in a
defiant tone, swore that he would not allow his uncle's servant
to be apprehended without his knowledge, and in his absence.
The commissioners replied sharply that they were determined
to do their duty, and not suffer the Royal warrant to be
resisted. High words were exchanged, and a serious scuffle
ensued, which was maintained for some time with great
obstinacy on both sides. The party that guarded Smith,
hearing a great noise in the town, killed him in order to
prevent his escape, and hurried in to assist their countrymen.
The inhabitants, who were not so well armed as their
opponents, finally gave way, and retreated to their houses.
John Sinclair of Stirkoke was killed, and James Sinclair
of Dunn severely wounded. James Sinclair of Durran saved
himself by flight. None of the Sutherland men were killed,
but many of them were badly wounded. Sir John Sinclair of
Greenland, who then lived at Ormlie, and the Laird of Dunn
arrived when the fray was concluded. Dunn proposed to
renew the attack, but Sir John Sinclair, considering what had
already happened, would not agree to any hazardous attempt
of the kind. The Sutherland men withdrew from the town,
and soon after proceeded homeward, carrying their wounded
along with them.

When the Earl of Caithness, who happened to be in Edinburgh at the time, was informed of the occurrences in Thurso,
he immediately instituted a criminal prosecution against the
Earl of Sutherland, Sir Robert Gordon, and Donald Mackay,
for the slaughter of his nephew, John Sinclair of Stirkoke;
while they, on the other hand, raised a similar process against
the Earl of Caithness, his son, Lord Berriedale, and their
coadjutors, for sundry past outrages, and particularly for
resisting, at Thurso, the King's commissioners, and attacking
those employed in its execution. On the day appointed for

their appearance at Edinburgh, the parties, with the exception of the Earl of Sutherland, met, attended by their respective friends. The Earl of Caithness and Berriedale were accompanied by Lord Gray, Sinclair of Roslin, the Laird of Cowdenknowes, a son of the sister of the Earl of Caithness, and his two brothers, Sir John Sinclair of Greenland, and James Sinclair of Murkle. Sir Robert Gordon and Mackay were attended by the Earls of Winton, Eglinton, and Linlithgow, Lords Elphinstone and Forbes, Munro of Foulis, and the Laird of Duffus. The Council spent three days in hearing the parties and deliberating upon the matters brought before them; but they came to no decision, and adjourned the proceedings until the King's pleasure should be known. The King proposed that their differences should be submitted to arbitration, and after some discussion, the parties were induced to sign a submission to that effect. Arbiters were accordingly appointed, but finding the parties obstinate, and determined not to yield a single point of their respective claims, they declined to act any further in the matter, and remitted the whole case back to the Privy Council. At a meeting of the Council, the Earl of Caithness preferred a very serious charge against Sir Robert Gordon. He said that he had procured the commission solely with the intention of ruining him and his house, and that previous to the affair at Thurso he had on one occasion lain in wait to kill him at the Little Ferry. Sir Robert, of course, indignantly repelled the charge. The dispute, from all that appears, was never settled; and the Earls of Caithness and Sutherland continued to maintain the same hostile attitude towards each other as before.

Connected with this case, I may here notice an occurrence which affords a striking instance of the manners of the period, and of the turbulent and pugnacious spirit of the parties implicated in it. At an early stage of the proceedings, Lord Gordon, son of the Earl of Huntly, who had been on some business in London, returned to Edinburgh. As soon as Sir Robert Gordon learned that he was on his way to Scotland, he went as far as the Borders to meet him, and accompanied him to town. This extraordinary attention on the part of the worthy baronet was not without a special object. He was exceedingly anxious to prepossess him in favour of the Sutherland side of the story before his relative, the Earl of Caithness, could have access to him; and it would seem that he was completely successful in doing so. The Earl was so offended at this that he declined to wait on Lord Gordon after his arrival in Edinburgh. At this time the High Street, one of the most picturesque thoroughfares in Europe, was the Pall Mall of the Scottish metropolis, and the grand promenade of the aristocracy, where they lounged and sauntered about when they had no other amusement or business on hand. It was then also fashionable for the male portion of the upper classes at least, if it was not rendered absolutely necessary by the lawless state of society, to wear defensive armour, and accordingly they seldom appeared in public or in private without their swords. An evening or two after Lord Gordon's return to Edinburgh, he and the Earl of Caithness, each attended by a number of his friends, happened to meet between the Tron Church and the Cross, when they began rudely to jostle and push one another into the strand. High words, as a matter of course, arose. Then swords were drawn, and a general scuffle ensued, which threatened to be attended with serious consequences. In the meantime, Sir Robert Gordon and Donald Mackay, accompanied by several followers, came running forward to the assistance of Lord Gordon. The Earl of Caithness, finding that he was likely to be overpowered by numbers, made a precipitate retreat with his friends from the scene of combat down one of the adjoining closes in which he lodged. Lord Gordon and his party followed them, and for some time paraded up and down before the Earl's lodgings, in order to provoke him to come out, but he very prudently remained inside. This melee, although such scenes were of frequent occurrence in the High Street, created not a little sensation in the city.

The next day the two lords were called before the council, when a reconciliation was brought about between them.

The Earl kept about him at Girnigoe a body of stout retainers, ready for all emergencies. Among others there was one named William Macangus Gunn, from Strathnaver, a fellow of a resolute spirit, and possessed of extraordinary muscular power and agility. Gunn was in many respects a most useful person to the Earl; but having the organ of acquisitiveness very largely developed, he was in the habit of appropriating to his own use whatever struck his fancy in the course of his visits to the neighbouring peasantry. Latterly he began to make free with property belonging to his lordship, and dreading the consequences of detection, he found it necessary to depart without taking leave. The Earl, as soon as he discovered how matters stood, despatched some of his people in pursuit of the delinquent; but having made a good start, and being thoroughly acquainted with all the fastnesses and hiding-places among his native hills, he completely eluded their search. A few weeks after he was apprehended stealing cattle in Ross-shire, and imprisoned in the castle of Foulis. Not relishing his confinement in this fortress, he jumped from the tower; but having unfortunately broken one of his legs by the force with which he came to the ground, he found himself unable to get up, and was once more taken into custody. The Sheriff of Tain, Sir W. Sinclair of Mey, a relative of Earl George, had him forthwith conveyed under a strong guard to Caithness, to be lodged in the castle of Girnigoe, and disposed of as his lordship saw meet. On his arrival there, he was duly secured and consigned to the prisoner's cell; but his limb having by this time become whole, he managed to free himself from his fetters, leaped from the castle into the sea, swam ashore, and immediately took to his heels, thus making an extraordinary escape for his life.

CHAPTER IX.

In the course of this same year (1612) a tragical disaster befell a body of Caithness men and their leader, Colonel George Sinclair, in Norway. Sinclair was a natural son of David Sinclair of Stirkoke, and nephew of the Earl of Caithness. Like many other Scotchmen of the period, he was a soldier of fortune, and had entered the service of Gustavus Adolphus, King of Sweden, who was then at war with Denmark and Norway. Having raised a regiment in his native county, amounting, it is said, to some 900 men, Sinclair embarked for Norway, and after a favourable passage of four days, landed on the coast of Romsdal. As a considerable part of the Swedish coast—all, indeed, from Nyborg to Calmar—was in temporary possession of the Danes, and as Stockholm was at the time invested by a large Danish fleet, he could not get to that city by way of the Baltic, and he was therefore obliged to land in Norway. His intention was to march across the country—in doing which he would have to pass the great chain of the Norwegian Alps—a difficult and perilous enterprise under the most favourable circumstances, but particularly so when the natives were his enemies. He was encouraged to make the attempt, however, from finding that Colonel Munckhoven, with an army of 2300 Scotchmen * had not long before landed at Trondheim, and succeeded in forcing his way over into Sweden. Sinclair accordingly pursued his route along the valley of the Lessoe, and, if Norwegian accounts can be credited, laid waste the country, and inflicted

* Chambers's, in his Domestic Annals of Scotland, says :—" As the King of Great Britain was brother-in-law of Christian IV. of Denmark, the troops were levied in a clandestine manner. The Privy Council fulminated edicts against the proceedings as most obnoxious to the King, but without effect."

much unnecessary cruelty on the inhabitants. The King's troops were at the seat of war, and there was no home militia to protect them. The peasantry, naturally brave, were roused to vengeance. Signal fires were lighted on every commanding height, and the budstick * was sent round to warn young and old to a general muster. A body of about 500 peasants assembled, armed with rifles, and axes, and under the leadership of one of their own number, named Berdon Seilstad of Ringeboe, resolved, as they had no chance of overcoming Sinclair in open fight, to endeavour to cut him off by stratagem. The mountainous nature of the country, to which the Scots were strangers, was regarded as particularly favourable for an attempt of this kind. Sinclair's movements, therefore, were narrowly watched by spies appointed for the purpose, and unceasing strategy was practised to lead him into an ambuscade. The part of the country through which he was now conducting his men bordered on the Dovre Field, and in the course of the march he arrrived (24th August) at a wild mountain gorge, called the Pass of Kringelen, which he must either go through or take a circuitous route of several miles in extent. The road along the pass, which was little else than a mere footpath, was exceedingly narrow, and overhung the precipitous banks of a deep and rapid stream that flowed underneath. While Sinclair paused, uncertain whether to make the attempt or not, a young man, in the garb of a peasant, came up, and voluntarily offered to be his guide. His seemingly simple and unembarrassed manner was calculated to lull suspicion. After some hesitation, Sinclair unfortunately trusted himself to his guidance. The Caithness corps now proceeded leisurely along the difficult and dangerous defile,

* "The Norwegian budstick, or message stick," says Laing, "answered the same purpose as the fiery cross in Scotland. It is of the size and shape of our constable's baton, is painted, and stamped with the royal arms, and made hollow with a head to screw upon one end, and an iron spoke on the other. The official notice to meet, the time, place, and object, are written on a piece of paper, which is rolled up and placed in the hollow. This is delivered from the public office or court-house of the district to the nearest householder, who is bound, by law, to transmit it to the nearest, and so on. The householder to whom it comes last brings it back to the office."

the stranger youth leading the way. When they had nearly reached the middle of the pass, the treacherous guide fired a rifle which he had concealed about his person, and immediately disappeared among the rocks. This was the preconcerted signal between him and the natives. In a moment after the discharge of the rifle, the Boors, who lay concealed in the rocks above, started up like Roderick Dhu's men from their ambush, and poured down a murderous volley on the unfortunate Caithness men. Others of the natives, who were not provided with fire-arms, hurled down large stones and trunks of trees, which literally crushed them to pieces. The slaughter was dreadful. Colonel Sinclair himself was among the first that fell. Many of the bodies of the killed tumbled into the river below, which was dyed with their blood. About sixty were taken prisoners. They were at first distributed among the neighbouring hamlets; but the savage Boors getting at length tired of supporting them, marched them off to a meadow, and cruelly murdered them in cold blood.* Of the entire nine hundred, only one or two escaped and got home to Caithness. Among these, tradition says, was Colonel Sinclair's lady, whose adventure on this occasion imparts a strong air of romance to the melancholy story. She was a young and beautiful woman, and being unwilling to part with her husband, to whom she had been but recently united, she accompanied the expedition, at first disguised in male attire, and did not reveal herself until the corps had landed in Norway. Strange to say, she was with them in the Pass of Kringelen, and escaped the fearful massacre. The tradition respecting our Caithness heroine seems to be well founded. Laing, an accurate and trustworthy writer, says, "A youth, who meant to join the peasants in the attack, was prevented by a young lady to whom he was to be married next day. She, on learning that there was one of her own sex among the Scottish troops, sent her lover to her

* The particulars of this horrible tragedy were furnished to the author by a gentleman, a native of Caithness, who had some time resided in Norway, and had visited the scene of the catastrophe.

protection : Mrs Sinclair, not understanding his purpose, shot him dead." The bodies of the unfortunate Caithness men, it is said, were barbarously left unburied, to become a prey to the wolf and the vulture. But some respect was paid to their leader's remains, which were decently interred. The Norwegians are proud of pointing out to strangers the spot in which he is buried. It lies in a remote solitude near the fatal pass, and over the grave is a wooden cross, with a tablet, on which is the following inscription, in the Norse language :—
" Here lies Colonel George Sinclair, who, with 900 Scotsmen, were dashed to pieces, like so many earthen pots, by the peasants of Lessoe, Vaage, and Froen. Berdon Seilstad of Ringeboe was their leader." Robert Chambers, who, in his tour through Norway, visited the place, says : — " In a peasant's house near by were shown to me, in 1849, a few relics of the poor Caithness men, a matchlock or two, a broadsword, a couple of powder-flasks, and the wooden part of a drum."

The author of a recent work, entitled " The Oxonian in Norway, gives a somewhat different version of this tragical story. The following, slightly abbreviated, is his account of it :—
" Colonel Sinclair landed, with 900 Scottish soldiers, at Vibelungsnaest, in Romsdal, and determined upon the hazardous experiment of marching across the country. As soon as the news of this invasion reached Lars Hage, the Lehnsman of the Dovre, he hurried to the parish church, where service was being held. Striding into the building, he struck thrice upon the floor, and cried, ' Listen ! the foeman is in the land.' The congregation upon this immediately broke up, and it was finally agreed to lay an ambush at Kringelen, which, from the precipitous nature of the ground overhanging the road, was well adapted for the purpose. A vast quantity of rocks were loosened, and so placed on the verge of the precipice as to admit of being easily hurled down at a moment's notice. On the opposite side of the river rode a peasant on a white horse, whose orders were to keep alongside of the advancing enemy.

K

A peasant girl was stationed on a hill over the water, with her cow-horn, who was to give a signal, by blowing her instrument, as soon as the Scots had fallen into the snare. These precautions were necessary, as, from their ambuscade, the peasants could not get a sight of what was passing below. Onwards marched the Scots, guided by one Peder Klunkenes, whom they had violently pressed into their service. Presently the strange and melancholy tones of an Alpine horn resounded from a distant height. At the same instant down thundered a mass of stones and trunks of trees upon the devoted Scots.* Berdon Seilstad, who had bitten one of his silver buttons into the shape of a bullet, so as to be sure of his man, who was supposed to bear a charmed life, took aim at Sinclair, and hit him over the left eye, killing him on the spot. The peasants were some 400 in number, of whom six only were slain. All the Scots are said to have been butchered but eighteen. But accounts differ."

There is a pretty long Norwegian ballad on the subject, entitled "Herr Sinclair's vise af Storm," that is, literally, Lord Sinclair's song by Storm, in which the prowess of the peasants is highly extolled. It is sung everywhere throughout Norway, and constitutes one of her great national airs. In it the number of Sinclair's men is said to have been 1400 ; but this is evidently a poetic licence, as, from the best accounts, as well as from the inscription on the monumental tablet, the real number was only 900.† The following is a free translation of the song from the original Norse, which, it may be remarked,

---

* A similar tragedy, on a larger scale, took place at the Potlatzer, in the valley of the Inn, in the year 1809. A whole division of the French and Bavarian army were there crushed under an avalanche of rocks, which tumbled down upon their heads at the Tyrolese signal—"In the name of the Holy Trinity, cut all loose ! "

† The historian of the house of Sutherland says that Colonel Sinclair had only 150 men. As Caithness was then thinly peopled, it is quite possible that this was all the number of men which he had with him belonging to the county, and that the remainder of the force consisted of recruits from other counties. Von Buch, in his "Travels," however, and all other writers who notice the event, with the exception of Laing, who reduces the number to 600, agree that Sinclair had a body of 900 men under his charge when he met with this sad catastrophe in Norway.

has no allusion to the hurling down of the stones, as if the poet thought this was too savage a piece of butchery for the muse :—

THE MASSACRE OF KRINGELEN.

To Norway Sinclair steered his course
    Across the salt sea wave,
But in Kringelen's mountain pass
    He found an early grave.
To fight for Swedish gold he sailed,
    He and his hireling band :
Help, God : and nerve the peasant's arm
    To wield the patriot brand.
'Neath the pale moon the billowy surge
    Around the tall ship broke,
When from the deep the mermaid rose,
    And thus to Sinclair spoke :—
" Speed back, speed back, thou Scottish youth ;
    My warning do not spurn ;
For, if thou touchest Norway's strand,
    Thou never shalt return."
" Vile wretch !" the angry chief replied,
    " Thou ever bodest ill ;
If I but had thee in my power,
    Thy heart's blood I would spill."
Three days he sailed the stormy sea ;
    The fourth day saw him land
With twice seven hundred stalwart men,
    Equipp'd with spear and brand.
He flung his banner to the breeze,
    Laid many a hamlet low,
And mark'd his route with blood and spoil—
    The mercenary foe.
The warriors of the land are far,
    They and their kingly lord ;
But shall her peasant sons not rise,
    And draw the avenging sword ?
On rock and hill the beacons blazed ;
    "Up, Northmen !" was the cry ;
And at the summons mustering strong,
    They met to "do or die."
In ambush close, 'mong Gulbrand's cliffs,
    Five hundred rifles lay ;
The vulture smelt the game afar,
    And hastened to his prey.

The fated band are in the pass ;
  Up rose the peasant's round,
And poured on them a storm of fire,
  When Sinclair bit the ground.
Woe to his hapless followers now !
  By hundreds dropping fast ;
They fell as thick as autumn leaves
  Before the polar blast.
In slaughtered heaps their bodies lay
  By Lange's darksome flood,
While the ravens from a thousand hills
  Gorged in the feast of blood.
They lay unburied where they fell—
  A sad and ghastly show,
Until the storm-king pity took,
  And shrouded them in snow.
O ! many a maid and mother wept,
  And father's cheek grew pale,
When from the few survivors' lips
  Was heard the startling tale.
A monument yet marks the spot
  Which points to Sinclair's bier,
And tells how fourteen hundred men
  Sunk in that pass of fear.

Before embarking for Norway, Sinclair was engaged in a
piece of business which, we suspect, will not be regarded as
having a tendency to exalt his character.   The circumstances
of the case are briefly these.   John, Lord Maxwell of Nithsdale,
having, it is said, treacherously slain Sir James Johnstone, a
neighbouring Border chief, first fled to France, and afterwards
to Caithness, where he lurked for some time.   Having, at
length, got a hint that his place of concealment was known,
and that a price was set on his head, he attempted to make
his escape out of the county, but was apprehended near its
southern boundary by Colonel Sinclair, sent to Edinburgh,
and executed.   Before committing the crime for which he
suffered, Lord Maxwell had quarrelled with the Government
about the Morton peerage and estates, which he claimed in
right of his mother, Lady Beatrice Douglas, daughter of the
celebrated Regent Morton.   This no doubt in the eyes of

Royalty aggravated his guilt. His " Good Night," a pathetic ballad, in which he takes leave of his lady and friends, is printed in the Border Minstrelsy.

1614.—This year, the Earl of Caithness was employed by Government to quell a species of rebellion which had taken place in Orkney. The notorious Patrick Stewart, Earl of Orkney, had been guilty of many grievous acts of oppression and violence both in that county and in Shetland, for which his memory is execrated to this day. He fearfully harassed the poor natives; and in an age remarkable for feudal tyranny, he was one of the worst and most despotic of tyrants. A serious misunderstanding had arisen between him and James Law, Bishop of Orkney. The bishop, at length, urged on by his own grievances and the crying complaints of the people, transmitted to the King a long list of the many crimes and misdemeanors committed by the Earl, who was in consequence imprisoned and divested of his titles and estates; and collectors were appointed by the Council to levy the rents for the Crown. Patrick, from his prison, sent special instructions to his natural son, Robert, to uplift the rents as usual, and pay no attention to the orders of Council. Robert did so, and forcibly expelled the collectors; while at the same time he took possession of the palace of Birsa, the castle of Kirkwall, the palace of the Yards, and the tower of the Cathedral, which he fortified as strongly as he could.

The Earl of Caithness, who happened to be in Edinburgh at the time, offered to proceed to Orkney, and vindicate the authority of the law, provided he were furnished with sufficient troops for the purpose. Government agreed to give him a requisite force; and the Earl, in the month of August, set sail from Leith with sixty soldiers and two pieces of cannon from the castle of Edinburgh. On arriving on the Caithness coast, the vessel brought up in Sinclair's Bay; and having procured some additional men from his own property, the Earl, accompanied by his natural brother, Henry Sinclair, sailed directly for Orkney, and disembarked his troops in the neighbourhood of Kirkwall. He then opened the campaign in true military style. He besieged and took in succession the different posts occupied by the insurgents. The last was the castle of Kirkwall, which Robert Stewart, with only sixteen men, bravely defended for the space of three weeks. The King's cannon made little impression on the iron walls of the fortress; and it was taken at last only through the treachery of a Patrick Halcro, one of the besieged. The prisoners were all brought south and executed, with the exception of Halcro; and very soon after, Earl Patrick Stewart himself was beheaded for high treason at the Market Cross of Edinburgh.

Before leaving Orkney, the Earl of Caithness delivered up the castle of Kirkwall to Sir James Stewart of Kilsyth, afterwards Lord Ochiltree, on whom, in the capacity of farmer-general, the King had conferred a new grant of the county. A few months after the siege, the Government ordered the castle of Kirkwall to be demolished. The work of destruction was set about and it was converted into a melancholy ruin, the more conspicuous and striking from its being situated on the west side of the main street, nearly fronting the Cathedral. This ancient fortress—the walls of which were of immense thickness, and so strongly cemented as to be almost impenetrable—was built in the fourteenth century by Henry Sinclair, the first of that name who was Earl of Orkney. It was called the King's Castle,* from its being the ordinary residence of the royal governors or chamberlains of the islands subsequent to their annexation to the Crown of Scotland. It was to this castle that Bothwell fled for refuge after parting with the Queen at Carberry Hill. But Balfour, the governor, refused to admit him; and in revenge he plundered the town of Kirkwall. Bothwell's subsequent history may be told in a few words. Having escaped the pursuit of Kirkaldy of Grange, who followed him to Shetland, he set out in an armed vessel

---

* This castle, says a native writer, was built "with such strength and skill, that the witch-haunted mind of the seventeenth century believed that only the devil himself could have been its engineer and architect!"

for the North Sea, and there supported himself and his associates for some time by piracy. He was at length captured by the Danes, and imprisoned in the castle of Malmoc, where he died, it is said, a raving lunatic in 1576. Lamartine in his "Mary Stewart" (page 53), states what we have not seen mentioned by any other historian, that Bothwell in his early youth was a corsair on the coast of Denmark. He says also that Byron, whose mother's ancestry was connected with the line of Lady Jane Gordon, has depicted him in his "Corsair;" but, he adds, "the poet is far behind historic truth, for the sovereign poet, Nature, outvies fiction by reality."

Among the writers who have related the story of the unhappy Patrick Stewart Earl of Orkney, there is a considerable difference of opinion regarding his criminality. Peterkin, in his "Notes of Orkney," while he allows that he was guilty of oppression, contends that he was illegally deprived of his estates, that he got no justice in his trial, and that his punishment was a "judicial murder." He represents Law,* the bishop, who collected the grounds of complaint, as a selfish and pliant ecclesiastic, who coveted the episcopal revenues which the Earl had obtained from the Crown, and who fed the insatiable vanity of the King by the most abject and ludicrous flattery. The archbishopric of Glasgow, he adds, was the reward of his services. Sentiments pretty nearly similar are expressed by Malcolm Laing, the historian. " It is probable," says that ingenious writer, "that Earl Patrick's oppression was exaggerated in the complaints of the islanders, or aggravated by the acrimonious report of their bishop. The episcopal revenues which he had obtained from the Crown were

---

* Law, who succeeded Archbishop Spottiswood, died in 1632. He was interred in the chancel of the Cathedral of Glasgow, where there is a monument erected to his memory by his second wife, who was a daughter of Boyle of Kilburn. He was esteemed a man of learning, and left behind him, it is said, in MS. a commentary on several parts of the Scriptures. The Bishops of Orkney would appear to have enjoyed a pretty considerable revenue. "The bishopric of Orkney," says an old writer, "was a greate thing, and lay sparsim throughout the haill parochines of Orkney and Zetland. Besides his lands, the Bishop had the tiends of auchteen kirks, and his lands grew daily as delinquencies increased in the countray."

solicited by the prelates ; and the king descended to the mean and unjust expedient of purchasing a large mortgage with which his estates were attached. As he refused to resign his right to the redemption of his property, his estates were seized. He was driven at length to the most desperate extremes. His son surrendered on the pious condition that no torture should be employed to extort a confession of his father's guilt; and yet the father was convicted on the son's confession." Dr. Barry, on the other hand, leans to the unfavourable view of his character ; and Mr Worsaae, the Danish writer, has the following strong remarks on the subject: —"Among those vassals (Crown vassals) none has left behind him a more despised or hated name than Earl Patrick Stewart, who from 1595 to 1608, or about thirteen years, oppressed the islands in the most shameful manner. He violently deprived holders of allodial farms of their right of possession, and converted almost all the freeholders into leaseholders. He arbitrarily changed the weights and measures,* so that the taxes and imposts were intolerable. Law and justice were not to be procured, for the Earl's creatures everywhere occupied the judgment-seats. To appeal to Scotland was no easy matter, as Lord Patrick's soldiers guarded all the ferries. In the Orkneys the Earl compelled the people to build him a strong fortress at Kirkwall, and in Shetland another at Scalloway, from which places armed men ranged over the country to punish and overawe the malcontents. The ruins of these castles form a still existing memorial of the wicked Earl Patrick, who for his tyranny was recalled to Scotland, accused of high treason, and beheaded." † His father, Robert Stewart,

* Mr Balfour of Trenaby, in his recent interesting work, entitled "Impressions in Orkney and Zetland," says that the two Earls, Robert and his son Patrick, and subsequent donatories, made an increase of 250 per cent. upon every denomination of weight and measure used at the time in Orkney and Shetland.

† Earl Patrick maintained great state in his household, both in Orkney and Shetland. He never went from any of his castles to church nor anywhere abroad through the islands without a guard of fifty musketeers. Three trumpeters always sounded as he sat at dinner and supper. On his palace at Birsa was inscribed the following motto :—"Robertus Stuartus, filius Jacobi

was also guilty of great oppression, tyranny, and treasonable intercourse with the court of Denmark, and had a narrow escape from the same fate during the regency of the Earl of Morton.

Sir Robert Gordon afforded at this time (1615) a strong proof of the jealous and bitter feeling which he cherished against the Earl of Caithness. Early in the month of January this season, the latter went to London to receive some reward from the King for his services in Orkney. His Majesty happened to be then at Newmarket. As soon as Sir Robert, who was at Salisbury with the Dean, his father-in-law, heard of the arrival of the Earl of Caithness at Court, he hastened thither, in order to prevent his Majesty, with whom he had great influence, from yielding anything to the Earl that he considered would be prejudicial to himself or to the house of Sutherland. In particular, he was most anxious that he should not obtain from James a promise of redress for the slaughter at Thurso of his nephew, John Sinclair of Stirkoke. In spite, however, of all that the malice of the baronet could urge against his lordship, the King granted him a full remission of all by-past offences, with an annuity for his services in Orkney. He also appointed him one of his Scottish Privy Council. But all these royal favours and honours the Earl subsequently forfeited by his imprudent and violent conduct.

Not long after, the very serious charge of incendiarism was brought against the Earl of Caithness. As the case is a curious one, a brief detail of the circumstances may not be uninteresting. George Sinclair of Dunbeath, as well as his grandfather,

Quinti, *Rex* Scotorum, hoc edificium instruxit. Sic fuit, est et erit." This motto gave great offence at Court; and it has been alleged that the Earl suffered the punishment of death more on account of it than for his so-called rebellion, and the tyranny and cruelty which he exercised towards the natives of Orkney and Shetland. "It is probable," says Sir Walter Scott, "that the only meaning of the inscription was to intimate that Earl Robert was the son of James V., King of Scotland, which was an undeniable truth; but putting Rex in the nominative, instead of Regis in the genitive, as the construction required, Earl Patrick seemed to state that his father had been the King of Scotland, and was gravely charged with high treason for asserting such a proposition."

William Sinclair, whom he succeeded, had suffered, it is said, much injury and annoyance at the hands of the Earl of Caithness. George was married to a sister of Lord Forbes; and there being no likelihood of his having any family by his wife, he conveyed the whole of his property, comprehending the lands of Dunbeath, Downreay, and Sandside, to his brother-in-law. Soon after the execution of the deed, he was seized with a fatal illness and died, when Forbes took possession of the estate. He appointed a William Innes, a native of Morayshire, as his chamberlain or factor over the property, who took up his residence at Sandside. Earl George felt highly indignant that his cousin's lands should go to a stranger in preference to himself, although from his conduct towards him he could have expected nothing else; and under pretence of discharging his duty as sheriff, he took every method of annoying the factor and distressing the tenants. Finding that all the mischief he could do in this way was not sufficient to gratify his spleen, he negotiated with two brothers, John and Alexander Gunn, and a cousin of theirs, named Alexander Gunn, and promised them an ample reward if they would undertake to burn the stackyard at Sandside. It is alleged that he first made the proposal in private to Alexander Gunn, the cousin; but that Gunn indignantly spurned the idea, and told his lordship that to gratify him he would undertake to assassinate William Innes, the factor, but that he would not burn the corn, a piece of work which he considered unworthy of a gentleman! After some hesitation, Alexander, brother of John Gunn, agreed to do the business, and going to Sandside in the dead of night, with two accomplices, set fire to the stacks of corn, and burnt the whole. A report was industriously circulated that some of Mackay's tenants in Strathnaver had caused the conflagration, which induced that chieftain to use every effort to find out the guilty persons. Strong suspicion rested on the three Gunns, who, a few days before the deed was committed, were seen going to Castle Sinclair. At length, Alexander Gunn, the cousin, in a private interview with Mackay and Sir Robert Gordon, on condition of being leniently dealt with, revealed to them all that he knew of the matter.   The three Gunns were cited to appear before the Lords of Justiciary at Edinburgh.   John Gunn and and his cousin, Alexander, obeyed the summons, but the other Gunn, the real perpetrator of the crime, did not make his appearance.   Both the Gunns, when examined by the Lords of Council, declared that the Earl of Caithness had bribed Alexander Gunn to burn Lord Forbes' corn, and that the affair had been proposed and discussed in their presence.   In the meantime, his Lordship stoutly denied the charge, and accused Sir Robert Gordon and Mackay of a design to bring him within reach of the law of treason, and to injure the honour of his house.   After a great deal of legal proceedings, the matter was finally compromised between the parties ; and a contract was drawn up, in which, among other things, the Earl agreed to pay Lord Forbes and Mackay the sum of twenty thousand merks Scots, which may be held as tanta-mount to a confession that he was guilty of the crime laid to his charge.   He also received a full remission from the King, but not without two galling and stringent conditions, the one that he should renounce his office of justiciary and sheriff ; the other, that he should give up and resign, in perpetuum to the Bishop of Caithness, the house of Scrabster, with as many of the feu lands of that bishopric as should amount to the yearly value of two thousand merks Scots, for an augmentation to the prelate's income.   These were hard terms ; but he found himself under the necessity of submitting to them.

On a review of the whole matter, it is hardly possible to avoid coming to the conclusion that the Earl was guilty of the crime imputed to him ; and yet there are circumstances in the case which admit of a doubt, and which a skilful pleader would turn to good account.   For instance, the Earl had in 1586 hanged the father of John and Alexander Gunn ; and as the spirit of revenge was at the time deeply cherished to the third and fourth generation, one would naturally think that his two sons would be the very last persons in the world that his lordship would take in his confidence and engage to perpetrate a crime of such a highly penal nature. Further, it appears that the three Gunns were tenants of Mackay, and that he gave John Gunn (a rather suspicious-looking grant) a life-rent lease of the lands of Strathy for his evidence against Earl George at Edinburgh.

During all this time the peasantry of the county were in a most wretched condition. Among other evils, Caithness was overrun with thieves. In 1617 a regularly-organised band of these vagabonds infested the borders of Sutherland and Caithness, where they waylaid and robbed travellers, and violated every unprotected female that had the misfortune to fall into their hands. Their principal haunt was the Ord of Caithness, a spot peculiarly adapted for their purpose. Scarce a week passed without the commission of some murder, rape, or robbery, in that quarter. Such, indeed, was the alarming state of matters, that people were afraid to cross the Ord, and all communication between the two counties was in a great measure suspended. The authorities on both sides were at length roused to a sense of the magnitude of the evil, and resolved to put it down. With this view, a strong posse of armed men were sent out to watch the movements of the gang, and to apprehend them. In a few days nearly the whole of the miscreants were seized and imprisoned, and after a summary trial sentenced to the gallows. A gibbet was erected on the highest part of the Ord, where, without benefit of clergy, they were all hanged as a terror to evil-doers. " By this exemplary punishment," says the historian of the house of Sutherland, " the country was rendered peaceable for a while after."

The restless and unhappy disposition of the Earl of Caithness was constantly involving him in trouble; and he was no sooner out of one scrape than he was in another. Another serious charge (1621) was now preferred against him, namely, that of being accessory to the slaughter of Thomas Lyndsay, half-brother of Robert Munro, commissary of Caithness. It has been mentioned that the Earl had been compelled to give up to the Bishop of Caithness a part of the Church lands which he held in feu. This forced resignation was a measure which deeply vexed and mortified him. Munro, the commissary, acted as chamberlain to the bishop. One of the first steps which he took, on being appointed factor, was to remove Sinclair of Durran, who was one of his lordship's tenants, from the lands which he occupied, and to grant a lease of them to his brother, Thomas Lyndsay. Sinclair adopted the Irish mode of revenge, and meeting soon after with Lyndsay in Thurso, he ran him through with his sword, and killed him on the spot. It was generally believed that he did this at the instigation of the Earl of Caithness. Sinclair immediately left the county, and hurried off to London to meet his kinsman, Sir Andrew Sinclair, envoy from the King of Denmark, who interceded with the King for a pardon to him; but his Majesty refused to grant it, whereupon, for better security, Sinclair fled to Denmark. In the meantime, Munro, the commissary, raised a criminal action against the Earl of Caithness and Sinclair of Durran for the slaughter of his brother. The parties were summoned to stand their trial before the Court of Justiciary at Edinburgh; but as neither of them appeared, they were both outlawed, and denounced rebels. Lord Caithness wrote the Privy Council, strongly asserting that he had no participation in the slaughter of Lyndsay, and that his reason for not answering their summons was fear of his creditors, who, if they found him in Edinburgh, would incarcerate him. His lordship was at this time far from being in an enviable situation. Troubles began to multiply around him from every quarter. He had disputed with his son, Lord Berriedale, who had lain five years in the jail of Edinburgh in consequence of engagements he had come under for his debts; and the Earl's nearest relations, and the principal gentlemen of Caithness, feeling disgusted with his conduct, which had done so much injury to the young nobleman, and kept the county so long in disturbance, warmly sympathised and sided with Berriedale. His creditors, too, were clamorous for payment; and their repeated complaints to the King respecting the breach of his engagements so incensed his Majesty, that he ordered a commission to be granted to Sir Robert Gordon and others to apprehend the Earl as a denounced rebel, and to take possession of his castles and fortresses for his Majesty's use. Proclamations were at the same time issued, interdicting all and sundry from having any communication with the Earl; and a ship of war was ordered to proceed to Sinclair's Bay to prevent his escape by sea, and to batter down his castles in case he should attempt to withstand a siege. The Earl at first resolved to resist the royal commission, and with this view he set about fortifying his castles, especially the strong tower of Ackergill; but on sober reflection, becoming apprehensive of the consequences should he be unsuccessful in his opposition, he despatched a messenger with a letter to Sir Robert Gordon, earnestly soliciting an amicable arrangement. In this document he begged to remind Sir Robert that he was a nobleman and a peer of the realm, who had once been a commissioner himself in his Majesty's service (alluding to his military services in Orkney); that no crime could be justly laid to his charge; that he was the first nobleman ever pursued as a traitor merely for falling into debt, and that all actions of a criminal nature brought against him were fabrications invented by his enemies, none of which were ever judicially proved. On these grounds he begged, if Sir Robert refused to negotiate with him, that he would at least give him time to represent his case to the Council before he adopted the extreme measure of invading the county. Sir Robert returned a long answer, expressing much affected regret for the unhappy situation in which his lordship had placed himself by his rebellious obstinacy and repeated breaking of his engagements, and concluded with saying that his lordship's sole object in proposing a negotiation was to waste time, and that if he did not at once submit himself unconditionally to the King's mercy, he would immediately proceed to execute the commission. The Earl, although he had still a good many friends and adherents in the county, when he saw such a heavy storm gathering round him, went on board a small fishing-boat in the night season, and made his escape to Orkney.

In the meantime, Sir Robert Gordon, his most active enemy, assembled a large body of Highlanders, and accompanied by his brother, Alexander Gordon of Navidale, and the principal gentlemen of Sutherland, crossed the Ord (1623), and proceeded in full military array on his expedition. His account of this bloodless enterprise, to which not the smallest opposition was offered, occupies several pages, and is, unintentionally of course, an amusing specimen of the mock-heroic. At Ausdale, near the border, he was joined by Lord Berriedale and James Sinclair, younger of Murkle, one of the commissioners, with about 300 Caithness men, consisting chiefly of the Calders and others who were favourable to Berriedale. At Latheron he was met by Sir James Sinclair of Murkle, Sir William Sinclair of Mey, the Laird of Rattar, Sutherland of Forse, and several other gentlemen of the county, who tendered their submission and obedience to his Majesty's commission, and offered their services to accomplish the object of the expedition. Sir Robert, with the Caithness men some half a mile in advance, continued his march to Wick. From Wick he proceeded to Castle Sinclair, thence to Ackergill Tower, and lastly to the Castle of Keiss, all of which, on the first summons, delivered up their keys to him in the name of his Majesty. At Keiss he had an interview with Lady Caithness, his cousin, who entreated him with great earnestness to use his interest to get her husband restored to royal favour, which he promised to do, provided the Earl would follow his advice. The keys of all the castles were delivered to Lord Berriedale, to be kept by him until the further pleasure of his Majesty should be known. A set of instructions was also drawn up at Wick by the commissioners for his future guidance in the government of the county ; and the result of the expedition was, that an annuity was settled on the Earl, and Berriedale got the entire management of the property.* When the storm had blown over, his lordship returned from Orkney, and finding that it was useless to contend any longer with the powers that be, he settled down into a peaceable subject.

The politic Sir Robert, who liked to have his hands full of business, was now entrusted by Government with the duty of putting the law in execution against poachers. It is supposed by some that the laws for preserving game are the growth of modern legislation. It would appear, however, that stringent enactments on this point were in force in Scotland † more than two hundred years ago; and in the north, persons guilty of poaching were more severely punished than at present. "In the year 1623," says Sir Robert Gordon, "divers of the inhabitants of Southerland and Catteynes were called to appear at Edinburgh befor the Lords of the Privie Councell for wearing of pistolls, and for shooting of deer and wyld fowl with guns, contrair to the Act of Parliament made thereanent." To obviate the necessity of attending at Edinburgh, a commission was granted to Sir Robert to summon all transgressors in this way within the diocese of Caithness to Dornoch, where they were severely fined and punished, and security taken for their not killing any game in time to come. "The inhabitants of Catteynes," says Sir Robert, "did much repyn that they should have been urged to give their appeirance and abyd their tryall in Southerland, considering that within the memories of some of them (during the minority of Earl Alexander) the inhabitants of Southerland did usuallie resort into Catteynes for

* In the bond fixing the annuity for the Earl the trustees stipulate that it shall be continued as long as he behaves himself dutifully to the creditors and their chamberlain. They, moreover, bind themselves to give him, when asked, "17 wedders and 200 poultry, as an augmentation of the rent." The Earl, on his part, "faithfully binds and obliges himself, upon the pain of perpetual infamy and damnation, never to be ingrate to his said creditors."

† In England the game or forest laws reach as far back as the time of the Saxon heptarchy. "William the Conqueror," says Hume, "enacted new laws, by which he prohibited all his subjects from hunting in any of his forests, and rendered the penalties more severe than ever had been inflicted for such offences. The killing of a deer or boar, or even a hare, was punished with the loss of the delinquent's eyes, and that at a time when the killing of a man could be atoned for by paying a moderate fine or composition."

decyding of their actions and controversies befor George, then Earl of Catteynes. This did they think a great alteration; so changeable and variable is the estate of all human affairs. Blessed are they," adds the worthy baronet, "that fear the Lord, and remit their vengeance to God."

In 1626 Sir Donald Mackay (afterwards Lord Reay) raised about 3000 men in different parts of Scotland to assist the Kings of Denmark and Sweden, who were now leagued together against Ferdinand of Austria, for the support of the Protestant cause in Germany. The long-continued sanguinary struggle which followed is known as the Thirty Years' War, and is eloquently described by Schiller, the famous German poet and historian. A considerable number of Mackay's auxiliary force belonged to Caithness. Several young men of family in the county volunteered as cadets, and, among others, John Sinclair, natural son of the Earl of Caithness; Francis Sinclair, son of Sir James Sinclair of Murkle; and John Innes, son of William Innes of Sandside. The whole of these cadets obtained commissions, and some of them rose to high rank in the service; Francis Sinclair became major, and John Sinclair and John Innes lieutenant-colonels. Colonel Sinclair was killed in the course of one of the campaigns; and, on the conclusion of the war, so many of the Caithness volunteers had fallen in battle that only a very few survived to return to their native county.

1634.—At this time great distress, occasioned by a famine, prevailed in Orkney and Caithness. Owing to tempestuous weather, the corn of the preceding year had not sufficiently filled, and much of it was cut down green. There was, in consequence, a great scarcity of meal; and from the want of seed nearly a half of the arable land in both counties remained unsown. To add to the prevailing dearth, the fish usually found in such abundance along the northern shores seemed to have wholly deserted them. Many of the poorer sort of the people were reduced to such extremity that to satisfy the gnawings of hunger they killed their very dogs and ate them, and greedily devoured sea-ware, or whatever would support life. Multitudes died in the open fields, while some, from sheer desperation, it is said, ran into the sea and drowned themselves. To mitigate the dreadful calamity the Bishops of Orkney and Caithness supplicated Government for food to the starving inhabitants. The Lords of the Privy Council at first recommended their case to the charity of their countrymen generally, but they afterwards sent them supplies of victual, "but not in time or quantity to save a deplorable mortality." *

Dearth of victual owing to the same cause, the badness of the weather, seems to have been a thing of frequent occurrence in the county. In 1671, the Presbytery appoint the 11th of October to be kept as a day of solemn fast and humiliation by all the congregations within the bounds, "because," says the minute, "of the present extraordinarie rains that threaten to consume and rott the fruits of the ground, and because of the abounding of sin that is like to procure us manyfold judgments." The years 1673 and 1674 were also characterised by a long continuance of tempestuous weather. In the Presbytery records for the latter year occurs the following remarkable entry :—" No meeting in July, in respect of the great scarcity of victual generally through the land, whereby delinquents are now rendered incapable to travel to the Presbyterie."

When Charles I. attempted to introduce Episcopacy with its entire ritual into Scotland, the spirit of opposition which broke out against this rash and unconstitutional measure extended to Caithness. John, Master of Berriedale, son of William, Lord Berriedale, warmly espoused the popular cause. After the meeting of the famous General Assembly at Glasgow (1638), he took the National Covenant, and persuaded many of his friends in the county to do the same. He was subsequently one of five commissioners appointed by the States to get the bond subscribed throughout the kingdom. This famous bond was at first subscribed in Greyfriars' Churchyard, Edinburgh. The original copy, says Arnot, in his History of

* Chambers's Dom. Annals, vol. ii., p. 73.

Edinburgh, is written on a piece of parchment four feet long and three feet eight inches broad.   His father and his grand-father, George, the old Earl,. who was still living, leaned to the King's side.   Among others who embraced the Covenant was his relative, Sir James Sinclair of Murkle, who raised a company of Caithnessmen, and joined the Covenanters in Moray, where about 4000 of them were assembled under the Earl of Seaforth.   The Earl of Seaforth afterwards forsook the Covenanters and joined the opposite party, and for this political backsliding he was excommunicated by the General Assembly, and had to stand in sackcloth in the High Church of Edinburgh.   This body of troops formed what was called the army of Covenanters north the Spey, and were intended to keep in check the Royalists under the Marquis of Huntly and his son, the Viscount Aboyne.   The Master of Berriedale, who took such an active part in the cause of the Covenanters, died at Edinburgh in the autumn of 1639, and was buried in the abbey church of Holyrood House.   The complaint which carried him off is said to have been spotted fever.   The death of this young nobleman, who would appear to have been an ardent friend of civil and religious liberty, was much regretted by the people of Caithness.   He had married a daughter of Colin, Earl of Seaforth, and by this lady he had two sons, one of whom succeeded to the earldom.   His relict afterwards married Sir Alexander Sutherland of Duffus, who, in 1651, was created Lord Duffus.*

As a curious illustration of the manners of the period and of the violence of spirit engendered by this politico-religious struggle, I may mention the following rather singular case which occurred at John O'Groat's.   In Wodrow's MS. there is a complaint to the General Assembly of 1639 by Andrew

* Kenneth Sutherland, third Lord Duffus, forfeited, in the rebellion of 1715, his title and estates.   Having fled to the Continent, he afterwards entered the Swedish navy as a flag officer, and married Charlotte, daughter of Eric de Seeblade, governor of Gottenburgh.   The title was restored, in 1826, by Act of Parliament, to Captain James Sutherland, son of Eric Sutherland, son of the attainted Kenneth.   On his death, in 1827, Sir Benjamin Dunbar of Hempriggs, second cousin of the restored Lord, assumed the title.

Ogstone, minister of Canisbay, against Sir William Sinclair, laird of Mey, in which Mr Ogstone complains that a solemn fast having been appointed to supplicate a blessing on the late General Assembly at Glasgow (the famous Assembly of 1638), he got none of his congregation except nine or ten to take part in worship ; that the rest remained outside in the churchyard all the time, and would not come into church, although he sent his officer repeatedly for them ; that, on the conclusion of the service, when he came out himself and rebuked them for their sinful conduct and contempt of God's word, they all with one voice exclaimed that the laird of Mey had commanded them not to enter the church that day ; that Sir William protected all sorts of delinquents, and kept them from satisfying church discipline ; that, having sent his officer to cite a servant of his to the Presbytery, Sir William took the summons from the man, beat him, and put him in prison for two nights ; and that, in addition to all these grievances, his own horse was this same year stabbed in the stable with a dirk ! The minister concludes his " pitiful story " by entreating their " godly wisdomes " to seriously consider his case, and " take such order " that he may henceforth be enabled to discharge in peace the sacred duties of his office. The Assembly referred the case to the Commission, but their deliverance is not given by Wodrow. The reason why Sir William bore such antipathy to the worthy minister is not stated in the complaint. According to the tradition of the place, Mr Ogstone had been Episcopal minister of Canisbay, and having conformed to the Presbyterian mode of worship, it is probable that he had thereby incurred the resentment of the laird of Mey, who, like many others in his rank of life, was no friend at heart either to the covenanting cause or to the rigid discipline of the church. He is the same person who, when a boy at the High School, shot the Edinburgh bailie.

Very few of the Caithness gentry embraced the cause of the King in the unhappy quarrel which ensued between him and his Scottish subjects. This was mainly owing to the zealous exertions of the late Master of Berriedale, who, being a great favourite with all classes in the county, was eminently successful in impressing upon them his own political and religious views. One Caithness proprietor, however, Mowat of Freswick, in Canisbay, or, as he was styled, Mowat of Bucholie, stood staunch to the King. When Montrose forsook the Covenanters, and raised the Royal standard, he joined him; and at the battle of Alford, in 1645, his name is mentioned as one of the officers that were killed on the side of the Royalists. The family of Mowat came originally from the south, but in what year is not exactly known. In 1410, William Mowat * of Loscragy, by a charter from James the First, made over to his son, John, a wadset of the lands of Freswick and Aukingill, in the parish of Canisbay. This John, nine years afterwards, was killed in the chapel of St. Duffus, in Tain, to which he had fled for refuge as a sanctuary, by Thomas Mackay of Strathnaver. For this murder, and next burning the chapel, Mackay was, by order of the King, apprehended and hanged at Inverness. The Mowat family, of whom none now hold any landed property in Caithness, are of considerable antiquity. In the year 1316, during the reign of Robert the Bruce, the name of William Mowat appears in the list of the Scottish chiefs and nobles who sent a missive to the Pope, firmly maintaining the civil and political independence of Scotland.

The Latinised name in ancient charters is "De monte alto." On acquiring the property of Freswick, the Mowats repaired and inhabited Sweyn the pirate's old stronghold, which was then called Bucholie Castle. The patronage of the church of Canisbay belonged to them, and in 1610 it is particularly mentioned that an incumbent who entered on the cure was presented by Mowat of Bucholie.

1643.—George, Earl of Caithness, distinguished by the not very flattering title of the "Wicked Earl George," died in

---

* In the papers of the Spalding Club, Patrick Mowat of Bucholie is mentioned as being witness to a testamentary deed by Andrew, Earl of Errol, at Slains Castle, 3rd of October, 1585.

the month of February this year, aged 79.   His son, William,
Lord Berriedale, died a few years before him.   Earl George,
by his tyrannical conduct, had procured himself many enemies,
and it is quite possible that his faults may have been thereby
much exaggerated.   Some of the crimes at least with which
he was charged were never fully proved against him ; and it is
clear, from the whole course of his history, that he had a very
bitter enemy in Sir Robert Gordon.   "The quietness and
moderation," says Mackay, "with which he appears to have
conducted himself during the last twenty years of his life
plead strongly in his favour."

The following year, Alexander Irvine of Drum, and his
brother, Robert Irvine, who were keen Royalists, to avoid
falling into the hands of the Covenanters, fled by sea to
Caithness.   As Lady Mary Gordon, the wife of Alexander
Irvine, was a near relative of the Countess-Dowager of Caithness, the two brothers naturally expected to find a safe asylum
in the county, but in this they were bitterly disappointed.
Having landed at Staxigoe, where at the time a Committee of
Estates happened to be sitting, they were immediately seized,
and "put in ward" in the castle of Keiss.   They were thence
conveyed to Edinburgh, under a strong guard, by Francis
Sinclair, son of the late Earl, and lodged in the Tolbooth,
where, among other persons of rank, they had Lord Reay as
a fellow-prisoner.   Robert Irvine died in prison ; and his
brother, the laird of Drum, who was under sentence of death,
was liberated by Montrose immediately after his victory at
Kilsyth.

1649.—In the course of this year the following affair took
place in Thurso.   A noted freebooter, of Irish descent, from
Strathnaver, named Donald Macalister, accompanied by some
eighteen or twenty followers, entered the town with the
intention of plundering it, and revenging some offence which
he had received from the inhabitants.   The day chosen for
this was a Sunday, when the greater part of the people were
at church.   The savage resolved to set fire to the building, and

burn all that were in it; and on some one remonstrating with him for contemplating such a wicked design on the Sabbath day, he is reported to have said, "In spite of God and the Sabbath both, Donald will spill blood!" Notice of his presence in the town being communicated to the congregation, they instantly rushed out of the church,* and, providing themselves with such weapons as came first to hand, attacked the party, headed by Sir James Sinclair of Murkle, who, such was the unsettled state of the county at the time, was in the habit of coming to the church armed. Sir James made a thrust at Macalister with his sword, but without any apparent effect, on which his servant, superstitiously believing that the vagabond was proof against steel, cut a silver button of a triangular shape from Sir James's coat, and with that shot him through the ear. The bandit staggered, and fell down mortally wounded, exclaiming, in Gaelic—"My curse upon the creature; he has deafened me!" After a hard contest, the gang were finally overpowered by the town's people, and the whole of them, it is said, were killed. Neil Mackay, the chief of the Clan Abrach, who happened to be in Thurso at the time, and who would seem to have sided with the Highlanders, was also killed in the fray. He was interred in the burying-ground of Thurso, opposite the Murkle aisle of the church, and a stone, with his arms cut on it, was erected over his grave.

* The church here mentioned, of which only a part of the walls is now standing, is supposed to have been founded by the celebrated Bishop Gilbert Murray. It was dedicated to St. Peter; and the Bishop occasionally ministered in it when he resided in his castle of Burnside, in the immediate neighbourhood of the town. Its appearance was cruciform, and in the pointed style of architecture, with a large window in the eastern end. Inside the walls at the heads of the pews were covered with pannelling, on which were here and there paintings of the very rudest execution. One of these represented the offering of Isaac. Abraham was dressed in something like kilt and hose, with a flowing surtout. A pot with fire stood in one corner, the ram bounded forward in another, while above appeared an angel eyeing the scene with an expression of countenance irresistibly comic. In 1726 [Origines Parochiales Scotiæ] the vestry was, by permission of the kirk-session, used by the magistrates as a court-house, and a vault connected with the building was made to serve the purpose of a lock-up or prison. From this it would appear that the good town at the period in question was pretty hard up for accommodation in the way of public buildings.

CHAPTER X.

THE late Earl, who had outlived his son William, Lord Berriedale, and his grandson John, Master of Berriedale, was succeeded by his great-grandson George, son of the latter. This George, the third of that name, was not distinguished by any remarkable qualities.

Passing over a few years unmarked by any incident of much moment, we come now to narrate an event which created a great sensation in the north. This was the landing in Caithness (1650) of the celebrated Marquis of Montrose from Orkney with a body of troops, for the purpose of making a last effort in behalf of the Royal cause. But before relating his proceedings in this county, it may be interesting to give a brief account of the circumstances which induced him to go first to Orkney, and of his reception and success in that quarter. Robert, Earl of Morton, who, on the death of his father, William, had succeeded to the government, etc., of Orkney, warmly espoused the cause of Charles II., and hailed with great satisfaction the intelligence of a contemplated invasion of the north of Scotland by the Marquis in support of the exiled prince. He invited him to make his first landing in Orkney, and promised him every assistance in his power. Montrose had collected on the Continent about 1200 men, the greater part of whom were from Holstein and Hamburgh. Early in September, 1649, the first division, consisting of a third part of the force raised, were embarked at Gottenburgh for the Orkneys; but the two vessels which conveyed them were wrecked in a storm on the Orkney coast, and all on board perished. Other two transports that were despatched with the second division, together with 1500 stand of arms and other munitions of war, arrived safely at Kirkwall about the end of the month. On board of one of the ships was the Earl of Kinnoul, his brother, and several officers. The Prince of Orange, who was friendly to the cause, had furnished most of the vessels. Kinnoul, on landing, was kindly received by the Earl of Morton and the county gentlemen. He took up his head-quarters in the castle of Birsay, and immediately proceeded to raise levies. Meeting with every possible encouragement from the proprietors, he soon got together a considerable body of young men from the different islands. Latterly he was somewhat checked in his progress by an unfortunate difference which took place between himself and the Earl of Morton. Morton died soon after, on the 12th November, and was speedily followed to the grave by Kinnoul. The temporary command now devolved on his brother, who assumed the title of Earl of Kinnoul. As Montrose himself was not expected in Orkney till spring, the troops were quartered in the mainland during the winter, and maintained chiefly at the expense of the landed proprietors. A writer* well acquainted with the civil history of Orkney gives the following graphic description of the arrival of Montrose :—" A sharp look-out was kept as the appointed time for his arrival drew near ; and one day early in March the beacon-fires gave warning that ships were in sight and approaching the islands. The town of Kirkwall presented a busy scene as the levies hurried in from the neighbouring parishes ; and the soldiers laboured hard to give the good old town somewhat of a warlike appearance, by mounting some great guns on the towers of the bishop's palace and on the rampier at the shore. This was absolutely necessary, as the town had been frequently attacked and plundered by English cruisers. The fears entertained as to the character of the approaching ships were set at rest when they entered the bay and made the preconcerted signals." The Marquis himself was on board a small frigate which had been presented to him

* George Petrie, county-clerk.

by the Queen of Sweden. He was accompanied by several officers, among whom were his own brother, Henry Graham, Lord Fendraught, General Urry, Colonel Hay, Majors Dalgetty and Whitford, and Sir George Drummond of Balloch. Having landed with the residue of his troops, numbering about 200 Dutch volunteers, Montrose proceeded to the "Palace of the Yards," where he and his companions took up their residence. Subsequently he removed to Noltland Castle,* in the island of Westray, and remained there during the greater part of the time he was in Orkney. The month of March was spent in raising additional men. In the beginning of April the Marquis mustered all his followers at Kirkwall, and then marched them to Holm Sound, to be embarked for Caithness. The whole amounted to about 2000 men, including a number of gentlemen's sons in Orkney. A Major Sinclair, a native of that county, interested himself very much in the cause, and accompanied the Marquis in the expedition. The weather fortunately happened to be favourable. The troops were transported across the Pentland Firth in boats, and disembarked at Duncansbay in the immediate vicinity of John O'Groat's. "On landing at Duncansbay," says Dr James Brown,† "the Marquis displayed three banners, one of which was made of black taffeta, in the centre of which was exhibited a representation of the bleeding head of the late King, as struck from the body, surrounded by two inscriptions, 'Judge and avenge my cause, O Lord,' and 'Deo et victricibus armis.' Another standard had this motto, 'Quos pietas, virtus, et honor fecit amicos.' These two banners were those of the King. The third, which was Montrose's own, bore the words 'Nil medium'

---

* Noltland Castle was built by Bishop Thomas Tulloch about the year 1460. In 1560, it was feued by Bishop Adam Bothwell to his brother-in-law, Gilbert Balfour of Westray, by whom it was repaired for the reception of Queen Mary, on her escape from Lochleven Castle, had she not been compelled to fly to the south. Balfour was Sheriff of Orkney, Captain of Kirkwall Castle, and Master of the Household to Queen Mary. By his son Archibald it was bequeathed to his nephew and chief, Sir Michael Balfour of Munquhanny and Westray, whose grandson Patrick was its proprietor at the time of Montrose's fatal campaign.

† History of the Highland Clans.

—a motto strongly significant of the stern and uncompromising character of the man." The unusual sight of so many troops at first greatly alarmed the inhabitants of the district, many of whom fled from their houses, and hid themselves among the rocks. The news of the landing spread like wildfire through the county ; and as soon as the report reached Dunbeath, Sir John Sinclair took horse and posted off direct to Edinburgh to communicate the alarming intelligence to the Convention of Estates, leaving his castle to be defended by his lady and servants.

Montrose proceeded to Thurso,* where he issued a manifesto strongly appealing to the patriotism of the people of Caithness, and exhorting them to rise along with him, and free the country from the tyranny of its present rulers in Church and State. But the call was not responded to. The proprietors, as a body, were indifferent or lukewarm in the cause, and made no efforts to induce their tenantry, or rather serfs—for they were little better at the time—to join Montrose. In this respect they acted very differently from their brother proprietors in Orkney. The only gentlemen in the county who came openly forward and tendered their services were Alexander Sinclair of Brims, and Hugh Mackay of Dirlot. They were soon after followed by Hugh Mackay of Scoury, in Strathnaver, who repaired to Thurso, and expressed his readiness to embark in the Royal cause. Montrose subsequently compelled the heritors and ministers to swear obedience to him as the King's lieutenant-governor, etc., by signing a bond to that effect. The only recusant was Mr William Smith † of Bower and Watten (then one parish), whom neither threats nor flattery could induce to sign the oath. Montrose, it is alleged,

* The house in which Montrose lodged was situated near the old church, in that part of the town called the "Fisher-biggins." It was, like most of the other domestic habitations of the place at the time, a mean, thatched hovel, which has long since disappeared.

† At the Restoration, when a sort of modified Episcopacy was established, Mr Smith was, on account of his opposition to the measure, ejected from Bower. He retired to Thurso, where he lived till the time of his death, being chiefly supported by his numerous friends and admirers. The other members of the Presbytery conformed to the new order of things, and stuck to their livings.

was so exasperated at the obstinacy of this clergyman that he caused him to be brought to Thurso, and in way of punishment, to be tied to the stern of a boat in the river, and dragged through the sea with only his head above the water, to Scrabster Roads and back again! After undergoing this bath, it is added, that he was fettered and thrown into prison, where he lay till the news arrived of the defeat and capture of Montrose. He was then liberated, and returned to his charge. There is proof that the worthy clergyman was confined, but there seems to be great doubt as to the truth of the story about his being trailed through the sea. The authority on which it rests is not given. The tradition is not common in the county; and it looks very like a pure fabrication invented by an enemy to blacken the character of the gallant Marquis. Such a piece of unmanly cruelty, which would only tend to injure his cause, was not in keeping with the noble and chivalrous spirit of the man.

The arbitrary way, however, in which Montrose dealt with the gentlemen of the county, does not appear to have advanced the object which he had in view, namely, the raising of additional men in Caithness; and having failed in this point, he resolved to proceed on his march southwards without any further delay. Indeed, he had remained too long already in the county, at a time when delay was full of danger. A consultation or council of war was therefore held as to the best route he should take. Sinclair of Brims and the two Mackays strongly advised him to march by the heights of Strathnaver, where the ground was inaccessible to cavalry, and possessed other natural advantages. But Montrose declined the proposal, assigning as a reason that his troops would be knocked up by a march through those trackless and rugged wilds, and he resolved on the eastern route through the Ord of Caithness. After instructing his brother Henry to raise what men he could in the highlands of the county, and then to follow him without loss of time, the Marquis set off for Latheron, and having arrived at Dunbeath, laid siege to the castle.

This is one of the few ancient edifices in the county which is still inhabited. Like most of the other castles along the coast, it is situated on a narrow, precipitous rock, projecting into the sea, which surrounds it on all sides, except towards the land. The neighbouring cliffs are from eighty to a hundred feet high; and when the sea is roughened by a breeze, the scene produced by the waves dashing against them, and boiling at their feet, is exceedingly wild. A tourist who visited the county about the year 1783, gives the following description of a cave connected with the castle :—" Underneath," he says, " is a large cavern below the foundation of the castle, running up from the sea, and into which the sea enters at a certain height of the tide, and approaches near to a dark, dreary vault—the bottom of which is about 50 feet deep from the surface of the rock on which the castle stands. From within the castle, the approach to this dismal place is by steps cut in the rock, formed like a narrow stair, twisting round and round as it descends into the vault. The entry to this stair is curiously covered from the sight of those who are not acquainted with it ; and at one side, within the vault, is a door, but concealed so nicely that a stranger could not perceive it, which opens to a passage that leads to the subterraneous cavern mentioned above. It is difficult," he adds, " to conceive what might be the original intention of it. It could not serve for a prison in times of barbarism, nor as a place of safety to retreat to when an enemy approached the castle, because the free ventilation of the air is so much excluded, that no person could live in it for any length of time. Most probably it was used as a passage to the sea, in order to escape in boats when the castle was besieged by an enemy. It was admirably adapted for concealing contraband goods." There is little doubt that it was used for both purposes. The precipice on which the castle stands slopes down nearly to a point. Between this point and the fortress, at the head of the rock, the remaining portion of the ground was anciently occupied as a garden. It was a perilous-looking spot, unprotected by any wall, with the billows beating on three sides. The castle seems to have undergone frequent repairs and alterations; and is now completely modernised, with a protecting wall or parapet built round the entire rock on which it stands. It appears in record as far back as 1439. In 1650 it was surrounded by a moat filled from the sea.

Montrose vigorously attacked the garrison; and the result was just such as what might have been expected in the circumstances. Lady Sinclair, who had neither the warlike spirit of the celebrated Countess of March, nor yet her means of defence, after holding out for a few days, surrendered on the condition that person and property should be respected. This was readily granted; and the lady, in the military phrase, came out with all the honours of war. The possession of this stronghold was deemed by Montrose to be of the utmost importance, in case he should meet with a reverse and be obliged to retreat to Caithness. A garrison was accordingly placed in it, and left in charge of Major Whitford. Montrose now pursued his march towards the Ord— of which he had taken previous possession by some 500 men sent forward for that purpose. This step was absolutely necessary to secure his entrance into Sutherland, as the Earl of that county had espoused the opposite side, and was in arms against him. During the siege of Dunbeath Castle, the Earl of Sutherland met the advanced division of Montrose at the formidable defile of the Ord, whose passage a few brave men—such as Leonidas had at Thermopylæ—could have disputed against a host; but finding himself unequal to the contest, and deeming discretion the better part of valour, he beat a quick retreat to Dunrobin, and not considering himself safe even there, he fled to Ross-shire, where he remained till the Marquis was a captive in the hand of his enemies.

The Committee of Estates, when they heard of the invasion of Montrose, were greatly alarmed, and immediately ordered General David Leslie to proceed to the north with 4000 men. Strahan was sent on before, with a body of cavalry, to check his progress. Montrose met with no serious interruption until he arrived at Carbisdale, on the confines of Ross-shire. Here he was unexpectedly attacked by Strahan, and, having no cavalry to oppose to that of the enemy, his raw and undisciplined foot soon gave way, and the issue was a disastrous defeat. Montrose made his escape to Assynt, a wild and mountainous district in Sutherland, where he wandered for several days without any food or shelter. At last he was apprehended in the disguise of a peasant by a party of men sent out for the purpose by Macleod of Assynt, and brought to his castle of Ardvrack. Montrose appealed to his humanity, and begged him to save his life, but the sordid wretch for the sake of twenty thousand pounds Scots—some say four hundred bolls of meal—delivered him up to Leslie. He was forthwith sent south, and, after a formal trial, was condemned and executed on a gibbet thirty feet high, at the Cross in the High Street of Edinburgh. By a barbarous sentence of the court, his head was ordered to be fixed on the Tolbooth of Edinburgh, his body to be quartered and his limbs to be placed on the gates of Glasgow, Aberdeen, Dundee, and Stirling.* "Such was the fate of a man," says Hume, "whose military genius shone forth beyond any that have appeared during those civil disorders in the three Kingdoms. The fine arts, too, in his youth, he had successfully cultivated; and whatever was sublime, elegant, or noble, touched his great soul." †

After the battle, Captain William Gordon of Dunrobin was despatched to Caithness in pursuit of Henry Graham, but he had the mortification to find that he had come a post too late. Just as he arrived at Thurso, Graham, who had been apprised of his brother's defeat, was setting off in a vessel from Scrabster Roads for Orkney. From Orkney he fortunately made his

---

* At the Restoration the mutilated remains of Montrose were collected, put into a splendid coffin, and interred in St. Giles. The Earl of Caithness was one of fourteen noblemen who were present at the funeral.

† The Earl of Kinnoul died of fatigue and hunger among the hills; but nothing is known as to what became of Major Sinclair, from Orkney, who was captured along with Montrose.

escape to Holland.   General Leslie soon after, accompanied by
the Earl of Sutherland, entered Caithness, and laid siege to
the castle of Dunbeath, which was bravely defended by the
few adherents of Montrose that were left in charge of it, and
only taken at last by cutting off their supply of water.   Leslie
summoned before him the principal gentlemen of the county,
and, after a brief examination, sent some of them to Edinburgh
to be dealt with by the Convention of Estates.*   The Church
took into her own hands the punishment of the ministers, who,
with the exception of Mr Smith of Bower, were all summarily
deposed by the General Assembly.   In the presbytery records
of Caithness it is minuted that they were thus punished for
" yr complyance with James Graham excommunicate in his
rebellion, and shedding the blood of the country."   The
deposing † of the ministers was manifestly harsh, as there
is hardly any doubt that they, as well as the proprietors,
subscribed through intimidation the written oath or bond
which Montrose had tendered them. ‡

The county of Orkney suffered severely for the assistance
which it had given to Montrose.   In a statement of grievances
drawn up by the heritors, it is said that, immediately after the
defeat of the Marquis, " one Captain Collace, by warrant of
General Leslie, came to the country, and violently quartered
his troop of horse and men through the country, destroying
and eating, trampling and abusing the growing corn in the
fields, and threatening for money, would not remove their
quarters till of some persons they got 500 merks, some 100,
some 54, some more, some less, amounting to the sum of
5000 pounds Scots or thereby.   That in 1651 the county
suffered great prejudice by several English men-of-war, which

* Sir George Drummond of Balloch, who was apprehended in Orkney, was
brought over and shot at a post in Caithness.

† The whole of the ministers of Orkney were also deposed, and one of their
number—-a Mr Aitkins—was excommunicated, and an order of Council issued
for his apprehension, on which he fled to Holland.

‡ Patrick Balfour, the possessor of the castle of Noltland, was fined £2000
by the Committee of Estates, and forced to fly to Holland, for his complicity
in the loyalty of the great Marquis.

plundered several houses and islands to the value of 10,000 merks ; and that, during the Usurper's abode in Orkney, they uplifted and violently took the sheep, cattle, and other victuals, as if it had been their awin, for little or nothing to pay to the great ruin of the land," etc.*

There was a double hardship in the case of the poor islanders. They were first punished by Leslie for the aid given to Montrose, and, after the Restoration, they were refused any compensation for the spoil committed through the country, and the large sums of money extorted from them during the time of the Commonwealth. This was quite in keeping with the careless and ungrateful character of Charles the Second. Mr Balfour, referring to this subject, says, " The islanders gave Montrose 2000 men and £40,000, and the Commonwealth (1650) exacted 300 horse and £60,000. Again, they raised another regiment and contribution to Charles II. (1651) ; and he rewarded their loyalty and their sufferings by a further exaction of £182,000 in 1662, and then surrendered the islands to the tender mercies of the Earl of Morton, the worst King Stork of all the Donatories."†

Caithness, also, it would appear, raised a body of men for the same purpose, who accompanied Charles on his expedition into England, and a number of them fell very soon after in the celebrated battle of Worcester. This interesting fact, as regards Caithness, is incidently made known by the records of presbytery, in which it is stated that the widows of several of the men who were killed appeared before that ecclesiastical judicatory at different times and petitioned for leave to marry again. On these occasions the women brought forward witnesses who were in the same engagement, and who declared upon oath, that after the action was over, they saw their husbands, some of them lying in the last agonies of death on

* They were reduced to great want, and, by an order of Synod, it is said, were partly supported by their successors in office. The ex-minister of Reay, after acknowledging his guilt, was allowed to preach, as he might be of use in the Gaelic language to his son, who succeeded him.

† "Oppressions in Orkney and Zetland." It will, of course, be understood that the sums stated by Mr Balfour are not sterling, but Scots, money.

the field, and the dead bodies of others thrown into waggons and carried off to be buried with the rest of the slain. I subjoin one of the minutes of Presbytery with the spelling modernised :—" Thurso, 4th July, 1666. Compeared Eupham Robsone, in Mey, in the parish of Canisbay, and supplicated the Presbytery for licence to marry, her first husband having gone to the wars, and now being absent for fifteen years. The Presbytery requiring testimony and evidence of his death, she produced her husband's brother, Gilbert Rosie, who declared that at ' Worcester fecht,' he left his brother in the pangs ; and the same was declared upon oath presbyterially long ago by other witnesses. Whereupon the Bishop and Presbytery gave the woman a licence to marry again."

The old county and burgh records, which rarely allude to the political condition of the country, or to any of the more important events of history, take no notice of the circumstance that Caithness furnished soldiers to assist Charles II. in his unfortunate campaign ; and what is stranger still, there is no account of any such thing handed down by tradition, which reaches much further back than the period in question. It is, therefore, impossible to say what number of Caithnessmen were actually in the royalist army on this occasion. The battle of Worcester (Cromwell's " crowning mercy") was fought on the 3rd of September, 1651. The Scottish army, which consisted of about 14,000 men, was completely routed ; and Hume says that the whole were either killed or taken prisoners. Those who attempted to escape were pursued and savagely cut down by Cromwell's Ironsides. It would appear, therefore, that amongst the prisoners taken by the English were the few surviving Caithnessmen that afterwards got home to their native county.

1651.—Sir John Sinclair of Dunbeath, who had taken such an active part against Montrose, died in the month of September this year. His lady,* who defended the castle in

---

* Lady Sinclair of Dunbeath afterwards married the first Viscount Arbuth-not. She was the great-grandmother of the celebrated antiquary, Walter Macfarlane. His works, which are in manuscript in the Advocates' Library,

his absence, was a daughter of Lord Lovat, and sister of the Countess of Sutherland. Her name was Catharine Fraser, and she was the second wife. Having no male heir, the baronet divided his estate, says the writer of the continuation of Sir Robert Gordon's history, "betwixt his brother Alexander's son and his own daughter's children; which daughter was married to the Baron of Kilbrake." His nephew succeeded to the title and became also laird of Dunbeath.

In the course of this season Cromwell's troops crossed the Spey, when Caithness, as well as the other northern counties in Scotland, received a visit from them. They planted a strong garrison in the Tower of Ackergill; and parties of them would seem to have been distributed here and there over the county, and to have remained in it for some time. From the following entries in an old session record of Canisbay, it would appear that a portion of those troops were, on three separate occasions, stationed in that remote parish. Thus, March 29, 1652—"No session holden by reason the Inglishe were quartered in the bounds; the congregation was few in number, and ther was not a sederunt of elders, nather was ther any delinquents." Again, May 2, 1652—"There not being a sederunt, by reason of a party of Inglishe horsemen being in our fields, whilk made the congregation fewer in number, and severall of the elders to be absent." And again, December 30, 1655—"Adam Seaton convict of drinking on the Sabbathe, and having masking plays in his house for the Inglishe men, he was ordained to make publick confession of his fault next Sabbathe." The record does not say why those troops were stationed in the immediate vicinity of John O'Groat's. It has been supposed that, on the three occasions referred to, they were on their way to Orkney. But the most

consist of two volumes of genealogical memoirs, copies of charters and records, and two volumes of a partly geographical, partly statistical, account of Scotland. Douglas, in his "Peerage," Chalmers, in his "Caledonia," and others, have all borne testimony to the great value of the information embodied in the Macfarlane MSS. After the death of this industrious compiler and in honour of his memory his portrait is preserved in the Antiquarian Museum in Edinburgh.

curious thing is what is mentioned about the Englishmen devoting the Sabbath to drinking and the amusement of masques. Cromwell's soldiers are represented in history as rigid sectaries of the most austere cast, to whom everything in the shape of amusement, and especially on the Lord's-day, was a heinous sin and an abomination, but it would seem that such of them at least as came to John O'Groat's were not so very strict.

The old register which I have mentioned throws not a little light on the condition of Canisbay at the period in question; and, judging from what is therein stated, great ignorance, superstition, and immorality, prevailed in the parish. The minister, whose name was William Davidson, appears to have laboured indefatigably to correct this state of things. The kirk-session, of which he was the head, pursued a most rigid system of discipline. That ecclesiastical judicatory met regularly every Sunday after divine service, for the despatch of business; and in addition to old scores not finally disposed of, they had seldom less than two or more fresh cases of delinquency at every sederunt to deal with. But the poor minister had much trouble, not only with his congregation, but with his elders. He had great difficulty in getting them to attend to their duty; and there are many grievous complaints interspersed through the manuscript respecting their absence from church, and from meetings of session. Nay, on one occasion one of those worthies had to appear before his own church court, and to be rebuked for a gross act of Sabbath breach,*

* This mistake of the elder of Canisbay would appear not to have been an uncommon one. An amusing story is told of a few families resident in a sequestered spot, called Dalvahn, in the highlands of the county, who were so thoroughly "obfuscated" in intellect and careless as to the flight of time that they frequently did not know when the Sabbath came, and were reminded of it in the following manner:—One of their neighbours, a man of some little substance and superior intelligence to the rest, who kept a correct reckoning of the time, had acquired among them the high title of "Lord of Dalvahn." This personage every Sunday morning regularly donned a long-tailed scarlet coat, and repairing to a small eminence near his dwelling, stood there for some ten minutes, to indicate to the community that the day of rest had come, when all labour, even to the grinding of grain on their querns, should be suspended. As soon as the signal was observed by his neighbours, they would run in, exclaiming in Gaelic, "Make haste, and lay aside your work. It is Sabbath; his lordship is out in his red coat!"

namely, drying malt on the Lord's-day! His apology was, that he had entirely forgotten that it was Sunday! One crying evil, the parent of many others, was intemperance. Whisky was then a rare beverage in the county, but there was a capital substitute for it in strong ale.* Ale-houses, as they were called, were plentifully scattered over the parish. There old and young congregated, got drunk, and quarrelled and fought; and as these breaches of the peace were also all brought before the kirk-session, the minister and elders had always plenty of business on hand. Nor was Canisbay morally and intellectually worse than any other parish in the county. In this respect all the parishes were on a par. Education, with its civilising effects, had as yet made but small progress; and Caithness, despite the labours of the clergy, was in a state of semi-barbarism, with the spirit of superstition and Popery clinging to her with desperate tenacity. Never was there a greater fallacy than the common saying—*the good old times.*

1668.—Mutual depredations, and those too on a more than usually large scale, were carried on even at this time between the two counties of Sutherland and Caithness. During the year 1667, the Mackays of Strathnaver made three separate raids into Caithness and carried off a great number of cows, sheep, and horses. Early next year, in way of reprisal, William Sinclair of Dunbeath, on whose lands the harrying had chiefly been committed, invaded Strathnaver with 1200 men, and returned home with 900 head of cattle! The parties on both sides raised actions at law before the Court of Justiciary at Edinburgh; but the lairds of Dunbeath and Murkle having failed to appear before the Court or to find caution for their appearance, were declared rebels, and a commission was granted to John Campbell, younger of Glenorchy, to pursue them with fire and sword. Glenorchy came to

---

* Much attention seems to have been paid throughout the county to the quality of the popular drink. In the burgh of Wick "tasters," as they were called, were appointed to try the strength of the ale which was to be sold in the public-houses, and if it did not come up to the proper test, the brewers of the same had to pay a certain fine.--"Burgh Records."

Caithness for the purpose. But the two Sinclairs betook themselves to the castle of Dunbeath, which was strongly fortified; and Glenorchy being unable to reduce it, or to apprehend the parties, failed in the execution of his commission. William Dunbar of Hempriggs, however, for "intercommuning" with Sinclair of Dunbeath, was imprisoned in Castle Sinclair, and was only set at liberty on finding caution to the amount of 5000 merks Scots. Dunbeath and Murkle, by the mediation of friends, soon after obtained a reversal of their sentence of outlawry. This was the first time that Campbell of Glenorchy, who afterwards figures so largely in the annals of the county, came to Caithness.

The Earl of Caithness of this period, although he gave no assistance or countenance to Montrose when he landed in the county, became a decided Royalist at the Restoration, and manifested great zeal in supporting the rigorous policy of the Government with regard to suppressing conventicles. He obliged all the principal persons in Caithness to sign a bond against these meetings, and the clergy were the individuals whom he appointed to see it subscribed in the different parishes. This appears from the following minute in the Presbytery records of Caithness, dated Thurso, 4th November, 1674 :—"The said day compeired the Earl of Caithness as one of his Majesties honourable privie councill, and by veirtue of ane commission granted to his lordship by the said honourable councill, enquired if yr was any conventicles keeped within the presbyrie and shyre of Caithness, and the brethren of the presbrie showed his lord yr was none, neither did they fear any to be, for qlk they *blessed God*. And the noble lord presented ane bond from the councill qlk should be subscribed by all considerable persons within the diocese of Caithness for preventing conventicles, and entrusted the brethren of the presbrie yrwith to see it subscribed. Moreover, the s'd noble lord, in name of his majesties honable privie councill, desired that the 29 day of May should be keeped a preached day in commemoration of his majesties hapie restauration to ye exercise of his royal dignitie and absents from the ordinance on yt day should be delated to his lordship, and he should present the same to the councill to be censured as their wisdom thought expedient." This was one of the last things which his lordship did in his official capacity as member of the Privy Council and lord-lieutenant of the county. He died at the castle of Thurso in the year 1676. His lordship was an elder in the church of Thurso at the time, and on his death-bed, his request that he should be publicly and privately remembered in prayer, is thus narrated in the records of Presbytery. "May 3rd.—Mr Andrew Munro, minister of Thurso, did represent that the Earl of Caithness, being visited with heavie sickness, did earnestlie desire that all the Brethren of the Presbie should remember him in their publick and private prayers to God, which desire was cordially entertained. His colleagues in the eldership were Sinclair of Brims, James Innes of Thursetter, Richard Murray, James Shilthomas, Alexander Oswald, and Alexander Rorrison."

CHAPTER XI.

THE late Earl, some time before his death, in 1676, having no male heir to succeed him and being greatly embarrassed in circumstances, sold his property, title and all, to Lord Glenorchy, who was one of his principal creditors. There were two dispositions, as they are termed, in favour of Glenorchy, the first dated 10th June, 1661, the second, 8th October, 1672, conveying all and sundry the lands, etc. The latter bears that, in case of non-redemption, Glenorchy and his heirs shall be holden and obliged to assume, wear, and use the surname of Sinclair and arms of the House of Caithness. "There can be no doubt," says Dr Henderson, "that this clause was inserted at the desire of Glenorchy to be used as a pretext for the assumption of the titles at a subsequent period. After this transaction, his chief means of support were derived from an annuity of 2000 merks which the purchaser had bound himself to pay him. Glenorchy married his widow—the Countess Dowager, a daughter of the Earl of Argyle and relation of his own, and assumed the title of the Earl of Caithness—the deed by which he acquired the estate and title having been confirmed by Royal charter under the Great Seal. In order to secure one influential friend in the county, he appointed Sir John Sinclair of Murkle sheriff and justiciary-depute of Caithness, as well as bailie of all the baronies on the Caithness estate. In the meantime, George Sinclair of Keiss, son of Francis Sinclair of Northfield, disputed Glenorchy's right to the title, and more especially to the lands of Northfield and Tister, which he inherited from his father. The claims of both were submitted to the four most eminent lawyers of the time in Scotland, namely, Sir George Mackenzie, Sir Robert

Sinclair of Longformacus, Sir George Lockhart, and Sir John Cuningham.* Their decision was in favour of Glenorchy, and forwarded to the King, who thereupon sent a letter to the Privy Council, ordering them to issue a proclamation prohibiting George Sinclair of Keiss from assuming the title of Earl of Caithness, etc., etc. Sinclair paid no attention to the interdict, and not only retained possession of the lands, which he claimed as his own by inheritance, but annoyed Glenorchy's chamberlains so much that they found it extremely difficult to collect his rents. Almost the whole of the gentlemen in the county espoused the cause of Sinclair of Keiss; but two of his warmest and most active supporters were David Sinclair of Broynach, and William Sinclair of Thura. They gave him all the aid in their power, and even went so far as to assist him in demolishing the castle of Thurso East, of which Glenorchy had taken possession. The common people were everywhere friendly to George Sinclair; and, in short, Glenorchy was generally looked upon as a usurper who had taken advantage of the necessities of the late Earl, and cheated him out of his title and property.

At length the Privy Council (November 11, 1679) passed an Act charging the " haill kin, friends, and followers of John, Earl of Caithness, to concurr and assist " in recovering the disputed lands. To carry this into effect Glenorchy next summer (1680) invaded Caithness with 700 men. This is the number generally stated, but Colonel David Stewart of Garth† says that Glenorchy's force amounted to 1100 men, including the followers of the immediate descendants of his family, namely, Glenlyon, Glenfalloch, Glendochart, and Achallader, together with those of his neighbour and brother-in-law, the

---

* This Sir John Cuningham was a native of Caithness. His father, John Cuningham, was admiral-depute of Caithness and Sutherland, and rented the lands of Geise and Ormly, in the neighbourhood of Thurso, under William, Lord Berriedale, after he had got the management of his father's estate. Sir Robert Sinclair of Longformacus, a descendant of the St. Clairs of Roslin, was also one of the creditors. The property which he held in Berwickshire was obtained by an ancestor of his in 1384, as appears from a charter of that date by the Earl of Orkney to his cousin, "James de Santo Clairo," of the lands of Longformacus.

† "History of the Highland Regiments."

Laird of Macnab. Sinclair of Keiss, as soon as he heard that the Campbells were passing through Braemore, on the confines of the county, resolved to meet Glenorchy in open field, and for this purpose hastily collected about 800 followers. Some accounts say that he had 1500. Many of them, however, it is added, were old men, while the whole were untrained and totally destitute of any knowledge of military tactics. The only gentleman with him, on whose experience as an officer he could depend, was Major Sinclair of Thura, who had served in the German wars. The hostile parties met near Stirkoke; but as the day was far spent, and the Highlanders were fatigued with a march of near thirty miles, Glenorchy declined battle, and withdrew to the hills of Yarrows. The place to which he retired was long known by the name of "Torran na Gael," or the Highlanders' Hill. The Sinclairs marched into Wick and celebrated their supposed advantage in a deep carousal, being liberally supplied, it is said, with drink by a secret agent of the Campbells. Pennant says :—"Glenorchy thought proper to add stratagem to force. He knew that in those days whisky was the nectar of Caithness, and in consequence ordered a ship laden with that precious liquor to pass round, and wilfully strand itself on the shore. The Caithnessians made a prize of the vessel, and in indulging themselves too freely, became an easy prey to the Earl." Such seems to have been the current tradition in the county at the time of Pennant's visit; and it is most likely founded in truth. Be that as it may, the Sinclairs spent the night in riot; but the Campbells acted more prudently. Glenorchy appointed a strict watch, and took every necessary precaution against a sudden surprisal. The men that were not on guard wrapped themselves in their plaids, and lay down to sleep on the bare heath. About eight o'clock next morning (July 13), Glenorchy quitted his bivouac, and crossed the river of Wick below Sibster, nearly opposite Stirkoke Mains. His men are said to have leaped across; and from the narrowness of the stream at one particular spot in this quarter, the feat would not seem impracticable to an agile, long-legged Highlander. The news speedily reached Wick, where it excited the utmost consternation and alarm. The Sinclairs, from the state in which they were found, were mustered with great difficulty, and then hastily led up the river side to meet the enemy. Glenorchy's intention was to proceed to Keiss, but as soon as he saw the Sinclairs advancing, he prepared for battle by drawing up 500 of his men on the haugh, some 200 yards farther up the river than the point where it is joined by the burn of Altimarlach.* This burn, or rather water-course, which in the summer season is quite dry, has steep banks on each side, and may be described as a huge gully. It lies about two miles to the west of Wick. Nothing could be better adapted for an ambuscade, of which Glenorchy with great tact availed himself. He accordingly ordered the remainder of his men to lie down and conceal themselves in this deep gorge, and not to stir from the spot until their officers should give them the word to rise. As the Sinclairs advanced, they made a detour to the right at some little distance from the head of the ravine, and of course did not see the ambuscade that was laid for them. Their object in this movement was to have the advantage of the higher ground, and thus to place the enemy between them and the river. In the meantime Glenorchy animated his men with the following short address, originally delivered in Gaelic :—" We are this day in an enemy's country. He that stands this day by me, I'll stand by him, my son by his son, and my grandson by his grandson; but if this day goes against us, he will be a lucky man that ever gets home, for long is the cry to Lochawe, and far is the help from Cruachan." When the two hostile bodies were within a few yards of each other, Glenorchy gave the signal for the attack, and the deadly strife commenced. The onset of the Campbells

---

* Altimarlach is a Gaelic compound, and has been usually rendered "Thieves' burn ;" but the author was informed by the Rev. Hugh Macalman of Latheron, an excellent Gaelic scholar, that it is a corruption of Altnamarbh clach, which literally signifies the burn of the stones of the dead, or the burn of the gravestones.

was so furious, that the Sinclairs, enfeebled as they were with
the debauch of the previous evening, instantly gave way, and
fled with precipitation in the direction of the burn of Altimarlach.   At this moment, the reserve corps of the Highlanders,
starting up from their ambush with a savage shout, met the
fugitives in the face, and being thus pressed in front and rear,
and at the same time outflanked on the left, the Sinclairs in
desperation made a rush for the river.   The Campbells chased
them into the water as they attempted to escape to the other
side, and committed such dreadful havoc, that it is said they
passed dry shod over their dead bodies.   Not a few of the
Sinclairs who endeavoured to save their lives by running for
the open plain were cut down by the murderous battle-axe and
broadsword of the infuriated victors.   Sinclair of Keiss himself,
Sinclair of Thura, and the other leaders of his party, who were
all on horseback, owed their safety to the fleetness of their
chargers.   The engagement did not last above a few minutes,
and was as bloody as it was brief.*   There is another account
of this affair which says that Glenorchy's men were advantage-
ously posted on the west side of the burn of Altimarlach, and
that the Sinclairs in their impatience to attack them, instead
of going round the head of the ravine, plunged recklessly down
into it, and attempted to scramble up the opposite bank.   In
this exposed and defenceless condition a great many of them
were slain.   Daunted at length by the difficulties of the place,
and the slaughter of their comrades, they fled in disorder
through the gully towards the river, whether the Campbells
pursued them, and massacred a great number of them without
mercy.   Of the two accounts, that of the former appears to
us the most entitled to credit.   We can hardly believe that
any body of men would be so foolhardy as to attempt climbing
up a steep and rugged bank in the face of a formidable enemy
ranged along the top.   Such was the issue of the famous battle
of Altimarlach, so disastrous to the county, and so humiliating

---

* In the Macfarlane MS. the number of Caithnessmen killed is said to have
been eighty, but it is believed that more than two hundred fell in this action.

to the pride of the Sinclairs.   It was the last great fight of the kind—originating in a family quarrel—in Scotland, and in this respect it possesses a general as well as local interest.

Glenorchy quartered a part of his troops in Caithness for some time, levying rents and taxes as in a conquered country, and subjecting the people to the most grievous oppression. The remainder of his men he sent home immediately after the battle in detached companies. With the last company was his chief bard and piper, Finlay MacIvor, who composed on this occasion the two well-known airs—" The Campbells are Coming," and " Lord Breadalbane's March." The latter was played for the first time at Altimarlach.   " In the heat of the battle," says Colonel Stewart, " and when the Caithness men were beginning to give way, Glenorchy's piper struck up a voluntary - the inspiration of the moment - when the sounds of the instrument seemed to express, in a very remarkable manner, the words bodach na briogais." This Gaelic phrase may be rendered the " bodies wi' the breeks," and is a sarcastic allusion to that part of their dress worn by the Sinclairs in this unfortunate fray. The Campbells, as genuine Highlanders, wore the kilt, and, like Dundee's men at the battle of Killiecrankie, were mostly all barefooted.

Glenorchy's piper, Finlay MacIvor, would appear to have been a man of more than ordinary talent in his vocation ; and the following anecdote is related of him while on his way out of the county :—The weather, it seems, was warm, and Finlay was afflicted with a disease very common among pipers, namely, an unquenchable thirst. Before crossing the Ord he and his party adjourned to a public-house at Dunbeath—then famed for the superior quality of its ale. The Highlanders were delighted with the drink, and did it ample justice in a sederunt of nearly two days. The third morning found Finlay there alone—his purse empty and his pipe pledged for the scores of the previous evening. Mine hostess was inexorable, and the poor man was in an exceedingly disagreeable plight. Had he and his countrymen been thrashed by the

" bodies wi' the breeks," the disgrace to him would have been
nothing compared with the loss of his pipes in such circumstances.   Fortunately, at this distressing conjuncture, a friend
unexpectedly came to his rescue.   William Roy MacIvor, a
countryman of his own, and one of Glenorchy's factors, who
lived near Dunbeath, having heard of the dilemma in which
Finlay had placed himself, called in just as he was making his
last appeal to the landlady.   The tally board was produced,
and the factor having glanced it over, generously paid the
whole reckoning, and ordered the pipe to be restored to its
rightful owner.   " Now, my good fellow," said the factor,
clapping him on the shoulder, and handing as much money
as would defray his expenses home, " I hope you'll be a little
more moderate in your potations in future, and not get into
such a fix again, at least before you reach the braes of
Glenorchy ; for, mind you, I will not always be at hand to
redeem your pipes."   The overjoyed bard could not express
his gratitude in words ; but he called to his aid his peculiar
talent, and rewarded his benefactor by composing a song in
his praise, and wedding it to a beautiful Gaelic air, named—
" Failt clan Ibhair."   The factor, a kind-hearted, hospitable
man, was not a little gratified with a strain which so happily
recorded his good qualities.   But it was like to have cost him
too dear ; for it is said the tune was never played in his
hearing without his treating the company to half an anker of
brandy !   He was the chief of the MacIvors in this county ;
and his name, embalmed in imperishable song, still lives in the
Highlands of Caithness.   Such is the immortalising power
of genius when it is aided by that most expressive and
delightful of all the sciences—music.

To return to the civil affairs of the county.   Nothing
daunted by the reverse at Altimarlach, George Sinclair of
Keiss, continued his opposition, and finally laid siege to Castle
Sinclair, which he took after a feeble resistance on the part of
those who had been left in charge of it.   Fire-arms, or some
kind of artillery, would seem to have been employed on this

occasion by the besieging party.   For this affair he and his three friends who assisted him, Sinclair of Broynach, Sinclair of Thura, and Mackay of Strathnaver, fell under the ban of Government, and were declared rebels.

At length, through the influence of the Duke of York, afterwards James II., George Sinclair finally secured his claim to the title of Earl of Caithness, and also obtained full possession of his patrimonial property.*   The sale of the earldom was manifestly an illegal transaction, and the decision of the Scotch lawyers in favour of Glenorchy is not a little strange.   " The earldom of Caithness," as is observed by Mackay, " was a male fee by the original grant, which would seem a bar in the way of its being gifted or disposed of to a stranger, and even of the King's altering its tenure, where there was no previous forfeiture."

Glenorchy was for about six years Earl of Caithness.   As a compensation for the loss of his title, he was created Earl of Breadalbane and Baron of Wick.   The Baron had little enjoyment in his Caithness property.   He was universally detested by the natives, who regarded him as a military butcher, and never forgot the slaughter of their friends at Altimarlach. They accordingly took every method of annoying him.   They waylaid and thrashed his factors ; they burned the corn, and houghed the cattle of his tenants ; and, even after his death, they vexed his successor so much that, despairing of bettering his affairs in the north, he divided the lands into separate portions and sold the whole in 1719.   The Ulbster family purchased the greater part of the Caithness estate.   It was a princely property, and at the present day would be valued at not less than from six to seven hundred thousand pounds. The whole debt lying on it, when it was sold to Glenorchy, does not appear to have exceeded twenty thousand pounds. The sheriffship of Caithness continued in the family of

---

* The lands of Keiss, Northfield, and Tister, which Sinclair claimed as his own by inheritance, are represented by him in a petition to Parliament (1681) as not exceeding 300 merks of yearly rent.   They have been since purchased at upwards of £30,000.

Breadalbane till the year 1735, when it was sold to George Sinclair, father of the late Sir John Sinclair of Ulbster.

From a curious old document dated 1750, and entitled "Observations by Harry Innes of Sandside upon the writs he has seen, and the information given him relative to the differences betwixt the deceased Sir James Sinclair of Dunbeath and John Sinclair of Ulbster," etc., Glenorchy would seem to have claimed, as his purchased property, the greater part of Caithness. In the paper in question, an inventory extending to about twelve pages folio is given of the various lands, etc.; and these comprise nearly all the principal townships, mills, multures, castles, towers, fishings, etc., etc., with the very hawks and hawks' nests on the Ord and Holburn-head. By all accounts, Glenorchy would appear to have been a grasping and unprincipled man, and there is no doubt that he claimed property to which he had no right by purchase.

I may here also mention that he was the Earl of Breadalbane so deeply implicated in the massacre of Glencoe. For this horrible deed a process of high treason was afterwards raised against him, and he was committed to prison, where he remained for some time, but was at last discharged without trial. He received £12,000 from Government to keep the Highlands quiet after the Revolution, the greater part of which he appropriated to his own use. And when the Earl of Nottingham wrote to him requesting him to account for the £12,000, which was given in order to be divided among the chiefs, his answer to that minister was, "My lord, the Highlands are quiet, the money is spent, and this is the best way of accounting among friends."

In a note appended to a memoir of the celebrated General Hugh Mackay,* Glenorchy is spoken of in the following

---

* Memoir by John Mackay of Rockfield, pp. 108, 109. The General Mackay above mentioned was the same who fought Dundee at the battle of Killiecrankie. He was a native of Sutherland, and nearly related to the Reay family. When a young man he entered the Dutch service, in which he greatly distinguished himself. He also displayed great military talent and bravery in Ireland during the rebellion which took place there to restore King James II. He was killed at the battle of Steinkirk in 1692.

terms :—" Returning to his own country of Breadalbane, and being a man of intrigue, he contrived to sow the seeds of dissension among his neighbours, and engaged them in expensive law-suits, which ended in their finding it necessary to sell their estates to him at an under-value, thus greatly enlarging his already extensive territories.   Though at heart no friend to the Revolution Settlement, he never avowed any hostility to it till 1715, when in the 80th year of his age, and last of his life, he sent 500 of his vassals to join the Earl of Mar."   The writer of the note, Tacitus-like, thus sums up the character of Glenorchy, " He was grave as a Spaniard, wise as a serpent, cunning as a fox, and slippery as an eel." Glenorchy was twice married.   His first wife was Lady Mary Rich, daughter of Lord Holland, with whom he received a large dowry.   " He brought her to Scotland," says one who chronicles this important event, " riding on horseback on a pillion behind him, attended by several Breadalbane clansmen fully armed, and the far-seeing John carried with him what was perhaps as near his heart as even his bride, a bag of gold, the tocher of Lady Mary, for there was no branch banks even in Edinburgh in those days through which to convey such a bagful by means of a cheque.   His second wife, formerly Countess Dowager of Caithness, died at Kensington in 1708.

George, Earl of Caithness, so famous for his dispute with the Breadalbane family, and the noble stand which he made for his title and his patrimonial rights, died at Keiss in 1698, and was succeeded in the earldom by his second cousin, Sir John Sinclair of Murkle.

CHAPTER XII.

DURING the time John Earl of Caithness governed the county, our local annals do not furnish us with any public events of much interest or importance. The event to which most interest attaches was the meeting at Thurso in 1700 of the Commissioners appointed by the General Assembly to visit Orkney, Shetland, and Caithness. Their names were Messrs John Brand, minister of Borrowstoness; John Sandilands, minister of Dolphington; James Hart, minister of Ratho, and Alexander Lauder, minister of Mordington. They met with the Presbytery of Caithness on the 20th of June, and continued in session, occupied with ecclesiastical business, for the four following days. The principal case that came before them was that of one Arthur Anderson, who is described as "a pretended preaching deacon," and who was in the habit of itinerating through Orkney and Caithness, and of making a trade of marrying and baptising irregularly. Among other parties, he had married David Sinclair of Broynach and a woman Janet Ewen, with whom Sinclair had cohabited for some time. A number of witnesses were cited and examined as to Anderson's imputed irregularities, and, after a full and lengthened investigation of the several charges brought against him, including that of drunkenness, he was unanimously found guilty, and deposed. The sentence bore that he was henceforth not to perform any ministerial function within the kingdom, under the highest penalty of the church. The great onus of Anderson's offence was, that he had married parties and administered the rite of baptism to the children of parties who had proved contumacious and refused to satisfy church discipline. In a paper of his which was handed into the court, for he did not appear there personally or by counsel, he signs himself late minister of Kilmeny, from which it would appear that he had a charge in the south before he came to Caithness. I have been the more particular in noticing this case of Anderson, from the circumstance that his marriage of David Sinclair of Broynach was afterwards pronounced irregular by the highest legal authority in the kingdom, and that it vitiated the claim of his grandson, James Sinclair, for the title of Earl of Caithness. Earl John died in 1705, and was succeeded by his son Alexander, who married Lady Margaret Primrose, daughter of the Earl of Rosebery. He was present at the last Scots Parliament in 1707, when the Treaty of Union was discussed, but he appears to have declined voting. Mr Dunbar, younger of Hempriggs, commissioner for the burgh of Wick, voted for the measure.

In the month of March, 1709, one of the magistrates of Thurso, named Lawrence Calder, was deliberately shot dead, in broad day light, on the principal street of the town, by William Sinclair, son of the Commissary of Caithness. Along with him were two accomplices, Robert Munro and William Macalister, both belonging to the parish of Reay. The three culprits managed to evade the punishment due to their crime by flight. The presbytery took up the case, and after solemn deliberation and prayer, passed on them the sentence of the greater excommunication. This sentence, once so fraught with terror, is engrossed at full length in the minutes of presbytery ; and as it may interest the reader to see the terms in which it is couched, we copy it verbatim :—" As by the word of God and the law of nations, the heinous guilt of murder and the shedding of innocent blood, renders the murderers liable to the highest capital punishment, so by the Acts of the General Assembly of this church, such as are guilty of atrocious, horrid murder are appointed to be excommunicated from the society of the faithful, and to be delivered over to Satan, for the punishment of the flesh, that the soul may be saved in the day of the

Lord. And the presbytery finding that William Sinclair, son to the late Commissary of Caithness, did, barbarously, feloniously, and deliberately, murder the body of Lawrence Calder, late bailie of Thurso, by shooting him with a pistol in the back; and, further, finding it proven by witnesses that Robert Munro in Reay, and William Macalister in Fresgo, in Sandside in the parish of Reay, were partakers with the foresaid murderer in this bloody tragedy; therefore the presbytery, after solemn prayer to God for counsel and direction, and being moved with zeal for the glory of God, the uttermost detestation of the foresaid villainy, for the purging the Lord's house and church of all such rotten, wretched, and corrupt members, did, and hereby do, according to the power committed to them by the Lord Jesus Christ, the great King and Head of this church, Excommunicate and Deliver over to Satan the fore-named persons, William Sinclair, Robert Munro, and William Macalister, obtesting and entreating all and sundry to whose ears this dreadful sentence shall come, to look on them as heathens and infidels, who by their horrid wickedness have cut off themselves from the mystical body of Christ Jesus, and are hereby Declaratively cut off, in His name, from the privileges and benefits of His house, ay and until they repent and abhor themselves, in dust and ashes, for their atrocious crimes, and make application to the judicatories of this church for having this dreadful sentence, so justly inflicted, taken off; and, finally, these are to give warning that none receipt, entertain, or harbour the foresaid murderers, or have any unnecessary correspondence with them, as they would not come under the same guilt, and be in God's account found liable to the same sentence."

The same minutes of presbytery also contain a copy of an address to the Queen (Anne) drawn up at the instance of the magistrates and Town Council of Thurso, in which, after setting forth the many murders and atrocities that are being daily committed in the county, it is humbly and earnestly solicited that her Majesty would be pleased to order some soldiers to be stationed within the bounds, so as to strengthen the hands of the magistracy, and enable them to put the law in execution against offenders.

About three years afterwards an occurrence took place in Caithness which created a considerable sensation in the county at the time. This was a duel which was fought by two of the proprietors—Alexander Sinclair of Olrig and William Innes, younger of Sandside. Sinclair of Olrig, who, it is said, was proud of his strength and moreover a man of a quarrelsome disposition, insulted the elder Innes at a public meeting in Thurso, and the result was a challenge from his son. The principals, with their seconds, met at a place called Tongside, about seven miles south from Thurso. Their weapons were swords; and after fighting for some time, Innes gave his antagonist a wound, of which he died in the course of a few hours. On this he and Sinclair of Dunn, his second, immediately fled the country. Innes went to Germany, and having entered the army there was promoted to the rank of captain. Meantime Donald Sinclair, son of the deceased, raised a criminal process against them before the Sheriff of Caithness for murder; but in consequence of the absence of the parties, it was not brought to any decision. After the lapse of a few years, both received a remission of the crime for which they had fled, and returned to Caithness. Captain Innes, however, was so much afraid of his life from the relatives of the man whom he had unfortunately slain that he ever after kept a strong muscular Highlander as a life-guard, who accompanied him wherever he went. He (Innes) died about the year 1747. He is said to have been a very stout man, and from his large stature was called "Captain More," or the big captain. Having no issue, he left his estate to his cousin, Harry Innes of Borlum. Since the publication of the first edition of this work, I have received the following additional particulars respecting this famous duel :— " The meeting at Thurso was that of the Michaelmas court in September. After the business was concluded, the whole of the gentlemen present dined together and indulged, it is said, very deeply in the bottle. James Innes of Sandside, who was well advanced in life, retired to another apartment of the house in order to take some repose. When the reckoning came to be paid, Olrig, without any ceremony, entered the room in which Sandside was sleeping, and dragged him by force to the drinking table to pay his share of the bill. The old man and his son, William, who was also present, highly resented the indignity, and the latter, on his father's behalf, challenged Olrig. On the morning of the day appointed for the duel, while on his way to Tongside, Innes called on the minister of Reay, Mr John Munro, and consulted him whether he would fight Olrig or not. The minister, it is said, advised him to go forward, adding that, with the Divine assistance, he would come off victorious ! Olrig had slept the previous evening at Dale, the seat of his father-in-law, Mr Budge. He was accompanied to Tongside by his seconds, William Sutherland of Geise and Henderson of Westerdale, and Sandside by his seconds, Alexander Sinclair of Dunn and Donald Gunn, his father's factor. They fought nearly an hour, when at length, taking advantage of a favourable opportunity, Innes gave Olrig a stab in the breast which eventually proved fatal."

The exiled Stuarts had many friends among the better class of families in Caithness, and in 1745* not a few of them warmly espoused the cause of "bonnie Prince Charlie." Circumstances, however, prevented them from giving him any effective aid. Alexander Sinclair, Earl of Caithness, who then lived at Haymar, and George Sinclair of Ulbster, the sheriff of the county, were both staunch friends to Government, and gave no countenance to the rebellion. Early in the spring of 1746, Lord Macleod, son of the Earl of Cromarty, entered the county with a body of the rebels under his charge, for the purpose of procuring men. They fixed their head-quarters in

---

* In the previous insurrection, in 1715, a similar strong feeling in favour of the Stuarts was manifested by a number of the Caithness proprietors. Sir Robert Dunbar of Northfield appeared with a party at the cross of Wick, and openly drank the health of the Chevalier ; while David Sinclair of Brabsterdorran joined the Earl of Mar, and was present at the battle of Sheriffmuir.

Thurso, where they billetted themselves on the inhabitants. From thence they went in detached parties through the several parishes, beating up and down for recruits, and endeavouring to enlist the sympathies of the people in behalf of the prince, whom they represented as the rightful heir to the throne. They wore white cockades in their bonnets, and were all armed. Their conduct was inoffensive, and they offered no violence to any one. Notwithstanding their peaceable deportment, the inhabitants in general, and particularly the women, unaccustomed as they were to the sight of armed men, and those armed men rebels, were greatly alarmed at their first appearance in the county. Several families hid themselves in caves and subterranean recesses along the coast; while others deposited their little money underground, and fled, some to Lord Reay's country, and some to the Orkneys. In order to expedite matters, Cromarty himself set out for Caithness; but he had scarcely reached the entrance into the county, when he heard of the advance of the Duke of Cumberland, and at the same time received instructions to hasten forward with all his available force to Inverness, where the main body of the Highlanders were assembled. Lord Macleod, with the party he commanded, hastily marched from Caithness to join his father in Sutherland, and both, in a day or two after, partly by treachery, were taken prisoners in the castle of Dunrobin. It would appear that on this occasion Cromarty, so far from exhibiting any tact as a leader, did not exercise even ordinary prudence and circumspection. Sir Walter Scott says :*—" The Earl and his son remained at the castle witnessing the tricks of a juggler; while his men, 350 in number, were marched under the command of subaltern officers, and with little precaution, on to the ferry, where they were to embark. Thither they were chased by comparatively a mere handful of the Sutherland militia, and the greater part of them were destroyed." In the Statistical Account of the Parish of Loth it is said that the Earl of Cromarty's men

* " Tales of a Grandfather,"

committed several outrages, and, among others, burnt the mansion-houses of Kintradwell and Crakaig. It is also added that two of his officers who had wandered into the glen of Loth after their return from Caithness were killed by three men who met them there. If the defeat at Culloden had not occurred so soon it is believed that a considerable body of Caithnessmen would have joined the rebels; but the news of this unexpected disaster came like a thunderbolt on the principal Jacobites in the county, and blasted all their hopes. "Many in Caithness," says Mackay, "had purposed to join the rebel standard, and were at considerable pains to persuade others, and several of them assumed the rank of captains, lieutenants, ensigns, etc., but a fear of being interrupted by the Royalists prevented them from marching southwards." Not a few of the ladies, to show their zeal in the cause, wore the prince's miniature suspended by a ribbon round their necks. About forty-five men joined Lord Macleod in Caithness, and before leaving the county the only compulsory measure he used was that of obliging the landholders to pay a part of the land tax. One of our Caithness proprietors, John Sutherland, Esq. of Forse, was a staunch friend of Government. This gentleman, grandfather of the present Mr Sutherland of Forse, raised a company of men on his own estate, had them enrolled among the "Loudon Highlanders,"* and was with them as their captain in the celebrated battle of Culloden. Caithness, therefore, may be justly said to have had her share in the achievement of that field which happily and at once placed on a firm foundation the civil and religious liberty of the country. After the battle a party of soldiers was sent to apprehend Sinclair of Scotscalder, who had rendered himself

---

* The "Loudon Highlanders" were raised in 1745. The regiment consisted of twelve companies, numbering in all 1250 men. Their colonel was John Campbell, Earl of Loudon, and their lieutenant-colonel John Campbell, Duke of Argyle. Only a part of the regiment was engaged at Culloden. The Earl of Cromarty and his son were both brought to London and convicted of high treason, but their lives were spared. Lord Macleod afterwards rose to the rank of Major-General in the British service in India, and the forfeited title and estates were restored to the family. He died in 1789 without issue.

particularly obnoxious to Government. Having got notice of their approach, he withdrew, and hid himself in the hills of Dorrery. When the party made their appearance at his house, his lady courteously invited them in, and regaled them with plenty of meat and drink. They seemed much pleased with their reception, and after a brief search they departed. The visit, happily for the laird, was not renewed; and his "meditation" among the hills is said to have cured him of his Jacobitism.

Alexander Sinclair, Earl of Caithness, died in 1765, leaving only one daughter, Lady Dorothea Sinclair, who married the Earl of Fife. He was succeeded in the property by Sir John Sinclair of Stevenson (Haddingtonshire), as heir-substitute under the entail executed by the Earl of his lands of Murkle and others. The estate is at present possessed by Sir John's grandson, Admiral Sir John Gordon Sinclair. On the demise of the late Earl, two claimants appeared for the title, namely, James Sinclair of Broynach* and William Sinclair of Ratter. A long process took place. The case was finally brought before the British Parliament, and in that last court of appeal Ratter carried the peerage in 1772.

At this time (1772) there occurred a striking instance of the disorderly and lawless habits of the natives of the parish of Reay. A vessel, called the "John," of Liverpool, laden with iron and deals from the Baltic, was wrecked in a storm near Sandside, and the greater part of the crew were drowned. A Mr James Hogg, a native of the south, who then occupied the farm of Borlum, treated the survivors with every possible kindness, and endeavoured to save as much of the cargo as he could for the behoof of the owners. The country people, as

---

* James Sinclair of Broynach, who claimed the earldom in preference to William Sinclair of Ratter, was son of David Sinclair of Broynach, cousin of Alexander, the ninth Earl. As a lineal descendant of Sir James Sinclair of Murkle, the eldest brother of George, the fifth Earl, he had undoubtedly a better claim to the title than William of Ratter, who was only a lineal descendent of Sir John Sinclair of Greenland, the Earl's second brother. Broynach's claim, however, would seem to have been vitiated by his grandfather's marriage with Janet Ewen not having been found valid, He died in 1788 without issue,

was usual in such cases, poured down in numbers to plunder the wreck. With the assistance of his servants and one or two constables from Thurso, Mr Hogg put a check to the pillage, and, moreover, made a rigid search in the houses of the peasantry for the recovery of what of the property had been carried away. This so exasperated them that they combined to destroy him and his family by setting his house on fire in the night time. The chief agents in this diabolical attempt were Alexander Macdonald, William Elder, George Miller, and Robert Farquhar, tenants in Isauld. They were indicted for wilful fire-raising, and tried before the Justiciary Court at Inverness. After a trial of eleven hours, the jury, with one voice, found the libel proven against William Elder and Alexander Macdonald. The Advocate-Depute having restricted the libel to an arbitrary punishment, they were sentenced to be publicly whipped in Wick and Thurso, receiving in each of these places twenty-five stripes on their naked backs, and thereafter to be banished to the Plantations. Mr Hogg, who was in daily terror of his life in a hostile neighbourhood, ultimately threw up his farm, and emigrated with his family to America.

About this time a band of robbers, consisting of some ten or twelve of the strongest men in the county, carried on a regular system of burglary by breaking into houses, shops, and granaries, and abstracting therefrom, money, goods, and meal, to a large extent. They were mostly all individuals in good circumstances; and it would appear to have been nothing but sheer covetousness that prompted to this dishonest course. They resided in different parishes, but they kept up a secret correspondence, and had certain places where they met from time to time, and concocted their villanous schemes. The county was then entirely destitute of anything in the shape of police. It had not even a sufficient prison or lock-up for malefactors; and such of the inhabitants as were possessed of any little means or money, lived in constant dread of a visit from the gang. There was a large granary at Murkle well stored with victual, belonging to the proprietor of the district. The robbers had forcibly entered it and carried off a rich booty in meal. Not long after this, one Swanson, an inhabitant of Thurso, nicknamed Canny, was returning home in the evening along with some other persons from a market in Olrig, and the conversation turning on the recent robbery, he happened to say that if he chose, he could tell who they were that broke into the store-house at Murkle. This being reported to some of the band, he was decoyed out one night after he had gone to bed, and the next morning was found lying dead at a short distance from the town, with seemingly the mark of a joiner's hammer on his forehead. In order to make it appear as if his death had been the result of accident, the body was laid to an old stone fence, with the feet uppermost, and the forehead resting on a sharp stone. This clumsy attempt at disguise excited the public suspicion more strongly. From the appear- ance of the wound and other circumstances, there could be no doubt that the poor man was foully murdered. A precognition was made, but it failed in bringing out any positive proof of guilt against the parties suspected.

The villains now laid a desperate plot to murder William Sinclair, the Laird of Freswick, who was believed to have a considerable sum of money in his repositories, which they resolved to seize on and divide among themselves. Mr Sin- clair, who was a man of peculiar habits, resided at the time in a large house which he had lately erected on the south side of the bay of Freswick. The following minute account of the discovery of the plot, and of the punishment of the robbers, is given by Robert Mackay :—" This gentleman (Mr Sinclair) had got into a habit of lying in bed awake all night, during which one of his numerous tenants alternately sat beside him. The murder and robbery were to be perpetrated on the night on which Donald Rugg, one of his tenants, who was one of the band, was to sit up with him, of which he was to give pre- vious notice to his accomplices. A few days before it came to Rugg's turn to attend his landlord—the latter having had occasion to send a bearer with a letter to Mr Henderson of Stempster on some business—Rugg sent a letter by the same bearer, addressed to John Swanson, joiner, in Thurso, another of the band, to whom he was to deliver it. When he arrived at Stempster, as he could not read, he gave both letters to Mr Henderson, who, on being informed that the one to Swanson had come from Rugg, both of whom were suspected to belong to the band, desired the bearer to return home, saying that he would convey the other letter to Thurso by a runner he was sending there. He broke open the letter, the import of which was that the '*black ox*' was to be killed on a certain night. He sent the letter to Mr John Sinclair, sheriff-depute of the county, who was son of Mr Sinclair of Freswick, with a list of the suspected persons. Mr Sinclair immediately despatched a party of twenty-four Highlanders from Dunbeath, who seized most of the band, some of whom afterwards turned evidence, by which and other means the plot was discovered. They were tried by a jury, and having been publicly whipped, were banished the county. Some of them had fled, and escaped punishment." Swanson, the joiner in Thurso, who was considered the leader of the gang, and was commonly known by the appellation of "Achgillan," was a tall, handsome, fine-looking man, and connected by marriage with a respectable family in the county. His mother-in-law, a woman of a proud spirit, felt very deeply the disgrace which he had brought upon them, and on the day on which he was to be whipped, came purposely to Thurso to witness the punishment. The town was full of people from all parts of the county, attracted thither by the novelty of the spectacle. While the culprit was being flogged, the old lady, his mother-in-law, stood looking on with much apparent satisfaction, and is said to have called out to the man with the lash, " Lay it well into the scoundrel, and don't spare ; he richly deserves all that he can get." Being a determined character, and possessed of more than ordinary talent, Swanson was transported to the Plantations ; and his success in after life was not a little

remarkable. When the Colonies rebelled against the mother
country, in 1775, he heartily espoused the cause, volunteered
into the service, and rose, it is said, in the revolutionary army,
to the rank of lieutenant-colonel. Rugg, the Canisbay robber,
escaped punishment by flight. He went to America, also, but
of his future career in that part of the world, whether he
became a reformed man, or committed deeds which brought
him to the gibbet, there is no account. His relatives in Caithness were very respectable people ; and he had a nephew,
David Rugg, who was many years an elder in the Church
of Canisbay. Another of the gang, nicknamed "Brunty," was
long known about Edinburgh as a common street beggar. He
was a rough-featured, dark-complexioned man, wore on his
head a soldier's bonnet, and generally took up his position at
the Tron Church, where he might be seen for hours impor-
tuning the passengers for money.

While on this subject, I may give some account of a celebrated bandit, named David Marshall, who flourished in the
county some time before the event which has just been
described, and who was in many respects an extraordinary
character. Marshall lived at a place called Backlas, in the
parish of Watten. His real name was Sutherland, and he was
a native of Kildonan, on the borders of Sutherlandshire. In
the traditional annals of Caithness, he is styled, *par excellence*,
the Robber of Backlas. This daring vagabond, who supported
himself entirely by robbery, was upwards of six feet in height,
stout in proportion, and possessed of extraordinary bodily
strength. It has been truly said that "none are all evil."
Nature rarely produces monsters in the moral world any more
than in the animal kingdom. The very worst characters have
often some good points about them ; and the Robber of Backlas
was not without some redeeming qualities also. To the poor
he was uniformly kind and generous, and seldom meddled
with anything belonging to them. It was the rich only,
or such as could spare a portion of their means, that he robbed.
His creed was that this world's goods were very unfairly

divided, and that the man who had not enough was perfectly justified in taking from him who had a superabundance.

Marshall openly attended all the country markets in the neighbourhood, equipped in full Highland costume, with dirk and broadsword; and when any of the small farmers or cottars of his acquaintance disposed of any of their live stock, they had such perfect confidence in his honesty in this matter, that they handed him their money as to a banker, in order to be kept for them until it was called for. Without this precaution, they ran the risk—such was the condition of the county at the time—of having their cash taken from them by other thieves before they reached home. In "Guy Mannering" the notorious Dick Hatteraick is represented as saying that he always acted honestly by his employers, and never cheated them of a stiver. The Robber of Backlas could have made a similar averment in regard to his conduct as banker for the poor. He never proved unfaithful to his trust, or appropriated to his own use a single farthing of their money.

Of the various anecdotes which tradition has preserved respecting Marshall, the following is perhaps one of the most curious and interesting. The proprietor of Pennyland sent one day for one of his tenants, named John Tait, whom he was in the habit of employing on confidential errands.

"John," said the laird, "there is a very particular business which I wish you to do for me. I have some money in the hands of a friend at Inverness, and you will have to go there for it."

John at first hesitated. He was willing, he said, to do anything in his power to serve his honour, but the journey was long and dangerous; and, should he meet with no accident in crossing the several rivers and ferries on the road, he was sure to be robbed on his way home, as soon as he came into Caithness, by David Marshall or some of his gang. David would to a certainty hear of the journey and its object, for there was nothing that he did not hear of.

"Nonsense," said the laird, "there is no fear of that; only

don't tell your wife where you are going, or anything about it. Women are so fond of gossiping, that not one in a hundred can keep a secret. Here is a good pocket pistol to carry with you for protection. Keep it well charged, and if any villain should attempt to rob you, use no ceremony with him, but draw the trigger, and give him the contents in his stomach."

John at length consented to go, and the necessary credentials were delivered to him.

" Now," said he, " if anything should happen to me, I hope your honour will look to my poor wife and family."

The laird promised that in such an event he would show them all the kindness and attention in his power. John arrived safe in the Highland capital, got the money, and was now on his way home ascending the steep mountain pass of the Ord, when whom should he see advancing towards him, with a smile on his countenance, but the dreaded David Marshall.

" Hollo ! John, is this you ? " cried David. " How are you ? You have been at Inverness, I understand."

John saw that it would be of no use to deny it, and replied in the affirmative.

" And you have got the money ? "

He said he had.

" And none attempted to relieve you of it by the way ? "

" None," said John.

" Well, I'm glad of that. Come, let us sit down and rest us here for a little."

John, although a man of more than ordinary nerve and courage, felt exceedingly uncomfortable. The old road, or rather foot-path, across the Ord at this time ran along the face of a sheer precipice overhanging the sea in a terrific manner. They were in the middle of this fearful pass ; and if the robber was inclined to take the money, and dispose of the bearer, he had nothing to do but to give him a push down, and he would be precipitated three hundred feet to the bottom. It was a dreadful situation for one to be in, and at the same time completely at the mercy of a determined outlaw. John instinctively put his hand into his coat pocket to take out his pistol, but on second thoughts he drew it back again, as he knew this would only serve to hasten his fate. Besides, the robber never went without a sword and a brace of pistols himself, and he was not a match for him in any way.

"I see, John," said Marshall, "that you would rather have met any one than me on the Ord, but don't be alarmed, my good fellow. I have no intention of taking a farthing of the money from you. You are a decent trustworthy chap, and though I am a villain myself, I have a respect for an honest man. Now, when I think of it, we will be no worse of a little refreshment."

So saying, he drew out of his pocket a flask of brandy and a small drinking-horn, and, treating himself to a bumper, he filled another to John.

"This is not bad stuff, friend," said he, smacking his lips, "I had it from the laird of Stangergill's cellar."

After chatting together for half an hour, they rose to depart.

"I'm on my way to Helmsdale," said Marshall, "and as it is possible you may meet some of my friends on the road, show them this (handing him a bit of soiled paper with the initials 'D. M.' rudely scrawled on it), and they will allow you to pass on without the least molestation. By the bye," added he, "one of my firelocks is getting rather the worse of the wear. If you please, I will relieve you of the one you have belonging to the laird, your master, and you may tell him, with my compliments, that I will keep it for his sake."

John gave him the weapon, very glad to get off so easily. They then bade each other good bye, shook hands at parting, and continued their respective journeys. John fortunately met with none of Marshall's associates, and had no occasion to make use of his passport. On reaching home, he repaired immediately to the residence of his master, delivered him the full sum of money, and astonished him not a little with an account of his adventure with David Marshall at the Ord.

In his more daring exploits as a robber, Marshall generally availed himself of the aid of accomplices. With their assistance he had twice broken into the castle of Keiss, and once into the castle of Dunbeath. In a second attempt on the latter castle a desperate encounter with fire-arms took place between the domestics and the robbers. The latter were in the end obliged to take to flight. One of the gang was killed by a musket shot; and Marshall, it is said, carried the dead body on his back all the way from Dunbeath to Dirlet, in the parish of Halkirk, where the man resided.

Many attempts were made for a long time to seize Marshall, but he either beat off the parties sent to apprehend him, or dexterously eluded their search. At length Sir William Sinclair of Keiss, who suffered much from his predatory visits, was determined, if possible, to take him, and put a stop to his lawless proceedings. With this view he got together twelve of the strongest men on the estate, and, heading the party himself, set off one night for the residence of the robber. They reached Backlas a little after daylight; and having ascertained that he was at home, Sir William ordered six of the party, to keep watch outside, while he with the other six forced open the door of the hut and rushed in with loaded pistols in their hands. Marshall had just risen from bed, and was in the act of combing his hair, which, not having been subjected to the scissors for years, was of great length.

"If you stir a foot, or make the least resistance," cried Sir William, presenting a pistol to his breast, "you are a dead man."

The robber for once appeared utterly confounded and paralysed. He made no attempt to resist the party, but quietly allowed himself to be handcuffed; and in this state he was marched off to Wick, and lodged in jail. His malpractices and deeds of robbery were so notorious that it was deemed quite unnecessary in his case to go through the formality of a trial. After remaining in durance for a few days, he was taken out, publicly whipped, and banished from Caithness.

He retired to his native county, but, as he still continued to follow his old profession, the authorities in Sutherland subsequently managed to get him transported to America. Another account says that Marshall and an accomplice of his, named Donald Miller, were tried before George Sinclair of Ulbster, the Sheriff, as heritable justiciary, and were condemned to be executed. Marshall procured a suspension of his sentence and was ordered to Edinburgh for trial, but contrived to escape from those who had charge of him in passing through Sutherland. Miller was hanged in Thurso ; and it is added, he was the last person who suffered capital punishment by the heritable sheriff of Caithness. Nor was burglary confined to the male sex. In a minute of the records of the burgh of Wick (6 Jany., 1710) there are no fewer than eight charges of this nature brought against one Agnes Reilly or Sutherland. One of these charges is entering the Manse of Wick at night, and stealing a guinea and some silver out of the breeches of the minister, the Rev. James Oliphant, while he was asleep ! Another of the charges is, in the words of the record, " coming to the dwelling house of Alex. Doull, bailie in Wick, and stealing furth thereof at severall times ane silver tumbler of twall ounces weight, ane pynt and chopin boule full of rum, nine table napkins, ane long muslen gravat (cravat), and certain quantities of meal and other things." The punishment she received is not known, as one or two of the leaves in this part of the record are torn from the volume.

William Sinclar, Earl of Caithness, died in 1782. His son John, Lord Berriedale, was at the time in America. He entered the army when a young man, and rose to be major of the 76th regiment, or, as they were called, the Macdonald Highlanders. It was the hottest period of the unfortunate war in the colonies. The Macdonald Highlanders were ordered to America ; and the command having devolved upon his lordship, he embarked with his regiment for New York, where they landed in the month of August, 1779. He was present at the siege of Charlestown, and was severely wounded on that occasion. Having on the death of his father become Earl of Caithness, he returned to Britain, and died unmarried soon after in London. The earldom then descended to Sir James Sinclair of Mey, in whose family it still remains.

During the first burst of the French Revolution, which threatened to overturn every kingdom in Europe, the national defences became a subject of anxious consideration to Government. At this fearful crisis, rendered still more alarming by the state of matters in Ireland, several patriotic noblemen and landed gentlemen throughout Scotland, prompted by a high spirit of loyalty, offered to Mr Pitt to raise fencible regiments for the general safety, in their respective counties, as auxiliaries to the line, and to take the command of them themselves. This offer was gladly accepted by the Premier, who issued letters of service accordingly. The patriotic example of arming in defence of the country was followed throughout the whole of Scotland. Every district had its band of armed citizens. Burns, in his impassioned song of the "Dumfries Volunteers," has happily expressed the martial spirit of the period—

> " Does haughty Gaul invasion threat?
>   Then let the loons beware, sir,
> There's wooden walls upon our seas,
>   And volunteers on shore, sir."

Among the first who nobly came forward in this emergency was the celebrated Sir John Sinclair. In the course of a few months he raised a body of 600 men—chiefly from his own estate in Caithness—and was invested with the full rank of colonel. They were appropriately named the Caithness Fencibles; but as Caithness and Bute then united in sending alternately a member to Parliament, and the Prince of Wales was pleased to grant permission that Rothesay, his chief seat in Scotland, should be added, they were subsequently called the Rothesay and Caithness Fencibles. Their uniform differed from that of the other fencible corps. It consisted of a bonnet and feathers, with a plaid thrown across the shoulders, tartan pantaloons, surmounted with a strip of yellow along the seams, a fringe of tartan on the outside of the thigh, and the same around the ankle. The regiment was embodied at Inverness in the month of October, 1794, and passed a highly-favourable inspection before Lieutenant-General Sir Hector Munro. In their handsome uniform they had a remarkably fine appearance; and the tallness of their officers, nineteen of whom exceeded six feet in height, attracted particular notice. The first station of the regiment was at Aberdeen, where they lay encamped for six months. They were ordered there by the Commander-in-Chief for the purpose of defending that city in the event of an invasion (which was then much apprehended) of the French army in Holland. After doing duty in different quarters through Scotland this battalion was reduced in 1799. In 1795, Sir John raised a second battalion of 1000 effective men, under the designation of the "Caithness Highlanders," whose service was extended to Ireland. Their uniform was the same as that of the first battalion. Captain Benjamin Williamson of Banniskirk was appointed Lieutenant-Colonel. After being inspected by Lieutenant-General Hamilton at Forfar, the Caithness Highlanders were immediately sent over to Ireland, where they did duty, in camp and barracks, during the whole period of the Rebellion. In 1798 an address was presented to the lieutenant-colonel of the regiment by Viscount Gosford, in name of the magistrates of Armagh, thanking the officers, non-commissioned officers, and men for their excellent conduct and efficient services. In 1802 the regiment returned to Scotland, and was disbanded in Edinburgh. "Sir John Sinclair," says the writer of a memoir of his life, "made them a farewell speech in front of his house in Charlotte Square, where refreshments were liberally served out to the regiment; and after three enthusiastic cheers for their much-honoured colonel, the soldiers then dispersed, though many of them enlisted immediately afterwards to serve abroad."

But the patriotic conduct of Sir John Sinclair was not the

only instance of the kind evinced by the remote county of Caithness, at a period so fraught with impending danger to the country.   In 1795 the late Lord Duffus, then Sir Benjamin Dunbar of Hempriggs, raised another fencible corps of about 700 strong, under the title of the "Caithness Legion."   Their uniform consisted of the usual red coat, with white facings, white breeches and leggins, and a helmet covered with bear-skin.   The acting colonel, when Sir Benjamin himself was not present with the regiment, was Lieutenant-Colonel William Munro, afterwards Lieutenant-General Munro.   William Innes of Sandside was major.   The legion went to Ireland soon after they were embodied, where they did duty for seven years, and were disbanded at Inverness in 1802.   About 200 men from the two fencible corps volunteered into the 78th, 92d, and 42d regiments, and went with them to Egypt.   Not a few of the Caithness common soldiers in this expedition, by their good behaviour and personal gallantry, rose to be commissioned officers.   Among others, the meritorious conduct of Sergeant Alexander Waters, a native of the parish of Olrig, who had volunteered into the 78th or Ross-shire Highlanders, is deserving of particular notice.   At the battle of El Hamet, which proved so disastrous to the small detachment of troops engaged in it, he saved, at a critical moment, and with great risk to himself, the life of Major Colin Mackay of Bighouse, then a captain in the 78th.   The circumstance is thus described by Colonel David Stewart of Garth.   "At length, when there were only eleven of the Highlanders, and an equally small number of the 35th left standing, Captain Mackay, seeing that further resistance would only expose the whole to speedy destruction, determined to make a desperate push to join the centre.   He charged through the enemy, when several succeeded in gaining the position, but others dropped on the way either killed or wounded.   Captain Mackay was wounded in two places before he pushed off to the centre.   When he had nearly reached the post, an Arab horse-man cut at his neck with such force, that had it not been for the cape of his coat, and a stuffed neck-cloth, both of which were unusually thick, his head would no doubt have been severed from his body. As it was, the sabre cut to the bone, and laid him flat to the ground, when he was taken up and carried into the post by his sergeant, now a lieutenant in the regiment, the only individual who escaped unhurt." On his retiring on half-pay, Lieutenant Waters married, and took up his residence in his native parish. He was a fine soldierly-looking man, and was much respected by all classes of the community. He died in 1830.

On the 25th December, 1806, Caithness was visited by a hurricane of unprecedented violence. Its occurrence forms an era in the annals of the county, and is still talked of as the "windy Christmas." The morning of that day opened without any appearances in the sky to indicate the near approach of such a fearful visitation. The wind began at first to blow from the west, but afterwards it changed to the north-west, and raged with a fury that threatened to carry every thing before it. The bay of Dunnet was tossed into mountains of boiling foam, and latterly its entire surface from side to side presented the appearance of one immense sheet of spray drifting towards the sands at the bottom of the inlet. The damage done to property throughout the county was incalculable. The houses of the peasantry were mostly all unroofed ; whole stackyards were thrown down, and their contents scattered and swept away by the resistless element. There were at the time several fishing smacks from Gravesend lying in Scrabster Roads. Most of the skippers and some of the crews had gone ashore to have a jollification in the public house at the "Rings ;" and when the hurricane came on, they could not get aboard their vessels. Three of the smacks that, from their position in the bay, were more exposed to the wind than the rest, broke adrift from their moorings, and, being unable to work out, were forced down the bay of Dunnet. One came ashore on the sands, near the burn of Garth, another below the house of Castlehill, and a third at Murkle. A sloop called the "Fisher," belonging to Thurso, was driven on the rocks below the castle of Thurso East. To the astonishment of every one, none of the hands in any of the four vessels were lost. But the most remarkable thing was the escape which one smack made by running to Orkney in the very height of the storm, and through a sea in which it was believed no vessel could live for any time. All the crew of this smack were ashore except one man and a boy. The man, whose name was James Mackay, was a native of Mey, in the parish of Canisbay. As the boy could be of no use to him in the circumstances, he shut him down in the cabin to keep him from being washed overboard, and after trimming the craft as well as he could, he lashed himself to the helm, and by an incredible effort succeeded in bringing her safely into Widewall bay—a feat, we venture to say, unparalleled in the history of seamanship. The extraordinary exertion, however, which he made seriously injured his constitution, which was naturally strong. He fell into bad health, and died not long after. Mackay was an unmarried man, quiet and reserved in manner, and of an excellent character. At the time of his death, he might be about 27 years of age.

CHAPTER XIII.

THE prelature of Caithness was founded about the year 1150. The first bishop of whom we have any distinct account was Andrew, who died in the year 1185. He is said to have been much at the court of King David I., and his two immediate successors, Malcolm and William. During his incumbency, mention is made of a rather curious tax which was imposed on Caithness, and which was, no doubt, considered by the natives at the time a very heavy and grievous one. Earl Harald, it would appear, being somewhat troubled in conscience, granted to the Roman See, for the redemption of his sins, a penny (unum denarium) from each inhabited house in the county. This grant, which had the twofold good effect of clearing off a debt of guilt, and at the same time replenishing the Pope's exchequer, was attested by Andrew. In the list of those elevated to the See of Caithness, there would appear to have been several eminent prelates, Popish and Protestant, besides Gilbert Murray, who enjoyed the dignity.

Among the most distinguished of the Protestant bishops was John Abernethy, who was ejected after the meeting of the famous General Assembly at Glasgow in 1638. He was the author of a religious work entitled "A Christian and Heavenly Treatise, containing physic for the soul, very necessary for all that would enjoy true soundness of mind, and peace of conscience." The book, which may be still seen in the libraries of the curious in antiquarian lore, is written in the quaint style peculiar to divines of that age, and in point of doctrine has been considered highly evangelical. The last bishop was Andrew Wood, who was ejected at the Revolution in 1688, and died at Dunbar in 1695, aged 76.

There would seem to have been a bitter feeling in some parishes at least in the county against episcopacy after it was finally superseded by presbyterianism. Of this popular dislike one very curious instance may be mentioned. On the gallery of the old church at Watten there was long a rude painting, evidently intended as a satire on what was then denominated "black prelacy." It represented the congregation met for worship, with the reader in the desk and the bishop, in full canonicals, in the pulpit. Immediately opposite was a grotesque figure of satan, no doubt in canonicals also, with cloven foot and horns, belching out fire and brimstone on the terrified audience. It is but justice, however, to state that episcopacy, or rather the modified form of it which prevailed in Caithness, did not merit the odium thus so uncharitably heaped upon it. It appears from the Presbytery records (the best and only authority on the subject) that the ministers were generally well conducted and diligent in the discharge of their duties, and that the bishops were in the habit of regularly visiting the different parishes, enforcing discipline where it was necessary, and doing all they could for the moral and spiritual welfare of the people. Indeed, if rigid discipline could have repressed immorality, there was no failure of duty in this respect. Delinquents were regularly made to stand in sackcloth before the congregation on Sunday; and one case is mentioned of a Donald Fraser who, for the edification of the natives, had to do penance in this garb in every kirk in the county! The crime of which this worthy confessed himself guilty was, in the words of the minutes of Presbytery, "counterfeiting himself to be dumb, and deceiving the people with lying signs of divination, as also for living in sin with a woman to whom he was not married." It was then universally believed by the vulgar, and the belief is not yet altogether exploded, that deaf and dumb persons or "dummies," as they were called, had the gift of prescience, and could foretell by signs whatever was to happen, whether of good or evil, to any one that consulted them.

There are no cartularies or documents,* extant at least in the county, to show the revenue of the see in popish or prelatic times; but from the thinness and poverty of the population, it could not be one of the richest. In Caithness, the bishop's lands were Scrabster, Lythmore, Stemster, and Dorrery, situated in the parishes of Reay and Thurso. Dorrery was used as a "grass room" or sheiling. Their present rent is £1882 8s. 3d. Among other lands belonging to the bishop in Sutherland was Durness, a parish equal in extent to a small county, being about 25 miles long and 12 broad, and (including all its lochs and arms of the sea) nearly 300 square miles in area. A bit of romance is attached to the history of this district. According to tradition, a Lewis chieftain of the name of Morison, having come to Thurso for a cargo of oatmeal, happened to fall in love with the bishop's daughter and sought her hand. Being a handsome, good-looking fellow, the young lady, nothing loth, agreed to take him, as the marriage ritual has it, "for better for worse." They were accordingly united in due form; and the bishop gave Morison, as a marriage portion with the bride, the whole of Durness! In addition to other property about the end of the 15th century, the castle and lands of Redcastle,† in Ross-shire (anciently called Ardmanach), passed into the hands of the bishop of Caithness by a grant from the Crown. They do not appear, however, to have been long possessed by that dignitary; for in 1524 James V. ganted them, along with the Earldom of Ross, to James, Earl of Moray.

* In a note which I was kindly favoured with on this subject from Professor Cosmo Innes, he says, "I do not think you will find more information of the diocese of Caithness, and its revenue and benefices than is given in the "Origines Parochiales Scotiæ." Bishop Gilbert Murray's foundation shows no great endowment before his time. But then you have traces of those old exactions and dues which preceded the acquiring of tithes. We have no "Antiqua Taxatio," nor "Verus valor," nor "Bagimont Roll" of Caithness.

† The crown lands are now under the management of the Commissioners of Her Majesty's Woods, etc. Before 1809 the rent was as low as £80. It was then raised to £700, and at present the lettings are as follows :— Scrabster, £925 ; Dorrery, with shootings, £442 10s. ; Lythmore and Stemster, £514 18s. 3d. ; in all, £1882 8s. 3d.—Henderson's Gen. View, 49th Rep. Com, Woods, etc.—"Cawdor Papers,"

SCRABSTER ROADS, THURSO.

The chapter of the cathedral of Caithness, as it was constituted by Gilbert Murray, consisted of ten members, the
bishop being the chief, and receiving the fruits of six parishes
for his use. The archdeacon had for his prebend the church
of Bower. Among the appointments of the undignified canons
one had for his prebend the church of Olrig, one the church of
Dunnet, and a third the church of Canisbay.

Before the Reformation, Caithness would seem to have been
intensely popish. Every parish in the county abounded with
small chapels dedicated to particular saints or saintesses ; and
of these there were images, chiefly of stone, which the ignorant
vulgar regarded as objects of worship. The common people
were in fact little better than rank idolaters   Such was the
deep hold which Popery had in the district, that many years
after the Reformed faith was introduced, some of the older
inhabitants were accustomed, at particular times, to visit the
old chapels, and kneel before the images. The Reformed
ministers, of course, did all in their power to suppress this
debasing superstition ; but they found they had to do with a
very "stiff-necked generation." The work was not only
difficult, but perilous. In 1613, Dr Richard Merchiston of
Bower fell a martyr to his zeal against this species of hagiolatry.
He was in the habit of going through the adjoining parishes,
and demolishing the images wherever he found them. The
people of Wick, at the time, would appear to have been still
strongly attached to the old superstition. In the course of a
crusade through that parish, the worthy iconoclast entered the
royal burgh, and broke a stone image of their patron saint, St.
Fergus.* The inhabitants were shocked and exasperated at

* St. Fergus was no legendary or fabulous saint, but an Irish missionary
who came to Caithness about the middle, it is supposed, of the eighth
century, and did much to convert the natives, who were then in a state of
heathenism, to Christianity. His residence would appear to have been in
Wick, or its neighbourhood. After labouring for some time in that district
he went to Buchan, in Aberdeenshire, and thence to Glammis, in Angus,
where he died. His remains were deposited in the Abbey of Scone. "The
great house of Cheyne," says Cosmo Innes, "so much connected with
Caithness, was proprietor of the parish in Buchan, which derives its name of
St. Fergus from the Caithness saint."—See note by this eminent archæologist

what they deemed an act of sacrilege, and with difficulty were restrained by the magistrates from doing violence to his person. They secretly threatened vengeance, however, and a party of them following him as he went home in the evening, caught hold of him and drowned him in the river of Wick. It was given out that it was the saints who did it, and that St. Fergus, in particular, was seen astride of the parson in the water, and holding him down! A further idea of the semi-barbarous condition of the natives, and of the little regard paid to outward decency during the religious services of the church, may be gathered from the following anecdote in the old statistical account of Halkirk, "Some time after the Reformation," says the writer, "during the incumbency of the Reverend Mr Cumming, the lettergae, as the precentor was called, was one Tait, gardener in Brawl. This Tait sung so loud, and with such a large open mouth, that a young fellow of the name of Iverach was tempted to throw a stone into it, whereby his teeth were broken and his singing stopped at once, and he himself almost choked. Iverach immediately took to his heels, the service was converted to laughter, two of Tait's sons overtook him, and the scene was closed with a most desperate fight."

It was some considerable time after the Reformation before all the parishes in the county were provided with ministers. In 1576 only four of the parishes—namely, Wick, Thurso, Halkirk, and Dunnet—had pastors. The other parishes were indifferently supplied by laics, who read to the people, and were thence called readers. All the incumbencies, however, would seem to have been filled up about the year 1600.*

It may be interesting to state that a Mr Zachary Pont was minister of Bower in the year 1605. He married Margaret,

in "Bannatyne's Miscellany," Vol. III. One of the fairs in Wick is named after this saint the Fergusmas.

* The ministers were for a long period very poorly paid. In 1658, the stipend of Olrig, for instance, was only a little more than £25 stg. That of Halkirk in 1685 was £36 ; and even as low down as the middle of last century, the stipends averaged only £52.

daughter of the celebrated John Knox, by his second wife, who was a daughter of Lord Ochiltree. The Ochiltree family bore the name of Stewart, and were related to the Royal House of Stewart. Robert Pont, the father of Zachary, was minister of St. Cuthbert's in Edinburgh, and an intimate friend of the great reformer. James VI. offered him the bishopric of Caithness, which he refused. Mr Pont, the minister of Bower, had a daughter who was married into the family of Bishop Honeyman of Graemsay in Orkney; and the Honeymans afterwards by marriage became connected with the Dunbars of Scrabster, the Hendersons of Stemster, and other families in this county.

Education made still slower progress in the county than the reformation from Popery. The heritors disregarded, or at least evaded, the Parochial School Act; and the ministers, it would seem, were not very troublesome in urging upon them their bounden duty in regard to this most important matter. The peasantry were literally serfs, and the lairds were not particularly anxious to expand their ideas, and elevate them above that condition. Wick and Thurso were not legally supplied with schools till 1706;* and, even so late as 1772, Reay was without a statutory school. In some cases the heritors gave the pittance of legal salary, but no school-room or school-house, and the schoolmaster not unfrequently taught in the church or in the steeple! The steeple of the church at Dunnet was many years used as a school-room. Owing to the culpable negligence of the heritors, in not affording the necessary accommodation and means of education, the great body of the people, about the beginning of the eighteenth century, were in a lamentable state of ignorance. Not one in

---

* Since the first edition of this work, I find that Canisbay also got a statutory school in 1706. The salary given to the teacher was a chalder of victual and twenty pounds Scots, to be paid by the heritors in proportion to the valued rent of their respective properties. The heritors at the time were Sir James Sinclair of Mey, David Sinclair of Freswick, John Sinclair of Rattar for his lands in Stroma, Sir Alexander Mackenzie for the "nether town" of Stroma, Margaret Sinclair (relict of Alexander Sinclair of Brabster), Donald Groat of Warse, and John Groat, portioner of Duncansbay.

fifty could either read or write. In 1701, when a call was "moderated in" to a new minister in Wick, it is stated in the session records that the "call was unanimously subscribed by the heritors and elders present, and consented to by a great number who could not subscribe." This is the more astonishing as we find from the Synod records that, in 1687, parents keeping back their children from school were to be rebuked by the session, and to be compelled to send them to it, at least three days in the week, and, further, that none be married who cannot say the Lord's Prayer, Creed, and Ten Commandments! This, we suspect, would be found a pretty severe test even in our own enlightened age.

At the present day Caithness, in the matter of education, is pretty much on a par with most other counties in Scotland. The parochial schools, where the parishes are large, are supplemented by schools belonging to the General Assembly of the Church of Scotland, to the Society for Propagating Christian Knowledge, and to the Free Church. There are also a few subscription and adventure schools, which are chiefly taught in the winter season. Were it not for this addition to the means of education provided by law a great portion of the people would have been totally uneducated. This would have been particularly the case in such a parish as Latheron, for instance, which is about twenty-seven miles long and from ten to fifteen broad. When the last statistical account of this parish was drawn up there were in it altogether no fewer than eighteen schools. Of these, fourteen were unendowed, and, it is said, of very inferior quality. This might, indeed, be expected from the smallness of the emoluments, which averaged only from £3 to £4, including fees! "What is wanted," the writer of the account very sensibly remarks, "is not so much additional schools as additional salaries. Without the latter it is hopeless to attempt to raise the character of the former."

On the 5th of January, 1838, some Caithness gentlemen residing in Edinburgh organised a society, entitled "The

Edinburgh Caithness Association," chiefly with the laudable view of promoting the spread of education, and raising its standard in their native county. Its principal founder was Mr Benjamin Mackay, late of the High School, a man of great learning and distinguished ability. He drew up regulations and a programme of the various branches for examination, copies of which were transmitted to the several heritors, ministers, and teachers in the county. By the rules of the Association, competitions were to be held annually in Wick and Thurso. All the schools, male and female, in the two districts were to be open to them ; and the clergy of the different denominations were to be the examinators, and to award the prizes to the successful competitors. No constitution could have been framed freer from sectarian or party bias or with a more benevolent object. The scheme was warmly approved of, and most of the gentlemen and clergy in Caithness, and a good many residing out of it, but connected with the county by property or otherwise, joined the Association, and remitted donations and contributions in order to raise a fund for defraying the necessary expenses. A handsome legacy of £100 was bequeathed to it by Mr Francis Sutherland, an old Caithnessman who had long resided in the United States. The Earl of Caithness was made honorary president. In the month of September, 1841, Mr Mackay attended himself the first competitions at Wick and Thurso, examined the pupils, and inaugurated the Association with great *eclât*. Everything promised to go on flourishingly, when the unfortunate Disruption in 1843 took place, and converted the whole of Scotland into an arena of bitter religious strife. The evil spirit got into the competitions, and, though outward decency was observed, there was little brotherly kindness among the examinators, and matters did not get on harmoniously. In awarding the prizes cries of partiality were raised, and broad insinuations thrown out of collusion between some of the examiners and the teachers. A system of cramming for the express purpose of carrying off prizes was known to be carried on; and many parents exclaimed against the practice of certain teachers, who, for several months every year, confined their attention to a few of their more advanced scholars, while the general business of the school was handed over to one or two of the bigger boys.

In 1845, the Free Church ministers and their teachers withdrew from the competitions, on the ground that the Committee of the Association at Edinburgh had arbitrarily appointed as chairman two gentlemen connected with the Established Church, whereas they ought to have left each meeting to choose its own chairman. The seceders set on foot a rival Association, and competitions under its auspices were held at Wick and Thurso for the first time in 1846, and continued for a year or two afterwards. The parent Association, however, by certain concessions, brought about a reunion, which continued until 1853, when a second *disruption* took place, and the rival association was reorganised. In 1857 the committee at Edinburgh obtained the assistance of Dr Cumming, Government Inspector of the Free Church schools, as examiner-in-chief at Wick and Thurso—an arrangement which they fondly hoped would unite all parties. But in this expectation they were disappointed; for the clergymen of both churches, generally speaking, kept away from the meetings, and but few schools sent pupils to them. The rival association, which betrayed symptoms of unhealthiness from the beginning, has ceased to exist; and the original competitions are still carried on, but they are not supported as they ought to be, and they have lost a good deal of the public interest which at first attached to them. Such is a brief history of the Edinburgh Caithness Association, or rather of the competitions at Wick and Thurso, which shows how extremely difficult it is to work out the most benevolent scheme when it has to contend with the jealousies and prejudices of human nature. It cannot be denied, however, that in spite of these unfortunate jarrings and divisions, the competitions have done good. They have given a stimulus to education in the county;

and they might have been productive of still greater benefits if the mischievous spirit of party could have been excluded from the proceedings.

To the honour of the Association it deserves to be mentioned, that since the competitions commenced, not fewer than 1500 volumes of literary and religious publications have been distributed as prizes, exceeding in value £200, besides £100 expended in bursaries to students from Caithness attending the University of Edinburgh. Mr Andrew Snody, a gentleman who had long taken a warm interest in the cause of education, has been secretary of the association from its commencement.

The accommodation of the parochial schoolmasters of Caithness is of a very inferior description. With one or two exceptions, their houses are strictly built according to what Professor Pillans somewhere terms the "villanous Act of 1803," which provides that the dwelling-house shall consist of not more than two rooms, including the kitchen. From a paragraph in Lord Cockburn's "Memorial of his Times," it would appear that the schoolmasters of Scotland may be thankful that they got even this small accommodation. Lord-Advocate Hope was the person who officially promoted the measure in Parliament; and Cockburn says:—"Hope told me that he had considerable difficulty in getting even the two rooms, and that a great majority of the lairds and Scotch members were quite indignant at being obliged to build *palaces* for dominies!" Comment on this is unnecessary. An amelioration of the condition of the parish schoolmasters is imperatively required. It is vain to talk of elevating the standard of education without elevating the status of the teacher. If the parochial school establishment is to be maintained, it must be greatly extended, and the salary increased to such amount as will render the office of schoolmaster an object worthy of a man of talent and literary attainment.

CHAPTER XIV.

Several of the Established schoolmasters and ministers of Caithness of a former age were highly-talented men. Among the more distinguished of the latter for learning and ability, may be instanced the late Alexander Pope of Reay, Thomas Jolly of Dunnet, Dr. Morison of Canisbay, and the two brothers, William Smith of Bower and James Smith of Canisbay. A brief account of each of these clergymen may be interesting.

ALEXANDER POPE OF REAY.

The late Mr Pope of Reay was in some respects a remarkable man. He was a native of the parish of Loth, in the county of Sutherland, of which parish his father, the Reverend Hector Pope, was Episcopal clergyman. Having adopted Presbyterian views, the son became a licentiate of the Church of Scotland, and on the 5th September, 1734, was ordained minister of Reay. The new incumbent was admirably fitted for the charge. He was possessed of great bodily strength as well as vigour of intellect; and strange though it may sound, he was not a little indebted to the former quality for his success as a moral and religious reformer. At the time of his induction, the parish of Reay might be said to be in a state of semi-barbarism. The natives were in general grossly ignorant, disorderly, and intractable, and in his intercourse with them Mr Pope had frequent occasion to avail himself of his physical powers. During the first year or two of his ministry, he never went through the parish, or even ascended the pulpit, without a good cudgel in his hand, either to defend himself in case of attack, or to inflict corporeal punishment on such reprobates as were inaccessible to reproof in any other way. Mr Carruthers, in his excellent memoir of Pope the poet, having occasion to allude to the minister of Reay, says, " He used to drive his graceless parishioners to church with a stick, when he found them engaged on Sundays at games out of doors.   Another of his reforming expedients was making all the rough characters of his parish elders of the church, so that, invested with ecclesiastical dignity and responsibility, they might be ashamed of vicious practices."

Touching this matter, there are several amusing anecdotes told of Mr Pope.   I will just mention one of them.   There was one resolute character, in the outskirts of the parish, who had hitherto defied all attempts to get him to come to church.   The minister had repeatedly sent messages to him, expressing a wish to see him at the manse, but Donald always declined the honour, and said that he had no desire or ambition to cultivate his acquaintance.   The parties as yet had not seen each other ; and as Donald would not visit the minister, the minister resolved to visit Donald.   Accordingly he set out one day, and arrived in the evening at the house of his refractory parishioner.   He passed himself off as a wayfaring man, and as Highlanders have at all times been noted for hospitality, he no sooner solicited quarters for the night than it was granted him.   He was provided with a homely but substantial repast, and he and his host chatted away very agreeably till bed-time. Donald then pointed to his couch, a primitive shake-down of heather, with a deer-skin for a coverlet, in one corner of the hut.   But the stranger declined betaking himself to repose until they had gone through the duty of worship.

" You will have to pray, Donald," said he.

Donald looked at the man with astonishment, and said he would do nothing of the kind ; he had no talent in that way.

" But you must pray," rejoined the stranger ; " I will make you do it, and on your knees too."

" Will you ?" said Donald ; " you'll be a clever fellow then ; no, Mr Pope himself, the minister, strong man though he be, will not make me do that."

" Well, I'm Mr Pope," said the stranger ; "and as you are an obstinate sinner, I order you to go to your knees instantly, or you'll repent it from every bone in your body."

Donald's wrath was now fairly kindled. Up he started to his feet, and up started the parson at the same time, and, without further parley, they set to with clenched fists in regular style. But Donald, though he fought like a hero, was no match for the minister ; and at length yielding up the contest, he said that he would try to do his bidding. He then knelt down, and uttered the following ejaculation :—" O Lord ! thou knowest herself cannot pray."

" That will do," cried Mr Pope ; " that is a very good beginning. I shall conclude the service of the evening myself with a few words of exhortation, after which we will retire to bed."

This singular visit to Donald was, under Providence, the means of producing a complete and happy change in his conduct. From that day henceforward, he became a reformed man ; and the minister, who felt a peculiar interest in his new convert, made him an elder of the church.

The worthy minister, with many solid and excellent qualities, had a strong dash of eccentricity and enthusiasm in his composition ; and one romantic adventure of his forms a highly interesting passage of his life. Mr Carruthers thus tells the story :—" The northern Alexander Pope entertained a profound admiration for his illustrious namesake of England ; and it is a curious and well-ascertained fact that the simple, enthusiastic clergyman, in the summer of 1732,* rode on his pony all the way from Caithness to Twickenham, in order to pay the poet a visit. The latter felt his dignity a little touched by the want of the necessary pomp and circumstance with which the minister first presumed to approach his domicile ; but after the ice of outward ceremony had in some degree been broken, and their intellects had come into contact, the

---

* There is an error of date here. Mr Pope was not minister of Reay in 1732, but was residing at Dornoch, and it must have been from the latter place that he rode to Twickenham.

poet became interested, and a friendly feeling was established between them. Several interviews took place, and the poet presented his good friend and namesake, the minister of Reay, with a copy of the subscription edition of the Odyssey in five volumes quarto."

Besides being an able and popular preacher, Mr Pope of Reay was a man of considerable literary talent, and a celebrated archæologist in his day. He translated from the Latin into English as much of the "Orcades" of Torfaeus as bears on the ancient history of Caithness; and he is the author of the Appendix, No. V., in Pennant's Tour, which gives a brief account of the antiquities and statistics of the several parishes in Caithness and Sutherland. He died on the 2nd March, 1782, after an incumbency of forty-eight years.

MR JOLLY OF DUNNET.

The late Mr Thomas Jolly, minister of Dunnet, was a native of Mearns or Kincardineshire, and was born on the 24th January, 1754. His parents belonged to the Scotch Episcopal Church, and he himself was, of course, bred up in that form of worship; but he changed his views, and joined the Established Church. This step, it is said, greatly displeased his relatives, who were keen Episcopalians, and looked upon the Church of Scotland as no church at all. He came first to Caithness as tutor to the late James Traill, Esquire of Ratter. In 1778 he was appointed assistant to Mr Traill's father, the Reverend Dr. Traill of Dunnet; and, on the death of that clergyman, was presented to the church of Dunnet, by the late Sir John Sinclair, and settled minister thereof in the year 1784. Mr Jolly was a most ingenious man, and an excellent scholar. Previous to receiving the presentation to Dunnet, he had been offered the professorship of humanity in one of the colleges of the United States—a situation for which he was eminently qualified by his high classical attainments, and his profound and accurate knowledge of the Latin language. He was perhaps the best Latinist of his time in the north of Scotland,

Being unwilling, however, to relinquish his views towards the ministry, he declined the honour of the academical chair.

At the time of his settlement at Dunnet, there was no medical practitioner nearer than Wick or Thurso; and having a good deal of medical skill himself, he was for many years both the physician and the pastor of his people. He always kept a stock of medicines, which he gave gratuitously to the sick; and his manner of treating diseases was so successful, that individuals came to consult him from all parts of the country.

Though highly esteemed by his congregation, Mr Jolly was not what is usually termed a popular preacher. He never indulged in vague declamation, or in any of those extravagances of gesture and expression that are so taking with the uneducated vulgar. He chiefly addressed himself to the understanding of his hearers; and while he gave due weight to the fundamental doctrines of religion, he always insisted on the practical effects which those doctrines were intended to produce. The matter of his discourses was always instructive, clear, and well arranged, and his style of composition singularly neat and chaste. In 1822 he published a sermon "On the Redeemed from the Earth," from Rev. xiv. 3. The leading idea is original, or at least not very common among divines; and the discourse is a remarkable production, full of ingenuity, and written in his usual chaste and perspicuous style. Dr. Andrew Thomson, in his review of the sermon in the "Christian Instructor," gave it all due praise as a most ingenious exposition, though he would not say the point was demonstrably established of that particular passage of the Apocalypse. Mr Jolly was also the author of a letter to Dr. Chalmers immediately before the Disruption, which letter, from its remarkable ability—for he was then verging on ninety years of age—and its mild but earnest tone of remonstrance, coming from an aged brother, who, it might be said, was calmly waiting his removal to a better world, excited at the time a good deal of public attention. Being zealously and conscientiously attached to the Established Church, as, in his view, the noblest and most perfect Christian institute in the world, he deeply deplored this calamitous event, which he considered calculated to embitter all the sources of social happiness and to exercise an injurious effect on the best interests of religion. He devoted much of his time to the study of the Scriptures in the original; and amongst his unpublished writings was found an elaborate treatise, entitled an "Essay on Justification," extending to upwards of 100 pages. It is divided into seven sections; and from the great care with which it is written, he would seem at one period to have had the intention of publishing it.

At the time of his death in 1845, he had nearly completed his 91st year, having held the incumbency for the unusually long period of sixty years. In person Mr Jolly was considerably below the middle size, but his head was large and well developed, and his eye keen and penetrating. In his habits he was remarkable for his regularity, and this must no doubt have greatly conduced to that uninterrupted good health which he so long enjoyed. He never had an assistant, and he preached until within a fortnight of his death. He was succeeded in the charge by his son, the Reverend Peter Jolly, a highly-talented man and an excellent preacher, who, at the time of his father's decease, was minister of Canisbay.

DR. MORISON OF CANISBAY.

Dr. John Morrison, the author of some of our finest paraphrases, was a native of the parish of Cairnie, in the presbytery of Strathbogie and county of Aberdeen. He was born in the year 1750. After finishing his academical course at King's College, Aberdeen, he came to Caithness in the year 1768, to teach the family of a Mr Manson of Greenland.* Having remained two years in Greenland, Mr Morison removed to the parish of Halkirk, and was tutor for three years in the family

* The Greenland mentioned above is the name of a township in the parish of Dunnet.

of Mr Williamson of Banniskirk.   After that he taught the
school of Thurso for about half a year.   On becoming a licentiate of the church he went to Edinburgh, where he resided
some months, improving himself in the art of elocution and
enlarging his knowledge of the Greek language and literature,
of which he was passionately fond, under Professor Dalziel.
While in Edinburgh he made the acquaintance of Dr. Macfarlane, who was afterwards appointed one of the committee for
making the selection of the paraphrases that were added to
the psalmody.   After leaving that city he went north, and was
engaged as tutor in the family of Colonel Sutherland of Uppat,
in the county of Sutherland.   While there he was fortunate
enough to meet Mr Sinclair of Freswick, sheriff of Caithness,
who formed such a high opinion of Mr Morison's talents, that
on the death of Mr Brodie, the minister, in 1780, he presented
him to the church of Canisbay, of which he was the patron.
There is another account which says :*—At Uppat Mr Morison
fell in with the bishop of Derry, in Ireland, who happened to
be on a tour through Scotland.   He accompanied the bishop
to Caithness, and was introduced by him to Mr Sinclair of
Freswick.   The worthy prelate, who had formed a high idea
of young Morison's literary attainments, interested himself so
much in his favour that he got Mr Sinclair to promise that he
would present him to the church of Canisbay when it should
become vacant.

As a preacher, Mr Morison was greatly distinguished for his
eloquence.   His command of language and liveliness of fancy,
it is said, were such that he seldom was at the trouble to
write out his sermons, but preached extempore, or at least
with very little previous study.   Of his uncommon readiness
in this way an interesting anecdote is told.   Being in Wick on
a certain occasion, Mr Sutherland, the minister, happened to
say that he would give him a text from which he would not

---

* This latter account, which appears to us as the correct one, is handed
down from a deceased clergyman of the county who was a contemporary of
Dr. Morison, and intimately acquainted with him.

be able to extemporise a sermon. Mr Morison said if it was a scriptural text he would try it. Accordingly on the Sunday forenoon, after he had ascended the pulpit, the precentor handed him a slip of paper on which was the following from Luke xiv. 34, "But if the salt has lost its savour, wherewith shall it be seasoned ?" When the introductory part of the service was over Mr Morison gave out his text, and, seemingly with the greatest ease, preached a most eloquent and instructive discourse, to the great delight of the congregation and the utter astonishment of their pastor.

On the 3rd of August, 1792, he obtained the degree of D.D. from the University of Edinburgh, on the recommendation of Professor Dalziel.

He sent twenty paraphrases to Dr. Macfarlane, who laid them before the committee. The merit of the whole was acknowledged ; but owing to the great number of contributors, and the limited number of pieces to be printed, only seven of Dr. Morison's were selected. One of his rejected paraphrases is the following, which we think equal in point of poetical merit to any of those that were admitted into the collection :—

ISAIAH xlii. 10, 13.

A new song to the Lord our God,
  All ends of the earth begin ;
In songs of praise break forth, ye isles,
  And all that dwell therein.

Ye rocks, with all your vocal tribes,
  Aloft your voices raise ;
Ye seas, with all your swarms, declare
  The great Creator's praise.

And ye that oft, in whelming floods,
  His works of wonder view,
O sing of Him whose saving light
  Beams marvellous on you.

In hallelujah's long and loud,
  To Him all praise be given,
Whose presence fills the spacious earth,
  And boundless waste of heaven.

The committee* at the same time expressed their regret that more could not be admitted, without seeming on their part to neglect or overlook the many contributions of others. His paraphrases are numbers 19, 21, 27, 28, 29, 30, and 35. Several poetical pieces of his on various subjects appeared in " Rudiman's Weekly Magazine," between the years 1771 and 1775, bearing the signature of "Musaeus." But these do not rise above the ordinary magazine poetry of the period, which, the student of English literature knows, was dull and mediocre enough. It is only as a sacred poet that Dr. Morison shone with any brilliancy. His genius kindled at the Christian altar. It seemed to catch inspiration from the divine theme ; and his compositions in this way are characterised by a beautiful simplicity and depth of poetic feeling that strike the most careless reader.

Among other amusements of his leisure hours he translated Herodian's history from the Greek, a part of which, as a specimen of the performance, he sent to professor Dalziel, who praised it very highly ; but from the original work not possessing any great inherent interest, it was never published. He also collected the topographical history of Caithness for George Chalmers' "Caledonia."

Soon after his induction to Canisbay, he married Miss Catherine Black, only daughter of Mr James Black, factor for the Duke of Gordon. By this lady he had a son and three daughters.

Dr. Morison died on the 12th June, 1798—comparatively a young man—in the forty-eighth year of his age and eighteenth of his ministry. The last time he appeared in the pulpit was during the war with France, when, the country being menaced with danger from her enemies at home and abroad, the church was, on some particular occasion, called upon to arouse the patriotic feelings of the people, and to set before them the

* In the list of members of this committee appear the names of Principal Robertson, Dr. Hugh Blair, Dr. Webster, Professor George Hill, Dr. John Ogilvie, and Dr. Alexander Carlyle of Inveresk.

many blessings and advantages, civil and religious, which they enjoyed under the British constitution. His text was from 1 Samuel x., 24, "God save the king." The subject was one peculiarly suited to his genius ; and his discourse is said to have been a masterpiece of eloquence, and to have electrified the congregation. The complaint of which he died was a decline brought on by exposure to wet and cold. His remains were interred in the churchyard of Canisbay ; and it is mortifying to think that not even a common slab indicates the spot where reposes the dust of one of the best poets of the Church of Scotland.

MR SMITH OF BOWER.

Mr William Smith was a native of the county, and the eldest son of the Rev. Alexander Smith, minister of Olrig. On the death of the Reverend James Oliphant of Bower, he was presented to that living, on the 17th September, 1788, by Miss Scott, eldest daughter and heiress of Major-General Scott of Balcomie, in whose family the patronage was then vested. The presentation was signed by commissioners appointed by Miss Scott, one of whom was the celebrated Henry Dundas, treasurer of the navy. At the time of his induction he was quite a young man, and for many years he was one of the most popular preachers in the county. He was particularly distinguished as a linguist. Besides being acquainted with several of the modern languages, he was a thorough proficient in Greek, Latin, and Hebrew. Latterly, he applied himself vigorously to the study of the Gaelic, under the instruction of an old catechist from the Highlands, and he made such progress in that language, that he fancied he could preach in it. At any rate, he was fully bent on giving it a trial. Accordingly, having on one occasion gone to Halkirk to assist at the communion (Gaelic and English discourses being regularly delivered there), he intimated to Mr Cameron, the minister, his wish to preach a Gaelic sermon to the people. Mr Cameron, a noted humorist, was amazed at the proposal, and it was with no little difficulty that he got him advised to give up the idea. He assured him that none but a born Highlander could preach in Gaelic, and that if he attempted to open his mouth in that tongue, he would, with his bad pronunciation and his blunders, set the whole congregation a-laughing at him.

With a vast fund of learning, much quaint and satirical humour, and a great knowledge of human nature, Mr Smith mingled a strong dash of eccentricity. One of his peculiarities was a fondness for travelling in the night season, and particularly in bad weather. If he happened to be at a meeting of Presbytery in Wick or Thurso, the darkest and stormiest night in winter would not deter him from setting out and proceeding on his journey homewards.

Allusion has been made to his knowledge of human nature. None knew better than he the habits, modes of thinking, prejudices, and superstitions of the peasantry of Caithness; and when he descanted on this subject from the pulpit, "holding the mirror up to nature," it was a perfect treat to hear him. In what may be termed moral anatomy, he was unrivalled as a dissector. His knife was blunt, but it did the work of cutting up effectually. He was particularly severe on those who gave long prayers, and made a great noise about religion, but whose conduct did not correspond with their profession. It happened that one of his own elders, a decent sort of man upon the whole, had, on one occasion, imbibed rather more liquor than was consistent with the dignity and responsibility of his office. The matter soon reached the ears of the minister, and the method he took to rebuke the erring member of his kirk-session was not a little strange. The next Sabbath, when the religious service was over, but before the pronouncing of the blessing, and when the elder in question was going round with the "brod," or ladle, for the usual collection for the poor, Mr Smith rose and thus addressed the congregation :—" My brethren, we are told in Scripture that the elders of old were filled with the Holy Ghost ; but now-a-days they're filled with John Barleycorn !" Having thus delivered himself, he resumed his seat in the pulpit. As the fama against the elder was widely known through the parish, every eye in the church was instantly turned on the poor man, and the congregation could not help giving way to a smothered laugh.

Mr Smith published one or two sermons during his lifetime ; but although they were highly evangelical and learned, they did not add much to his literary fame. He was unfortunately a careless composer, immethodical, and digressive ; and his discourses wanted that connected train of thought and elegance of style so necessary to secure the attention of the better class of readers. He died in 1846, in the seventy-eighth year of his age.

MR JAMES SMITH OF CANISBAY.

Mr James Smith, who succeeded Dr. Morison, was a most amiable and accomplished man, and an excellent classical scholar. Before his appointment to Canisbay, he was for a short time tutor at Barrogill Castle, in the family of the Earl of Caithness. Mr Smith was a man of fine taste. His sermons, which he wrote with great care, were models of elegance, and reminded one of the style of Blair. They were, indeed, too fine for his audience ; and the consequence was that he was not popular as a preacher, though in every other respect he was much esteemed and beloved by his people.

Mr Smith's life presents few incidents or salient points of much biographical interest ; but the following anecdote may be given as a proof of his kindly, unsuspecting nature :— Living as he did so near John O'Groat's, and being noted for his hospitable disposition, Mr Smith had occasionally a visit from some of those tourists who, in the summer and autumn months, came to see that celebrated locality. One forenoon a stranger gentleman called at the manse, and, addressing the minister in Latin, told him that he was a native of Hungary, a Protestant, and a Professor of Humanity in one of the colleges in that country, and that he was at present travelling through Britain chiefly for the benefit of his health. He had only a few words of English, but he knew his reverence was a scholar, and would be able to converse with him in the good old Roman tongue. Mr Smith felt interested, and, brushing up his Latin, said he was happy to make his acquaintance, and asked him to remain and take dinner with him, which he readily consented to do. The conversation was carried on in Latin—rather stiffly at first on the part of the minister, who was often at a loss to give the Latin terms for common things. The professor, considering that he was a valetudinarian, played a capital knife and fork, and relished very much his tumbler of toddy, declaring that the man who first invented it should have had a statue erected to his memory! To entertain his host he sung with great spirit some of the odes of Horace; and, in short, proved so intellectual and fascinating a companion that Mr Smith—who was then untroubled with the cares of matrimony—kept him at the manse for about a month, during which time the professor enjoyed himself greatly, and made a rapid proficiency in English! On taking his leave, the kind-hearted clergyman expressed himself as sorry at parting with him, and said he sincerely hoped he would get safe home to his own country. But the good, worthy man was in this instance imposed upon. The professor was not the "genuine article," for it was afterwards found out that he was an accomplished rogue and a Jesuit in disguise.

Mr Smith died in 1826, at the comparatively early age of 51.

The Established Church and the Free Church embrace the greater part of the community in Caithness. The other religious denominations are the Original and U.P. Seceders, the Baptists, and Independents, with a small body of Reformed Presbyterians, and another of Episcopalians. The Romish Church has no footing in the county, and there is not, we believe, a single pervert to Romanism among the entire population. There is a chapel in Pulteneytown for the accommodation of such strangers of that communion as come to Wick at the time of the herring fishing, which usually lasts about three months, but except for that brief period the chapel is seldom opened or used as a place of religious worship. The Original Seceders and the Baptists have long been established in the county. One of the first ministers of the former was a Mr Dowie, whose memory is still held in great veneration by that body. He was settled in Thurso about the year 1771, and died in 1797. The founder of the Baptists in Caithness was Sir William Sinclair of Keiss, who belonged to the Dunbeath family, and was, properly speaking, baronet of Dunbeath. His lady was a daughter of Sir James Dunbar of Hempriggs. On embracing Baptist views, Sir William went to London, and was there formally baptised, and admitted a member of his adopted church. He commenced preaching in Caithness about the year 1750, and continued to do so with great zeal for the space of fourteen years. He formed a church at Keiss, over which he regularly presided as pastor. In 1765 he left the county and went to Edinburgh, where he died two years afterwards. Sir William published in his lifetime a small collection of hymns of his own composition, sixty in number, which are still sung—or were till very lately—at the meetings of the Baptists for religious exercises at Keiss. In this peculiar department of sacred literature the worthy baronet did not shine. The hymns contain no poetry properly so-called, but they indicate a mind imbued with deep and fervent piety. Sir William, we have heard, was in his younger days a short time in the army. While there, he learned to become an expert swordsman ; and touching his skill in this way the following curious anecdote is related :—A good many years after he had retired from the service, and while he was one forenoon in his study intently engaged in perusing some treatise bearing on his peculiar religious views, his valet announced that a stranger wished to see him. The servant was ordered to show him into the apartment, when in stalked a strong muscular-looking man, with a formidable Andrea

Ferrara hanging by his side, and making a low obeisance, thus addressed the baronet :—

"Sir William, I hope you will pardon my intrusion. I am a native of England, and a professional swordsman. In the course of my travels through Scotland, I have not yet met with a gentleman able to cope with me in the noble science of defence. Since I came to Caithness, I have heard that you are an adept at my favourite weapon, and I have called to see if you would do me the honour to exchange a few passes with me, just in the way of testing our respective abilities."

Sir William was not a little astonished and amused at this singular request, and replied that he had long ago thrown aside the sword, and except in case of necessity, never intended to use it any more. But the stranger would take no denial, and earnestly insisted that he would favour him with a proof of his skill.

"Very well," said Sir William, "to please you I shall do so."

And rising and fetching his sword, he desired the fellow, who to appearance was an ugly-looking customer, to draw and defend himself. After a pass or two, Sir William with a dexterous stroke cut off a button from the vest of his opponent.

"Will that satisfy you," inquired the baronet, "or shall I go a little deeper and draw blood ?"

"O, I am perfectly satisfied," said the other. "I find I have for once met with a gentleman who knows how to handle the sword."

The story ends here ; but there is little doubt that the worthy baronet, before he allowed his visitant to depart, would seize the opportunity of reasoning with him on the folly of his conduct, and directing his attention to a more rational and Christian course of life. The Caithness Baptists cherish with affectionate regard the memory of Sir William. The Independents in Caithness owe their origin to the visit of the celebrated Messrs Haldane and Aikman to the county in 1797. Their first minister in Thurso was the late Mr Edward Mackay, a native of Perthshire.   In 1805 Mr Mackay adopted the views of the Baptists, went to Edinburgh in order to join that body, and on his return to Thurso became the pastor of the congregation in that town.   He was a superior preacher, and a most amiable and worthy man.   He died in 1845.   The Reformed Presbyterians have existed among us for some time back ; but the Episcopalians are of recent introduction, and consist principally of strangers from the south.   Their preaching station is in Wick.

CHAPTER XV.

In this chapter I purpose to give a brief account of a few of the most distinguished laymen that Caithness has produced, at the head of whom deservedly stands

SIR JOHN SINCLAIR.

Sir John was the son of George Sinclair of Ulbster and Lady Janet, daughter of William, Lord Strathnaver of the House of Sutherland, and was born at Thurso Castle on the 10th of May, 1754. His father died in the prime of life, when the young proprietor, then only sixteen years of age, was left under the sole guardianship of his mother, fortunately for him a shrewd, able, and managing woman. His first tutor was Mr John Logan, afterwards distinguished as a poet and divine, whom the celebrated Dr. Hugh Blair of Edinburgh had recommended as a person every way qualified for the task.* Nature is often capricious in her gifts, and Logan's physique was not in his favour. His appearance, manners, and dialect were all uncouth; and Lady Janet, apprehensive that her son might catch, in some measure, the rusticity and awkwardness of his tutor, stated to Dr. Blair her anxiety to have him placed in other hands. The accomplished professor of rhetoric took a very different view of the matter. "Your ladyship," said he, "in selecting a tutor for your son, should prefer a scholar to a dancing-master." In the case of Logan, Lady Janet, with all her shrewdness, failed to discern the fine genius that lay

---

* In drawing up this notice of the late Sir John Sinclair, I have been indebted for several of the leading incidents and particulars to his "Life," written by Archdeacon Sinclair, and also to a "Memoir" of the deceased from the pen of Miss Catherine Sinclair, the accomplished authoress.

hid under an uncouth exterior. The future poet,* who must have seen that his appearance and manners were distasteful to his employers, did not remain long at Thurso Castle. Lady Janet had the good sense, however, to give her son all the advantages of an excellent education. After a due course of elementary instruction at the High School, he attended the Universities both of Edinburgh and Glasgow, and finally completed his studies at Oxford. It was at Glasgow, while attending the lectures of the celebrated Dr. Adam Smith, that he is said to have imbibed a taste for the science of political economy.

In 1780, when he had attained his 26th year, he was returned member of Parliament for his native county, and in that noble assembly of legislators he soon distinguished himself by his zealous advocacy of every measure that he considered to be for the national benefit. When he entered into public life, the agriculture of Great Britain was at a very low stand, and he was among the first, if not the very first, that gave it an impulse. By his exertions, the Board of Agriculture was established, of which he was with great propriety elected president. His first step, on the establishment of the board, was to open a correspondence with all the most distinguished cultivators of the soil, both in this country and on the Continent. The varied and highly-important information which he thus received he afterwards arranged and published in a work entitled the "Code of Agriculture."

* Logan was born at Soutra, in East Lothian, in 1748. In 1773 he was ordained minister of South Leith. While there he published a volume of poems, and a tragedy entitled Runamede, which was acted in the theatre at Edinburgh. In Scotland, a large section of the laity, as well as the clergy, have, on moral grounds, always entertained a strong prejudice against theatrical representations ; and this drama of the minister of South Leith, along with some imprudencies of conduct, rendered him so unpopular with his congregation that he found it necessary to resign his charge, and, on obtaining a retiring allowance, he went to London in 1785, and eked out a little to his income by writing for the press. He died there in 1788 at the early age of 40. When students at the University of Edinburgh, an intimacy, founded on a similarity of literary tastes, took place between him and Michael Bruce, the poet of Lochleven. It has long been disputed which of them is the author of the Ode to the Cuckoo, one of the sweetest little poems in the language ; but the general belief seems now to be that it is the production of Bruce.

In 1786 he received the honour of knighthood from George the Third. At this time he made a tour of the Continent, for the purpose of enlarging his sphere of knowledge and seeing men and manners abroad. He visited Sweden, Denmark, Russia, Prussia, Holland, France, etc., and was everywhere received with much flattering distinction. Among other foreign potentates to whom he was presented was Catherine, the celebrated Empress of Russia, from whom he had a most gracious reception. In the course of his travels, he formed an acquaintance with several of the most eminent political and literary characters on the Continent, and he collected a great deal of useful information, especially on his favourite subjects of finance and agriculture. Some of the scenes which he witnessed in "high places" abroad are not a little amusing. When at Berlin he supped one evening at the house of Count Finkenstein, the prime minister. After supper the party engaged in the game of "blind man's buff," in which the worthy baronet joined. "The dinners," says Sir John, "were miserably long and tedious, and the guests ate most voraciously. The old custom in Germany was to get up between the services, and to walk about in another room until the second service was put on the table and ready to be devoured. The longest dinner I ever witnessed was at the house of the Prince de Lachen, where the company sat eating for nearly five hours!" Sir John's patriotic exertions in raising two fencible battalions, the one in 1794 and the other in 1795, have been already noticed. They were such as tended greatly to exalt his character in the estimation of the country.

Sir John was a most indefatigable writer. One of the earliest of his productions was a collection of Scotticisms. This brochure was written with the laudable purpose of assimilating the conversational language of England and Scotland, and preventing the use of those solecisms on the part of the natives of North Britain which expose them to the ridicule of their southern neighbours. Of the liability of even well-educated Scotsmen to commit themselves in this way, Miss Sinclair gives the following anecdote :—" Lord Melville had one day asked Mr Pitt to give him a horse the *length* of Richmond, to which the minister facetiously replied that he had none quite so *long*."

Among his various publications was a work entitled the " Code of Health and Longevity," which was embellished with prints of the longest-lived persons throughout Europe.   They were all frightfully ugly.   Of this production a celebrated critic is reported to have said, that to read it through was sufficient to throw one into a consumption.   It is, however, notwithstanding this bit of critical sarcasm, an excellent compilation of its kind, and contains many useful hints and suggestions on diet and regimen, and the best means of prolonging health.

But Sir John's most celebrated work, and that on which his fame chiefly rests, is his Statistical History of Scotland.   The idea of this undertaking was quite original.   Nay, the very term statistics itself—taken from the German *statistik*—was new to the language.   The work, which was one of incredible labour, was begun in 1790, prosecuted for the space of seven years, and finally published in January, 1798, in twenty-one thick volumes.   Sir John had great difficulty in bringing it out.   " In order to complete the work," says one of his friends, " he required answers to 160 queries from nearly 1000 ministers. To many of them such topics were strange or distasteful ; and all of them encountered difficulties themselves in the shyness and sometimes in the supersition of their informants.   Tenants would not tell the produce of their farms, for fear that their rents should be raised ; and Highland shepherds would not count their flocks, lest their vain curiosity should entail judgment on the fleecy people."   Several parishes did not make any returns ; and to these Sir John was obliged to send persons at his own expense, whom he styled " statistical commissioners," to draw up reports.   Add to all this, many of his best friends prophesied that the undertaking would not succeed and that it would be so much labour and money thrown away. But no discouragement could damp Sir John's zeal and perseverance ; and he had the satisfaction at last of seeing his labours crowned with the most complete success. When the work made its appearance, its great merits were at once acknowledged, and every one lauded the indefatigable industry and patriotic spirit of the enterprising editor. Even the most captious critics were forced to admit the immense value of·a work which gave a particular and succinct account of the topography, agriculture, antiquities, customs, and manners, and, it might be said, the morals of every parish in Scotland. Many important benefits resulted from its publication. Among others, several oppressive feudal burdens were abolished, and a great impulse was given to the improvement of Scottish agriculture. The clergy of the Established Church were also benefitted by it. A law was passed for regulating the augmentation of their livings, either from the parochial funds or, where the tithes were exhausted, from a parliamentary grant in their behalf. By this enactment it was provided that £150 per annum should be the lowest stipend of a clergyman of the Church of Scotland. The whole of the profits arising from the sale of the publication were generously assigned to the Society for the Sons of the Clergy in Scotland.

The following anecdote, which we quote from an excellent writer, affords a remarkable illustration of Sir John's benevolent disposition and energetic promptitude in relieving commercial distress at a critical period in the history of the country :—" In 1793 the stagnation produced by the war led to an unusual number of bankruptcies, and many of the first houses in Manchester and Glasgow were tottering, not so much from want of property, but because the usual sources of trade and credit were for the time shut up. A period of intense distress among the labouring classes seemed imminent, when Sir John urged in Parliament that Exchequer Notes to the amount of five millions should be issued immediately as a loan to such merchants as would give security. This suggestion was adopted, and his offer to carry out his plan, in conjunction with certain members named by him, was also accepted. The vote was passed late at night, and early next morning Sir John, anticipating the delays of officialism and red tape, proceeded to bankers in the city, and borrowed of them, on his own personal security, the sum of £70,000, which he despatched the same evening to those merchants who were in the most urgent need of assistance. Pitt, meeting Sir John in the House, expressed his great regret that the pressing wants of Manchester could not be supplied so soon as was desirable, adding, ' The money cannot be raised for some days.' It is already gone ! it left London by to-night's mail,' was Sir John's triumphant reply ; and in afterwards relating the anecdote, he added with a smile of pleasure, ' Pitt was as much startled as if I had stabbed him !' "*

Sir John's principal original work is his History of the Public Revenue of Great Britain, which is allowed by competent judges to display a thorough knowledge of the intricate subject of finance, and to be very ably written. Sir John's mind was one of that active cast that seems to be continually on the stretch for information. Of this insatiable thirst for knowledge, the following anecdote, taken from a work entitled " Anecdotes of Painters," affords a lively instance :—" Happening one day to dine in company with Sir David Wilkie, the painter, that distinguished artist was asked, in the course of conversation, if any particular circumstance had led him to adopt that profession. Sir John enquired, " Had your father, mother, or any of your relations a turn for painting, or what led you to that art ?' Sir David replied, ' The truth is, Sir John, it is you that made me a painter.' ' How I !' exclaimed the baronet. ' I never had the pleasure of meeting you before.' Sir David then gave the following explanation :—' When you were drawing up the Statistical Account of Scotland, my father, who was a clergyman in Fife, had much correspondence with you respecting his parish, in the course of which you sent him a coloured drawing of a soldier of your Highland fencible regiment. I was so delighted with the sight of it, that I was constantly drawing copies, and was thus insensibly transformed into a painter.' "

During the famous Ossianic controversy, Sir John warmly supported the side espoused by Dr. Blair and others of that school. On this point Miss Sinclair says, " Never indifferent to the fame of Scotland on any subject, the zealous patriot took infinite pains to collect evidence on the genuineness of Ossian's poems, found what he supposed to be the original manuscript in Gaelic, which he placed in the hands of the Highland Society of London, and published them with a pre-face showing that Macpherson was only the translator."

There never yet was a great or celebrated man without his weak points, and Sir John Sinclair was no exception to the general rule. The worthy baronet was full of projects, some of them, it must be admitted, not a little amusing, and not easily reconcilable with his naturally sagacious and philosophic turn of mind. He was a great advocate for the improvement of British wool; and one of his schemes was the introduction of Spanish sheep into Caithness. The native sheep are subject to a disease called the "rot," arising chiefly from wet and cold; and, to secure the interesting strangers against this malady, and keep their feet warm and dry, he ordered a sufficient quantity of leather, and had them all equipped in boots ! It is needless to say that the sanguine baronet was disappointed in his expectations. The boots did not preserve the sheep from the rot, and the whole thing turned out a miserable failure.

Another of his schemes* was a plan to enliven Caithness with the music of nightingales ! "He employed London bird fanciers' to procure nightingales' eggs, and Caithness shepherds to find the nests of the equally soft-billed robin redbreast. The London eggs soon displaced the Caithness ones, and robin carefully hatched and reared the embryo melodists. In sum-mer, numbers of young nightingales were seen about the

* It is quite possible that this latter story may be without any real founda-tion, but it appeared not many years ago in a respectable publication.

bushes ; but at the autumn migration they disappeared, never to return." In these two instances the worthy baronet, in his zeal for improvement, seemed to forget the lessons of natural history, and to overlook the obvious influences of climate on the animal creation. Caithness was never intended by nature to be the *habitat* of Merino sheep or of nightingales.

A third scheme of his had no better success. " In the year 1798," says Captain Henderson, " Sir John being determined to give a fair trial to the bee husbandry on his Langwell estate, ordered twenty-one hives, with a stock of bees, from the southern counties, and employed a person who was recommended to him to superintend them. They were brought to the garden of Langwell, situated in a warm valley, sheltered from the north and west by the Morven mountains. The superintendent was supplied with a stock of honey to feed the bees through the winter and spring. The result, however, was that all the bees died, it is said in consequence of the superintendent or manager having taken the honey for his own purposes and neglected the bees."

Sir John continued to represent his native county in Parliament for the long period of 31 years. In 1811 he vacated his seat, and was succeeded by his son, Sir George, then Mr Sinclair, younger of Ulbster, a most accomplished scholar and a man of fine talents. As some reward for his public services, he was appointed cashier of the Excise, with an income of £2,000 a year. Never was a Government appointment more deservedly bestowed. Sir John died at Edinburgh on the 24th December, 1835, in the 81st year of his age, and was buried in the Chapel Royal of Holyrood. The magistrates of Edinburgh and a deputation from the Highland Society of Scotland testified their esteem by attending his funeral. Sir John was twice married. His second wife was the honourable Diana, only daughter of Lord Macdonald, the lineal representative of the ancient Lord of the Isles.

Sir John's reputation during his lifetime was greater abroad than at home. So highly were his works esteemed by eminent foreigners, that he received diplomas from no fewer than twenty-five learned and scientific societies on the Continent.

The grand distinguishing feature of Sir John's character was an ardent desire, which animated him to the last, to promote the public good, and to be useful in his day and generation. All his literary undertakings, and even the most fantastic of his schemes, had this benevolent object in view. He was a patriot in the truest sense of the word. Those who envied his reputation, while they could not deny the immense good that he had done, alleged that his great leading principle was vanity ; but his vanity—of which he, no doubt like other men, had his share—was of an unselfish and disinterested nature, and might be said to be sublimed into a virtue.

MR TRAILL.

The late James Traill, Esq. of Ratter, Sheriff of the county of Caithness, was borne at the manse of Dunnet, on the 2nd June, 1758. His father, the Rev. George Traill, D.D., was minister of the parish. Dr Traill, was a native of Orkney, and possessed a small property called Hobbister, in the island of Sanday. Mr James Traill, after a course of due instruction at home, was sent to Marischal College, Aberdeen, where he had the good fortune to have as private tutor the late Rev. Thomas Jolly, minister of Dunnet, then a young man pursuing his studies at the same seat of learning. He afterwards studied law at Edinburgh, and passed advocate in 1779. In the year 1788, he succeeded John Sinclair, Esq. of Freswick, as Sheriff-depute of the county of Caithness, the duties of which office he discharged for many years with great ability and to the general satisfaction of the community. In his judicial capacity, and in every business in which he engaged, he was distinguished for a remarkably sound, penetrating judgment and great quickness of comprehension. He was not, however, a ready speaker, and in this respect he was much surpassed at public county meetings by Sir Benjamin Dunbar of Hempriggs, afterwards Lord Duffus, who, in addition to a fluent and eloquent elocution, and considerable knowledge of the law, possessed a wonderful power of argument, which he could employ with equal dexterity on either side of a question.

Mr Traill began at an early period of life to direct his attention to matters of public utility. He was the first who commenced the modern system of agricultural improvements, etc., in Caithness, for which the county is now so much distinguished. While Sir John Sinclair theorised and wrote books, Mr Traill laboured with unwearied industry as a practical improver, and set a noble example to all the other landed gentlemen in the county. When he became proprietor of Castlehill, there was not a single tree on the whole property. He immediately engaged a forester, and commenced planting. The scheme was laughed at, and looked upon by many as quite utopian. He persevered, however; and the young shoots being protected from the sea blast, throve, and the plantation has now a respectable appearance and gives Castlehill quite an air of the south. The trees are principally ash, plane, elm, oak, mountain ash, and larch. Some of them have attained to the height of fifty feet. The writer of the new Statistical Account of the Parish of Olrig very justly observes:—" Mr Traill may well be called the author of all improvements in the county, which a single view of his property in this parish, after surveying Caithness, will sufficiently testify, either as regards culture, plantations, buildings, harbours, roads, live stock, or crops. Indeed, what he has accomplished could scarcely be credited as being the work of one individual, and is, and will be, a great example to Caithness in all time coming."

Of the readiness with which he could apply his practical mind to any particular art or profession, and master its details, the following instance is a proof:—In 1801, when the volunteer force was embodied for the defence of the country, Mr Traill took a very active part in raising the Caithness volunteers. He was appointed their colonel, and although previously quite unacquainted with military matters, he, in the shortest time, learned the whole science of drilling soldiers as then practised in our army ; and the precision and accuracy with which he put the Caithness volunteers through their various evolutions, excited the astonishment and admiration of the general officers who were occasionally sent from the south to inspect the corps. Among those who came north on this duty, was the famous General Duff, who had served for several years in India. He was a very stout man, of prodigious strength, and was commonly known by the name of " Tiger Duff," from the remarkable circumstance that, being on one occasion attacked by a tiger, when he happened to be without any defensive armour, he, by dint of sheer physical force, managed to throttle the savage animal.

Mr Traill originated the pavement trade of Caithness, which is now so extensively carried on in the county. The works at Castlehill were commenced in 1824,* and the first shipment of stone was made in 1825. The number of men employed is upwards of 300. Between 700,000 and 800,000 feet of stone are shipped annually, requiring about 7000 tons of shipping to carry it to market. The pavement is sent to all the principal cities in Great Britain, and to many places abroad. A steam engine, with powerful machinery, has lately been erected for cutting and polishing the stone, etc., by which a great deal of manual labour is saved. Several gentlemen in the county have since followed the example of Mr Traill and opened quarries on their estates. The trade has, in consequence, become one of great importance : its annual value amounting, it is said, to about £30,000.

The following remarks on this stone, by Sir Roderick Murchison, are interesting in a scientific point of view :—" The flagstones of the Caithness quarries," says this eminent geologist, " are highly valuable for many uses, and must prove eminently durable from the nature of their composition. The well-known durability is attributable, in part, to the large portion

* The pavement trade at Castlehill has been under the able management of Mr James Macbeath from its commencement.

of bitumen they contain, which has been produced by the abundance of fishes which existed at the time those rocks were deposited—the fossil remains of which still abound. Tar and gas may be distilled from them." And Hugh Miller says :—" The animal matter of the Caithness ichthyolites is a hard, black, insoluble bitumen, which I have used more than once as sealing wax."

Mr Traill married Lady Janet, second daughter of William Sinclair, Earl of Caithness, whose residence was Ratter House, in the parish of Dunnet. He subsequently purchased the estate of Ratter, which, it would appear, was encumbered, and which, in default of male heirs, had become the property of Lady Isabella Sinclair, the eldest daughter. Mr Traill had, by his lady, a fine family of sons and daughters. Lady Janet died at Edinburgh, we believe, in the year 1805, and being a descendant of the illustrious house of St. Clair, was interred in the chapel of Roslin. Mr Traill, who was deeply attached to his lady, never married again. He survived her many years, and died at the House of Castlehill, on the 19th July, 1843, at the advanced age of 85. He was succeeded in the property by his eldest son, George Traill, Esquire, who has been many years member of Parliament for the county, and is highly esteemed by the constituency for his strict attention to their interests, and his firm adherence to his principles as a Liberal representative.

The late Mr Traill was essentially a man of business. Though possessed of excellent talents and extensive information, he seemed to have no turn, like Sir John Sinclair, for bookmaking, and he disliked political writings. When it was first proposed to start a newspaper in the county, he was consulted on the subject; but he disapproved of the idea of getting up anything of the kind. His opinion was, that such a publication would be made a vehicle only for political squabbling and personal abuse, and it would set the whole county by the ears. Caithness would not support a paper, and did not require one. In this instance Mr Traill's otherwise excellent judgment was at fault; and his prudential caution was carried to an extreme. The *John O'Groat Journal* was, notwithstanding, started by Mr Peter Reid in 1836; and it gradually forced its way into notice, and obtained a large circulation. The evil predicted by Mr Traill and others has not happened. On the contrary, the publication has, in various respects, been of immense benefit to Caithness; and by his enterprising spirit as projector of the press in the "far north," Mr Reid's name will have an honourable place in any future literary record of the county. And here it is but right to mention Mr Benjamin M. Kennedy, a native of Wick, who was the first editor of the *John O'Groat Journal*. Possessed of excellent abilities, a great fund of original humour, with a lively fancy, and much command of language, Mr Kennedy rendered the paper, as long as it was under his management extremely popular. It is a remark of Dr. Johnson, that "the mass of every people must be barbarous when there is no printing." It would be absurd to say that the great body of the inhabitants of Caithness were in this condition immediately before the introduction among them of the printing press; but there can be no doubt that since then they have risen vastly in intelligence and public spirit. The press has in one sense acted the part of a schoolmaster, and made the people to read and to think, and it has been the means of calling forth native talent which but for it would have lain in obscurity. Mr Traill's repugnance to starting a newspaper was no doubt in some measure owing to his strong Conservative politics, which he shared in common with most of the leading proprietors of the county. But in all other respects his conduct merits the highest praise. As an excellent sheriff and a man who did much to develop the material resources of his native county, his memory will be long cherished in Caithness.

JAMES BREMNER, CIVIL ENGINEER.

James Bremner, the most remarkable man for mechanical ingenuity which the north perhaps ever produced, was born at

Keiss, near Wick, on the 25th September, 1784. His parents' names were James and Janet Bremner, and he was the youngest of a family of nine children. His father enlisted when a young man into the 3rd regiment of the line, the well-known Buffs. With this corps he embarked for the West Indies, where he was thrice wounded in action, and after a servitude of ten years, returned to Britain with his few remaining comrades. The regiment, when it first went abroad consisted of 850 men, and out of this number only 27, of whom Bremner was one, were destined to see again their native country. The rest had all found graves on a foreign shore. The Irish Rebellion having broken out soon after his return to Britain, Bremner was sent to Ireland, and served there for some time, when, through the influence of a superior officer who had known him in the West Indies, he was appointed to conduct a party of the leading rebels, who had been taken prisoners, to Fort-George. On getting his discharge from the army he removed to Caithness, and settled in his native parish. He is said to have been a steady, well-conducted man and possessed of great energy of character.

James, the subject of our notice, was in due time sent to school, but all that he learned there was simply to read and write, and that very imperfectly. Education in Caithness was then at a low stand. Except in one or two parishes, there were no statutory schools; and in the country districts the instruction of the young was chiefly entrusted to females, or to men with the merest smattering of learning, who, being incapacitated by physical infirmity from following any other vocation, set up as teachers. The classics and the higher branches had, of course, no place in the scholastic programme. As the writer of a memoir of Mr Bremner truly observes, grammars and lexicons, globes and maps, were quite unknown, and the pupil who could read through the Proverbs of Solomon without stammering, and write pretty quickly, whether he could spell or not, was considered fit for any situation.

Young Bremner's predilection for ships and nautical matters

discovered itself at a very early period; and the writer of the memoir relates the following singular and perilous adventure of his when a boy:—"Among the crags and rocks of his native district none were half so venturous. Fear was not in his vocabulary; and so we find him one fine morning complacently paddling himself through Sinclair's Bay, sitting in a large tub! Fortunately for him there was not a breath of wind; and one of his brothers having raised the alarm, he was picked up and safely brought ashore."

Having expressed a strong desire to learn the art of ship-building, interest was obtained to get him into the building-yard of the Messrs Steele of Greenock. He accordingly went to that place in his sixteenth year, and was bound an apprentice for six years. At the expiry of his apprenticeship he made two voyages to America. He then returned to his native county, and being young, active, and of a highly enterprising spirit, he resolved to prosecute his trade in Pulteneytown, which had just been established as a settlement by the British Fishery Society. He obtained a building-yard on a life lease, near the harbour, and during the time he occupied it, he built upwards of fifty-six vessels, ranging from forty-five to six hundred tons.

But he did not confine himself to his own particular profession. Being endowed, as has been already mentioned, with great mechanical ingenuity, he commenced engineer, and while engaged in this line, he planned, built, or improved no fewer than nineteen harbours. Among these was the new harbour at Pulteneytown. One remarkable instance of his persevering and indomitable spirit, while he was employed on this work, is related by the writer in the *Northern Ensign*:—"In one night, at Pulteneytown harbour," says he, "during a terrific gale, works which cost £5000 were thrown down and rendered useless. Any ordinary man would have sunk beneath the disaster. Not so did James Bremner. Eight times during that disastrous night was he prevailed on to go home and get his clothes shifted, and as often in a few minutes was he seen

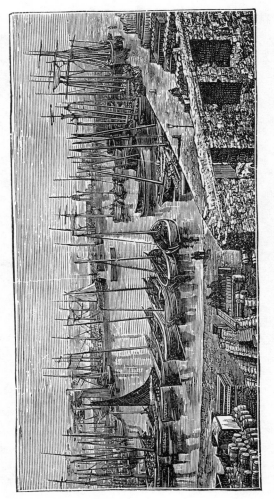

OUTER HARBOUR, WICK.

at the head of his men, cheering them on in their efforts to save as much of the property as possible.   His fame as an engineer was by this time widely spread.   Having been ordered up to London, he was examined before a Committee of the House of Lords on the subject of harbours of refuge, and obtained a patent for harbour building.

Mr Bremner now began to attain great celebrity as a raiser of wrecked and sunk vessels.   The total number which he raised in deep water, or took off the strand, is said to have amounted to 236.   On this point the writer of the memoir gives the following interesting statement :—" Of those raised in deep water, the most remarkable was a large vessel which had sunk at Broadbay, in the Lews.   Her name was the 'Unicorn,' of Sunderland, carrying 700 tons of coal.   She went down in eleven fathoms, and the aggregate weight of vessel and cargo was upwards of 1100 tons.   After the vessel had lain embedded in the sand for about two years, and after three other individuals had successively undertaken and failed to raise her, Mr Bremner succeeded by employing means much the same as those for which he obtained a patent for harbour building.   Not less triumphant, and far more heroic, was his effort in raising the 'Orion,' of Pillau, at Watersound in Orkney, in 1825.   This vessel's cargo consisted of 40,000 feet of timber, which, with the wreck of the ship, he constructed into a raft 450 feet long, 22 broad, and 16 deep, on which he constructed paddles wrought by manual labour, erected poles with sails, and after being twice driven through the Pentland Firth, he succeeded in bringing the whole to Pulteneytown harbour."   But in this department the crowning triumph of Mr Bremner was the taking the "Great Britain" off the strand at Dundrum Bay, Ireland, in the month of August, 1847, after some of the most eminent engineers in the kingdom had exhausted all their skill in fruitless endeavours to remove her.   In this undertaking he was ably assisted by his eldest son, Mr Alexander Bremner, now of Aberdeen.   The "Great Britain" was at the time the largest ship in the world, being 3500 tons register, and built of iron.

Mr Bremner was, for the space of twelve years, agent at Wick for the Aberdeen, Clyde, and Leith Steam Shipping Company. In conveying goods and passengers to and from the steamboat he was, from the exposed nature of the bay, often placed in situations of great danger; but such was his presence of mind and knowledge of boatmanship, that during the entire period of his management, no accident involving loss of life or property occurred.

The celebrated Hugh Miller, in a geological visit to Caithness, was introduced to Mr Bremner at Wick, and in one of his publications he says of him:—"I was conscious of a feeling of sadness as, in parting with Mr Bremner, I reflected that a man so singularly gifted should have been suffered to reach a period of life very considerably advanced in employments little suited to exert his extraordinary faculties, and which persons of the ordinary type could have performed as well. Napoleon—himself possessed of great genius—could have estimated more adequately than our British rulers the value of such a man. Had Mr Bremner been born a Frenchman, he would not now be the mere agent of a steam company in a third-rate seaport town."

Mr Bremner married in early life a very amiable woman, by whom he had a numerous family of sons and daughters. One of his sons, named David, who acted as engineer for the Clyde Trustees, was cut off in the prime of life. He inherited much of his father's talent, and, had he lived, would undoubtedly have attained to eminence in his profession. The loss of this promising son, and subsequently that of his wife, affected him very deeply. His constitution, which was naturally strong and had hitherto withstood toil and fatigue before which thousands would have fallen, began rapidly to break down, and it was evident to all who saw him that his journey of life was near a close. He died in the month of August, 1856, having survived his wife only a few months. Mr Bremner was admitted a member of the Institute of Civil Engineers in 1833. He communicated to that body several valuable papers, for which he received one of the Institute's medals. .By his professional brethren his opinion on engineering matters was greatly esteemed. In the execution of the Thames Tunnel, Dover harbour, and other great undertakings, he was frequently consulted; and his correspondence included many illustrious and well-known names of historical fame. Sir Charles Napier, as a mark of his respect, presented him with a massive gold finger-ring.

In his particular department, indeed, Mr Bremner was universally allowed to be a man of more than ordinary genius. His readiness of invention was wonderful. He knew little or nothing of the theory of mathematics, and, as has been well observed, " all his efforts as an engineer were but the bringing out of natural mechanical power."

In person Mr Bremner was rather above the middle size, with a strong and robust frame of body and a thoroughly Scotch cast of countenance. In conversation he appeared occasionally absent, and he was by no means gifted with a fluent or ready utterance. His temper was naturally hasty, but the gust of passion soon passed off. Of him it might be said, as of Cassius in the play, that he was—

> " Yoked with a lamb
> That carried anger as the flint bears fire,
> Which much enforced shows a hasty spark,
> And straight is cold again."

Like most people of quick and hasty temperament, he had great tenderness of heart. In saving the lives of others in cases of shipwreck, he often risked his own; and when any distressing accident took place before his sight, he has been known to shed tears like a woman. He was at the same time remarkable for his generosity and hospitality, especially to strangers. To his board all of respectable character were welcome, and none more so than the cast-away sea captain.

His idea of hospitality was that of the genuine old school. Such was Mr Bremner in private life.

Viewed in his professional character, he affords a remarkable instance of the force of natural talent, unaided by education, overcoming all obstacles and pushing its possessor forward to high distinction. He was a man of whom Caithness may well be proud, and his name will live in the annals of engineering science.

Some years before his death several of the inhabitants of Wick, in order to testify the esteem in which he was held, presented his family with his portrait at full length. The County Hall of Wick very properly contains the portraits of the late James Earl of Caithness, Sir John Sinclair of Ulbster, James Traill of Ratter, etc., and we think it a pity that the portrait of Mr Bremner has not been added to the number. Though not an aristocrat by birth, he belonged to the "aristocracy of nature;" and as a man of scientific eminence, who did much good in his day and who reflects lustre on his native county, his memory deserves to have received the honour.

JOHN FINLAISON,
LATE ACTUARY OF THE NATIONAL DEBT, AND GOVERNMENT CALCULATOR.

Thurso has produced many clever men, and several excellent scholars. The inhabitants are naturally acute and intelligent, and for a long period back they have paid great attention to the education of the young. The parish school, which is situated in the town, has generally had able and well-qualified men for teachers.* Among those who have taught in this school may be mentioned the late Rev. Dr. Morison of Canisbay, the Rev. William Smith of Bower, and the Rev. William Munro. The last-named gentleman, who died in the year 1813 while he still held the office, was perhaps the best

---

* This would appear indeed to have been the case more than two hundred years ago. In the Presbytery records, 1658, occurs the following entry :—The Presbytery appoint Hew Monro, who has been appointed schoolmaster of Thurso, to have ready against next meeting an oration "de educatione juventatis, and to expone and analyse the first epistle of Horace in order to take tryal of his humanities."

teacher Thurso ever had.   He was an accomplished scholar and an admirable drill, and, among other things, he inspired a taste for the classics which exists in the place to this day. Mr Finlaison,* the subject of our memoir, was one of his pupils.   He was the eldest son of Donald Finlayson and Isabella Sutherland, and was born at Thurso on the 27th day of August, 1783.   His father went to sea when he was quite a boy, and after being some time in the coasting trade, he gave up that employment and betook himself to his native town, where he married and settled down as a fisherman.   He died from an attack of brain fever on the 28th of November, 1790, at the early age of twenty-nine, leaving his wife a widow, with three children—John, seven years ; Christian, three years ; and William, four months old—all wholly unprovided for.   "The rearing of the family," says a relative of theirs, "was thus cast upon the widowed mother at an age when the children were entirely helpless ; and she must no doubt have had a hard struggle with 'pinching poverty' to support herself and them. But she was a woman of discreet judgment, and of careful and industrious habits ; and though her means were scanty, she sought something higher for her boys than the dangerous and unprofitable calling which had been pursued by her husband. All honour to her memory for her laudable ambition, and her noble self-sacrificing toils."

John, her eldest boy, was early placed under Mr Munro, who was then ably assisted by Mr John Macdonald, afterwards the celebrated Dr. Macdonald of Urquhart.   The young pupil showed great quickness and aptitude for instruction, and soon became a favourite with his teacher.   Books and study were more attractive to him than the boyish games of his companions ; and thus it was, that though he took a proud place in the school-room, he was content to take a less distinguished one on the sands—the school-boy's usual play-ground.

At the age of fifteen he was removed from school, and

* On his removing to the south he signed his name Finlaison, instead of Finlayson, as it is commonly spelled.

apprenticed to Mr Donald Robeson, a writer in Thurso, in whose office he acquired a considerable amount of professional knowledge and, what was of still more value to him in after life, regular business habits. In the meantime, his passion for books—although he could not be strictly called a book-worm—was heightened rather than otherwise by the dry technicalities of law, and accordingly much of his leisure hours was devoted to reading and the storing of his mind with useful information. But in gratifying this laudable desire he at first met with obstacles such as could not have been experienced by any young man at the present day; and in his case it might be truly said to have been "the pursuit of knowledge under difficulties." At the period in question, books in Thurso were scarce and dear. There was no circulating library in the town; and, if there were private libraries among the upper classes, no stray volume from their shelves by any chance found its way into the cottages of the poor. In these circumstances our young student made the acquaintance of a baker who happened about this time to come to Thurso. The baker's brother was connected with Mackay's circulating library in Edinburgh; and boxes of books found their way periodically to the little town in the far north, and were feasted on by the baker, by Mr Finlaison, and by such of his companions as had a taste for reading.

At this time, too, he diversified his studies by cultivating an acquaintance with the theory and practice of music, of which, like most people of high intellect, he was passionately fond. His favourite instrument was the flute, which he soon learned to play with much taste and skill. He frequently practised out of doors; and on a fine summer evening, when the beautiful bay of Thurso lay spread out as smooth as a mirror and the sun was setting in all his glory in the Atlantic, and casting a golden radiance over sea and land, it was his custom to go out in a small boat with one or two young friends, and while they gently plied the oar, he would play now some lively air, now some slow, plaintive melody, whose notes might be heard floating along the waters, mellowed into exquisite sweetness. In recreations of this kind, as innocent as they were delightful, and surrounded with the magnificent scenery of Scrabster and Holborn-head, he passed, it is said, many a happy leisure hour.

On the expiry of a four years' apprenticeship with Mr Robeson, he was appointed factor for Sir Benjamin Dunbar (afterwards Lord Duffus) at Ackergill, in the neighbourhood of Wick. He held this appointment for about twelve months, and in August, 1804, proceeded to Edinburgh, where he obtained a clerkship in the office of Mr Glen, a Writer to the Signet. He remained in Edinburgh only six weeks, but during this brief stay he wooed and won his first wife. The circumstance which led to his acquaintance with her was somewhat singular. Being at dinner one day with Mr Glen, his employer, the dress of á young lady, one of the party, accidentally caught fire, and being near her at the time, Mr Finlaison had the presence of mind to tear up the crumb-cloth, and throw it round her, and thus extinguished the flames. Gratitude, followed by a more tender feeling, sprang up in the young lady's heart towards her gallant preserver, which met with a glad response in his; and in a short time it was arranged between them that they should link their lot in life together. To prevent the possibility of opposition from relatives, they informed no one of their intentions, but went to London in September, 1804, and were married there. The young lady was Miss Glen, the sister of Mr Finlaison's employer in Edinburgh. Many a novel has been founded on a less romantic incident.

In 1805, Mr Finlaison obtained a situation in the Admiralty. The story of his subsequent career in that office will be best given in the following summary, taken from the *Times:*—" Mr Finlaison speedily distinguished himself by a plan which was adopted for the entire reorganisation of the system under which the vast correspondence of the department was then imperfectly carried on. The Navy List was first compiled in its present semi-official form by him, and was published under his superintendence. A scheme for the establishment of a widow's fund in the civil service, and a similar plan (afterwards carried out) on behalf of the widows of the naval medical officers, drew Mr Finlaison's attention, in 1817, to the study of vital statistics. The information then extant on this question was extremely meagre and unsatisfactory; but resorting to the official records of the Exchequer, where certain classes of life annuities had long been payable, Mr Finlaison established from authentic data those deductions which enabled him successfully to point out the unfitness of the tables then made use of by Government for the sale of annuities. Mr Finlaison's representations met with a favourable reception from Mr Vansittart, Chancellor of the Exchequer at that time, and ultimately led to the establishment of a sounder system that brought about an immense pecuniary saving to the country. The immediate result of his general services on this question was his appointment, in 1821, to the office of Government Actuary. From this time forward until his retirement in 1851, his counsel and calculating powers were generally put in requisition when any of the public measures involved considerations of political arithmetic. Some of the principal subjects in which he was consulted may be enumerated in the order of their occurrence. The negotiation with the Bank of England for its acceptance of the charge for public pensions, in consideration of the dead-weight annuity; the investigations in 1825 and 1827, by select committees of the House of Commons, into the general condition of friendly societies; the preparation of his report, in 1829, on the evidence and elementary facts on which his new tables of life annuities were founded. This important parliamentary document contained twenty-one new observations of the law of mortality, and one of the law of sickness prevailing among the labouring classes in London; vast computations of the duration of slave and creole life, with reference to the emancipation of slaves in 1834, and the West India loan raised for that purpose. Mr Finlaison's report on the late Mr Hume's resolutions on that loan is a

Parliamentary paper of that date well worth perusal. In the measures emanating from the Ecclesiastical Commission in 1835, the steps leading to the 'appropriation clause' in 1836 and those preceding the discussion of the Church Rate question in 1837, Mr Finlaison's services were called out to an extent greatly beyond what is generally known to the public. He was also consulted on certain points connected with the establishment, in 1837, of the registration of births, deaths, and marriages ; and the closeness of his estimate of the deaths which would be registered in the first year (falling within 14 of nearly 330,000) attracted much notice at the time when mentioned in the Registrar-General's first annual report. The demands made on his mental powers about this time affected his health, and thenceforward he was obliged to exercise more caution in his devotion to the public service. His professional researches were, however, still assiduously carried on for some years, and from time to time he was frequently called upon to give evidence before Royal Commissioners and select committees of both Houses of Parliament, until he finally retired in August, 1851, from his position as actuary of the National Debt and Government Calculator. For the last nine years his studies were directed to Scripture chronology, and to the universal relationship of ancient and modern weights and measures. His researches, which were exceedingly profound on the latter subject, led him to form opinions decidedly adverse to the introduction of a decimal system of coinage and metrology into this country."

Very soon after his appointment in the Admiralty office, Mr Finlaison settled a competent annuity on his mother, which relieved her from anxiety and toil for her subsistence during the remainder of her days. About the same time, also, he procured a midshipman's commission for his brother William, who shipped on board H.M.S. Beagle at the early age of fifteen. In this ship, Captain Fitzroy (afterwards Rear-Admiral Fitzroy) circumnavigated the globe on a voyage of scientific discovery. The expedition was out four years; and the celebrated Mr Darwin, whose work on "The Origin of Species created such a sensation among physiologists and critics, accompanied it as naturalist. William afterwards served on board the Morgiana, Nimrod, and Hydra, and ultimately attained the post of commander. After a brief retirement, he was appointed governor of the island of Ascension, but the climate not agreeing with his constitution, he was obliged to resign the situation. He died in 1851.

The last few years of Mr John Finlaison's life were passed in comparative ease and tranquillity. He was at length unexpectedly seized with congestion of the lungs, and after a brief illness, died at his residence, Nottinghill, London, on the 13th April, 1860, in the 77th year of his age. He had been nearly fifty years in the Government service. Mr Finlaison was no common man. He possessed extraordinary abilities as an accountant, and was long regarded as the most expert and correct calculator in the kingdom.

RICHARD OSWALD, AND THE OSWALD FAMILY.

The Oswalds of Auchincruive and Scotston are of northern origin. In a pedigree of the family in our possession, their ancestor is mentioned as James Oswald of Kirkwall, in Orkney, who died about the year 1660. His son, James Oswald, was one of the magistrates of Wick, and married Barbara, a daughter of Coghill of that ilk. He had two sons, James and George, the former of whom became minister of Watten, and the latter minister of Dunnet, in the county of Caithness. Richard and Alexander, sons of Mr Oswald of Watten, went to Glasgow, and adopted the mercantile profession, in which they succeeded so well that they realised an ample fortune, and, about the year 1739, purchased the estate of Scotston, in Renfrewshire. They were, it seems, strong Jacobites; and, when the Pretender's army came into the neighbourhood of Glasgow, they, together with some other gentlemen of the same way of thinking, were asked by the citizens to negotiate terms with the Prince, in order to prevent the occupation of the town by his Highland troops.   To this, on the payment of a sum of money, the Prince agreed; and the Messrs Oswald received the thanks of the provost and magistrates for their services, as appears by the records of the Town Council.   One of the sisters of these gentlemen, named Isabella, was married to Campbell of Lochend, in Caithness. James, eldest son of Mr Oswald of Dunnet, succeeded his father as minister of that parish, but was translated to Methven, where he died in 1793.   Richard,* the other son, who afterwards attained to such high distinction, went to Glasgow to his cousins, and after being some time with them, he proceeded to London, where, by steady industry and success in business, he became a wealthy merchant and a leading man on 'Change.   His high position in the mercantile world—his fame as a capitalist, and his excellent character, were of course a passport to the best society in the British metropolis.   In 1750 he married Miss Mary Ramsay, only daughter and heiress of Alexander Ramsay, Esquire of the island of Jamaica—a cadet of the family of Balmain.   During the famous Seven Years' War on the Continent, he took extensive Government contracts; and finding that they were mismanaged, he accepted the appointment of Commissary-General to the allied armies, and served with them through several campaigns.   In 1759 he purchased the estate of Cavens, in Kirkcudbright, and that of Auchincruive, in Ayrshire.   At the latter place he completed the mansion house, which was in course of being erected by Mr Murray of Broughton, from whom he had bought the property; and he afterwards lived alternately at Auchincruive, and at his house in Great George's

* In the first edition of this work, I stated on the authority of the old statistical account of Thurso, written by Sir John Sinclair, that Richard Oswald, the Plenipotentiary, was in his younger days a rejected candidate on a comparative trial for the office of parochial schoolmaster of Thurso.   I have since found that this is a mistake.   R. Oswald, the son of the minister of Dunnet, was born about the year 1704; and in the Presbytery records of Caithness it is particularly mentioned that the comparative trial took place in November 1706, when he was only an infant.   The rejected candidate of the same name, Mr Henderson thinks, would be a grandson of Alex. Oswald, bailie and elder of Thurso in 1647 and afterwards.

Street, Westminster. In 1782 he was, through the influence of Lord Shelburne, with whom he had long been on terms of intimacy, appointed Plenipotentiary for Great Britain, and sent to Paris to conclude a treaty of peace with the United States of America, and there he signed the treaty in question with the celebrated Dr. Benjamin Franklin, on the 13th November, 1782. It is abundantly evident that Mr Oswald must have possessed more than ordinary talent and political sagacity before he would have been appointed to sit at the same council board with such a man as Franklin, and on a matter of such vast national importance as the ratification of a treaty of peace between this country and the new transatlantic republic.

Dr Franklin and he were on a very intimate and friendly footing; and as a proof of the high esteem which the great American philosopher and statesman had for Mr Oswald, he presented him with his (Franklin's) portrait, which is to be seen at Auchincruive. Mr Oswald died there in 1784 without issue, leaving the whole of his property in life-rent to his widow. On her death, in 1788, by the terms of the will, his nephew, George Oswald, succeeded as heir to one portion of his extensive estate, and his grand-nephew, Richard Alexander Oswald, to the other.

In Franklin's "Memoirs" are to be found several letters that passed between him and Mr Oswald during the time they were negotiating the treaty of peace at Paris. The same work contains also a copy of the commission under the Great Seal appointing him Plenipotentiary for Britain. It is too long and cumbered with law phraseology to be quoted entire, but I subjoin a brief extract from it :—

"George the Third, by the Grace of God, of Great Britain, France, and Ireland, King, defender of the faith, and so forth. To our trusty and well-beloved Richard Oswald of our City of London, Esquire, greeting. Whereas by virtue of an Act passed in the last Session of Parliament, intituled An Act to enable His Majesty to conclude a peace or truce with certain

Colonies in North America therein mentioned," etc., etc. "Know ye, that We, reposing especial trust in your wisdom, loyalty, diligence, and circumspection in the management of the affairs to be hereby committed to your charge, do nominate, appoint, constitute, and assign you, the said Richard Oswald, to be our Commissioner in that behalf to use and exercise all and every the powers and authorities hereby entrusted and committed to you, the said Richard Oswald," etc., etc. . . .

"Witness our self at Westminster, the 21st day of September, and the 22d year of our reign.

"By the King himself."

Dr. Carlisle, in his autobiography, thus speaks of Mr Oswald when he was with his cousins in Glasgow:—"This gentleman was much confined to the house by sore eyes, and yet was able to pass his time almost entirely in reading, and becoming a very learned and intelligent merchant, and having acquired some thousand pounds by being prize agent to his cousins, whose privateer had taken a prize worth £15,000, he, a few years after this period (1743), established himself in London, and acquired a large fortune."

Caithness has reason to be proud of having produced such a man as Richard Oswald, and of being the birth-place of the ancestors of a family so highly respectable as the Oswalds, all of whom are now resident in the south. John Henderson, Esquire, Thurso, who has kindly furnished the writer with much interesting information on this and other matters, says— "Mr Traill and the Oswalds are related by marriage, thus: The Reverend Dr. James Oswald of Dunnet (afterwards of Methven) and the Reverend Dr. Traill of Dunnet, grandfather of the present Mr Traill, married sisters, daughters of Murray of Clairdon. A third sister was married to my great grand-father, the Reverend Mr Brodie, minister of Latheron." And he adds—"There are tenements in Wick and Thurso still known as 'Oswald's tenements,' and a burial-place in Thurso as 'the Oswald's tomb.'"

Inside the church of Watten there is a marble tablet to the

memory of the Rev. James Oswald, with the following inscription in Latin :—Hic conduntur cineres Jacobi Oswald, probati pastores ecclesiæ apud Watten ; placido sed virili aspectu, ingenio plus quam vulgari ; mirabilis ei concionandi felicitas, dum menti persuderet, cor movebat. Generosi comitatem ornabat sanctitate, cæterisque virtutibus sacerdotes dignes, perfugium miseris, conciliator pacis. Hinc illi apud omnes magna auctoritas, cujus ope, imperitorum mentibus ad prudentiam formandis et inimicitiis potentiorum sedandis plurimum valebat. Natus die Januarii 26, 1654, ad sacra vocatus 1682. Uxorem duxit Mariam Murray, filiam Richardi Murray, orti ex honesta familia de Pennyland, Decembris die 28, 1683, Obiit 4 Novembris, 1698. Vidua marito superstes pietati et educatione liberorum dedit, quos reliquit fama et opibus florentes. Obiit Maria 29 die Junii 1738, cum conjuge eodem in tumulo sepulta. Hoc monumentum, parentum memoriæ et cineribus sacrum, constituerunt duo filii, Richardus et Alexander, negotiatores Glasguenses.

"Here reposes the dust of James Oswald,* the worthy pastor of the church of Watten, a man of a pleasant countenance, and of a genius above what is common ; who possessed a wonderfully happy power of addressing an audience, and who, while he convinced the understanding, also moved the heart ; kind and affable, adorned with sanctity, and all those other virtues which became him as a minister of the Gospel ; a friend of the distressed, and a peacemaker. Hence he had great influence among all parties, both in moulding the minds of the ignorant to prudence, and in reconciling those who were at enmity. He was born 26th January, 1654 ; was called to the ministry, 28th December, 1682 ; married in 1683, Mary, daughter of Richard Murray, of the honourable family of Pennyland, and died the 4th November, 1698. His surviving

---

* James and George Oswald, the sons of the Wick bailie, were of different churches. James was Episcopal minister of Watten, and George was Presbyterian minister of Dunnet. The latter was appointed to Dunnet in 1697, and died in 1725.

widow occupied herself in piously educating the children whom he had left, blessed with plenty, and a comfortable residence. She died June 29, 1738, and was buried in the same tomb with her husband. Her two sons, Richard and Alexander, merchants in Glasgow, reared this monument, sacred to the memory of their parents." The Oswalds have been particularly distinguished for their deeds of charity and benevolence ; and in the exercise of this virtue, they have not been unmindful of Caithness. They have at sundry times given sums amounting in all to about £1800 to be mortified for the behoof of the poor in the several parishes of the county. This benefaction has preserved, and will long continue to preserve, the memory of the family in the north.

I here conclude my sketch of the History of Caithness, in which there will, doubtless, be found errors of "omission and commission." I have endeavoured, however, as far as possible, to give a true and impartial account of all the matters touched upon ; and although the work has cost me a good deal of arduous research, often in musty tomes and out-of-the-way nooks and corners, it has been to me notwithstanding, I may truly say, a labour of love. I only regret that the performance is not more worthy of the subject. To the county, I feel naturally a strong attachment. It is the place of my nativity ; it is the residence of all my best and dearest friends, and it contains within its bosom the ashes of my kindred.

> " Land of my sires ! what mortal hand
>   Can e'er untie the filial band
>   That knits me to thy rugged strand ? "

APPENDIX.

No. I.

ANCIENT STATE OF HUSBANDRY, HANDICRAFTS, ETC., IN CAITHNESS.

It is a curious circumstance that in the reign of David II. of Scotland, more than five hundred years ago, the weights and measures of Caithness were the standards of Scotland. By a royal ordinance, or Act of that monarch, entitled the "Regiam Majestatem," it is statuted, "that ane common and equal weicht quilk is called the weicht of Caithness (Pondus Cathaniæ) sall be keeped and used be all men in buying and selling within this realm of Scotland." This is a sufficient proof that Caithness, notwithstanding its remote situation, was, at the early period in question, a place of considerable commercial importance. The inhabitants had already begun to apply themselves to agriculture ; and at a later period they carried on a regular traffic with Norway and Denmark. Thurso, on account of its safe and excellent roadstead, was the principal sea-port. From it great quantities of malt and meal were annually shipped for the Baltic, from which wood, iron, etc., were imported in return. This is the more remarkable, when we consider how imperfect must have been the system of agriculture, and all the operations connected therewith, at the time. Previous to 1780, there was not a single cart in the whole county of Caithness. "Crubbans," a kind of wicker baskets, were the principal substitutes for carts. Two of these, one on each side of the horse, were hung from a wooden saddle, called a "clibbar," beneath which was a cushion of straw to protect the animal's back. A sort of bags made of straw, called "cazies," were used instead of sacks for holding corn. Two of these, capable, when filled, of containing each half a boll of grain, were fastened to the crook saddle on the back of a garron, and hung down, one on each side of the beast. "Six or seven horses thus loaded," says Henderson in his Agricultural Survey of Caithness "might be seen going in a kind of Indian file, each tied by the halter to the other's tail, a person leading the front horse, and each of the others pulled forward by the tail of the one before him. After the driver arrives at the destined place, the horses are unloaded, and the halter of the front horse is tied to the tail of the rear horse, by which means they cannot run away, as they can only move in a circle where they stand." Such was the simple mode of carriage before the introduction of the cart into the county.

The old Caithness plough, called the "thrapple plough," was of a very primitive construction. With the exception of the coulter and "sock," it was entirely of wood, with wooden pegs for nails, and it had only one stilt. To this machine four miserable garrons, with perhaps a pair of oxen, were yoked abreast. The person who held the plough had a sheep-skin tied round his right thigh, to which he held the stilt to keep the plough steady in its course. A second person pressed his whole weight and strength on the middle of the beam, to keep the plough in the soil; and the third, the driver, walked backwards between the two foremost beasts, leaning his arms on their necks to prevent his falling. The driver was not unfrequently a woman. The price of the thrapple plough was only four shillings, and the quantity of soil it turned up in a day was not much above a quarter of an acre. "The one-stilted plough," says a statistical writer, "though a fertile subject of ridicule, was the ancient plough of Rome, Egypt, and even England."

That Caithness, long before the introduction of the present improved system of husbandry, produced no inconsiderable quantity both of grain and stock, we have the recorded testimony of three intelligent tourists. Brand, who formed one of a deputation sent by the General Assembly of the Church of Scotland in 1700 to visit the north, says of Caithness :—"The county is very fertile, abounding with grass and corn, hence yearly there is a great quantity of victual exported, as anno 1695,* there were sixteen thousand bolls embarked and taken out, for which end it is much frequented by barks from the Forth, Clyde, and other places, for ordinarily, when there is no scarcity or dearth, the meal is sold here at 3 or 4 or at most 5 merks per boll." He then adds—"The cattle and fish also are to be had very cheap, as good kine often in the shambles, such as the country doth afford, for 3 or 4 shillings sterling, and sometimes they say for 2 shillings; so that, as I have heard some of the more intelligent inhabitants observe, here is the cheapest market in the world. And the gentlemen can live better here upon 1000 merks than they can do in the south upon 4000 per annum."

"The county," says Pennant (this was in 1769), "produces great quantities of oatmeal; and much whisky is distilled from barley (bere). The great thinness of the inhabitants throughout Caithness enables them to send abroad much of its productions." What Pennant says in regard to the distillation of whisky is fully confirmed by the following extract from the county records :—"At a meeting of the Justices of the Peace and Commissioners of Supply of the county of Caithness, held at Thurso, 21st May, 1776, it was, *inter alia,* agreed to discountenance, as far as in their power, the pernicious practice of distilling whisky,† so very prejudicial to the morals and the constitutions of the people, there being from *eighty* to *ninety stills* in the county, which, at a moderate computation, consume from 100 to 150 bolls of barley each." Before whisky began to be distilled in the county, the

---

* As a farther proof that the export trade of Caithness was very considerable at the time, I may mention, on the authority of a Morayshire paper, the "Forres Gazette," that in the year 1694, there was purchased by Sir James Calder of Muirton, in that county, from Bailie Robert Calder, and others in Wick, beef, tallow, tongues, and salt hides, to the amount of L.8678 19s. 4d. Scots, the whole of which commodities were, according to the bill of lading, to be shipped for "Camphore, in Zealand, by the good ship the Ludovick & William of Findhorn."

† Whisky is mentioned for the first time in the Session records of Wick in 1758. That would appear to be the period when it began to be distilled in the county.

great beverage of the people was ale.   It may be here mentioned, as a curious statistical fact, that in the year 1668, no less than 1749 bolls of malt were brewed into ale in Caithness—a goodly quantity certainly, considering the limited amount of population at the period in question. The duty charged to the revenue, at 2 merks per boll, was £156 0s 6$\frac{3}{4}$d sterling, which, from the great difference in the value of money, would be nearly equal to £1000 at the present day.

Wright, author of the "Husbandry of Scotland," has the following statement regarding the county, which he visited about the year 1783 :—"The inhabitants are reckoned at 25,000, and yet, from the parsimony of the people and the want of manufactures, there are exported annually about 25,000 bolls bere and meal.   In Wick, curing and salting fish is a considerable branch, as also salting and exporting beef.   Provisions are cheap and plentiful : beef at salting time a penny per pound ; mutton three halfpence.   There is a good inn, everything at a moderate rate, and excellent claret for half-a-crown the bottle.

The farms at the period in question were generally small ; but one gentleman would seem to have occupied, as middleman, the whole of Murkle.   "Mr Macleod, the Sheriff-Substitute of the county," says Wright, " rents the farm of Murkle, for which he pays £275 of rent. Has under him thirty sub-tenants, and eighteen cottagers.   The rent is paid partly in money, and partly in victual.   The cottagers pay of rent from one to two bolls of victual, and perform services—shearing in harvest, for example—which they are obliged to do without any victuals.   Here is slavery in perfection, without any alleviating circumstance."   When the imperfect state of husbandry at the time is considered, the wonder really is that the county produced so much grain as it did.   As has been already observed, the tenantry had only small patches of land ; and these were intermingled in the oddest way imaginable—one having a piece here, and another a piece there—in what was called rig-and-rennel, or run-rig.   This barbarous custom was originally adopted, it is said, in order to prevent neighbours at enmity from setting fire to each other's fields of corn, and to cause the whole of a township to band together to protect their crops and their cattle from the Highland reivers.

As nearly the whole of the rent was paid in kind, the grain exported belonged solely to the proprietors, who had storehouses or granaries for receiving it.   When the Earls of Caithness lived in the Castle of Girnigoe, they had two large storehouses for this purpose at Staxigoe. These contained four meal-girnels, each capable of holding 1000 bolls of meal ; and four lofts, each capable of holding 1000 bolls of bere. About the year 1770, says Captain Henderson, the wages of farm servants, such as were fit to hold the plough, &c., did not exceed from £6 to £8 Scotch, that is from 10s to 13s 4d stg. in the half year. Women servants had only from 3s 6d to 5s in the half year.   In 1790, a fat hen was bought at from 3d to 4d, a cock at 2d, and a dozen of eggs might be had for a penny.   All the other necessaries of life were cheap in proportion.

The following account from the Old Statistical History of Caithness, published in 1793, will give some idea of the extent of services and of the customs, as they were called, which the lairds exacted from their tenants.   They tilled, dunged, sowed, and harrowed a part of an extensive farm in the proprietor's own possession.   They provided a certain quantity of peats for fuel, carried feal and divot, thatched a part of his houses, and furnished ropes made of hair and simmons (straw ropes) for that purpose, as well as for securing his corn in the stack-yard, weeded the land, led a certain quantity of midden feal from the common for manure to his farm, mowed and ingathered his hay, the spontaneous produce of the meadow and marshy grounds, and cut down, ingathered, thrashed out in part, manufactured, and carried to market the growth of the farm. Besides these services, the tenants paid vicarage, or small teind, viz., meat, lamb, wedder, poultry, and eggs out of each house, with teind geese and mill gault. Grass farms in the Highlands paid veal, kid, butter, cheese, &c. Tenants on the sea-coast paid a certain quantity of fish (kater fish, as it was called) and oil out of each boat belonging to them, and carried sea-ware for manuring the proprietor's farm. Amongst other articles of rent, the parsonage or great teind—being the tenth sheaf of the tenant's produce —was also till lately drawn by the laird in some places in the county. Tenants also wintered a beast or more, each according to the extent of his possession ; and their wives spun a certain quantity of lint for the proprietor's lady, who likewise had from them a certain portion of wool annually. All these different payments obtained generally in the county of Caithness previous to 1793. Nor were the towns exempt from their share of burdens. "The inhabitants of Thurso," says Dr Henderson, "were formerly liable to be called out by the superior to cut down his crops at Thurso East, and for other services. This was done by tuck of drum, and under pain of poinding the *tongs* or best *blanket*. This vassalage was rigidly enforced by Lady Janet Sinclair, Sir John's mother, till at length a sturdy citizen named Sandy Murray put an end to it by driving his staff through the drum and desiring the drummer to tell Lady Janet that he had done so."

How the poor people contrived to live under all these burdens is not a little surprising to us at the present day. The condition of the slaves in America and the West Indies was infinitely preferable. And yet, as the balance of happiness is pretty nearly equal in all conditions of society, we have no reason to think that they were without their own share of the comforts and enjoyments of life.

Some sixty or seventy years ago comparatively little corn was grown in the Highlands of Caithness, the inhabitants thereof having chiefly devoted their attention to pasturage and the rearing of cattle. They kept a number of cows, and made considerable quantities of butter and cheese. These valuable products of the dairy were usually manufactured in the summer season, at what was called the shielings, that is, places affording abundance of common hill pasture, and frequently situated a good many miles distant from their own habitations. This seems to have been quite a common practice also with the peasantry in Norway and other hilly countries. The author of the Agricultural View of the County gives the following graphic account of the Caithness shielings :—"About the 20th of June, the housewife and maid set out with the milch cows, perhaps from ten to twenty in number, to the shielings, where a booth or cabin was previously prepared for their reception ; another for the milk vessels, and a small fold to keep the calves from the cows during the night. There they passed a complete pastoral life, making butter and cheese, and living on curds and cream, or a mixture of oatmeal and cream, seasoned with a glass of whisky before and after meals, dancing on the green and singing Gaelic songs to the music of which, at milking time, the cows listened with apparent

attention and pleasure. Here they remained for a month or six weeks at least, while there was good pasture for the cows." Potatoes were introduced into the county about the year 1754, and for some years after were cultivated only in the gardens of the better classes. From 1760 till 1786 the tenantry planted a few of them annually in what were called "lazy beds." Regarding this valuable esculent there is the following curious note in Chambers's Traditions of Edinburgh :—
" There was long, as we have been told by a very venerable personage, a prejudice in Scotland against the potato for two reasons—1st, That it was a species of the night-shade ; 2nd, That it was a provocative to incontinence !"

During the latter half of the last century, and even down to about 1809, the handicrafts in Caithness were in a state of primitive simplicity. Shoemakers and tailors were itinerant, and were fed and lodged by those who employed them. The farmer generally found both the leather and the cloth. The leather, which was tanned by himself, cost very little ; and the whole family were furnished with " brogues " at the rate of twopence per pair, and with shoes at from one shilling to one shilling and sixpence per pair. Farmers and their servants wore also in the labouring season a kind of half-boots, called " rillens," made of untanned horse or cow leather, drawn together round the foot by thongs, and with the hairy side out. For clothing, every farmer and cottager had a small flock of sheep of the native breed. "These," says the local writer* from whom we have already quoted, " annually supplied a fleece or two of good wool, which the gudewife and her family carded and spun into yarn either for blankets or blackgrays (a kind of broad cloth), or for Highland tartan for the wear of the family. When the web was returned from the weaver it was washed in warm water, and if it was necessary to full it, that operation was thus performed :—The house door was taken off the hinges, and laid on the floor ; the web was then laid on it hot out of the water ; then three or four women sat down around it on a little straw at equal distances, and all being ready bare-legged, by the signal of a song, each applied her soles to the web, and they continued pulling and tumbling it on the floor with their feet until the web was sufficiently fulled ; then it was stretched out to dry, and was ready for the family tailor or for sale, as the case might be."

No. 2.—Page 3.

MEMORANDA CONNECTED WITH PUBLIC ROADS IN THE COUNTY OF CAITHNESS.

The first attempt at road-making on a large scale in Caithness was by the late Sir John Sinclair, who called out the statute labour of the district to form a road or tract from the hill of Bein Cheilt, across the moss or bog called the Causeway Myre, towards Thurso.

The calling out the inhabitants to perform the statutory service of six days' work at roads was found so unprofitable and oppressive, that an Act (33 *Geo. III.*, *cap.* 120) was obtained in 1793 to commute

---

* " Henderson's Agricultural View of the County."

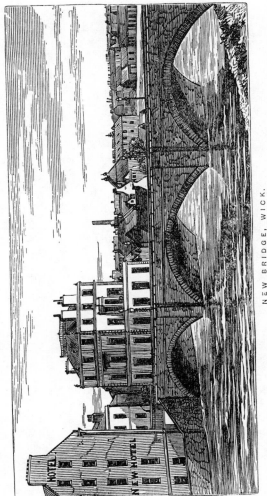

NEW BRIDGE, WICK.

the statute labour into a money payment by occupants of land, at the rate of 30s sterling for every £100 Scots of valuation held by them, by cottagers and the inhabitants of towns at the current rate of wages for the six days' work. This would produce about £500.

In 1803 an Act (43 *Geo. III.*, *cap.* 80) was passed, appropriating £20,000 for that year towards making roads and bridges in the North of Scotland, "whereby its fisheries may be encouraged, and the industry of the inhabitants greatly promoted." It being provided that one-half the cost of the roads and bridges shall be paid by the county or district.

In 1806 an Act (46 *Geo. III.*, *cap.* 138) was passed, authorising the making six roads in the county of Caithness, of which one-half was to be paid by the Parliamentary Commissioners under the previous Act of 1803, and the other half by the county. Of these six roads, one only, that from the Ord to Wick, and thence to Thurso, and known as the Parliamentary Road, was made under this Act—half the cost, amounting to £16,437 9s 9d, having been paid by the owners of lands throughout the county. The bad harvests of 1816 and 1817 prevented the other five roads in the Act from being made at that time, and no adequate provision was made for roads in the county until 1830, when an Act (11 *Geo. IV.*, *cap.* 102) was obtained to provide for the proper repair of the old roads and the making of new ones by an assessment on owners and occupiers of lands amounting to about £1500 a-year, exclusive of the commutation on occupiers of cottages and inhabitants of towns. Under this Act, 137 miles of roads were made, and the communications throughout the greater part of the county opened up. The assessment on occupants under the Act (1830) was found to be adequate for the future maintenance of the roads, if expended, over all the leading lines without the limitation of districts and parishes, but there were not funds sufficient to pay off the money borrowed to make the roads. To provide a sum sufficient to pay off the debt in twenty-one years, the proprietors of land agreed to double the assessment payable by them, and an Act (1838, 1–2 *Vict.*, *cap,* 79) was got to effect this, and to place 137 miles of the leading lines of roads under the management of the Commissioners for the repair of Highland roads, as the only means of partially consolidating the roads and parishes into one trust.

In 1859 the Act of 1838 expired, and with it a large proportion of the funds.

An Act (1860, 23—24 *Vict.*, *cap.* 201) has been obtained laying a uniform assessment on the real rent of all lands and heritages in the county, payable half by owners and half by occupants ; consolidating all the funds and roads into one trust and system of management, and giving power to remove tolls when a fair and adequate substitute for the revenue they produce shall have been provided.

Under this Act, in addition to the former, road trustees being proprietors, one or more tenant farmers are elected by each parish.

To provide for the maintenance of the Parliamentary roads in the Highlands and in Caithness, an Act was passed in 1819 appropriating to that purpose the sum of £5000, to be paid annually by the Barons of the Exchequer in Scotland, and requiring the balance in each county to be asssessed on the proprietors of land and of houses in the county and burghs, according to the returns of rentals for the property tax in 1814.

The whole of this assessment in Caithness fell on the landward heritors, there being at that time no owner of house property in the towns who was assessed for income tax, and hence the towns, at that time so insignificant, have been raised to their present prosperity and importance by means of communications between themselves and with the south, to which they have up to this date contributed nothing.

Amount paid for making and maintaining county roads since 1830, ...	£68,406	18	0
Half cost of making fifty-four miles of Parliamentary Road and proportion of repairs	28,853	9	8
	£97,260	7	8

Whereof paid by owners of land exclusively—					
Half cost, making fifty-four miles Parliamentary Road, ...	£16,437	9	6		
Proportion of maintaining do., do.,	12,416	0	2		
Assessment for county roads, 1830—38, .	6,354	17	3		
Do., do., do., 1838 to 1859	31,537	12	8		
Bridge money, ...	2,900	0	0		
Total paid by owners of lands, ...				69,645	19	7
Do. do. occupants and by towns . . .				27,614	8	1
				£97,260	7	8

Say in round numbers, £100,000.

SUPERSTITION IN CAITHNESS.

Perhaps in no county in Scotland, with the exception of Orkney, did superstition more abound than in Caithness. The clergy tried to grapple with the evil; but in some respects they were as superstitious themselves as the people. One imaginary source of crime in the existence of which they firmly believed was witchcraft, and to it frequent reference is made in the Presbytery records. For instance, in 1698, "the Presbytery being informed that sorcery and witchcraft abounded much in the parish of Wick, and that sorcerers banished out of Orkney lurked there, recommend seriously to the heritors and magistrates to banish all such out of the town." Again, in 1719, "several persons in Thurso being suspected of witchcraft and formal compact with the devil," the Presbytery ordered the minister to write to the sheriff and church agent for commissions to try them. The Presbytery, at the same time, resolve to hold a general fast "on account of the abounding of all vice, and the practice of that mysterious wickedness of witchcraft, sorcery, and other handiworks of the devil." "The circumstance," says Dr. P. B. Henderson, "which gave rise to these proceedings was the story of Margaret M'Gilbert. The tradition is that a person named Hugh Montgomery, in Scrabster, was much annoyed at the unaccountable consumption of his ale. Resolved to ascertain the cause, he one night kept watch in his cellar, and at last saw a company of cats stealing into the room. He waited patiently for a time, but when they commenced an attack upon his ale he could contain himself no longer. He valiantly assaulted the intruders with his sword, and cut off the leg of one of them. Very soon after a rumour arose that a venerable dame living at Oust, in the parish of Thurso, who had long the reputation of being 'no canny,' was ill in bed and without a leg. Conjecture ripened into belief, and it was speedily decided that she was the identical cat that had been deprived of her leg in Montgomery's cellar. She was forthwith apprehended and conveyed into town. The sheriff was soon on the spot, and took a precognition of the affair. This, the most nonsensical, says Sir W. Scott, in his work on 'Demonology,' of all the nonsensical papers ever written on such a subject, was remitted to the Lord Advocate (Robert Dundas), who severely censured the sheriff for taking up the case, and ordered the proceedings to be quashed. In the meantime the poor old creature had been left neglected in prison, and actually died of the ill usage she had experienced." Pennant, who heard of this ridiculous story when making the tour of Caithness, gravely asks what part of the old lady would have been wanting had the cat's tail been cut off? To this very puzzling question Robert Mackay, the historian of the Clan Mackay, indignantly replies, "Both the inquiry itself, and the question whether or not it was witty, might have been suspended until it was ascertained that *such cats had tails!*"

Dr. Charles Mackay, in his "Popular Delusions," gives a different version of this story, which I slightly abbreviate. He says that Montgomery was a carpenter who had a mortal antipathy to cats, and somehow or other these animals generally chose his backyard for their caterwaulings. He puzzled his brains for a long time to know why he above all his neighbours should be so pestered. At last he came to the sage conclusion that his tormentors were not cats, but witches. The next time the unlucky tabbies assembled in the backyard he rushed out among them with an axe, a dirk, and a broadsword, mortally wounded two of them and maimed the leg of a third with his axe, but did not capture any of them. A few days afterwards two old women of the parish died with the marks of wounds on their bodies. The third, Nanny Gilbert, was found in bed with her leg broken. She was brought to Thurso, and being put to the torture, confessed that she was indeed a witch, that the two old women recently deceased were witches also, besides about a score of others whom she named. From the ill usage she had received she died the next day in prison. Happily for the persons she had named in her confession, Dundas of Arniston, at that time the King's Advocate-General, wrote to the sheriff-depute, one Captain Ross of Littledean, cautioning him not to proceed to trial, the "thing being of too great difficulty, and beyond the jurisdiction of an inferior court." He himself examined the pre-cognition with great care, and was so convinced of the folly of the whole case that he quashed all further proceedings.

THE DWELLING-HOUSES, DRESS, ETC., IN CAITHNESS.

The houses of the Caithness peasantry in the olden time were such as would have thrown a connoisseur in architecture, like Mr Ruskin, into convulsions. They were wretched hovels of turf and stone with a divot roof, and consisted generally of two rooms, a "but and a ben," or, as they were provincially termed, the "fire-house and cellar,"

The fire was in the middle of the floor; and the smoke issued out at an aperture in the roof, not unfrequently at the door, and in short, wherever it could find an egress. The byre formed a part of the main dwelling; and the domestics and cattle entered at the same door, and were only separated from each other by a flag or two in the way of partition, and by a straw mat at the one end, which by being lifted up or moved aside served the purpose of a door, and admitted you to the sitting apartment. A canopy of smoke commonly rested over the heads of the inmates from which by long custom they seemed to feel no sort of inconvenience or discomfort. On the contrary, they considered that it added greatly to the warmth of the place, and there can be no doubt that dwellings of this description were much warmer in the winter season than finer houses that were provided with chimneys, and built of stone, with slate roofs. The supporting couples or rafters were black as ebony with soot, which hung also in festoons from the roof. The inferior bipeds and quadrupeds had free access to the fire house. Hens and ducks freely mingled there; and the pig walked about very familiarly among the pots and pans in quest of dainties, or lay enjoying a siesta by the hearth. Occasionally too, when the weather was cold, a cow with a young calf at her feet might be seen ruminating in one corner of the apartment. Nor was there an ill-natured collie wanting to salute you with a growl as you entered. The cellar, which was the bedroom of the family, had no fire in it summer or winter. The principal bed in which the good man and his better half reposed, was shaped like a large square box and called a "close bed" from its being every where shut in except in front. This was furnished with a folding door which was always drawn close to when the parties retired to rest, for it never occurred to them that the admission of free air was necessary for the preservation of health. The barn and kiln were attached to the upper end of the house.

The midden was always in front, and the back was the kail-yard, which was usually well supplied with cabbage, with the addition, perhaps, of a few sybots, some camomile, and southron-wood, and one or two saughs or bowtrees.

In some of the houses belonging to the higher grade of the farmers there was an additional room off the "cellar" which had a chimney, and was styled the "chamer" (chamber). It was never used except on great occasions, such as christening or catechising, or when the family received a visit from some of their wealthier and more respected friends. In a recess in the wall was the family library, which consisted of the big ha' Bible, the "Pilgrim's Progress," Boston's "Fourfold State," and the "Crook in the Lot," with perhaps "Jack the Giant Killer," "Goody Two Shoes," and a few ballads, the property of the junior members of the family, purchased from some travelling packman.

The houses of the poorer sort of the people in the highlands of the county were mostly altogether of turf, and generally consisted of but one appartment, with the family in the one end, and the cattle in the other. The roof was thatched with heather, and not unfrequently with rushes. The couples, which were of undressed birks, rested on the clay floor, and to these the cattle were attached by a binding of twisted withes, called "nasks."

Tallow being expensive and oil not to be had in the district, the peasantry used for light bogwood, that is, decayed fir, in which there is much resinous matter, dug out of the mosses. This was cut up into small pieces, and one of these when ignited served as a candle, could be carried conveniently in the hand, and in a dark winter evening showed the way to the barn or any of the premises outside. A good rousing fire afforded abundance of light for all domestic purposes indoors.

Nor could much be said in praise of the houses of the gentry. They were large ungainly erections, generally of two storeys, with small windows and high-peaked crow-stepped gables. The seat of the late William Sinclair, Earl of Caithness, at Ratter, which was standing not many years ago, was an unsightly lump of a building, more resembling an old granary than the mansion of a nobleman. With the exception of the dining-room, the apartments were small, and the whole were unfurnished with anything in the shape of sofas or carpets. To most of the houses was attached what was called a "loupen on stane," 'for the benefit of such ladies and gentlemen as could not otherwise get easily on horseback. The old gentry, however, paid some attention to horticulture, and they had very passable gardens, modelled somewhat after the Dutch style, in most of which were to be seen a dove-cot and a stone dial.

About eighty or ninety years ago, and before the introduction of potatoes, the diet of the lower classes was very poor, consisting gene-rally of brose or porridge to breakfast, of cabbage boiled with a mixture of oatmeal for dinner, and of bere bread and brochan (water gruel) for supper. Butcher meat, with the exception of a little pork, rarely appeared at table. Sowens, when it was to be had, was a favourite dish for breakfast, dinner, or supper. Another favourite dish was "bursten," which was prepared by a portion of oats and bere being hastily dried in a pot over the fire, and then ground in a hand-quern.* The kind of meal thus produced, when taken with milk, formed a very palatable dish, and was by many preferred to the ordinary porridge. The inhabitants along the sea-coast, when fish was to be had, got on pretty well; but when they were prevented by rough weather from going to sea, or when, as sometimes happened, the fish appeared to have left the coast, they had recourse to shellfish, such as limpets, mussels, and periwinkles, which were but an indif-ferent substitute for the other. One luxury, however, they had which their descendants, by the stringency of the revenue laws, are deprived of, namely, good home-brewed ale. There was scarcely a family without this wholesome beverage.

The gentry, on the other hand, though without the refinements and luxuries of modern life, lived well and sumptuously. They had plenty of roasted and boiled, and abundance of wine, particularly claret; and when whisky punch became the order of the day, they did ample justice to it, commonly drinking it out of large china bowls. One of these relics of the good old times the writer saw in the Castle of Dunbeath. It was a magnificent article of its kind, about forty-eight inches in circumference, and deep in proportion.

The dress of the lower order of both sexes was very plain, consisting entirely of woollen stuffs of home manufacture. The men wore coats,

---

* In a Pict's house at Kettleburn, in the parish of Wick, A. H. Rhind, Esq. of Sibster, found among other relics two querns, a proof that at a very early period corn was to some extent grown in Caithness.

vests, and breeches of black or hodden gray, and those who could not conveniently get metal buttons used ones made of wood, which they called "knobbies." For Sunday attire they had a finer stuff, called manky, which was generally dyed blue. The women wore plain gowns of drugget. Silk and straw bonnets were totally unknown. Before marriage young lasses went bare headed to kirk and market, with only a narrow stripe of ribbon—Scottice, a snood—round the brow, while the hair was secured by a large comb which extended from ear to ear, and was termed a "kepping comb." Their chief finery was a string or two round the neck of glass beads of various colours. The headgear of the married women was a plain "toy," and that of a matron in full dress a "box-plait mutch," or cap puffed out at the top and encircled with a broad flashy ribbon. Elderly females wore scarlet plaids, and the writer remembers to have seen his grandmother go to church habited in a plaid of this colour. One piece of dress frequently worn by the women, and which had a picturesque appearance was a blue short gown with long red sleeves.

At the time of which we speak, when there were no roads or bridges in the county, travelling, which had to be performed either on foot or on horseback, was often attended with much danger, especially in the winter season. In 1620, the eldest son of Sir John Sinclair of Greenland and Ratter was drowned in attempting to ford the Burn of Reisgill, when it was overflowing its banks after a heavy fall of rain. When a lady travelled she rode on a pad behind her husband or a servant. The greatest difficulty was in crossing moors. To obviate this in some measure, the rider usually carried a bundle of heather at the saddle bow, and when he encountered a boggy step he threw on it some of the heather, and then led his pony over it. Notwithstanding these drawbacks and inconveniences, there was much visiting and sociality among both the upper and lower classes. A visit was a visit in those days, and not a mere formal call of a quarter of an hour or twenty minutes. When a family of the better sort visited another, they commonly remained with them a week or a fortnight, faring on the best, and whiling away the hours that were not devoted to festivity in dancing, in playing at cards, or "blindman's buff," which were the chief indoor amusements of the period. People were not then in the habit of reading. Indeed there was nothing to read except long-winded stories, such as Richardson's "Pamela," or Smollet's "Roderick Random," and Fielding's "Tom Jones," which last, though amusing enough, were certainly not calculated to improve the mind or mend the morals. A stray newspaper from Edinburgh perhaps found its way into the county once a month. With much boisterous hilarity and freedom of manners there mingled at the same time a good deal of formal etiquette and ceremony, the going through some of which was rather trying to one who happened to be afflicted with what the French term *mauvais honte*. For instance, when a gentleman visited a family, he had to kiss all the ladies in the house. This was no doubt a pleasant enough ceremony so far as regarded the young ladies of the establishment, but it was not quite so agreeable to have to salute in this way the elderly ladies, especially if they took snuff, which in these days they very generally did. From Dr Somerville's autobiography, it would appear that the fashion of snuffing prevailed to a much greater extent among the fair sex in the south of Scotland than in the north. "Many young ladies," says he, "and perhaps the greater number of married men and women carried snuff boxes.   The habit prevailed so generally that it was not uncommon for lovers to present their sweethearts with snuff boxes, which were to be purchased for that purpose adorned with devices emblematical of love and constancy." The worthy doctor also mentions that acquaintances of both sexes, when they met after long absence, and sometimes even on the occasion of visiting, saluted with a kiss."

The " Virginian weed" seems to have found its way into Caithness at a very early period.   In the old Session Register of Canisbay, from which I have quoted in a preceding part of this work, there is a curious entry of date 1655, mentioning that one of the congregation was fined for taking snuff during "the time of singing the psalm." The clergy, indeed, both Catholic and Protestant, would seem from the first to have been much opposed to snuffing during divine service. "In 1624," says Dr Macnish, " Pope Urban VIII. published a bull excommunicating all persons found guilty of taking snuff when in church."   At a comparatively recent period, a great deal of tobacco was clandestinely introduced into Caithness and manufactured into it. Some people had hand mills for the purpose of grinding the tobacco.

I have alluded to the ancient social habits of the people.   They were fond of congregating to drink and "trip it on the fantastic," and to such a height was this carried, particularly in Wick, that the church there deemed it necessary to apply a check to the growing evil. In the records of the burgh there is a curious entry to this effect.   On 2nd February, 1787, the Rev. William Sutherland and kirk-session send in a strong petition to the magistrates against the "keeping of disorderly houses for dancing and drinking" within the burgh, whereupon the civic functionaries issue the following edict :—" The magistrates did and hereby do enact that in time coming every householder within the burgh who keeps disorderly houses for dancing and drinking, etc., shall, on a complaint to the magistrates from the kirk-session of Wick or the procurator-fiscal of the burgh, be liable in the sum of ten pounds Scots each, *toties quoties.*   That each musician or piper who shall take it upon him to play at such meeting shall forfeit the sum of six pounds Scots for each trespass.   That no public dances are to be allowed within the burgh except Christmas Day and New Year's Day, and that only to continue till ten o'clock each night, under the penalty of twelve pounds Scots, to be paid by each piper or musician who shall play after that hour," etc., etc.   The same records afford a number of curious entries, of which the following is one :—In 1741, "William Callum, fisherman in Wick, guilty of sheep-stealing, is liberated from prison, etc., on agreeing to become common hangman and executioner for the burgh, etc., and he binds and obliges himself to execute and perform everything proper and incumbent on him in that office, as he shall be ordered and authorised by warrant of the magistrates or of the sheriff of Caithness and his depute.   And as he cannot write, he empowers William Calder, notary public and clerk of the said burgh, to subscribe the enactment and obligation for him."

I have in a former work, " Sketches from John O'Groat's," given a description of most of the old superstitions, and of the peculiar customs that were observed at marriages, funerals, etc., by the common people in the county.   One ancient custom to which I alluded was that of having a white flag carried before a funeral.   Dr Henderson mentions a curious practice which, in the case of funerals, prevailed in Thurso in his younger days. "The kirk officer," says he, "perambulates the streets with a small deep-toned bell in each hand; at intervals he raises the one, then the other, as he goes along, causing them to send forth a very solemn sound. At the corners of the streets he stops and invites all 'brothers and sisters' to attend the funeral of the person mentioned by him. As it is not the custom for females to attend funerals in this county, it is possible that this form of invitation has been handed down from Popish times, or at all events from the period when Episcopacy prevailed. When the funeral took place the officer preceded it with the bells, which ever and anon sounded their sad notes, while the church bell tolled at measured intervals. The whole scene was calculated to arrest the attention of the most unthinking passenger."

It was also one of the duties of the sexton to go through the town on the Sunday forenoon ringing a small hand-bell to warn the people of the hour for public worship. Both these customs have now fallen into desuetude.

No. 3.—Page 14.

EXTRACTS FROM OLD INVENTORIES OF THE TITLES OF THE ESTATE OF MALCOLM GROAT OF WARSE.

These Inventories are in the possession of the Clerk of Supply of Orkney.

1. JOHN GROT, son to HUGH GROT, 1496.—*Charter* from William De St Claro, Earl of Caithness, to John Groat, son to Hugh Groat, of one penny land in Duncansby, paying therefor yearly *tres modios Brasii* at Martinmas. Dated at Girnigoe Castle, 14th March, 1496.

2. WILLIAM GROAT, younger, 1507.—*Charter* from William Oliphant and Christian Sutherland, his spouse, to William Groat, younger, of his halfpenny land in Duncansby, for the payment of five shillings Scots at two terms. Dated the 12th May, 1507.

3. JOHN GROAT, 1515.—*Precept of Sasine* by Jo. Sinclair, Earl of Caithness, for infefting John Groat in ane penny land in Dungsby. Dated at Nose, 5th Oct., 1515.

4. JOHN GROAT, 1515.—*Sasine* in favors of John Groat of ane penny land and miln in Duncansbay, proceeding on a precept of Sasine from John, Earl of Caithness, to him thereanent. Sasine dated 12th Oct., 1515.

5. WILLIAM GROAT, 1515.—*Sasine* to William Groat in a farthing land in Dungsby, proceeding on a precept from John, Earl Caithness. Sasine dated 12th Oct., 1515.

6. WALTER GROT, son of WILLIAM GROT, 1521.—*Precept of Sasine*, John, Earl Caithness, for infefting Mr Walter Groat, son and air of umquhile William Grot, in a farthing land in Dungsby. Dated 28th Sept., 1521.

6-2. WILLIAM GROT son to JOHN GROT, 1521.—*Precept of Sasine* by Andrew Oliphant of Berrydale, and Superior of the fourth part of Caithness, to William Groat, son to John Grot on the land in Duncansbay called the penny land, dated at Auldwick, 22d Nov., 1521. The Precept proceeds on a Charter formerly granted.

7. JOHN GROAT, 1523.—*Precept of Sasine,* Jo. Sinclair, Earl

Caithness, for infefting Jo. Groat in one penny land in Dungsby conform to a Charter granted yr anent. The precept is dated at Girnigoe, 22nd Oct., 1523.

8. DONALD GROAT, 1536.—*Sasine* in favor of Donald Groat on the lands of Skirsary, upon a precept of sasine granted to him by Pat. Mowat of   and Freswick, relative to a disposition granted by him to the said Donald mentd in the said precept. The Sasine is dated 16th July, 1536.

9. JOHN GROAT, eldest son of WILLIAM GROAT, 1540.—*Precept of Clare Constat*, George, Earl Caithness, in favours of Jo. ·Groat, eldest son and heir to William Groat, for infefting him in a farthing land in Duncansbay, dated at Mey, 8th March, 1540, before witnesses. These honest men, John Sinclair of Dun, Walter Mowat of Rattar, Malcolm Groat of Warse, and another honest man, Mr Jo. Dunnot, Rector of Canasbay, and seul oyrs.

10. HUGH GROAT, 1540.—*Charter* dated 11th March, 1540, granted by Hugh Groat, portioner of Duncansbay, with consent of Mariot Bane, his spouse liferentrix thereof, in favours of William Bane, in Papingo of a fourth part of his two-penny land, called in the Charter *unam obolatam*, in Duncansbay, with his whole part of the field called Stamster, for the payment of a penny *blench*.

11. GILBERT GROT, son of WILLIAM GROT, and HUGH GROT, 1543. —*Instrument of Resignation* by Mr Gilbert Grot, son and apparent heir of William Grot, in favours of Hugh Grot his brother, of two-penny land in Dungsby, in the hands of Laurence, Lord Oliphant, as Superior thereof, dated 24th May, 1543.

12. DONALD GROAT and his son JOHN GROAT, 1547.—*Disposition* on parcht, Be Dod Groat in Duncansbay, in favour of his son John Groat, of his half-penny land in Skirsary, for the payt of 65 mks, contained in the Reversion of the said lands to Pat. Mowat of Bagirholly, Superior thereof, and of his two-penny land in Cannasbay, for the payment of a 100 mks to the Earl of Caithness, Superior, as contained in the Reversion thereof. Dated at Dunnet, 5th August, 1547.

13. JOHN GROAT, son of FINLAY GROAT, 1549.—*Precept of Clare Constat* from Geo., Earl Caithness, to John Groat, son to Finlay Groat, for infefting him in the ferry-house and ferry, and 20 feet round about the said house. Dated at Wick, the   day of Nov., 1549.

14. WILLIAM GROAT, 1557.—*Precept of Sasine*, Laurence, Lord Oliphant, for infefting William Groat in ane Octo land in Dungsby, as contained in a Charter granted to him thereanent. The precept is dated 7th June, 1557.

15. HUGH GROAT, 1557.—*Charter*, the Master of Oliphant to Hugh Groat and the heirs procreat betwixt him and Catherine Ratter, his spouse, on the land in Duncansbay called the penny land, and another penny land there, making two penny land, for the yearly payt. for the land called the penny land Ten Sh. Scots, and for the other penny land a penny blench. Dated at Auldwick, the 11th June, 1557.

16. *Precept of Sasine* on said Charter, dated 11th June, 1557.

17. Sasine on Charter and Precept of Sasine, No. 15 and 16, dated 16th June, 1557, under the subscription of Jo. Stevenson, N.P.

18. JOHN GROAT, 1557.—*Precept of Sasine* from Laurence, Master of Oliphant, for infefting John Groat in ane halfpenny land, called *unam obolatam*, in Dungsby, as contained in a Charter granted there-anent. The precept is dated at Auldwick, 12th June, 1557.

19. WILLIAM GROAT, son of FINLAY GROAT, 1557.—*Charter* from the Master of Oliphant, dated at Auldwick, 12th June, 1557, in favors of William Groat, son to Finlay Groat, upon ane Octoe of land of Duncansbay, for the yearly payment of 15 pennys Scots at two terms in the year.

20. JOHN and FINLAY GROAT, 1576.—*Charter*, John Groat, portioner of Dungsby, to Finlay Groat on a farthing land at Dungsby, and the heirs male of his body, which failing, to the said John and the heirs male of his body, paying therefor yearly three pecks with two cops and half a cop bear, dated at Dungsby, 15th Nov., 1576.*

20. *Sasine* thereon, dated 16th Nov., 1576.

21. HUTCHEON GROAT, 1572.—*Letter of Reversion* from Malcolm Groat of Tankerness to Hutcheon Grot òf Dungsby, for redemption of ane halfpenny land in Dungsby, and his haill part of the field called Stemster, disponed by the said Hutcheon to the said Malcolm, by payt. of 40 Sh. Scots in the Kirk of Cannasbay, or in his house of heritage in Dungsby, upon any day 'twixt the sun-rising and down-passing of the samen, dated at Dungsby, 30th August, 1572.

22. HUGH GROAT and JOHN GROAT, his son, 1589.—*Charter of Resignation.*—Laurence, Lord Oliphant, to Hugh Groat in Duncansbay, and Marion Mowat, his spouse, and longest liver in liferent, and John Groat, younger, eldest son, and the heirs male of his body, which failing, to his nearest and lawful heirs male and assignees, qt'soever of his land in Duncansbay called the Pennyland, and also of one penny land more in said town extending to two penny land, which formerly belonged to the said Hugh Groat holden of the said Lord Oliphant, paying yearly for the penny land 10 Sh. Scots, and for the oy'r penny land a penny blench with Scat and S   to the Cathedral Church of Kirkwall as use is. Dated at Auldwick, 29th January, 1589.

23. JOHN GROAT, grandson of JOHN GROAT, 1590.—*Sasine* in favour of John Groat in Dungsby, oye and heir to John Groat, elder there, proceeding on a precept of *Clare Constat* from Laurence Lord Oliphant for infefting him in a halfpenny land, called *unam obolatam ferrarum de Dungsby*, which belonged to the said Jo. Groat, elder, his grandfather—dated 16th November, 1589. The Sasine dated 6th June, 1590.

24. HUTCHEON GROAT, 1593.—*Letter of Reversion* from William Groat of Tankerness (in Orkney) to Hutcheon Groat of Duncansby, for redemption of ane halfpenny land in Duncansbay, and a part of a the field called Stemster disposed by the said Hutcheon Groat to the said William for payment of £24 Scots at any time in the Kirk of Cannasbay, and upon any day 'twixt the sun-rising and down-passing thereof. Dated 30th August, 1593.

25. HUGH GROAT, 1595.—*Charter* from Hugh Groat, feuar of 2d land in Duncansbay, and John Groat, his eldest son, with consent of Marion Bane, his spouse, to George Sinclair of Mey, and James Sinclair, his second son, and the heirs male of his body, which failing, to John Sinclair, his third son, and the heirs male of his body, whilks failing, to the said George Sinclair, his heirs and assignees whatsome'r, of three farthing land of their lands in Duncansbay, paying therefor yearly to the Lord Oliphant, superior, of 10 Sh. Scots if asked allenarly.

* There is in the possession of G. Petrie a discharge by Malcolm Groat of Tankerness to his guid friend Jon Grot of Dongsby of all maills and duties of ane penny land, with the pertinents and the mill of Dongisby, which the said John had in tack, and assidation of the said Malcolm. Dated at Dungasby, 11th Mch., 1570.

Dated 26th September, 1595.   N.B.--A nott: signs for them with three subscribing witnesses.

26. JOHN GROAT, son of umql. HUTCHEON GROAT, and ADAM GROAT, brother of JOHN, 1603.--*Charter* in English, Jo. Groat, lawful son and heir of umquhil Hutcheon Groat, portioner of Duncansby, to Adam Groat, his brother-german, his heirs and assignees qt'soer bearing and retaining the sirname of Grot and nane other, all and haill these his proper two penny land in Duncansbay, holden of the Lord Oliphant, and paying therefor yearly to the said Jo. Groat and his heirs of ane penny blench and 10 Sh. and one penny Scots to the superior, at the usual terms redeemable for the pay't of the sum of . Dated at Kirkwall, 18th Nov., 1603.

27. ADAM GROT and JOHN GROT, brothers, 1606.—"*Sasine* wrot on paper" in favours of Adam Grot proceeding on a Charter, granted to him by John Grot, his eldest brother, portioner of Dungsby, of his two penny land in Dungsby, then in the possession of the said Adam and Donald Grot of Warse. The Sasine is dated the 11th August, 1606. Reg'rat in the Books of the Sheriffdom of Inverness and Cromaity, at the Chanonry of Ross, upon the 21st of said month of August.

28. DONALD GROAT to JOHN GROAT, son of umql. FINLAY GROAT, 1607.—*Charter*, Donald Groat of Warse, and portioner of Dungsby, to John Groat, lawful son and apparent heir of umquhil Finlay Groat, portioner of Dungsby, and the heirs male of his body, which failing, to return to the said Donald Groat and his heirs male on his farthing land in Dungsby, formerly disponed by John Groat, his father, to the said Finlay Groat, and was at the date of the Charter possessed by John Groat, Finlay's son, paying therefor yearly three pecks, two cops, and half a cop of bear at Marts. yearly, in name of feu farm. Dated 2d Jan., 1607.

29. JOHN and ADAM GROAT, brothers, 1612.—*Ane Instrument* taken by Jo. Groat, agt. Adam, his brother, upon Adam's surrendering one of the two penny lands to him, in consequence of the reversion mentioned in the Charter No. 26.   Dated the said instrument, 21st Feb., 1612.

30. MALCOLM GROAT of Warse, 1617.—*Liferent Sasine* in favours of Marion Doul, spouse of Malcolm Groat of Warse, on the one penny land of Warse and Smiddies, and one penny land in Duncansbay. Dated the   day of July, 1617.

31. JOHN GROAT, son of FINLAY GROAT, 1626.--*Sasine* in favours of Jo. Groat, son to Finlay Groat in Duncansbay, proceeding on a precept of *Clare Constat* granted by Jo., Bishop of Caithness, for infefting the said John in ane tenement in Wick, *ex boreale parte ejusd.*   Sasine dated 27th day of   1626, and reg'rat.

32. MALCOLM GROAT, 1656.—*Sasine*, Malcolm Groat, the late ferryman's father, upon his land in Duncansbay.   Dated 20 and 26 days of Jan., 1656.

NOTE.—JOHN GROAT.—The ferryman referred to here was probably John Groat, described as "the Ferryman" in a document belonging to about the same date as the Inventory in which No. 32 is entered.

32a. MALCOLM GROAT and DONALD GROAT, his son, 1642.—*Inhibition.*—Malcolm Groat, and Marion Doul, and Donald Groat, his son, agt. Sir William Sinclair and Sir James, his son, for not implementing the Contract upon the lands of Wares, 1642.

33. JOHN GROAT FINLAYSON.--*Inhibition.*—Jo. Groat Finlay's son, being the late ferryman's grandfather, agt. Sir James Sinclair of

Cannasbay, and Sir William Sinclair of Cadboll, his father, proceeding upon and contract of sale of Jo. Harper's D. land in Duncansby, by them in favours of him.   No date.

NOTE.—The John Groat above mentioned is the same referred to in No. 28 as Finlay's son.

MALCOLM GROAT *of Wares*, mentioned in No. 32a, had a *son* DONALD, who appears to have been succeeded by *Malcolm Groat*, whose son, *George Groat*, on 16th March, 1715, disponed all his lands in Duncansby, and in the Parish of Latheron, together with the ferry-house, ferry, and ferry-boats of Duncansby, and lands pertaining thereto, to Malcolm Groat, his son, and his heirs male ; whom failing, to other parties of the name of Groat, mentioned in the Deed, and their heirs male respectively.   The Disposition does not appear to have been recorded.

Malcolm Groat, last mentioned, became embarrassed, and on 1st August, 1741, a fitted account, showing an arrear of £8352 17s. 8d. Scots, of teinds and other duties due by him, was subscribed by him and by Mr William Sinclair* of Freswick,'and an obligation was annexed thereto, binding Mr Sinclair to accept of £4000 Scots in full payment of said arrear, for which a Bond was granted of the date of the account by Malcolm Groat to Freswick.   The original Disposition and the fitted account, both on stamped paper, are in my possession.

GEO. PETRIE, Clerk of Supply.

KIRKWALL, 9th October, 1860.

No. 4.—Page 42.

The oldest extant valuation of the county is dated in 1707.   It was subsequently amended and revised at various intervals, and in 1760 and 1798 the valuation stood as follows :—

Landward part of the county,	...		...		...	...	£34,972	8 6
Burgh of Wick,	...	...	...	...	...	...	166	13 4
Town of Thurso,	...	...	...	...	...	...	666	13 4
Total, Scots money,		...	...	...		...	£35,805	15 2

At Whitsunday, 1860, the valuation on real rent stood thus :—

Landward part of the county,	...		...	...	...	£86,753 18 0
Town of Thurso,	...	...	...	...	...	4,429 0 0
Parliamentary Burgh of Wick—						
Royal Burgh, ...	...	...	...£3,694 18 0			
Pulteneytown,	...	...	... 10,355 4 0			
Louisburgh, etc.,	...	...	... 2,328 10 0			16,378 12 0
Sterling, ...	...	...	...	...	...	£107,561 10 0

The amount of real rent of the county in 1814 upon which property tax was levied was £29,484 14s. 10d.

---

* This Mr Sinclair of Freswick was the second son of John Sinclair, fifth laird of Ratter.   It was he whom the band of Caithness thieves had plotted to rob and murder. His memory is still fresh among the inhabitants of the district in which he resided. He would appear to have possessed great astuteness and force of character, and was altogether a person of much local celebrity in his day.

No. 5.—Page 105.

EARLS OF CAITHNESS OF THE SINCLAIR FAMILY, AFTER CAITHNESS WAS DISJOINED FROM ORKNEY AND ERECTED INTO A SEPARATE EARLDOM.

1. William Sinclair, Chancellor, grandson of Henry Sinclair, the first of that name, Earl of Orkney, was invested with the Earldom of Caithness in 1455.

2. William, second son of the Chancellor—his father having resigned the earldom in his favour—became Earl in 1476. He fell at Flodden in 1513, and was succeeded by his son John.

3. John was killed at the battle of Summerdale, in Orkney, in the year 1529, and was succeeded by his son George.

4. George died in 1583, and was succeeded by his grandson George, son of John, Master of Caithness, who died in prison at Girnigoe in 1576.

5. George, having survived both his son and his grandson, died in 1643, and was succeeded by his great-grandson George.

6. This George, being encumbered with debt, and having no male issue, sold his title and estates to John Campbell of Glenorchy. He died in 1676. The title was disputed by George Sinclair of Keiss, a descendant of the fifth Earl by his second son, who ultimately obtained the earldom.

7. George of Keiss, now Earl of Caithness, died unmarried in 1698, and was succeeded by his second cousin, Sir John Sinclair of Murkle.*

8. John, died in 1705, and was succeeded by his son Alexander.

9. Alexander, died in 1766 without male heir, and was succeeded by William Sinclair of Ratter, who was lineally descended from Sir John Sinclair of Greenland and Ratter, second brother of the fifth Earl.

10. William of Ratter, died in 1782, and was succeeded by his son John, Lord Berriedale, a major in the army.

11. John, died unmarried in 1789, and was succeeded by Sir James Sinclair of Mey, the ninth in lineal descent from George Sinclair of Mey, youngest son of the fourth Earl.

12. James, died in 1823, and was succeeded by his son Alexander.

13. Alexander, died in 1855, and was succeeded by his son James, the present Earl, and the fourteenth of the Sinclair family who have inherited the earldom of Caithness. His Lordship was elected one of the Representative Peers of Scotland in 1858.

ARMORIAL BEARINGS OF THE EARLS OF CAITHNESS.

Quarterly—1st azure, a ship at anchor, her oars erected in saltyre within a double tressure counterfloured, or; 2nd and 3rd or, a lion rampant, gules; 4th azure, a ship under sail, or. And over all a cross engrailed, dividing the four quarters, salt. Crest on a wreath, a cock proper, two griffins armed and beaked, or. Motto—"Commit thyself to God."

---

* The lands of Murkle appear to have been first bestowed on James Sinclair, second son of John, Master of Caithness. His son Sir James was created a baronet of Scotland and Nova Scotia in 1636. Sir James' eldest son John (afterwards Earl of Caithness) left four sons—Alexander (who succeeded him), John, Francis, and Archibald. John studied law, and became a judge of the Court of Session, with the title of Lord Murkle. The first James Sinclair married Elizabeth Stewart, daughter of the Earl of Orkney, and their son James, the baronet, married Jean, daughter of Stewart of Mains and Burray, also in Orkney.

PEDIGREE OF THE MEY FAMILY.

WILLIAM SINCLAIR, elder brother of George, son of the 4th Earl.	GEORGE SINCLAIR, died about 1610, mar. Margaret, daughter of William, 7 L. Forbes.	
Sir WILLIAM, created 1631, married Katharine, dghtr. of Ross of Balnagown.	JOHN SINCLAIR, kn'td. 1631, d. 1651, pur. Geanies, Stemster Brabstermyre, & Dunbeath (vide Dunbeath)	MARGARET, mar. Wm. Dunbar of Hempriggs, cr. 1698, d. 1741, now represent-by Sir Geo. Dunbar.
Sir JAMES, mar. Elizabeth, 2 dgtr. of John Ld. Lindores.		
Sir WILLIAM, mar. Margaret, d'tr. of Geo., Earl Seaforth.	ROBERT SINCLAIR of Durran, 2 son of Sir Jas. & 1 Durran f'mly.	GEORGE SINCLAIR of Olrig, 4 s'n of Sir Jas. ances. Olrig Sinclairs.
Sir JAMES, m. Frances, daughter of Sir John Towers.		
Sir JAMES, m. Mary, daughter of James, Lord Duffus.		
Sir JAMES, m. Margaret, daug. of Jn. Sinclair, Barrock.		
Sir JOHN, m. Charlotte, daug. of Eric, Lord Duffus.		
Sir JAMES, 12th Earl of Caithness, m. Miss Campbell, Barcaldine.		
ALEXANDER, 13 Earl, m. Frances H. Leigh, dr. of Dean Hereford.		
JAMES, 14th Earl, m. Louisa G. Phillips, dr. of Sir Geo. Phillips.		

NOTES.—Durran remained in the family of Sinclair until purchased by the late Earl of Caithness.

The male representatives of this branch are Augustus Sinclair and Charles Sinclair, sons of the late Lieut.-Colonel John Sutherland Sinclair, R.A.

The Estate of Olrig remained in the family till the time of Charles Sinclair of Olrig. He left a daughter, Fenella, who married Mr Cullen, barrister-at-law, and left several children. Whether Mrs Cullen, or her father, sold the estate, I have not been able to ascertain.

LETTER OF MR SINCLAIR OF FORSS TO THE AUTHOR.

FORSS, 13*th November*, 1860.

DEAR SIR,
         I send you pedigree of the Sinclairs of Forss, who are descended from David Sinclair of Dunn, cousin-german to the Earl of Sutherland, whom, when a minor, he rescued from falling into the hands of the Earl of Caithness, and placed under protection of Lord Huntly, for which "valuable service" the Earl of Sutherland gave him the lands and mill of Forss and Baillie. The Sinclairs of Dunn (not Southdunn) settled in Caithness about the time Henry Sinclair was created Earl of Orkney (in 1379), and held the lands of Dunn previous to the earldom of Caithness (1455) and until 1745, when the then possessor, having been baulked by his mother in keeping an engagement to join the Stewart family, shot himself, and the property was sold. The younger brother had gone into business and made sufficient to retrieve it, but was drowned in the river of Thurso, at the place called "Sinclair's Pool," * when attempting to ride across it from Thurso East.

I have not been able to trace how David Sinclair was connected with the Earl of Sutherland, but there is no doubt of the fact, as the charter bears to be to David Sinclair of Dunn, "*our cousin by consanguinity.*"

Yours truly,

JAS. SINCLAIR.

Mr J. T. CALDER.

PEDIGREE OF THE FORSS FAMILY.

David Sinclair of Dunn acquired Forss by gift from John, the fifth Earl of Sutherland, in 1560. He had three sons—1, Alexander ; 2, William ; and 3, Henry.

William Sinclair of Forss, second son of David Sinclair of Dunn, had two sons. David, eldest, married Janet Murray, and died without issue.

Alexander, second son, succeeded his father infeft in 1607 ; married Margaret, daughter of Sinclair of Mey, and had two sons. David, the eldest, infeft in 1628, died without issue. George, second son, married — 1st, Jane, daughter of William Sinclair of Dunn ; 2nd, Mary, daughter of Sinclair of Murkle. He had, by first marriage, Margaret, who married Malcolm Groat of Warse ; by second marriage, John, married—1st, Janet Sutherland of Giese ; 2nd, Barbara, daughter of John Sinclair of Ratter ; 3rd, Elizabeth, daughter of Murray of Pennyland. He had, by first marriage, George of Forss, who died without issue ; John, eldest son by second marriage, succeeded his brother, was minister of Watten in 1733, married Esther Sinclair, daughter of Sinclair of Olrig, and had an only son, Alexander

* This was the Mr Richard Sinclair mentioned in a preceding part of this work, whose apparition was said to have been seen by Mrs Sinclair at the time he was drowned.

of Forss, who died unmarried, and was succeeded by his uncle, James of Holbornhead.

James Sinclair of Holbornhead, afterwards of Forss, succeeded his nephew Alexander, and married a daughter of Robert Sinclair of Giese. He had three sons—Robert of Freswick ; William, a surgeon in the army, died unmarried ; and James. Captain Robert Sinclair of Freswick died without issue.

James of Forss married Joanna M'Kay, daughter of Bighouse, issue four sons and five daughters ; was succeeded by his eldest son.

James Sinclair of Forss married Jessie, eldest daughter of W. S. Wemyss of Southdunn, and had issue, James and other sons.

William Sinclair, physician in Thurso, fourth son of John of Forss by second marriage, married Barbara, daughter of Robert Sinclair of Giese, advocate, and had a son, William Sinclair of Freswick, by second marriage.

No. 6.—Page 105.

TESTAMENT OF ALEXANDER SUTHERLAND OF DUNBEATH, IN CAITHNESS.

(From the Bannatyne Miscellany.)

THIS Testament is dated 15th November, 1456, at Roslin Castle, the seat of the testator's son-in-law, William, Earl of Orkney, afterwards created Earl of Caithness, and at that time one of the most affluent and powerful of the nobility of Scotland. The lady, Dame Marjory Sutherland, who is mentioned in it, was the second wife of the Earl of Orkney; and their issue branched out into the families of the Sinclairs, Earls of Caithness, the Lords Sinclair of Herdmandston, and the Sinclairs of Roslin. She had usually been considered as the daughter of Alexander, eldest son of John, ninth Earl of Sutherland, until Lord Hailes, in his Additional Case for Elizabeth, Countess of Sutherland, proved her real parentage by referring to the following Testament. At the close of the seventeenth century, Father Richard Augustine Hay, Canon of St Genevieve, Paris, and Prior of St Pieremont, compiled the "Genealogie of the Sainte Clairs of Rosslyn ;" and among other original deeds which he had in his possession, and transcribed, was the following Testament. Father Hay's MS. Collections are preserved in the Advocates' Library ; and the portion that contains the Genealogy of the Sinclairs was published at Edinburgh, 1835, small 4to, in a volume edited by James Maidment, Esq., Advocate. The original Instrument containing the following Inventory and Testament (along with a large number of Roslin Charters), having recently been discovered in private hands, it was thought advisable to insert it in the present volume, in a more accurate form than it appears in Father Hay's Collections. It is written upon a large sheet of parchment, attested in the usual form by two Notaries Public. As the deed itself mentions, it was sealed by the granter ;"but the seal is now lost, and the parchment partially soiled, so that the writing in some parts is not very legible.

The titles of the parties having been prefixed, the Testament proceeds :—

In the Fyrst, xxiiij oxyn in Catheness ; Item, in ky iiijxx young and ald, wyth Ennyn Prest in Blenser, wythoutyn caluyfs ; Item, in Turs-burst[er], wyth Bulan, xx ky ; Item, wyth his son in Clanok, xx ky ; Item, wyth Aytho Faurcharson, xl ky ; Item, xxiiij fra the smyth wyth Makboyenauch or Faurchar Donaldon ; Item, xl schep in Turs-buster wyth Poyl Colanson ; Item, sex rydyn horss in Dunbeth ; Item, sex horss in Turbuster, and iiij rydyn horss ; Item, xij merys and stagges ; Item, in utensil and domycyl, xx markis ; item, in grangeys, xxiiij chaldyr of beyr, xxxv chaldyr of atis.

Item, in Siluer, sex hundreth markis, and iiijxx of poundis, tharof with Sir James in Werk twa hundreth poundis in sex peny grotis, wytnes Sir John of Strabrok. Item, wyth the Abbot of Feyrn, a hun-dreth pundis of sex peny grotis, and four score of pundis of bonath grotis, wytnes Donald Brontuch. Item, a hundreth pund wyth myself.

Item, in Clethyng, a goun of Dowa blak furryt wyth funyeis ; Item, a goun of Inglys broun, furryt wyth funyeis ; Item, a syd goun of Dunde gray ; Item, a rydyn goun of Dundee gray ; Item, a goun of broun gray to the smal of the leg; Item, a doublat of blak satin; Item, doublat of blak semys lethyr ; Item, a doublat of fustyan, and a cot of greyn ; Item, a hud of Ynglys broun, and an uthir of Scottis blak ; iij payr of scheytis in Tayn, and iij payr wyth myself ; twa blankatis, twa coveryngis. Item, in to Tayr, iij kystis full of gere, and al my charteris, wyth the Abbot of Feyrn ; Item, a kyst in Dunbeth, wyth part of geir ; Item, a fethyr bed wyth Sir Wiliam Monelaw ; Item, a compt burd, a bouster, a nopsek, a furryng of quhyt, and a Primar buk ; Item, in Werk, a kyst, wyth diuers thyngis tharin.

Hec sunt Debita que sibi debentur.

In the Fyrst, thre hundreth wedeys of yrn, that I lent to the Byschop of Catheness, bourous Alexander Malcum Saulsons son, and Wiliam of Devan, conjunctly and seuerly. Item, xx lib. of siluer that I lent to the said Bischop, for the qubilkis I haf Tom Mudy and Wat of Carnegeys obligaciouns ; Item, xij lib. the said Bischop tak of myn fra Donald Clerk at the markat ; Item, my fee the said Bischop is awand me sen he fyrst enteryt, that is to say yerly xx lib. Item, Alexander the Crounaris son aw me for the tend of Dail Thurro, and the byrun, wyth uthyr gudis that he tuk of myn, that cummys to iiijxx of markis and mair. Item, Henry the Crounaris son aw me for tendis and ky that he tuk of myn xl markis and mair, as vetail wes sauld in the countre that tym. Item, al my dettis of Catheness and Suthyrland, as they are wrytin in my compt bukis. Item, the Earl of Suthyrland tuk of my gold, silver, jeoullys, clething, fermys, mal, yrn, and uthir gudis, mair than a thusand pundis, quhat fyrst, quhrt last, atour his lettres and feil and bodylyk athis, befor natable witnes, the quhilkis I have to schaw for me. Item, the Vicar of Tayn had my meel that I left in myn ynns in Tayn, and all the beir that I had grouand in Tayn. Item, Master Wiliam of Ross aw me x markis that I lent him, borouys Alexander Mychelson, Donald Maktyrysson, and and Henry Donald Begson. Item, a hundreth pundis that I lent to Sir Androu Tulaych umquhil Chantour of Murray, for the quhilkis I have my Lordis of Ross oblygacion and my Lord of Orknays ; tharof wes payd to me xx lib. be my Lord of Ross. Item, Nycol of Tulauch

John of Hauyk, and Eduard of Tuluach aw me xx lib., the quhilk I
have thar oblygaciones of, for the Ersden of Orknay.   Item, the Erle
Huntle aw me for xviij chaldyr of bere and thre chaldyr of quheyt,
and a hundreth wedy of yrn, the quhilkis bere and quheyt I sold to
Rychard of Ruthyrfurd for half a mark ilk bol of bere, and the quheyt
for viij s. the bol, and ilk wedy of yrn for ij s. ; Item, xl lib. aucht me
be the said Erle of Huntle that I lent hym, for the quhilkis I have
twa obligaciones of hym under his seil patent.   Item, the Lard of
Loranstone, my sister son, aw me iiijxx of lib., for the quhilkis I have
his obligacion, and xxiij s. for xiiij wedy of yrn, bourth Alexander
Froyg.   Item, Master Walter Idyl aw me fourty markis.   Item, Henry
Bannermays ayrs iij lib.   Item, Theman of Abirden ij chalys ; Item,
a chalys in my kyst in Tayn.   Item, John Bullok v lib. of the ald
dettis, and xij lib. for a hundreth wedy of yrn.   Item, the Lord of
Hyrdmanston xx lib., the quhilkis gif he payis nocht fal ryn apon the
Landis of Noss.   Item, Sanderis Frog aw me xxviij s.   Item, Sir
Androu Wyschart aw me aucht pundis.   Item, Huchon Alexanderson
aw me for his wyfis hosttend bayth of siluer, gold, corn, horss, ky,
oxyn, jeoullis, and uthyr gudis.   Item, the Lard of Tuleuard aw me
vj lib. that I lent hym.   Item, Makyntoys aw me iiijxx lib. of my
malls of Clauyetharn, that tym that I had the thryd of Murray, and
Wat Tomson of Inuerness, John Makyntagart, and Thom Angusson,
borouss for the said iiijxx of pundis.

Hec sunt Debita que debet.

In the Fyrst, to the Vicar of Werk for tendis a mare ; and til
Eduardis barnys iiijxx of lib. outtakand fa mekle as I have payt til
Kenyouch his son.

I, Alexander of Suthyrland of Dunbeth, seyk in body, hayl in
mynd, makis my Testament in this manner.   In the fyrst, I gif my
saul til the Almychti God of hevyn, and till his blessit modir the
gloriouss Virgyn Mary, and til al the haly company of hevyn ; my
body to be gravyt in the College Kyrk of ane hie and mychti Lord,
Wilyam Erle of Catheness and Orknay, Lord Sinclar, &c., in Rosslyng,
ner quhar hymself thinkis to ly, quhar the said Lord Erle thinkis
spedful.   Item, I gif and 1 leyf til a prest to sing perpetualy for my
saul in the said College Kyrk x pundis of anual rent yeirly ; that is to
say, vj markis and vj s. of anual rent that I had fra Robyn Gray of
Leyth, of the quhilkis vj markis thar lyis fifty s. worth yeirly in
Louranston besid Leyth, and xx s. of the Landis of Leyth in the self,
the quhilkis wes the said Robin Grays, and xxvj s. yerly of the lands
wes James Taylouris lyand in the Canongayt :   And gif it happynys
the said landis to be quyt out, I gif and I assigne the mone to my
Lord Erle of Orknay and Catheness, &c., and til his ayris, to by fa
mekle anual as the mone extendis to.   Item, I gif a hundreth lib. to my
Lord Erle to by ix markis of land or of anual, to fulfil furth the said
feftment :   And gif it happynys that the said sex markis vj s. of anual
may nocht be bruikyt be law to the feftment of the said Chappellan, I
ordan myn executoris and myn ayris, to fulfill to the said Lord and
the said College, vj markis worth of anual, in als convenable a place,
or else als mekle mone as wil by als mekle anual in als gaynand
places :   And gif it happynys at the said hundreth pundis wil nocht
by the ix markis worth of land or anual, I ordan myn executoris to
gif als mekle mar to the said Lord Erle as fulfill the ix markis worth
of land forsaid or anual ; and the said Lord to ger the said Chappellan

incontinent syng for my saul as he wil answer befor God. Alsua, I
gif and I leyf a hundreth poundis of mone that the Abbot of Feyrn
hafis in kepyn, to the byggyn and reparatioun of the said College
Kyrk, and the said Lord to by me throuch stane to lay upon myn
grave.   Item, I gif and I leyf of the landis of Ester Kyndeiss yeirly,
til a prest to syng for me, and the Lady my wif in to the Chanonre of
Ross perpetual ; the quhilkis vj markis fal be tan up be myn ayris or
assigneis, and fal be payd at twa usual termes of the yer, that is to
say, Witsonday and Mertymes, to the said Chappellan.   Item, I gif
and I leyf to the Chanonis of Feyrn for a Mess, wyth not of the
Requiem, to be done dayly for my saul perpetually, vj markis of usual
mone of my landis of Multayth and Drumnern, and falyeand of thame
of my landis of Dunbeth, to be delyverit at twa termes of the yer, as
is befor said, to the said Chanonis be myn ayris or assigneis.   Alsua, I
gif and I leyf to my son, Master Alexander of Suthyrland, Ersden of
Catheness, the twa hundreth pundis that Sir James of Werk hafis in
kepyn of myn, my said Son passand for me in pilgrimage to Sant
Peter of Rome, and to do the thyngis for me and my saul that I have
chargit him under confessioun, as he will answer befor the hyeast
Juge upoun the day of Doum, as he wes oblist to me.   Item, I gif and
I leyf to be brynt in wax in the day of my sepultur viij stan.   Item, I
ordane thrie eln of brayd clayth to wynd me in.   Item, xviij pennys
til ilk prest that cummys to myn erdyng and says Messe for me, and
ij s. to thame that cummys ofer, and vj d. til ilk an that redis the
Salter for me.   Item, I ordane xxxti Trentallis to be said for my saul,
of the quhilkis viij in the Chanonre of Ross, iiij in Feyrn, iiij in Tayn,
iiij in Dornouch, iiij in Kinloss, and vj in Orknay.   Item, I gif and I
leyf to my Lord the Erle of Ross xl lib., xviij chalder of bere, the bol
sald for half a mark, thre chalder of quheyt, the bol sald for viij s.,
and a hundreth wedy of yrn, the wedy sald for viij s., the quhilk the
Erle of Huntle aw me, of the quhilk I have his obligacioun of xl lib.,
and the bere, quheyt, and yrn, he tuk fra my childyr in Abyrden.
Item, I gif to my Lord Erle of Ross xl lib. of it at Makyntoyss aw me,
he beand gud lord, manteynar, supplear, and defendar to my barnes
executoris and assigneys, and all my kyndmen and servandis, and to
supple my executoris in the gettyn of my dettis.   Item, I gif and I
leyf to my Lord Erle of Catheness and Orkney, and Marjory my
douchtir, and to the barnys gottyn and to be gottyn betuix thame, the
thusand lib. that the Erle of Suthyrland hes of my, and is awand me,
or quhat at may be recoveryt tharof.   Item, I gif, I leyf, and assignys
to the barnes gottyn and to be gottyn betuix my said Lord Erle of
Catheness and Orknay, &c., and my douchtir Marjory, al the landis
that I have in wedsettyng of the said Lord Erliis wythin the Erledom
Catheness, togidder wyth al the richt and clame of wedsettyng that I
have and had to the landis of Noss, wyth the pertinents, and to the
landis of Turbuster, wyth the pertinets : the maylls and profitts of the
said landis to remain to the use of my said Lord and Douchtiris
barnys, ay and quhil thay be quyt out be thame or thair ayris that
layod thaim on me ; and quhat tym at the said landis be quyt out the
mone to be disponyt and turnit to the use and profyt of the said barnys,
the quhilkis I have made my assigneys to the said landis, males, and
mone, as my letter of assignatioun mar fermyllie proports in the self.
Item, I gif and I leyf and assigneys to my son Robert, half the landis
of Jaxton, and half Skaldouthmure, liand in the Meyrnys, quhil at he

be payd apon a day as the letter of reversione proportis of the some. Item, I gif and I assigne to my son Nycolace, Dallyanye and Berydal, quhil he be payd of the some of xviij markis, and thre yeris maie bygane. Item, I gif and assigne to my son Edward al my landis of Catouch and Broenach, quhil he be payd of the sum as the letters of reversion proportis. I leyf and assigneis to the said Edward, Gillye-callomgil and Strabrora, quhil he be payd of the some as the letters of reversion proportis. Item, I gif and assigneis to my son John, the landis that I have in wedsettyng of the Medylton, in the Meyrnys, and xl s. worth of land yerly that I suld have of the Lard of Kynnard, quhether the said John wil have it in Kynnard, or of the bord-land of Skelbow, quhil the said John be payd as the letters of reversion pro-portis. Item, I gif and assignes to Donald Brontouch half the ayllous of the tour of Gouspy, quhil he be payt of samekle as it drawys to. Item, I gif and assignes to my douchtir Marion al the lave of my landis that I have undisponyt upone, and sa mony ky, ald and yong, as I have wyth Aytho Faurcharsone, or wyth Mackay Benauch, and sa mony ky as scho aucht to have of Wiliam Polsonys ky. Item, I leyf til Kateryn of Chaumer, and Elynor my douchtir, xxxti ky. Item, Kateryn my douchtir xii ky and xl lib. of it at the Lard of Louranston aw me, I gif, leyf, and assignes til her marriage. Item, to Jonet, my douchter, xvj ky. Item, to Marjory, my douchtir, xxiiij ky. Item, I gif, levys, and assignes to my son the Ersden, all the ky that I have in Cianok, and my gray hors, the quhilk ky and hors wes gevin and sald to hym ij yeris sen, for the quhilkis I put this in his awn place in kepyn for the froytis that I tuk of his benefice. Item, I geve and I leyf to the Crounar a horss. Item, to Robert, Nycolace, Edward, and John, my sonnys, ilk ane of thame a horss. Alsua, I geve and I leyf to my Lordis the Bischopis of Orknay and Ross, the remanent of the hundreth lib, that I have thair obligaciones for, ilk ane of thame fyndand a prest for me to syng ij yeris, and for the layf to gar do for my saul, as thay will answer befor God, as sum tyme I trustit in thame. Item, I leve xl lib. to the Lard of Loranstoun, of the some he is awand me. Item, I leve to Kateryn of Chaumer, the aucht pundis quhilk is the Ersden of Orknay aw me, and the xx lb. that Nycol of Tulauch, John of Hawyk, and Edward of Tulauch, aw me. Item, I gif to Donald Bruntouch, iij ky and a mere; Item, to Will Baxter iij ky; Item, to the Shera a kow; Item, to Safe, v s.; Item, to the wyf at kepis me, v s. Item, I leyf al my clethyng in to the disponyng of my son and executour the Ersden of Catheness, to dispon thame as I chargit him. Item, I gif and I leyf to my said Lord Erle of Catheness and Orknay, xl pundis of the bonage grottis at the Abbot of Fern has of myn, and fyfty lib. worth of my corn, catel, and uthyr gudis and dettis that are aucht to me in Catheness and Orknay, that are undisponit upon, for his gud Lordschyp done to me, and for to be done to my barnes, executouris and assigneys, and for the expenses that he has made upon me, ann in my querelj. Item, I gif and leyfs to my son the Ersden, xl lib. of the bonage grottis that the Abbot of Fern has of myn, and fyfty lib. worth of my corn, catel, dettis, and uthyr gudis that I have in Cathenes sand Orknay that are undisponit upon, he to be gud trayst and helplyk freynd til his Moder, Brotheris, and Sisteris, and to do and fulfyll certane thyngis quhilkis I commandyt him to do for my sayd Lord Erle as they bayth knawys. Item, I gif and I leyf ane of the chalys that Theman has to the

College Kyrk of Roslyng ; Item, I gif the tother chalys that Theman has to Sant Mawnis altar in Kyrkwayl, and the said chalys to be giltyt. Item, quhat gold, joells, or uthyris gudis that I have nocht expremit in my Testament, na nocht disponit on befor my discesse, or or foryet in ony mannys handis or kepyn, I will and I ordane that my said Lord Erle of Catheness and Orkney, and my son the Ersden of Catheness, dispone upon the said gold, joellis, and uthyr gudis be thair discresciounes for my saul, and uthyr wayis as thay think spede-full.   Item, I gif and I leyf to the Bischop of Catheness and to the reperacione of Sant Gilbertis Kyrk, al my fee that he is awand me sen he wes fyrst Bischop, except xl lib.   Item, I gif and I leyf to the said Bischop to syng for my saul and to confyrme my Testament xx lib. Item, I gif and I leyf my croys of gold to Marjory my dochtir, and at sche ger do a trentall of messis for my saul.   Item, I gif and I leyf my sylvar collar to Sir Gilbert the Haye, and he to say for my saul x Salteris.   The lave of al my gudis expremyt in my Testament that I have nocht disponyt upon, I put in the disposicion of myn Executouris, quhilkis I ordane a venerable fadir in Crist Fynlay Abbot of Feyrn, Master Thomas Louchmalony Chancellar of Ross, Master Alexander of Suthyrland my son Ersden of Catheness, and Alexander of Stratone Lard of Loranston my sister son, that thay dispone upon the forsaid guidis as they will answer befor the Hee Juge on the Day of Doum. In wytnes of the quhilk thyngis my seil is toset to thys present Testa-ment, the day, yeir, place, and wytnesses before writyn.   And to the mar certificatione wytnessyng, I procuret the signes and subscriptiones of twa worthy men, Master Thomas Thorbrand and Sir Robert Haly-well, publyc notaris, etc.

The attestation of the witnesses, in Latin, follows.

Explanation of some of the old phrases and contractions in the above document :—
"Wedeys of yrn," measures of iron ; "Bourth," cautioner ; "throuch stane," flat tomb-stone ; "stan," stone ; "trentallis," masses for the dead ; "xxiiij," four score ; "Ersden," Archdeacon ; "unam obolatam,' one halfpenny ; "oyrs," others ; "croys of gold," cross of gold.

No. 7.—Page 106.

MUTINY OF THE HIGH SCHOOL BOYS—YOUNG SINCLAIR OF MEY.

1595. Sept. 15.—The "scholars and gentlemen's sons" of the High School of Edinburgh had at this time occasion to complain of some abridgement of their wonted period of vacation ; and when they applied to the Town Council for an extension of what they called their "privilege," only three days in addition to the restricted number of fourteen were granted.   It appears that the master was favourable to their suit, but he was "borne down and abused by the Council, who never understood well what privilege belonged to that charge.   Some of the gentlemen's sons resolved to make a mutiny, and one day the master being on necessary business a mile or two off the town, they came in the evening with all necessary provision and entered the school, manned the same, took in with them some fencible weapons, with powder and bullet, and renforcit the doors, refusing to let [any] man come there, either master or magistrate, until their privilege were fairly granted.''—*Pa. Anderson.*

A night passed over. Next morning, "some men of the town came to these scholars desiring them to give over, and to come forth upon composition, affirming that they should intercede to obtain them the license of other eight days' playing. But the scholars replied that they were mocked of the first eight days' privilege, . . . they wald either have the residue of the days granted for their pastime, or else they wald not give over. This answer was consulted upon by the magistrates, and notified to the ministers ; and the ministers gave them counsel that they should be letten alone, and some men should be depute to attend about the house to keep them from vivres, sae that they should be compelled to render by extremity of hunger."—*H. K. J.*

A day having passed in this manner, the Council lost patience, and determined to use strong measures. Headed by Bailie John Macmoran, and attended by a posse of officers, they came to the school, which was a long low building standing on the site of the ancient Blackfriars' Monastery. The bailie at first called on the boys in a peaceable manner to open the doors. They refused, and asked for their master, protesting they would acknowledge him at his return, but no other person. "The bailies began to be angry, and called for a great jeist to prize up the back door. The scholars bade them beware, and wished them to desist and leave off that violence, or else they vowed to God they should put a pair of bullets through the best of their cheeks. The bailies, believing they durst not shoot, continued still to prize the door, boasting with many threatening words. The scholars perceiving nothing but extremity, one Sinclair, the chancellor* of Caithness' son, presented a gun from a window direct opposite to the bailies' faces, boasting them and calling them *buttery carles.* Off goeth the charged gun. [The bullet] pierced John Macmoran through his head, and presently killed him, so that he fell backward straight to the ground, without speech at all.†

"When the scholars heard of this mischance, they were all moved to clamour, and gave over. Certain of them escaped, and the rest were carried to prison by the magistrates in great fury, and escaped weel unslain at that instant. Upon the morn the said Sinclair was brought to the bar, and was there accused of that slaughter ; but he denied the same constantly. Divers honest friends convenit and assisted him."‡ The relatives of Macmoran being rich, money offers were of no avail in the case : life for life was what they sought for. "Friends threatened death to all the people of Edinburgh (!) if they did the child any harm, saying they were not wise that meddled with the scholars, especially the gentlemen's sons. They should have committed that charge to the master, who knew best the truest remedy, without any harm at all."

Lord Sinclair, as head of the family to which the young culprit

---

* "Chancellor of Caithness" was merely a titular office, which was kept up some time after the Reformation.

† Patrick Anderson's History, MS. He adds—"I was at the time by chance an eye-witness myself."

‡ Hist. K. Ja. 6.

belonged, now came forward in his behalf, and, by his intercession, the King wrote to the magistrates, desiring them to delay proceedings. Afterward, the process was transferred to the Privy Council. Meanwhile the other youths, seven in number, the chief of whom were a son of Murray of Spainyiedale, and a son of Pringle of Whybank, were kept in confinement for upwards of two months, while a debate took place between the magistrates and the friends of the culprits as to a fair assize, it being alleged that one composed of citizens would be partial against the boys. The King commanded that an assize of gentlemen should be chosen ; and, in the end, they, as well as Sinclair, got clear off.—*From Chambers's " Domestic Annals of Scotland."*

Dr Steven's account of this affair, in his history of the High School, differs from that of Chambers's in some particulars, but in the main they agree. The doctor says, that some days before the autumnal recess, the boys had been very disorderly, and that the head master, Hercules Rollock, required his utmost exertion to maintain discipline.

Bailie Macmoran was the wealthiest merchant of his time in Edinburgh, but exceedingly unpopular with the inhabitants, from the circumstance that he exported victual to the Continent. He had been at one period a servant of the Regent Morton, and afterwards what is called a messenger, or sheriff's-officer. His house is still standing in Riddel's Close, in the Lawnmarket. In May, 1598, the town of Edinburgh gave an entertainment in it to the Duke of Holstein, the queen's brother, at which the king and queen were both present. The room where the Duke was banqueted is now used as the Mechanics' Library.

There is another circumstance which, in a local point of view, imparts an additional interest to this unfortunate affair of young Sinclair of Mey and the Edinburgh bailie. In the " Origines Parochiales Scotiæ " it is stated that, in 1624, John Macmoran was served heir to his father, James Macmoran, merchant-burgess of Edinburgh, in a yearly revenue of £411 6s, from the lands and baronies of the earldom of Caithness, including the lands of Clyth and Greenland. Although the book to which we have referred says nothing about the relationship of the parties, there seems to be little doubt that the two Macmorans, father and son, here mentioned, were the immediate descendants, or at least near relatives, of Bailie John Macmoran who was shot by Sinclair of Mey. How the revenue was acquired is not said. But, as the Earl of Caithness of the period had a host of creditors in the south, it is highly probable that he had borrowed money from the first John Macmoran or his immediate heir, and, in way of repaying the loan, had mortgaged or pledged a portion of his property for the yearly sum of £411 6s.

THE MOWATS OF BUCHOLIE.

Page 165.

The Mowats are of old standing in Caithness, and appear to have possessed landed property in Aberdeenshire at an early period. The name of Buchollie or Balquhollie, in the parish of Canisbay, was evidently taken from the original family estate of the same name in the parish of Turriff, Aberdeenshire, now called Hatton, and which was united with the Caithness estate of Freswick, Auckingill, and others, into the barony of Buchollie. In 1519 the Mowats were possessed of Brabstermire, which was subsequently acquired by Sir John Sinclair of Dunbeath; and in 1627 Magnus Mowat of Buchollie executed at Buchollie a deed, relating to the tiends of Brabstermire, in favour of "John Sinclair, now styled of Dunbeath, my son-in-law." In 1650 Brabstermire was disponed by Sir John to his nephew, John Sinclair, in whose descendants it still remains. In 1661 the estate of Freswick was acquired from Magnus Mowat of Freswick by William Sinclair of Greenland and Ratter, grandson of George fourth Earl of Caithness, and it still remains in this family of Sinclair of Freswick.—J. H.

POSTSCRIPT.

COLONEL GEORGE SINCLAIR.

THE following extract from a letter, to Sir George Sinclair of Ulbster from a Norwegian gentleman, relative to the melancholy fate of Colonel George Sinclair, and the body of men under his command in Norway, in the year 1612, will be found interesting. It is without date, but its authenticity may be depended upon :—

Dr Kraag, a Norwegian, now on a visit to this country, is desirous to obtain information regarding the invasion of his country by a body of Scots, chiefly Sinclairs, in the year 1612. His father is Dean of the district where the invasion took place.

The Doctor has seen Sir Robert Gordon's history, as well as an account of the expedition given by Laing in his work entitled a "Residence in Norway in 1834, '35, '36." Laing, whose account is in some respects incorrect, suggests that the Sinclair families in Caithness may have traditional information which would be highly interesting in Norway, where the defeat of the Sinclairs is still dwelt upon as a great national exploit. The object of the expedition was to assist Gustavus Adolphus in the conquest of Norway. Munckhoven's corps succeeded in joining the Swedes. The Sinclairs landed more to the south. Their commander or colonel was brother of Sir John Sinclair of "Stirkay" (Stirkoke), nephew of George, fifth Earl of Caithness. The second in command was Alexander Ramsay, who had two lieutenants under him—Jacob Mannerspange and Henrick Brussy (probably Bruce). Was the Colonel a legitimate descendant of the Earls of Caithness ?

He was accompanied by Fru (or Lady) Sinclair. The title of Fru implies that she was his wife, and she is still affectionately remembered by the Norwegians. In their songs it is alleged that after the defeat she rushed into a rapid river, in which many of the soldiers were drowned, but being supported by her ample robes she was even able to carry her infant son safe across in her arms. When the child died she adopted a young Norwegian. A mermaid appeared to Colonel Sinclair by night, and threatened him with death in case he should advance. The Colonel replied, "that when he returned in triumph from the conquest of the kingdom, he would punish her as she deserved." The mermaid's name was Ellen, and some allege that she was Fru Sinclair herself in disguise.

The Norwegians are very desirous to know her name, and whether she was really married. An entry in the registry of the parish proves that she and at least two others survived. In another account the number of survivors is increased to three officers and fifteen men, including Ramsay and his two lieutenants. Is there any tradition in Scotland that either she or they returned home? One of the Sinclairs, a prisoner, who was about to be murdered, rushed up to a peasant on horseback, exclaiming, "Protect me; I am not prepared to die!" The peasant saved him, and Sinclair afterwards sent a stained glass window to Norway representing an angel protecting a suppliant. The window has been preserved, and is highly valued by the people.

An insolent speech of Colonel Sinclair's is still repeated by the Norwegians with great indignation : "I'll recast the old Norway lion, and turn him into a mole that will not venture out of his burrow!"

I enclose the music which the Sinclairs played as they advanced through the defile. The bass has been added, and is not good. Is the tune known in Caithness?

NOTE.—All the accounts of this tragical affair we have seen, including that in the above communication, differ from each other. So far as we know, there are no family papers in the county to throw any light on the subject. Colonel Sinclair was a natural son of David Sinclair of Stirkoke, and brother of John Sinclair, who was killed at Thurso in 1612.

That the Caithness men were cheered with music as they advanced through the defile, is a new feature in the story. If such were the fact—and it is not at all improbable—the instrument must have been the bagpipe; and it would afford a melancholy interest to know the particular tune that was played, and which on this occasion might be well termed their own "dead march."

THE following is a list of most of the Caithness proprietors and wadsetters in 1668 :—

George Sinclair, Earl of Caithness ; Sir William Sinclair of Mey ; John Sinclair of Murkle ; George Sutherland of Forss ; William Dunbar of Hempriggs ; Francis Sinclair of Stirkoke ; Patrick Sinclair of Ulbster ; Alexander Bain of Clyth ; John Murray of Pennyland ; Alexander Sinclair of Telstain ; David Sinclair of South Dunn ; William Budge of Toftingall ; William Bruce of Stanstill ; William Sinclair of Thura ; John Sinclair of Brabster ; George Sinclair of Barrock ; John Sinclair of Stangergill ; Robert Sinclair of Durren ; George Sinclair of Olrig ; George Sinclair of Assary ; Alexander Calder of Newton ; David Calder of Scouthel ; Charles Calder* of Lynegar ; James Sinclair of Holburn-head ; John Bruce of Ham ; James Innes of Sandside ; Donald Henderson of Achalibster ; Donald Sinclair of Lybster ; David Murray of Clairdon ; David Coghill of that ilk ; Francis Sinclair of Latheron ; and David Sinclair of Freswick.

---

* Chalmers, in his "Caledonia," has the following note on the name Calder :—"The name of the parish of Cader (Lanarkshire) and of the lands of Cader appears in the charters of the 12th and 13th centuries in the constant form of Cader. In modern times it is called Calder, obviously derived from the British Cader signifying a fortress." The Caithness Calders are said to have come originally from Morayshire, and their first place of settlement in the county seems to have been Watten.

LIBERTIES OF THE TOWN OF THURSO.

I, John Earl of Caithness, Viscount of Bredalbin, Sinclair, Borridie, and Glenorchy, heretable proprietor of the said Earldom and Baron, burgh of Thurso, annexed thereto. For as meikle as the deceast George Earl of Caithness, and our predecessor, be his order, warrant and commission made and granted be him to the baillies of Thurso, and their successors, baillies thereof, councelors, and inhabitants of the samen, tending to their weal and good government of in common will, within the said baron burgh, to be used and put in execution by the present bailies then for the time, and their successors, containing all prevelidges, liberties, and powers belonging and incumbant to any burgh of barony, to be used and execute to the said baillies, with advice of the counselors elected, and to be elected, within the said burgh, as the said commission, warrant, and order of the date the twenty-ninth day of December jaixii and fifty-nine years, in itself at length bears. And now seeing we find it very necessary that in such an Incorporation the same government in common will within the said burgh be used, and be put, execute, and kept in due and lawful execution hereafter be the magistrates and councelors thereof tendant to the glory of God, his Majesty's laws and authority, and the good and weil of us their superior, we give, grant full power, commission, liberty, and warrant to James Innes of Thurso, Thomas Sinclair, merchant in Thurso, and James Campbell, merchant there, present baillies, and their successors, baillies thereof, and councelors of the samen, and to the several articles aftermentioned.

First. That the baillies and councelors be assisting to the minister and elders of the said burgh in maintaining the kirk, kirkyard dykes, keeping of the Sabbath, maintaining of schools, masters thereof, and all other things tending to God's glory and worship, and in curbing and punishing of all vice and sin opposite thereto, to their power.

Secondly. We give, grant full commission, power, and warrant to them and their successors to decide cognitions, and decern in all civil actions, questions, controversies, for debts, buying, selling, lending, borrowing, feeing and untying of servants, and all other wrongs and injuries arising betwixt the inhabitants resident and trafecting within the said burgh ; and to determine and settle the same according to the burgh laws of any burgh of barony.

Thirdly. That the said magistrates decern and give out decreet against all inhabitants within the said burgh for whatsoever debts, sums of money, and other goods restand to others ; arrest and stress for the same until they make satisfaction of what other of them shall be found justly restand to others, at least to find caution for forthcoming as law will, the said being within forty shillings sterling money.

Fourthly. That the said magistrates suffer no merchant, nor other inhabitant of the said burgh, to buy victal or other commodity, that shall be coming to the market, until it be first presented on the ordinary market-place, except it be for old debts, for their own rents, and for sustaining of their families and houses, under the pains falling under the compass of any burgh of barony, to be inflicted upon the contraveeners, as they shall think convenient.

Fifthly. That when merchants, shippers, or owners of goods shall come with goods to the said burgh, by sea or land, to be sold in greate, that no inhabitant shall make any bargain therewith, until the baillies and councelors refuse the same ; and that the said magistrates, upon the neat payment thereof, without fraud or guile, make offer to the merchants, craftsmen, and inhabitants of the said burgh, that they may have their proportion of the same, according to their necessitys and ability ; and that none make merchandise in buying and selling privately or openly, in prejudice of the said merchants, craftsmen, and other inhabitants, under the pains of such laws as the said magistrates shall impose and inflict upon the contraveeners, both sellers and buyers, competent, according to the laws of the burgh.

Sixthly. That all carcases of beef and mutton that shall happen to come to the market to be sold, shall have therewith their hides, skins, and tallow, and that the beef and mutton shall not be minched, cut, or spoilt, under such pains as the said magistrates shall enjoin, sett down, and uplift, upon the contraveeners.

Seventhly. That no stranger, merchant, or chapman traveller, shall take booths or shops to sell their goods within the said burgh and liberty thereof, without special licence first had of the magistrates ; and also of the said merchants and chapmen to consend and agree with the magistrates for their liberty of buying and selling within the said burgh, for such and such convenient days and times as they shall happen to condescend upon, under such pains and pecuniary sums as they shall inflict upon the contraveeners, for increasing upon the libertys of the said burgh.

Eighthly. We grant full commission, deputation, power, and warrant to the said magistrates to take, order, and execute justice upon all persons, inhabitants of said burgh, committors of riots, blood, blood-witts, plays, and all other inormities, as well to strangers as others without the said burgh, as the inhabitants committing the same within the said burgh and bounds thereof : and upon breakers of kail-yards, dykes, stealing of peats, kail, and other goods, casting down of dykes, lymming of hides and skins, meddlers with their neighbour's moss, muirs, banks, peats, unorderly loading of peats under night, and anent the peat leaders with horses ; and to make setts, acts, and orders thereanent as shall be found convenient, and to uplift the fines and penaltys thereof incumbent to any burgh of barony.

Ninthly. That the magistrates take an special care of all calsays, streets, and wynds, common property, to cause them to be bigged and repaired, kept clean, and the filth and gudding removed from the High Street to convenient places ; and cause remove stranger beggars, and all sorts of vagabonds, unlawful persons setting of houses to unlawful tenants, and mainteners of them, and to appoint marcate places for selling of meal and fishes, and setting prices on the fishes, ale, beer, and aquavite, bread, and candles,—upon all sorts of craftsmen's works, and sufficiency thereof,—upon workmen, and weavers, and to nominate surveyors for that effect, and to inflict penalties and punishments upon the contraveeners, as shall be thought meet. The said magistrates uplift and apply the same to the use and utility of the said burgh.

Tenthly. That the said magistrates take order of all unsufficient measures—liquid and dry—and with all weights, all yards, firlochs, pecks, and cause seal the sufficient with the town's mark, and fine all users of unlawful measures and weights, upon tryall and conviction thereof.

Eleventhly. That the said magistrates are to receive count and reckoning from the collectors and all other receivers and uptakers of all cess and other stint imposed upon the said burgh, heritors, and inhabitants thereof ; what the same extends to, how the same was paid and disbursed upon, and to be satisfied by them of the surplus, if any be, and apply it for the common well of the said burgh ; and upon their disobedience and neglect to make count, reckoning, and payment to the treasury of the burgh that shall be nominate to fine and refine the recousants, ay, and while they have not obtempered the said order.

Twelfthly. That the said baillies shall go diligently and actively about the haill former acts, commission, and instructions, in putting of the same to due ejection, with all other acts, statutes, and ordinances anywise belonging and incumbent to kirk and burgh, made or to be made, pertaining or that may pertain, and come under the priveledge and liberty thereof. Penalties and fines upon all contraveeners to inflict, uplift, and apply the same to the behoof of the said burgh and inhabitants thereof.

*   *   *   *   *   *   *   *

Fourteenthly. We also order and ordain that the haill inhabitants within the said burgh, of all degrees of persons dwelling and trafecting in the same, shall give assistance and obedience to the said magistrates in all lawfull affairs, and expedients belonging to the said burgh, and good and lawfull government thereof, as they shall be required ; and whatsoever person be disobedient to them or their officers, and break their lawful anectments, and convicted thereon, shall be fined and cashiered at the said magistrates' deliverance and will, according to the greatness and measure of their offence and guiltness.

Fifteenthly. The said magistrates and council shall be lyable to count for their intromissions, and how they are or shall be employed, relating to what stints shall be imposed upon the said burgh by them, either for repairing of the streets, or any other necessary convenience, Whilk commission, deputation, power, warrant, and order respective above mentioned by the said John Earl of Caithness, we shall warrant, hold firm and stable to the said baillies in all and haill things in form and effect as is above mentioned, at all hands whatsomever.

We have subscribed these presents, with our hands, at Thurso, the fourteenth day of October, one thousand six hundred and eighty years, before these witnesses, Alexander Campbell of Bredalbin, and William Campbell, notary public.

The above deed would seem, from the date, to have been drawn up about three months after Glenorchy had defeated Sinclair of Keiss at the burn of Altimarlach. It is in several respects a curious and interesting document, and throws not a little light on the state of matters in Thurso a hundred and eighty years ago. Some of the regulations which it contains are excellent, and as necessary to be enforced, in not a few places, at the present day, as they were in 1680 ; as, for instance, that which enjoins the keeping of the streets clean, and the removal from the town of " stranger beggars and all sorts of vagabonds." Among the several rights and privileges the reader will be amused with one, namely, the plenary power given to the magistrates to fix and regulate the prices of work, and of all commodities and necessaries of life brought into the town, even to the very fish of the sea! The obvious intention of this was to keep things at a moderate rate for the inhabitants. The motive was good, though certainly not in accordance with the principles of free trade and a sound political economy.

THE CAITHNESS FENCIBLES.

THE following are the names of the officers belonging to the Caithness Fencibles, taken from an Edinburgh almanac of the year 1799 :—

Rothesay and Caithness Regiment.

First Battalion—Colonel, Sir John Sinclair ; Lieutenant-Colonel, David Rae. Major, J. Sinclair. Captains—George Dawson, George Swanson, William Falconer, William Brodie, George Sutherland, J. M'Gregor, D. Campbell, S. Davidson, C.L. Lieutenants—John Sinclair, sen., John Sinclair, jun., John Yetts, George Taylor, A. Evans, James Brown, Benjamin Sinclair, J. Bethune, William Yetts, R. M'Killigen, Robert Hall. Ensigns—John Pringle, A. Sutherland, A. Matheson, J. Thomson, A. Campbell, R. Stewart, Alexander Sinclair, John Mackay, William Innes, P. Nicolson, D. Campbell, G. Sutherland, S. Pringle, M. Russel. Second Battalion—Major D. Darrock. Captains—B. Williamson, J. Williamson, A. Henderson, H. Ferguson, James Dudgeon, John Dudgeon, Alexander Orr, J. Henderson, G. Williamson. Lieutenants—C. Reynell, John Matthews, J. B. Johnston, James Thorburn, John Sinclair, James Young, Robert Darling, D. Campbell, J. Henderson, M. Fraser. Ensigns—Simon Fraser, Jacobus Hojel, A. Fraser, J. Neismith, D. Sinclair, J. Sinclair, James Mould, D. Henderson, John Kay, —— Martin, A. Fraser, J. Anderson, J. B. Johnston.

Caithness Legion.

Colonel, Sir B. Dunbar ; Lieutenant-Colonel, W. Munro. Major, W. Innes. Captains—Hugh Innes, Robert Sinclair, John Taylor, John Burton, Alexander Strange, R. Kennedy, J. Yardley, D. Miller. Lieutenants—George M'Beath, John Watson, W. Terrence, Joseph Nield, Peter Innes, W. M'Pherson, A. M'Pherson, Robert M'Kay, G. Mackenzie, G. Carrick, W. Paton, G. M'Kenzie. Ensigns—J. M'Kenzie, J. Barton, J. Sweetman, S. Mason, John Blake, James Calder.

In connection with the Caithness Fencibles, there is an interesting anecdote of Sir John Sinclair not generally known, which places in a very striking light his humanity and kindness of heart. The story was communicated to the writer by a gentleman in Glasgow, who had the particulars some years ago from an aged individual who had been a soldier in the corps. After the first battalion was embodied at Inverness, they were a short time quartered at Fort-George. It happened that one of the soldiers, a youth belonging to Caithness, of respectable parentage, was, for some slight disobedience of orders, put into confinement. The officer in command, a strict martinet, and a rigid disciplinarian of the old school, had the youth tried by a court-martial, and he was sentenced to receive five hundred lashes ! The men of the regiment were shocked at the cruelty of the sentence, and expressed great sympathy for their comrade, whose fault was less owing to intentional disobedience than to inacquaintance with the rules of the service. Fortunately the sentence could not be carried into effect without the sanction of Sir John, the head colonel, who was then in London, attending to his parliamentary duties. As soon as the document requiring his signature reached him, Sir John posted direct for the north, and scarcely halted till he arrived at Campbell-town, about two miles from Fort-George. It was close on midnight when he came to the village inn, and being greatly fatigued he went to bed. In the morning it was whispered in the garrison that their much-respected colonel had arrived during the night at Campbelltown. The news fled like a wild-fire from one company to another. A simultaneous impulse seized them. The whole regiment, in defiance of officer and martial law, turned out, rushed past the sentries, and marched at a quick step to the village, where, as soon as they saw the worthy baronet, they rent the air with their exclamations. They then carried him shoulder high into the Fort. Having assembled the Fencibles on the usual parade ground, Sir John warmly censured the officer in command for the barbarity of the sentence, which he ordered to be cancelled from the regimental books. He ordered the prisoner at the same time to be liberated from his confinement. The acting colonel, whose pride was deeply wounded, immediately left the regiment ; another was appointed in his place ; and Sir John, after remaining a day or two at Fort-George, retraced his steps back to London.

LORD CAITHNESS'S STEAM CARRIAGE.

THE present Earl of Caithness is a nobleman of high scientific acquirements, and honourably distinguished for his mechanical talent. Among other ingenious contrivances, he has invented the steam carriage, or at least constructed it so perfectly that it can be easily managed, and run on roads. The experiment, indeed, is allowed to be a complete success. Last season his Lordship brought it from London to his seat of Barrogill Castle, near John O'Groat's ; and we understand that he and Lady Caithness travelled in it a good part of the way ; at all events, they came in it from Inverness to Wick, and thence to Barrogill Castle, a distance of some hundred and thirty miles. His Lordship encountered no difficulty on the road ; and the steep and still somewhat dangerous passes for wheeled vehicles at the Ord of Caithness, Berriedale, and Dunbeath, with a gradient in some parts of one in twelve, were surmounted with the greatest ease. The rate of speed was from seven to eight miles an hour. On their arrival at Wick in their novel carriage, Lord and Lady Caithness, who are both great favourites in the county, were loudly cheered by the inhabitants of the burgh.

The subjoined description of this remarkable invention we copy from a periodical entitled the *Parlour Journal*, which contains an excellent engraving of the carriage, after a photograph executed by his lordship. Had the print come sooner into our possession, we would have had great pleasure in embellishing our book with an engraving of the carriage :—

"The success attending Lord Caithness's experiment with his steam carriage for common roads, has drawn general attention to the invention ; we therefore present an engraving, after a photograph con descendingly executed by the noble Earl for our use.

"It will be seen that the front view is that of a phaeton placed on three wheels, and made a little wider than ordinary, so as to have room for three or even four abreast. His Lordship sits on the right hand side and drives, resting his left hand on a handle at the end of a bent iron bar, fixed, below the front spring, to the fork in which the front wheel runs, and guiding with ease the direction of the carriage. Placed horizontally before him is a small fly-wheel, fixed on an iron rod, that, passing downward, works at the lower end by a screw, through one end of a lever, attached at the other end to a strong iron bar that passes across the carriage, and has fitted on it a drag for each of the hind wheels. By giving the fly-wheel in front a slight turn with his right hand, his Lordship can apply a drag of sufficient power to lock the hind wheels and stop the carriage on the steepest declivities of common roads. Inside the carriage, in a line backward from his right hand, is placed a handle, by which the steam is let on, regulated, and shut off at pleasure.

"The tank, holding about 170 gallons, forms the bottom of the carriage, and extends as far back as the rear of the boiler, where the water is conveyed from it into the boiler by a small force-pump, worked by the engine. There are two cylinders, one on each side, six inches diameter and seven inches stroke. These, and all that is necessary to apply the power to the axle, are well arranged and fitted in, so as to occupy the smallest possible space, between the tank and the boiler, and appear at first sight insufficient to exert nine horse-power. The coal, one cwt. of which is sufficient for twenty miles on ordinary road, is held in a box in front of the stoker, whose duty it is to keep up the fire, see that there is always sufficient water in the the boiler, and that the steam is up to the required pressure, as seen by the gauge on the top of the boiler.

"The power of the engine, and the perfect control his lordship has over it, enabled him on several recent occasions, to make long journeys over rough and mountainous roads at the rate of eight miles an hour ; there can therefore be no doubt that carriages propelled by steam can be used for the purpose of traffic on common roads. A journey of 140 miles made in two days, at a cost of less than 1d per mile for fuel, proves this ; and the fact that no accident to man or beast was caused by the steam carriage during the whole journey, answers the objections as to frightening horses.

"His lordship continues to use the carriage, and is most kind and courteous in explaining its construction and working. It is to mechanical science that much of our country's greatness is due, and it is truly gratifying to see the Earl of Caithness lending the influence of his distinguished rank and talents to assist in fostering the improvements of his country.

THE BATTLE OF ALTIMARLACH: A BALLAD.

'TWAS morn ; from rustic cot and grange
   The cock's shrill clarion rung ;
And fresh on every sweet wild flower
   The pearly dew-drop hung.

Given up to thoughtless revelry,
   In Wick lay Sinclair's band,
When suddenly the cry arose,
   " Glenorchy's close at hand !"

For now the Campbell's haughty chief
   The river Wick had crossed,
With twice seven hundred Highlanders—
   A fierce and lawless host.

" To arms ! to arms !" from street to lane
   The summons fast did go ;
And forth the gathered Sinclairs marched
   To meet the coming foe.

Where Altimarlach opens up
   Its narrow, deep ravine,
Glenorchy's force, in order ranged,
   Were strongly posted seen.

They meet, they close in deadly strife,
   But brief the bloody fray ;
Before the Campbell's furious charge
   The Caithness ranks give way.

Flushed with success, Glenorchy's men
   Set up a savage cheer,
And drove the Sinclairs panic-struck
   Into the river near.

There, 'neath the Campbell's ruthless blade
   Fell more than on the plain,
Until the blood-dyed stream across
   Was choked up with the slain.

But who might paint the flood of grief
   That burst from young and old,
When to the slaughtered Sinclair's friends
   The direful tale was told !

The shrieking mother wrung her hands,
   The maiden tore her hair,
And all was lamentation loud,
   And terror, and despair.

Short time Glenorchy Caithness ruled,
   By every rank abhorred ;
He lost the title he usurped,
   Then fled across the Ord.

While Keiss,* who firm upheld his claim
   Against tyrannic might,
Obtained the Sinclairs' coronet,
   Which was his own by right ;

That coronet which William† wore,
   Who loved his Prince so well,
And with his brave devoted band
   On fatal Flodden fell.

---

* Sinclair of Keiss.   † The second Earl of Caithness of the Sinclair line

GLEANINGS FROM DOUGLAS PEERAGE OF SCOTLAND, AND OTHER SOURCES.

EARL OF CAITHNESS.—This title is of great antiquity, Dungaldus, Earl of Caithness, occurring in the year 875, in Torfæus' History of Orkney.—*Douglas Peerage.*

The compiler of this elaborate and valuable work says that much obscurity hangs over the early history of the earldom of Caithness. He mentions the names of only a few of its Scandinavian "Jarls" or Earls, but he enters very fully into the genealogy of the Sinclair family and its collateral branches.

WILLIAM SINCLAIR, EARL OF CAITHNESS.—William, who fell at Flodden, had two sons—John, who was slain in Orkney, and Alexander (styled of Stempster), who in the year 1529 obtained for himself and his spouse, Elizabeth Innes, by royal charter, the lands of Dunbeath, Reay, and Sandside, which were united into the barony of Dunbeath. In 1507 the township of Dunbeath was possessed by Alexander Innes of that ilk.   Prior to this, in 1429, Alexander Sutherland * obtained a grant of the lands of Dunbeath on his marriage with Mariota, sister of Alexander, Earl of Ross and Lord of the Isles.—*Douglas Peerage.*

JOHN, MASTER OF CAITHNESS.—John married Lady Jean Hepburn, only daughter of Patrick, third Earl of Bothwell.   She was the sister of James Hepburn (the notorious Earl of Bothwell), the widow of John Stewart, Prior of Coldinghame, and mother of Francis Stewart, afterwards Earl of Bothwell.   This Francis Stewart, and John's son George, fifth Earl of Caithness were therefore (as has been already mentioned) half-brothers on the mother's side.—*Ibid.*

SIR WILLIAM SINCLAIR OF MEY.—This was the William Sinclair who, when a pupil at the High School, shot the Edinburgh bailie. He obtained a remission for the crime under the great seal of Scotland, and was afterwards knighted by James the Sixth.   He married Catherine, daughter of Ross of Balnagowan.   His brother John was bred a merchant, and acquired great wealth.   He was knighted in 1631.   He purchased the lands of Geanies in Ross-shire, and those of Dunbeath and Brabster in Caithness.   He married Christian, daughter of Mowat of Bucholie, Laird of Freswick.   By her he had a daughter, Margaret, married to Hugh Ross of Kilravock, to whom he gave, at her marriage, lands in Ross-shire and 50,000 marks as a dowry.—*Ibid.*

JOHN, MASTER OF BERRIEDALE (son of William, Lord Berriedale), who espoused the cause of the Covenanters in opposition to his father and grandfather, died of fever at Edinburgh in 1639, and was buried in the Abbey Church of Holyrood.—*Ibid.*

GEORGE, SIXTH EARL OF CAITHNESS.—He married, at Roseneath, 22nd September, 1657, Lady Mary Campbell, third daughter of Archibald, Marquis of Argyle.   "Was committed prisoner to the Castle of Edinburgh for the slaughter of a soldier sent to quarter for deficiency of cess and excise.   Sold, before his death, his title and property to John Campbell of Glenorchy, his debts extending, as is said, to more than a million of marks."—*Ibid.*

BATTLE OF ALTIMARLACH.—"The Council, 7th June, 1680, issued

---

* This was the Alexander Sutherland whose Testament will be found in the Appendix, page 292.

an order to General Dalzell to assist, with a party of His Majesty's troops, in the execution of their order. The Earl (Campbell of Glenorchy), raising his friends and followers, and attended by a detachment of the King's troops, marched from the banks of the Tay, and engaged the Sinclairs at Old Marlach (Altimarlach), when victory declared in favour of the Earl."—*Ibid.*

No other writer has mentioned, so far as I know, that the King's troops were employed on this occasion to assist Glenorchy; but, as the author of the Peerage had access to the best sources of information, there can be no doubt of the truth of the statement; and it is therefore not to be wondered at that the Sinclairs were so easily overcome by the Campbells, aided, as they would seem to have been, by trained soldiers. Altogether, this story of Campbell of Glenorchy and Sinclair of Keiss is a curious one, and gives us anything but a favourable idea of the law proceedings, and of the Government measures of the day.

CAITHNESS.—The district anciently known as Katanes, or the Nes, included the modern earldoms or counties of Caithness and Sutherland. Sutherland was termed Sudrland, or South Caithness.— *Origines Parochiales Scotiæ.*

THE CHEYNES OF CAITHNESS.—Reginald Cheyne, third of that name, is styled in ancient charters "Ronald, Lord Schen."—*Ibid.*

ST. BAR.—The original parish church of Dornoch (not the cathedral), the date of whose foundation is unknown, was dedicated to St. Bar, a native of Caithness, and Bishop of Cork, in Ireland.—*Ibid.*

Sir Robert Gordon, in his History of the House of Sutherland (sec. 1, page 25), says that St. Bar was appointed Bishop of Caithness by Malcolm Canmore in 1079, but this statement does not seem to be correct, more especially as the prelature of Caithness was not established till about the year 1150.

ABBEY OF SCONE.—The Abbey of Scone, near Perth, was, from an early period, peculiarly connected with Caithness. One of the Earls of Orkney and Caithness (Harold) granted a mark of silver yearly to the canons of Scone, for the weal of the souls of himself and his wife, and for the souls of his predecessors.*—*Cosmo Innes, Liber de Scon,* 58.

STATE OF MATTERS IN CAITHNESS IN 1801.—"This year was remarkable in three different respects:—1st. A great crop, and yet victual at from 35 to 45 shillings per boll. 2d. Most part of the men in the county fit to bear arms trained to the exercise of war. 3d. That a resolution has been entered into by the land proprietors of Caithness to enforce winter herding, the sowing of grass and turnip seed on the open fields, and enclosing the commons, by which the use of feal for manure and building is prohibited."—*Extract from the Session Records of Dunnet.*

AGRICULTURAL SOCIETY. — The Caithness Agricultural Society originated in 1829. It gave the first impulse to the improvement of stock in Caithness. At the period in question there was not a single Tees-water, and few or no Leicester sheep in the county. The Society has two general meetings, one at Wick in the month of February, when the county fiars are struck, and the other on the last Wednesday of July, on the Georgemas Market, where the competitions for the premiums given by the Society take place.—*Local Paper.*

* The mark was equal in value to 40 shillings sterling.

ANCIENT CUSTOM.—Of old it was customary in Caithness (and the practice in some degree still continues) for beginners in the farming line, who had not much capital, to go about begging seed-corn, or, as it was delicately termed, "thigging." On this occasion, the "thigger" threw over his shoulders a large sack, and having provided himself with a well-filled snuff-box, commonly one of horn, he called at every farm-house as he went along, when he received more or less, according to the generosity of the giver or the tact he had in exciting it. The thing was so common that there was no disgrace in thus soliciting a mite for a beginning. The same custom would appear to have prevailed in some of the other northern counties. The following amusing anecdote is given in the *Banffshire Journal*:—"An old man, who had frequently tried the thigging, used to say with glee—'I kent fu to dee with them (the farmers); I had aye on a clean, ruffled sark, and as I gaed in ower to the toon, I drew out my ruffles, got my snuff-box in my hand, ready to present to the guidman finiver I sud see him; syne, gin there happent to be ony lasses, I was sure to be frankest wi' them—reised them oot for being clean, clever, bonny queans, and promised to tak my second wife oot amon them; and syne laying a clap at this ane's cheek, an' a smack at the next ane's mou', keepit them in sic humour that I cam aff wi' a good thigging; and gin the guidman's snuff-box happent to be teem, I never suffered by tumblin' a pickle intill't.'"

"LIMBS OF THE LAW."—The following is an extract from the old statistical account of Thurso (of date 1798), and, judging from it, the spirit of litigation would appear to have been very active in the "far north" about the end of the eighteenth century:—"There are a greater number of limbs of the law in Thurso than in many places of much greater extent. There are no fewer than eight public notaries, five of whom are messengers-at-arms, and there is besides one messenger who is not a notary. One half," says the writer, "would be fully adequate to the business in town and county."

At a subsequent period the whole of these "limbs of the law" would appear to have been needed. "In the ten years ending 1832," says Dr. Henderson, "there were no less than 6934 cases decided in the justice court for the Thurso district, embracing the parishes of Reay, Thurso, Halkirk, Olrig, Dunnet, and Bower, and involving transactions to the amount of £9854. This gives an average of 639 cases and £985 for that district; and if we suppose, at least, as many for the Wick district comprehending the remaining parishes of the county, we have 1278 cases before the justices annually with £1970 in dispute. Add to this, 3000 cases before the sheriff's small debt court, involving £4500, and the whole will amount to 4278 cases and £6470." In the "good old times," most of these cases would have been decided by the *stick*. A great improvement has taken place in this as in other things; and there is now as little litigation in Caithness as in any county in Scotland.

TRADITION RESPECTING THE EARL OF CAITHNESS WHO WAS KILLED IN ORKNEY.

The Earl in his flight from the field outran his pursuers, and entered a farm house to solicit refuge. There was nobody in but an old woman who was sitting before the fire, and spinning from a distaff. The Norse tongue was then the language of the common people, but the Earl, by means of signs and the magic power of a few pieces of money, contrived to make her comprehend the purpose of his visit. She rose from her seat, led him to the far end of the byre which was quite dark, signed to him to lie down, covered him with straw, and then returned to her work. A little after, a party of ten entered, and asked the old woman if he was in the house. She replied, "he is not here," but while she said so, she pointed with her finger to the spot where he lay concealed. Thither they accordingly went. Finding that he was betrayed, the Earl started up, and with his drawn sword defended himself for sometime with unshrinking courage. At length, however, he was overpowered and slain, but not until four of his cowardly assailants had fallen down mortally wounded before him. He was buried in a field not far distant from the cottage, and a slab was erected over his grave, which was afterwards broken and carried away for some domestic purpose. The tradition says nothing about the sending of his head to Caithness. It would appear, however, to have been by no means a bloodless victory to the Orkneymen, though by their acquaintance with the ground, and being well prepared for the contest, they possessed many advantages which the invaders did not.

Note.—The above interesting tradition was communicated to the author by Mr Alex. Louttit, a native of Caithness residing in Glasgow. He had it from a relative of his, a Mr George Louttit, who was parochial schoolmaster of Birsay in Orkney. The Louttits belonged originally to that county; and the schoolmaster of Birsay had an ancestor James Louttit who was in the battle of Summerdale on the side of the Orkneymen, and had particularly distinguished himself on that occasion. This family tradition, handed down from father to son, in which they must all have felt a pride and an interest, appears to me to bear the impress of truth.

EXPEDITION OF THE CAITHNESS VOLUNTEERS TO ORKNEY.

The weather during the following month of January (1807), proved more than usually boisterous. About the 12th of the month, a Dutch transport with troops and stores for Curacoa in the West Indies went ashore in a snowstorm at a place called the Holms of Syre, in the island of Sanday in Orkney. The whole of the troops, amounting to 500, were saved, but a great many of them died of cold and fatigue among the rocks soon after landing. At first, the presence of so large a body of the enemy—for Holland was then in league with France—created great alarm among the inhabitants, and an express was sent from Kirkwall to the Lord-Lieutenant of the county of Caithness requesting him to send over without delay the Caithness volunteers for the protection of the island. The regiment, under Colonel James Sinclair of Forss, speedily mustered at Thurso, and was embarked in companies in some fishing smacks (then in Scrabster Roads) which had been engaged to transport the corps to the island of Sanday. Soon after the smacks left the roadstead a violent storm of wind arose, nearly equal in fury to that of the 25th of December, and it was with great difficulty that they reached Orkney. One or two of the vessels were in imminent danger of being foundered. After all, the services of the volunteers were not required. On Colonel Sinclair's arrival in Elwick bay, near Kirkwall, he learned that the poor Dutchmen, who were in great distress and were objects of pity rather than of fear, had peaceably delivered themselves up to the authorities in Orkney. In these circumstances, finding it unnecessary to proceed to Sanday, Colonel Sinclair shortly after returned home with his men to Thurso. Such was the pacific issue of the Caithness volunteers to Orkney.

The Dutchmen lay in prison for some months in Kirkwall. They were afterwards sent to Leith. About 95 of then volunteered into the British navy, and the remainder were put on board the Norfolk sloop of war, 22 guns, and conveyed away home to Holland.

NOTES TO SECOND EDITION.

BY T. SINCLAIR, M.A.

PAGE 1.—The Rev. Timothy Pont, A.M., minister of Dunnet, in his admirable maps of Scotland, drawn by him at great fatigue of personal survey, 1608 *et seq.*, makes the north-western boundary of Caithness to be the river of Halladale up to Achridigle, thence to the top of Ben Ra, and south towards Morven. With him Drumholisten was not the low hills now so named beside the sea, but the range beginning with Ben Ra and running southward. The encroachment of Sutherland was caused by the purchase of land in Reay by Sir Donald Mackay of Farr, from the profits of British levies he raised for the Thirty Years' War of Germany.—See "An Old Scots Brigade," by John Mackay, chiefly compiled from Munro's "Expedition," but having additional original documents. Some unpublished letters in the British Museum were recently printed which gives illustrations of Lord Reay's money affairs. In 1628 he got this peerage title from his Caithness chief property. If ruin had not overtaken him the whole of Reay parish would have been carried away from its proper county. It has to be remembered that Sutherland was then divided into Sutherland and Strathnavernia, the latter being much the larger. In some state documents of 1626, the Bighouse and Halladale properties are entered under the heading of Caithness. Pont's accuracy on these geographical and historical points is incontestable. The anomaly of one parish in two counties would seem to have thus its explanation. In the " Athenæ Cantabrigienses " is a notice of another geographer: —" John Elder was born in Caithness, and studied twelve years in the Universities of St Andrews, Aberdeen, Glasgow, and afterwards resided at Cambridge. He was in England shortly after the death of James V., when he made and presented to Henry VIII. a plot or map of Scotland. He wrote books which are extant in the British Museum."

P. 3.—Road money, under the old system, as appears from a Sandside estate-book of date 1794 to 1800, was charged to the tenants with the rent, the scale of assessment being from 1s 6d for those paying about £1 sterling yearly, to 7s or 8s for those rented at £8 to £10, who were the large farmers of the time. In 1799 there was a charge of 1s up to 5s or 6s, according to rent for the building of Thurso bridge, nominally subscription but practically assessment. Cotters' service to the landlord could then be commuted or converted at 3d a day. If a cotter had to give 60 days' work in the year, and chose in preference to compound for his absence, this meant 15s added to his rent. When he kept a swine, he had to pay 5s a year of rent or fine.

P. 7.—Holborn Head is called by Ptolemy, 140 A.D., in one passage, Orcas; but, as he guessed only of the north, there is difficulty in identifying his names with the places. Faro Head in Strathnavernia is mentioned as Orcas or Tarvedrum, Strathy Head was Virvedrum, and Duncansbay Head, Veruvium or Virvedrum or Betubium Dunnet Head also claims to be the Orcas, from which came the description of the Orkneys as the Orcades. Holborn Head has caves which open at some distance inland like deep shafts, after the manner of the famous ones on the north-west of the chief island of the Shetlands. On the top of the promontory is an ob lisk-shaped pillar twelve feet high, commemorating the supposed suicide of Captain Sclater, Thurso, at that part of the sheer cliff. A woman took the fatal leap about this spot. Uttersquoy was the old name of Holborn Head House and property.

P. 9.—The phrase *fanum Donati in Cathanesia* is to be found in an Elezevir Latin selection from George Buchanan and Camden.

P. 10.—The best of all mermaid stories is that of Miss Mackay, daughter of Rev. David Mackay, Reay. At the beginning f this century, she and two other witnesses saw one in Sandside Bay and her experience was discussed throughout the whole kingdom by the scientific and learned world. The Rev. William Munro, A.M., schoolmaster of Reay and afterwards of Thurso, published the fact of a similar sight in the same quarter by himself at an earlier period. Full details of dates and letters, quoted from the *Scots Magazine* and other authentic sources, were recently printed.

P. 15.—Agatha, daughter of Hugh Groat of Southdun, married the second laird of Dun, John Sinclair, and Margaret Sinclair of Forss, of the same Duns by her father and mother (who contracted 11th July, 1645), married Malcolm Groat of Warse, whose son was Donald Groat of Warse. There is no reason to doubt the Dutch origin of the family. Hugo De Groot, better known as Grotius, the great European jurist and Latinist, born in 1553, was of Holland ; and the London historian of Greece, George Grote, traced himself to the same country. Donald Groat of Warse and John Groat of Duncansbay were Commissioners of Supply in 1702. On 15th February, 1649, Malcolm Groat of Warse was made one of the commissioners on the committee of war in the county.

P. 16.—There is an extraordinary description in Latin of the Pentland Firth in the " New Chorographic Description of the Orkneys," published in 1654.

P. 18.—For the story of Gow read Scott's "Pirate," Peterkin's " Notes on Orkney," Mackay's " History of the Mackays," " John Gow, the Pirate," in the *Newcastle Chronicle*, " The Newgate Calendar," Tudor's " Orkney and Shetland," *Chamber's Journal* for January 1883, and " Services of Heirs for Scotland." Henderson, in his " Caithness Family History," gives the best account of the pirate's sweetheart, Kate Rorison or Gunn, afterwards Mrs Gibson, Stroma, the Gibsons being related to the Earls by marriage. Gow was a native of Scrabster or Stromness, and was hanged in chains at Execution Dock on the Thames, August 11th, 1725, with seven of his crew. A tragic sea-tale of the present reign, was that of Captain Johnson of Dunnet. He shot and stabbed to death five or six of his officers and crew, who, he said, were mutineers. Tried in London for murder, he was condemned to be detained as a lunatic during Her Majesty's pleasure in Bethelem Hospital, best known as Bedlam. He protested his sanity for many years, but without avail, and published a stout pamphlet of details to secure his release, which was ultimately granted. His only sleep for six weeks of the fatal voyage was on his cabin floor, girt with pistols and cutlass, his head against the door for fear of surprise.

P. 21.—The laird of Halcro, South Ronaldshay, in the seventeenth century had a good yearly return from feeding cattle on the largest of the Pentland Skerries of which he was proprietor.

P. 23.—For details about castles, especially those on Sinclair's Bay, see "The First Contest for the Earldom" in *Northern Ensign.*

P. 27.—In Pont's map of 1608, Loch Calder is Loch Orient, from a house of this name on its south side.

P. 28.—Seven distinguished Edinburgh Caithness students, twenty years or more ago, secretly named themselves the Corriechoich Brotherhood, after the valley near Morven. This n ay have biographic and perhaps historical interest. See p. 30 *infra*, lines 8 and 9.

P. 29.—The bridge is drawn in one of Cordiner's books published 1780. It was not erected in 1761 when Bishop Pococke was in Berriedale. In the register of Privy Council of 1566, there is an account of lively doings at Berriedale Castle, then one of the homes of Lord Oliphant. Five Sutherlands, with accomplices, had slain Alexander Ison in Lapok, and several others, on 27th August, 1565, burning the house of Andrew Bain in Easter Clyth. Earl George, as justiciary, called upon them to underlie the law. They were put to the horn, in other words, sold out, but fled to Berriedale Castle, and defended themselves against the law. The Earl took the place by storm, but complained to the Privy Council that Lord Duffus secretly sent Sutherlands of his kin, who retook the castle by surprise and then held it. The Council ordered it to be delivered to Laurence, the Lord Master of Oliphant, within ten days, on pain of being declared rebels and at the horn. Alex. Sutherland of Duffus was specially charged. The Sutherlands about that time complained to the Council of the slaughter and mutilation of their kinsmen by Earl George on the plea of exercising justice. See p. 115 *infra* for what seems to have been a different version of the earlier stage of that which turned out to be a long feud between the Sinclairs and Sutherlands, the latter aided by their relatives the Murrays and Gordons of Sutherlandshire.

P. 30.—In 1608, Wick, judging from Pont's map, was divided into four rather straggling groups of buildings, the smallest nearest Proudfoot Point, and the two largest opposite an island in the river. The The church stood in the fourth group, which was also somewhat large. On the east side of the church the road went, which crossed by a bridge to Newton. The whole town was less than a mile in length. It would take a volume to do justice to the history of the burgh, the materials being unusually plentiful. Its records from 1660, opening with the quaint introductory, "In the name of the Father, Son, and Holy Ghost," are now being published, and give much insight into the town's past. The relations of the Ulbster family to the Provostship are in the yet unpublished portion, and especially Harpsdale's doings, James Sinclair, Thrumster House. The proposal of the inhabitants to John of Ulbster to become hereditary provost, in 1723, accepted by him, is a curious and lengthy document. He was to recover the Hill of Wick for them from the Dunbars of Hempriggs, pay the town's debts, set burghers up in trade, &c. In the "Acta Parliamentorium," the burgh's rights are printed, but it seems to have been for long periods unaware or deprived of them. Among the members it sent to the Scottish Parliament the name of Alexander Manson of Bridgend, in 1694, is notable. His daughter, Sydney, married Lythmore, one of the Barrack family, and their son, Robert Manson Sinclair of Bridgend, Watten, played a large part in town and county affairs during middle of last century. The fullest recent account of Wick is in the "Ordnance Survey Gazetteer of Scotland," which has a cut of the town's seal. Gough's "Topography" gives references to Macfarlane's "Geographical Collections," in the Advocates' Library, Edinburgh; "A Geographical Description of Canisbay and Wick, by Mr Sinclair of Hempriggs, in 1724," (from whom Henderson quotes); and "A Description of Wick by its minister, the Rev. James Oliphant, in 1726." See *infra* p. 210. Mr Oliphant also wrote of Thurso, Olrig, Bower, Watten, and Reay. Mr Oliphant had a son who was minister of Bower. The old and new "Statistical Accounts" give much interesting information of Wick, published, the first from 1790 to 1799, and the second in 1845. The parochial register begins in 1701, and makes, up to 1820, three volumes. The Wick register, though more than fifty years later in beginning than the oldest in the county—the invaluable one of Thurso—is fruitful of historical matter. The ministers of Wick since the Reformation were—Andrew Philp, before 1567; Thomas Keir, before 1576; Alex. Mearns (reader), Thomas Pruntoch, John Annand, before 1636; David Allardyce, in 1638; John Smart, in 1638, ejected 1650, and afterwards minister of Dunnet; William Geddes, in 1659, ejected in 1675, restored in 1692. William Geddes published several poems, one of these under the quaint title, "The Saints' Recreation upon the Estate of Grace." Patrick Clunas, in 1676, who died in 1691; Charles Keith, in 1701, dying in 1705; James Oliphant, in 1707, who died in 1726; James Ferme, 1727, dying 1760; James Scobie, 1762, dying 1764; William Sutherland, in 1765, dying in 1816; Robert Phin, 1813, dying 1840; and Charles Thomson, placed the same year, who compiled the interesting account of Wick in the "New Statistical Account of Scotland." This list is given chiefly to compare some of the names with those in the Burgh Records, several of the ministers' descendants being citizens, and sometimes not the most reputable.

P. 33.—Of Pulteneytown it must be enough here to say that "Jack" Sinclair, sister's son of Major Innes of Thrumster, has the credit of building its first house, his energetic temperament having taken him besides into millwright, carpentering, and other work, in which he employed seven or eight men.

P. 35.—Lybster has perhaps most interest as being the home of the Sinclairs of Lybster for two centuries, the first of them being John, bailie of Latheron, son of John Sinclair of Assery and Scrabster, a son of Sir James Sinclair of Murkle. Lieutenant-General Sinclair of Lybster was, last century and the beginning of the present, one of Sir John of Ulbster's earnest coadjutors in advancing the agriculture of the county. He sowed wheat in 1806 experimentally. (See Henderson's "View.") This appeared in a London newspaper:—"On 6th May, 1884, at 3 Dunham Terrace, Westbourne Park, London, Isabella, widow of Jeffrey Amherst Sinclair, Surgeon-General, Bombay Medical Service." Jeffrey, who appears to have been the last of the Lybsters was one of the heirs of entail of the estates of the Ulbster family in a summons of declarator by the late Sir George for the Court of Session, of date 19th June, 1839. The elder brother, Frederick Temple, was also a possible heir, failing nearer relations. John Sinclair of Lybster was an heir in the original entail of 1709, as well as John Sinclair of Assery.

P. 36.—In his "Antiquities and Scenery of the North of Scotland," published 1780, the Rev. Charles Cordiner has a description and cut of Oldwick Castle. It was discussed by antiquarians with respect to its masonry as a transition between such buildings as Dundornadilla, Coningsburgh Castle, near Doncaster, and the Scottish baronial castle. Its possessors for the longest time—the Oliphants—have a good historian, Dr. Joseph Anderson ; and in Caithness and State records their names and doings occur continually. The Privy Council Register (which see) has several striking passages about them which are of county interest. In 1569, Lord Oliphant was in Wick on 27th July, after a dinner with Thomas Weir, when the Master of Keith's men, to twenty-four, set up a quarrel, and his lordship got with difficulty to Auldwick. He sent his servants back to protect Weir, whose house was beseiged by sixty persons, but they were shot at "by seven bowmen standing in arrayed battle at the market cross of Wick." A fight followed, and John Sutherland was slain, and many wounded. Next day, John, Master of Caithness, and the Sutherlands, besieged Auldwick for eight days, till Weir and others were taken for the Earl to put them to an assize. John Sutherland was grandson to Catherine, daughter of Bishop Sinclair of Caithness, brother of one of the earls. (See Anderson's "Oliphants.") In his contributions to the *Celtic Magazine*, G. M. Sutherland has references to this and various other incidents in the lives and affairs of the Oliphants ; and " Origines Parochiales Scotiæ" gives abundant details about their properties. Lord Oliphant of 1549 got from Mary, Queen of Scots, the ward and nonentry—in other words, the rent—of Shurery, Brawlbin, Skaill, Borrowston, and Lybster, which the Crown had held for 120 years, namely, since the death of Ranald, Lord Cheyne. Their Wick and other lands were also large.

P. 37.—The most important record in writing belonging to Thurso seems to be its parish register, at Edinburgh, which ought to be printed, for greater safety of preservation and for the use of investigators into county facts. As the largest town north of Inverness for centuries, it must have had much written burghal and legal record. In print it has had abundant notice, in particular from Sir Robert Gordon in his "Genealogical History of the House of Sutherland," and Mackay in his "History of the Mackays." For convenience of being near the centre of affairs, the earls had Thurso East Castle erected. There is a good notice of the town in the "Ordnance Survey Gazeteer of Scotland."

P. 40 (a).—The founder of the Miller Institution, Alexander Miller, was the son of Daniel Miller, Skinnet farm, and Janet Sinclair, daughter of Patrick, tacksman of Giese, who died in 1807, aged 77, an illegitimate son of Alexander, Earl of Caithness. She was born in 1769, and died in 1801. Her son died some years ago, leaving, it was said, a quarter of a million ; but this could be easily authenticated by reference to wills.

P. 40 (b).—The bridge of Thurso is said to have been built by Robert Tulloch, master mason, son of John Tulloch and Christina Sinclair, of the Ulbster family of Brims, whose daughter Elizabeth was baptized 15th April, 1759. John came from Orkney before 1737, the date of his first marriage, to be factor to Alexander, Earl of Caithness (Lord Hemer), who died in 1765. He held the position twelve years. Robert was married to Christian Gunn, in Halkirk, on 1st January, 1796. His brother James was father of Professor John of Aberdeen and five ministers. Their mother, an early widow, brought them up with difficulty at Achrascar, near Achinabest, and they got their education at Reay under the Rev. William Munro, A.M., afterwards schoolmaster of Thurso. A third brother, John, was a Caithness schoolmaster. Robert's sons were John, also a county teacher, and Murdoch. The late Principal Tulloch was said to be descended from a brother of the earl's factor.

P. 41.—For mysterious stories, Professor George Sinclair of Glasgow University, appointed 1672, in his "Satan's Invisible World Discovered," may be mentioned. The work has a preface of Sinclair genealogy. See Sir Walter Scott's introduction to "Woodstock," where the Professor is called the "approved collector" of ghostly tales. Unfortunately, Thurso has, from one fact, the credit of having had too much belief in the supernatural. Margaret Gilbertson, in Ourton, Lythmore, was killed by a Thurso crowd as a witch in 1718. The horrid tale is told in great detail by Mackay in his "History of the Mackays," his informant, Bailie Paterson, having had the legal proceedings in his possession. The Rev. T. F. Thistleton Dyer, in the *Gentleman's Magazine* of May, 1882, states that there was a judicial inquiry held in Thurso on the point of witchcraft, at the instance of a William [or Hugh] Montgomery, Scrabster, who had been "reduced to a remarkable condition by the gambols of a legion of cats [drinking his ale, etc.] His man-servant affirmed that the cats spoke amongst themselves. Montgomery attacked them with broadsword and axe. Two old women died immediately, and a third lost a leg, which, having been broken by a stroke of the hatchet, withered and dropped off." No doubt it was the third who, after being dragged to court, was done to death by the witch-hunting mob, the others dying from age, and not from blows. The most civilised parts and individuals of the globe had been long lost to the delusion that the devil gave his direct services to some people. One of the Caithness tests of such communion was that when asked to say Paternoster or the Lord's Prayer, they invariably said "Our Father which *was* in heaven."

P. 42 (a).—The first Lord Reay's brother, John of Strathy, had Dirlet till his death in 1645. (See the "Dairy of Samuel Pepys" for a discussion of second sight in which he and others of the locality figured.) There is a burying-ground at Dirlet sacred to the Gunns. (See "A History of Dirlet Churchyard," in *Northern Ensign*, by Dr. William Gunn, Futuna, New Hebrides; and also an eloquent passage on it, written in 1834, by the Rev. John Munro, the second of the name, of Halkirk, in the "New Statistical Account.")

P. 42 (b).—Captain Henderson's "Agricultural View of Caithness" published in 1812, gives much information. The rent of the county in 1702 was not much above £3000 sterling. He describes the manufacturing scheme of 1788 at Thurso, linen, rope, and tanning; the building of Sarclet by Captain Brodie, designated Brodie's Town on the plan;

and the trade to the east in corn, and also a trade to the West Indies from Thurso. In 1810 there were 250 straw-plaiters in the town. Ten years before its population was 1952, and Wick 1749. The Crown lands were let on the lease to 1809 at £80 sterling. Tacksmen used to pay £200 to £800 to the proprietors, and sublet to the tenants. Of natives of the south who aided the development of the county, John Paterson, Borlum, ought to be mentioned, even though in Highland clearance literature he ranks with the Lochs and Sellars of sheep-raising notoriety. He was born at Oxnam, Roxburghshire, in 1780, and came a poor shepherd to Caithness in 1804. Becoming sheep-manager and then factor for Major William Innes of Sandside, he lived in his service, mostly at Borlum House, forty-one years. He died at his farm of Skinnet in 1853, leaving £39,000 of money, besides the stocked agricultural and sheep-farms of Downreay, Skaill, Borrowston, Lybster, Skinnet, Melness, Armadale, and others in Caithness and Sutherland. His evictions about 1810 in West Caithness were numerous, but his energy tended much to the development of the natural resources of the county. The very original business faculty he had did not come down in so large a measure to his descendants. Of the numerous and valuable recent improvements by other than native intellect, those of W. Reid Tait, factor for Sir Robert Sinclair's estate of Isauld and Murkle, have been remarkable.

P. 47.—As patriotism of the Stornoway and Lapland kinds can become unscientific, it may be useful to add that the Rev. James Hall, in his book, published in 1807, gives quite as harsh an account of the emaciated people and poor food of the county then as Chambers does of the scenery in 1831.

P. 48.—The allowance was £5 Scots per day while attending Parliament. Sir George Sinclair of Clyth, M.P., charged the barons and freeholders of the shire, in his will, at this rate for the session from 26th June to 23rd September, 1706, "with eight days coming and eight days going," £515 Scots altogether. For the session of 1703-1704 four landlords were charged £92 Scots each, others having probably paid.

P. 49 (a).—About the *tumuli* or tullochs of Caithness, see the "Archæologia Scotica," Samuel Laing's tractate on Caithness skeletons, and the learned works of Dr. Joseph Anderson. A Latin description of Ulster, in Ireland, during the early period of English conquest, shows the Celts there to have had somewhat similar community homes of the circular form.

P. 49 (b).—The treaty of St. Clair, on the river Epte, France, in 912 gave Rollo the dukedom of Normandy. It is certain that this St. Clair, as well as the more important one near St. Lo, was given, after the manner of the period, to a near relative, who thence took the local surname now known as Sinclair. The Lord of St. Clair who fought at the battle of Hastings in 1066, and the "Romance of Rollo" says, "overthrew many of the English," may have been French, but it is much more probable that he was Norse, like William the Conqueror himself, his near relation also by marriage. The Rev. Alban Butler, in his "Lives of the Saints," gives the origin of the name:—"St. Clarus was an Englishman by birth, of very noble extraction. He was ordained priest, and leaving his own country, led many years an angelical life in the county of Vexin, in France. He often preached the truths of salvation to the inhabitants, and died a martyr of chastity, being murdered by two ruffians employed by an impious and lewd lady of quality, about the year 894. He is named in the Roman and Gallican Martyrologies, and honoured with singular veneration in the dioceses of Rouen, Beauvais, and Paris. The village where he suffered martyrdom, situate upon the river Epte (which separates the Norman and French Vexins), nine leagues from Pontoise, and twelve from Rouen, bears his name, and is become a considerable town by the devotion of the people to this saint. His rich shrine is resorted to by crowds of pilgrims, who also visit a hermitage which stands upon the spot which was watered with his blood near the town. Another town in the diocese of Coutance, in Normandy, which is said also to have been sanctified by his dwelling there before he retired to the Epte, is called by his name St. Clair." It was from the latter that the Conqueror's companion-in-arms was called the Lord of St. Clair, but the other one seems also to have been his property. Two of his sons founded great houses in England, their titled descendants taking prominent part in the events of English history as far down as the accession of the house of Stuart to the united throne in 1603. In the "History of the Scottish Expedition to Norway in 1612," p. 127, there is new information, such as the following:—" The noble Swedish family is said to be descended from the St. Clairs of Freswick and Dunbeath." See the *Scots Magazine*, vol. ii., 1740, for account of the murder by the Russians in Silesia, while returning with despatches from Turkey, of Count Major Malcolm of this branch in 1739, and letter of the Czarina herself on the subject, in the time of "the Caps and Hats." Carlyle, in "Frederick the Great," writes of him :— "The royal Bruces seem to have reached Normandy likewise from Caithness, Orkney, and Norway."

P. 53.—See the paper in the transactions of the Society of Antiquaries, by the Rev. Alexander Pope, A.M., of Reay, on the horse shoe circle of standing stones at the loch of Stemster, who has astronomical theories about them. It was printed recently in the *Northern Ensign.*

P. 57.—It would be a pity to destroy so keen a source of amusement as fairy tales by stating that the green folks are only embodiments of what poets think of vegetation. Shakspeare, with Bottom, the weaver, straying in the greenery to meet Titania and the rest of the gay company, is of this opinion in "Midsummer Nights' Dream."

P. 64.—As the earlier history of Caithness is nearly all taken from the "Orcades" of Torfæus, published 1697, and the "Orkneyinga Saga," it is enough to say that there is an English translation of the former from Latin, as far as connected with Caithness, in an appendix to Pennant's "Tour," by the Rev. Alexander Pope of Reay, while Dr. Joseph Anderson has translated the Saga for English readers. Sweyn, the viking, is the ancestor of the Swansons, who are by no means destitute of his courage ; and they are therefore blood relations of the equally daring, or, as Sir Robert Gordon said, desperate Gunns. It is an anomaly that the latter, being of purely Teutonic stock, should have been thought a clan, even though they did for most part speak Gaelic.

P. 74.—One of the earliest notices of Assery, after that by Torfæus, is by a MS. in Stirling's Library, Glasgow, giving a list of donations to the Church :—" In 1533, Henry Rattray of Pitf . . . . to the kirk of Caithness, the mill of Forsie, and £20 out of the mill of Assery or Baluny."

P. 79.—It was in Brawl Castle that "Mr" John Sinclair, the first of the line of Ulbster, usually did his teaching duties. He calls himself in an agreement with his brother Patrick, of date Girnigo, 10th Feb., 1603, "pedagogue to William, Master and Fiar of Caithness."

P. 85.—See "National Dictionary of Biography," article "Baltroddi," a bishop of Caithness, for the Bishop's castle and some of its associations.

P. 92.—The chief authorities on the history of the Gunns are Sir Robert Gordon in his genealogical history ; Rev. Charles Thomson of Wick, in the "New Statistical Account," through aid of the MSS. of Dr. Patrick Brodie Henderson ; the late John Henderson, W.S., in his "Caithness Family History ;" Mr G. M. Sutherland in the *Celtic Magazine ;* Mackay in his "History of the Mackays ;" George Sutherland Taylor of Golspie in the "New Statistical Account ;" and William Mackenzie of Inverness in his "History of the Macdonalds." Their battles, first with the Keiths, then with the Macivers and Abrach Mackays, and lastly with the Sinclairs, have had many historians. Rev. Alexander Pope of Reay, in his appendix to Pennant's "Tour," has notes of them. There is no mention of the Gunns in the "Acta Parliamentorum" till 1647, which shows that they had small ruling importance. "Alexander Gun of Calelnan" is put on the Committee of War for Caithness and Sutherland that year.

P. 102.—Torfæus gives an account of the investiture by King Haco of Henry Sinclair, baron of Roslin, to the principality of the Orkneys in 1379. One writer says that Ernegol Swanson was temporary governor or titular earl before him. He is now said to have been the first historic discoverer and coloniser of America. See the story of his Venetian admirals, the ducal Zenoes in Hakluyt's "Voyages." It is noticed in Pinkerton's "History of Scotland." Henry, his son, was guardian to James I. of Scotland. For the Roslins see Father Hay's MS. (printed by Maidment); Van Bassan's MS., the Danish Schiern's "Life of Bothwell," Nisbet's "Heraldry," Wallace's "Orkney," Douglas's "Baronage," Nisbet's "Appendix," aided by Hearn's "Antiquities of Great Britain," Crawford's "Lord Chancellors," the Peerages of Burke, Foster, Walford, and Collins, with many other works. Mrs Pffeifer had a long poem in the *Contemporary Review* of 1879 on The *Prince's* Pillar, the Roslins wearing a royal coronet for the Orkney and Shetland Isles. Principal Campbell of St Andrew's and Oxford has also written verse on Roslin. The literature, both English and foreign, on the subject is endless. Billings is one of the fullest authors on the architectural and free-mason topics, the Roslins being the hereditary heads of Scottish freemasonry till William Sinclair, Scott's model for the Douglas of "The Lady of the Lake," gave up the position in 1736. See the *Gentleman's Magazine,* vol. xl., 1778, the year of his death.

P. 107.—The drum-head charter given to the Earl of Caithness by King James IV. on Flodden Field was traced by Mackay in his "History of the Mackays" to the charter chest of the earls of Fife. It is not an historic myth, and no great acumen was required to show how it found its way among the Duffs. Alexander, the second Earl of Caithness of the Murkle line, who died on 9th December, 1765, at his castle of Hemer, near Thurso, had it among his charters. His only daughter, Lady Dorothy, married James, the second earl of Fife, on 5th June, 1759, and on her father's death she and Lord Fife had the possession of his papers and charters. A law suit took place between Lady Dorothy and Sir John Sinclair of Stevenson, Haddingtonshire, ancestor of the present Sir Robert of Murkle, for the lands of Murkle, Isauld, and others, which, on the interpretation of a single word, she lost, and which the Stevensons have held ever since. (See p. 201 *infra.*) Sir Robert in writing and personal conversation has affirmed that his agents have none of Lord Hemer's charters or estate documents. The inference is clear that Lady Dorothy secured them. Through her divorce from Lord Fife they may have been scattered, but the presumption is that many documents of the Caithness earldom and of the Murkle and Isauld estates are in the strong boxes of the present Earl of Fife. It would be a great find in the way of county history if this should prove to be fact. But in any case there is sufficient written and printed evidence as to the real existence of the drum-head charter.

P. 108.—Earl John acquired lands in the Helmsdale valley from Adam Gordon, second son of the Earl of Huntly, and the daughter of James I., when, as some said, he was usurping the earldom of Sutherland. He had married Elizabeth Sutherland, and then repudiated her only brother's claim as being a bastard. Further light is thrown on things if it is true that Earl John of Caithness was married to Adam's sister, after the death or divorce of his first wife, Mary Sutherland, daughter of Duffus. The authorities for this are William Gordon in his "History of the Gordons to 1690," published in 1726, and C. A. Gordon in his "History of the House of Gerston," published at Aberdeen in 1754. Earl Adam's fifth sister was married to the Earl of Caithness, who could be no other than John. Adam's eldest sister married Perkin Warbeck, the pretender to the throne of England, as being one of the York little princes, and who, he asserted, escaped from the Tower of London from the murdering uncle, Richard the Third. It was in 1495 that "Richard Plantagenet of York," as Warbeck, dubbed himself, came to Scotland, "where the King, James IV., gave him his kinswoman, Katharine Gordon, in marriage." After his execution, "his beautiful wife, 'the White Rose,' as she was called, became an attendant on Henry's Queen"—Henry VII. of England. The dates of the life of John Earl of Caithness alone agree with this narrative, and the interesting item may be accepted as a real addition to the county history at a distant period. In Robert Forsyth's "Beauties of Scotland," published in 1802, the fifth volume dedicated to Sir John of Ulbster, there is a story of Earl John's time. Robert Gunn, tacksman of Braemore, killed Sutherland of Langwell with bow and arrow for the love he had to his wife, whom he married. He contrived a marriage between the son, "big Sutherland," and his daughter to ward off revenge. John Earl of Caithness sent John Sinclair of Stirkoke to get the rent from Gunn, but he was wounded, and his party defeated by the unpleasant tacksman. Forsyth has much information about the provostry and council of Wick.

P. 118.—On the same two Gordons' authority, the lady blamed for the tragedy at Helmsdale was Elizabeth Sinclair, daughter of the first laird of Dunbeath, Alexander, brother of John Earl of Caithness; the second laird, William, being her brother. She had three sons, John, Patrick, and Gilbert, with several daughters, her husband being

Gilbert Gordon, as in the context. Sir Robert Gordon, the historian, names her Isobel, but makes her sister of William.

P. 119.—George, the fourth earl of Caithness, got the wardship of the young earl of Sutherland as being a near, if not the nearest, relation; a great privilege of those times, because nonentry or rents went with the tutorship, as it was sometimes called. Feudally he had also the marriage of his ward, and did nothing unusual in marrying him to his daughter. The truth of the Earl's whole family life has been garbled by Sir Robert Gordon, the bitterest of enemies, because an angry and earth-hungering relation. Even the tragedies said to have occurred in the cases of the two sons seem to have been misread to his discredit. He was the absolute justiciary of the two counties, using habitually the power of capital punishment; but there is no proof that he exercised it against his eldest son, though the master crowned disobedience and conspiracy with the hurting of his brother William to the death. See Galt's "Entail" for a version of the tragic tale different from that of Sir Robert Gordon. Gunn, a schoolmaster at Wick, is made the narrator; and as Galt knew the Ulbster family descended from William's illegitimate but legitimated son "Mr" John, he may have got his information through them and their direct traditions. Jealousy of father and son about a Mackay lady is said to be the cause of their supposed quarrel of years.

P. 123.—Robertson, the historian of Scotland, quotes the Fordyce MSS. as showing that it was Lady Bothwell who sought the divorce in 1567, after a few months' marriage, because of Bothwell's adultery with Bessie Crawford, her servant; but the historian makes a mistake in saying that she afterwards married the Master of Caithness instead of Alexander, Earl of Sutherland. The full text of the divorce is in an appendix. Bothwell on his side put in the plea of too near blood.

P. 126.—The Bannatyne "Miscellanies" have "An Opinion of the Nobility" of date 1583. This was the year of the death of George, Earl of Caithness; and the following is the forecast of his grandson and successor:—"George Sinclair, half-brother to this Earl of Bothwell, by the mother's side, is a youth of seventeen years of age, and in the tutory of the Earl of Gowry, who has his wardship, a cause of the late unkindness and heart-burning between him and Bothwell (Stewart, grandson of James V.) Of his religion and inclination there is yet little trial. His power extends over the bounds of Caithness, though the Earl, Marshal Keith, and Lord Oliphant, are portioners with him of that country."

P. 127.—In the triangular duel which went on actively for more than a century between Caithness, Sutherland, and Strathnavernia, George, the fifth Sinclair Earl of Caithness, took perhaps the most prominent position. The houses of Sinclair, Gordon, and Mackay fought each for its own hand, though the closest ties of relationship existed between them. It was family quarrelling throughout, and none the less bitter of this. G. M. Sutherland, in the *Celtic Magazine*, has indicated best the general condition of things. The immediate relatives of the three houses, who were the stewards and tacksmen, had little of the brunt of the fighting, leadership at intervals alone putting them in danger. The Abrach Mackays for Lord Reay, the MacIvors or Campbells, imported from Argyle, for the Caithness earls, and the Gunns in the interest of the Dunrobin Gordon, were the fighting and defending elements. Through whatsoever changes of that which may be called the local politics, and though these vassals sometimes reversed sides, the rule of attachment was as above. It is important towards understanding the position to remember that these tribes, made up mostly of those then called broken men, were placed on the borders of the triple province which had the inclusive name of the diocese of Caithness, and over which the Earls of Caithness had for long the hereditary justiciaryship. The details of these boundary wars are numerous, and bloody fights have many silent memorials on the hills and in the valleys near the marches. It was only now and again that members of the ruling families headed these sanguinary and needless struggles. Raids for goods and cattle were the variations to tribal contests.

P. 134.—In 1590 the MacIvers, under David Sinclair of Stirkoke, fought and defeated the Gunns at Craig Mohr, near Achinabest. A standing-stone and about a score of grave-heaps mark the scene of the battle, which ended in a flight, the last Gunn but one being slain at the Caa, Sandside. Donald Gunn escaped to Strathy, though wounded by sword and pistol, through leaping over a rock on the south of Craig Mohr, as Sir Robert Gordon says, "fifteen fathoms in height." On Upper Downreay there is a similar standing-stone, and either a graveyard or battlefield ; while above Borlum there is a double grave-yard, as if the resting-places of enemies, the stones in straight lines, and numbering about one hundred. Sir James Sinclair of Murkle was a prominent leader in the fights of that period with the Gunns. They had killed several MacIvers, and in one of his expeditions seven Gunns were killed by his men at Strathy in 1594. The incidents of the Gunn, MacIver, and Mackay warfare were as numerous as sanguinary. What intensified the fighting then was the defeat in 1586 at Auldgown. (See p. 129 *infra.*) The following very interesting document, the year of date 1586 or 1587, illustrates the situation :—"At Girnigo, the 16th day of June, ... years. It is agreed by a noble and potent lord, George, earl of Caithness, taking the burden on him for his whole kin, friends, dependants, and partakers whatsoever on the one part, and Sir Patrick Gordon of Auchindoun, knight, taking the burden on him for a noble and potent lord, Alexander, earl of Sutherland, and the said Earl of Sutherland for himself, and taking the burden on him for his whole kin, friends, dependants, and partakers whatsoever on the other part : Forasmuch as it is notoriously known to all men, of the cruel, undutiful slaughter and murder committed in June, 1586 years, by those of the name of clan Gunn upon the said George, earl of Caithness's special kinsmen, friends, and dependants, and of the said clan Gunn, the committers of the said slaughter, being his Majesty's rebels, repairing and being daily received within the bounds of Caithness and Sutherland, to the great grief and contempt of the said earl of Caithness, the same being greatly to his lordship's dishonour to behold, he has deliberated, with God's assistance, they being his Majesty's rebels, as said is, to seek, seize, and pursue, even to the death, wherever they or any of them may be apprehended. In the doing of this, the said noble and potent lord, Alexander, earl of Sutherland, by the mouth of the said Sir Patrick Gordon, promises faithfully on his lordship's honour and credit to concur, assist, and take plain pact by himself and his aforesaids with the said earl of Caithness and his aforesaids, in the pursuit of the said clan Gunn to the death. For the upright, true, and

forward doing of which by the said Earl of Sutherland and his aforesaids, with the said Earl of Caithness and his aforesaids, both the said
earls are contented and faithfully promise to enter into special favour
and goodwill with each other, and to convene and put their forces
together between this and the end of this present month of June, and
to pass forward to the pursuit of the said clan Gunn wheresoever they
may be apprehended, and from this time forth both the said earls to
continue in friendship and true amity for ever; and acts, quarrels,
and chances whatsoever which have fallen out, or yet shall happen
to fall out, between the said earls or their dependants, to be remitted
and considered by the judgment of discreet and indifferent friends
within the diocese of Caithness or sheriffdom of Inverness, or any
others who may be chosen by the said earls. And for faithfully
observing and keeping the promises, both the said earls have subscribed these with their hands, and the said Sir Patrick the burden on
him, as said is, day, year, and place aforesaid, before witnesses,
James Sinclair, Master of Caithness, and John Sinclair of Dun solely.
Signed, CAITHNESS; PATRICK GORDON, of Auchindoun; JAMES
SINCLAIR, Master of Caithness, witness; JOHN SINCLAIR, of Dun,
witness." This James is Sir James of Murkle, who figures so
prominently in the punishment of the Gunns thus devoted to extir-
pation.

P. 142.—The tragic story of Colonel George Sinclair has been fully
told in Michell's "History of the Scottish Expedition to Norway in
1612," published 1886. The author's theory that the younger Ramsay
was the actual leader through the fatal pass is wrong; but he has printed
so many original documents in his volume that readers are enabled to
form their own judgment; and all must feel indebted to him for his
successful researches in Britain, Norway, Denmark and Sweden.
His mistaken attempt to reverse tradition is condemned by the following from a letter which he gives out of the State archives of Norway,
by Chancellor Ove Bjelke to the Stadtholder Iver Krabbe, asking
him to help Peder Eckre, of date so near the expedition as 20th
December, 1651:—"I knew his father, who was the man that beat
Hr. Georgium Sinclair, who wanted to lead the Scottish folk through
Gudbrandsdalen." Mr Michell does not make him but his father
David illegitimate, who, however, was legitimated in 1588. No tale
has more dramatic or historic interest than that of the 550 Scots,
chiefly Caithnessmen, who died the soldier's dreaded death of ambush
in Norway. There is valuable Sinclair genealogy on page 126 et passim.
Colonel, then Captain, Sinclair's seizure of Lord Maxwell of Nithsdale
for murder was an ordinary unavoidable executive duty for his uncle,
the earl, as justiciary. The Maxwells had no claim upon Sinclair to
aid them to escape from law, if for nothing but their despicable
betrayal of Oliver of Roslin at Solway Moss.

P. 150.—Queen Mary's husband, the Earl of Bothwell, made Duke
of Orkney, was the son of Agnes Sinclair, sister of William, second
Lord Sinclair; and as his sister, Jane Hepburn, was married to John,
the Master of Caithness, who died in the dungeon in Girnigoe in 1576,
it is easy to understand how and why he fled to the north in his
necessity. See Schiern's "Life of Bothwell."

P. 153.—So much has been printed about the burning of the Sandside
cornyard in 1616, that only something new and hitherto unpublished
gives a reason for reference to it. These letters are their own recom-

mendation:—"To the right honourable, his assured good friend, Sir Robert Gordon, tutor of Sutherland, these ; Right honourable sir and truest friend, Finding the commodity of the bearer, your sister's son, the laird of Mackay, I thought good to make you foreseen of that which has past between me and him concerning the Clan Gunn, as likewise about his agreement with the Earl of Caithness. As for his agreement, I will suspend my judgment of it till time try the effect. But concerning the Clan Gunn, I cannot know by Mackay that he has any evil will at any of them except John Robson, who, as he alleges, deserves the same at his hands, as has been proved before yourself. Mackay complains greatly to me that you have taken John Robson's maintenance against him, as likewise that you have given him land by promise since Mackay's away-coming. You know best yourself if these things be true or not. But this far I will say, as a neutral friend, who wishes both your standings, that neither of you will do well to maintain or defend any man against the other, who is known notoriously to have justly offended. I know by Mackay that he is most willing to keep duty in all respects to the house of Sutherland, providing that he get a meeting to himself and his friends. You should be loath to lose him, willingly or any other way ; for you may take example by your neighbours what it is to be in trouble or variance with your own, without great reason. And if Mackay breaks duty any way to the house of Sutherland, you may be assured there shall not be a friend living who will be further against him than myself. Mackay likewise has been very earnest with me seeking a discharge to John Robson for the burning of the corn of Sandside. This I have granted conditionally that John, according to his promise, shall deliver the three factors of that burning, as likewise find security that I and mine shall incur no harm by him and his in time coming. Otherwise, I assure you that I will follow John to the uttermost for that fact, and for all other things that I may lay to his charge so far as law will. But the men being delivered and surety found, as said is, I assure you by these presents, that I will be a friend to John and all his, till they deserve the contrary again. But in case you see John make any subterfuge in doing that which the laws will compel him to do, I pray you to give his answer to Mackay, whereby I may be advertised thereof with diligence. And although he would refuse the same, I doubt not that if you and Mackay please to concur together, you may get the malefactors apprehended, which I am assured you will both extend your means to do, as I have been and shall be ready to pleasure any of you. If the wrong had been done to any of you which has been done to me, and the malefactors so often in my bounds as these men have been in yours, they had not escaped their condign punishment until now. As for a warrant to apprehend them, Mackay has a caption lying beside him in Strathnaver which will serve you both, as Mackay will inform you at meeting. I am informed likewise that John Robson is very evil disposed in his speeches against William Innes and others of my servants in Caithness. If this be true, it marvels me ; for I think John should rather press to make amends for bygones, than to urge or incense me to further wrath against him. So I rest, committing you with my Lady, your mother, your bedfellow, and all your friends, wherever they are, to the love and favour of God, your assured good friend at power, ARTHUR L[ORD] FORBES."

Driminor, 13th April, 1618.

Mackay informs me that he is to sell or wadset part of his lands of Edderachilis, and that he is to make you the first offer thereof, and if you will not accept the same that he will end with his ally, the clan M'Kenzie, for the said lands. Therefor my counsel is that you will do herein what you may, before you let other neighbours enter among you. L. FORBES.

The next is a scroll in Sir R. Gordon's hand:—" I, Arthur Lord Forbes, assignee constituted together with Sir Donald Mackay of Strathnaver, knight, by William Innes of Sandside, to the action of the burning of the corn of Sandside, which fact of burning was committed, as is alleged, by Alexander Gunn, *alias* Robson, and his accomplices, by these presents discharge and forgive *simpliciter* the said Alexander Gunn thereof, and of all the things that may flow thereupon for ever, and oblige myself that I shall never pursue the said Alexander Gunn for the same by laws or by law, directly or indirectly. And, further, I oblige myself, by the truth of an honest man, that I shall do my diligence and best endeavour to persuade the aforesaid William Innes of Sandside never to pursue the said Alexander Robson for said fact of burning, directly or indirectly, and that I shall move the said William so far as I can to discharge the said Alexander thereof for ever. And, further, I promise that neither myself nor any other by my means shall be the advocate's informer, directly or indirectly, against the said Alexander Gunn for the said fact of burning. And for the more security hereof, I am content and consent that these presents be inserted and registered in the Books of Council, to have the strength of a decree of the lords thereof, that letters of horning may pass thereon in a simple charge of ten days only, and to that effect I constitute . . . my lawful procurators, to consent to the registration hereof, *promittere de rato, etc.*, by these presents, written by Sir Robert Gordon, tutor of Sutherland. I have subscribed the same with my hand at . . the . . day of March, 1619 years, before these witnesses . . .

P. 156.—David Sinclair in Lybster, Reay, while from home, had all his cattle stolen by robbers, who drove them over Shebster Hill, and rested in the deep hollow on the Strathnaver side, near a small loch which was there at that time. On his return, David took a boy with him, and pursued till he came to the Yellow Moss. There he secreted the boy in a peat-stack, telling him he was going over Shebster Hill, and that if a whistle was heard he was to follow. If no whistling reached his ears in an hour or so he was to return to Lybster. After thus providing for the boy's safety and the possibilities of a death struggle, he went after the reivers, armed with a sword. He found them all five asleep. Two he killed on the ground, a third got his quietus when rising, and the remaining two he mastered in a running fight, the last cut down about a hundred yards from where the surprise took place. Where they fell was marked by five heaps of stones and sod, which still remain prominent on the heath.

P. 161.—See Munro's " Expedition," " An Old Scots Brigade " by John Mackay, &c. In Munro's book there is a Latin epitaph by a Dutchman, Dr. Narsius, to the son of the earl.

P. 162.—On Caithness covenanters consult " The Inneses of Sandside " in the *Northern Ensign.*

P. 165.—The " Nova descriptio Cathanesiæ," published 1654, mentions the " Mowats or, more exactly, the Monte-Altoes," as strangers holding property in Caithness, much of which they got by writ from the Keiths. The Mowats had Harpsdale for a long time. They appear in English and Welsh history.

P. 167.—See *Northern Ensign* for details, through State papers, on the fight at St. Peter's, Thurso, and also for other history connected with this ancient church.

P. 171.—It was John Sinclair of Brims, and not Alexander, his father, who joined Montrose. Alexander was descended from the old Dunbeath family, and married in 1619, Ann Mackay, sister of the first Lord Reay, dying in 1625. Hugh Mackay of Dirlot was his first cousin.

P. 174.—In describing the defeat near Tain in 1650, Monteth in his history, published in 1735, says, "Montrose swam over the river accompanied by the gallant Sir Edward St. Clair and St. Clair of Brims, a gentleman of Caithness. Montrose got into a very deep valley, and having continued two days, he sent Brims, who knew the country, to look for some provisions, but he having betrayed him, a party of the country people came upon him immediately thereafter, and having promised him all manner of good usage, basely sold him to David Leslie." There is this note by the French translator of Monteth to the above evidently false statement :—"Bishop Wishart, author of Montrose's Life, writes that it was Macleod of Assynt who betrayed him." The royalty, after their return to power, did all they could to ruin Macleod, who was said to have had 1,000 bolls of meal for Montrose ; but nothing is heard of Brims, though he lived in Sutherlandshire at Rigibil, which is proof positive that he had no blame in the matter. Macleod was long imprisoned, and only escaped with his life, losing ultimately his lands, and suffering in many ways through the cloud that was over him. In an unpublished paper of date 1758, there is a long account of how he and his people were dispossessed. It is protested there that Macleod at his trial in Edinburgh proved an *alibi*, being at the time sixty miles away from where Montrose was taken. Sir William Sinclair of Mey and Cadboll, is put down as one of his relentless enemies, having imprisoned Assynt in Mey Castle, the Seaforth Mackenzies being the chief. Worlds of discussion open on this question. But there is no ground to charge Brims with the "cruel, barbarous action." He was the last of the old Dunbeath family who resided at Brims Castle. In the Inquisitions-General a son, John, heirs his mother, Christina Mein, spouse of John Sinclair of Ribigil, on 28th Feb., 1691, but this was in Strathnaver under their relatives the Reays. The Ulbsters followed at Brims Castle till the notorious Patrick (the model of Byrons Manfred, his tale probably communicated at Harrow School by the late Sir George Sinclair) sold it in 1726 to Lord Hemer, Earl of Caithness. No place in the county has more extraordinary historical associations than this castle, a door and two or three walls of which alone remain, on a moderate rock over the northern seas. One of Patrick's victims was The White Lady, who, being poisoned, haunts it still.

P. 175.—In a book published at Edinburgh in 1833, of which only 60 copies were printed, entitled "Historical Fragments relative to Scottish Affairs from 1635 to 1664," there is " A Note of the Letters taken out of the Trunk that came to Dunbeath ; with Copies of two Letters from Colonel Gordon and the Earl of Kinnoul to the Marquis of Montrose, 1649." It was Lieutenant General Leslie that took them out, and they consisted of a letter which came from the King of Denmark to the King, 15th Sept., 1649, referring all to James Graham [Montrose]; another of the same tenour; one from the Marquis of Brandenburg to Graham; Sir John Cochrane's story of his negotiations at Hamburg; a paper of Urry's resolution (see p. 170 *infra*) to follow James Graham; a letter of Crawford to Urry, complaining of Montrose's great undertaking without effect; and various other documents of general historic importance. One of local interest was " James Graham's warrant subscribed under his hand, that he was to come to Caithness to relieve the country from burdens, and that he would proceed against all rebels who did not concur with him." The preface speaks of Montrose's betrayal by Macleod of Assynt, and says that Dunbeath Castle, the proprietor of which was an enemy, was occupied in order to provide for a retreat. Colonel Urry, to whom it had been surrendered, placed in it what he conceived to be a sufficient garrison, and then joined Montrose. It appears that for greater security a box or trunk of papers containing a variety of valuable documents belonging to the Marquis, had been placed there, which upon the subsequent rendering of the castle fell into the hands of General David Leslie, afterwards Lord Newark,"

P. 179. (*a*).—This nephew was William Sinclair, M.P., the ancestor of the second or Mey family of Dunbeath. His struggles with the sixth Earl of Caithness about the sheriffship were described recently in the *Northern Ensign*, on information from the Lauderdale MSS. of the British Museum.

P. 179. (*b*).—The Causeway Mire is said to have its name from a road put down by Cromwell's soldiers. A murder about the beginning of this century took place there, done, it was said, by one of the Gunns, called "Minearts."

P. 181.—In "The First Contest for the Earldom" will be found a valuable series of original letters and documents from the Duke of Lauderdale's unpublished papers; and, by the added explanatory writing, the whole period of the Glenorchy occupation, with sometime before and after, is covered. The titles of many books, and numerous indications of other sources of knowledge are given; but the field has much still to be gleaned. Murkle and Dunbeath's fatal quarrel with the Mackays is told there, as it is in Mackay's History less fully. Murkle, who afterwards became Earl John, having been wounded in the neck.

P. 191.—The real importance of the Ulbsters dates from the marriage of John Sinclair of Brims, as Collins in his "Peerage of England" puts it, "great grandfather's father of the present Sir John of Ulbster, member for Caithness," the first baronet, to Miss Goldman, "of the family of Sandford, of English descent." The English connection may or may not be, but the following from the *Inquisitiones Generales* seems proof of Scotch origin, and certain evidence of where the money was made which bought most of Glenorchy's usurped lands:—*Jan.* 18, 1639, *Margareta Goldman, haeres Jacobi Goldman, mercatoris burgensis de Dondie, patris*—"Margaret Goldman, heiress of James Goldman, merchant, burgess of Dundee, her father." On the same date she was served heiress to William Goldman, lawful son of the aforesaid James Goldman. It was the other daughter who married the ancestor of the Ulbsters. Margaret married James Wedderburn, second son of the first Baron Kingennie, and "with this lady," says

Collins, "he got a great portion in money." It was the like portion which enabled the Ulbsters, who were always provident, to become the largest proprietors in the county. The father was Provost of Dundee, and, it is said, made his money by trading in tallow. No doubt the town records, if they exist, give his history incidentally. But some of these points have been touched before.

P. 194.—As a sequel to the "First," "The Second Contest for the Earldom," which is nearly ready for publication, will enter into full particulars of the protracted legal struggle between James Sinclair, grandson of David of Broynach, and William of Ratter, who ultimately succeeded to the earldom in 1772. Robertson's "Proceedings," the *Scots Magazine*, a poem by "P. P." of Caithness, but above all a printed legal proof taken by Ratter at Thurso, and now in the British Museum, are the chief sources of information. The claimants had to give notice to Lady Dorothy Sinclair, Countess of Fife, at certain points of the seven years' fight. No passage in the county history is more interesting, but here it can only be hinted at.

P. 195.—This remarkable story seems to be the same as a tradition attaching itself to Isauld, which made a William Sinclair kill some one in a market brawl. It was explained that Thurso markets used to be held between Reay and Isauld for convenience of Strathnaver, and this may mean the same thing as the shooting on "the principal street of the town." It must have been a fight, for even a presbytery could hardly be so illogical as to blame three for what they say one did. The "partakers with the aforesaid murderer" were, strangely enough, from the neighbourhood of Isauld. Is it possible that the Commissary or his son was tacksman here? Unfortunately there is no getting the estate books or charters of Isauld, else this point might at once be settled ; but some of the local lawyers or factors could perhaps gather incidental evidence to establish the identity of the two Williams. The Commissary is often mentioned in parish registers and county records. Much interest attaches to this inquiry. The date of 1709 fits the tradition. See Henderson's "Caithness Family History" on the Commissary's lineage.

P. 197.—There are other versions of this notorious duel. Some say the cause of offence was Olrig reproving Innes, then a big young fellow, for drunkenness. A red stone moved a little for the railway, on to a small farm at Tongside, is a memorial of the affair. Innes and a tall servant, Gunn, were first on the ground. Olrig was cutting Innes every stroke, who was going backwards, parrying, till Gunn said to him that he was like a woman before horses in the yoke. He then attacked, and drove his sword through Sinclair. He fled to Crosskirk, and waited in a boat outside for a vessel which took him to the Continent. Mackay says he found refuge at Tongue, in the first instance. Surely enough a warrant was issued against him, and this document or a copy of it, is said to be now in the possession of Alexander Gunn, Newton, Watten, late in Braehour, found among old papers in Westfield House. If so, it ought to be published and pre-served. Innes, whose father James must have been the son of the great Mr James, M.P., got a remission, it is said because of accepting the challenge of an Italian duellist, and, through the training of Colonel Baillie, killing him. At his death he gave express orders to have no memorial over his grave for fear of insult to it from the kin of Olrig. He was secretly interred in the Reay Churchyard, where the high road now runs, or even still more towards the sea, near the buried town. The Rev. John Munro mentioned was the last of the three Munro ministers, successively of Reay, Mr Alex. Brodie coming next, immediately before Pope, in whose time Innes died.

P. 200.—Wm. Gordon Forbes, schoolmaster of Reay, afterwards in America, says in his report, in the "New Statistical Account," that in a cave 25 feet by 10, in Ben Frectan, or Hill of the Watch, Shurrery, two families disaffected to the Hanoverian Government, took asylum in 1745. They were Sinclair of Scotscalder and Sinclair of Assery, the latter family having changed politics since 1660, when James was fined £600 by the Stuart Royalists as a Covenanter. From the "Services of Heirs," they were both named John. In March, 1771, John of Assery died, and his son Robert heired him with benefit of inventory; in other words, leaving nothing behind him unless it might be debts. The heir and his brothers became handsome army officers. One of them died in a lodging at the Horse Market, Thurso, about 1825 ; another in a poor person's house near Clysterfield ; and a third at the house of Innes of Ulloclet. Misfortune made the three all but insane. The last of the Scotscalders was Captain James of the Royal Artillery, who used to reside much at Scrabster House with his cousin, the late Alexander Dunbar, the last of the Caithness real Dunbars. James's father, Robert of Scotscalder, lost the property, and became the farmer of Dounreay and Borrowston, at which latter place he died 15th May, 1815, aged 65 years, after a rakish life. He was the Rev. Charles Cordiner's enthusiastic guide when he visited Caithness about 1779.

P. 201 (a).—Though the Stevenson family, represented by Sir Robert Sinclair, Baronet of Murkle, are usually considered new to the county, having secured the lands of Alexander, Earl of Caithness, as late as 1765, it is by no means the fact. Sir Robert of Longformacus, one of them, took a principal part in the Glenorchy struggle, and at one time had proprietory and legal rights, absolute and prospective, in Caithness. The Longformacus (Berwickshire) baronets were a distinguished line, the last of them, Sir John, a writer, dying in 1798, in the Canongate, Edinburgh, so poor, it is said, as to be able to pay only 3s 6d a week for a little room there, the baronetcy becoming then extinct. See Stoddart's "Armorial Bearings." The relationship between them and the Stevensons is clear. Matthew Sinclair of Longformacus was served heir to his father James in 1553. He was married to Elizabeth Swinton, and had four sons—Robert of Longformacus ; George, the progenitor of the Stevensons ; Thomas, "who died before the year 1622, which appears by a charter of confirmation under the Great Seal, *quondam Thomæ Sinclair, filio quondam Matthæi Sinclair de Longformacus, terrarum de Over Bilpster, etc.*—to Thomas Sinclair, son of the deceased Matthew Sinclair of Longformacus, of the lands of Upper Bilpster—dated the last day of February, 1622 ;" and a fourth son, James. This Thomas is buried in the Sinclair aisle, Wick churchyard, with the inscription :—" Here lies an honourable man, Thomas Sinclar of Bilpster, third son to the laird of Longformacus, master-stabler to an honourable lord, George Earl of Caithness, Lord Sinclair of Berriedale, who departed at forty-two years of age, the 26th day of October, 1607. Remember death." His arms are on the memorial, supported by the letters T. S. There is also the phrase, "Regard ! Good service will get reward ! A.B.M.R.M." Sir Walter Scott's edition of Lord Fountainhall's "Chronological Notes of Scottish Affairs" has a pursuit, at the instance of Sir Robert St. Clair of Stevenson, against Sir James Sinclair of Kinnaird, Fifeshire, as heir to Thomas Sinclair of Bilbster, his uncle, for payment of a jointure to Mr Thomas's widow, Anna Foulis, 27th Jan., 1686. There is more on the Stevensons in Fountainhall's "Decisions," published 1759. They are a branch of the Roslins senior to the Caithness earls. From an ancient funeral escutcheon, their arms were argent, an engrailed cross, saltire, gules, five bezants, or; but when Alexander, Earl of Caithness, disinherited his daughter, Dorothy, Countess of Fife, in their favour they took his arms with a slight difference. They have had constant connection with Scottish high legal offices. In Thomas Thomson's "Eminent Scotsmen," the famous Dundas, Lord of Session, and Lord Melville, are said to have owed their legal talent to "Meg Sinclair," their ancestress, one of the Stevensons. The Caithness property has been a somewhat insecure possession, because of the very distant kinship to Lord Hemer. Quite recently a Swedish Sinclair threatened, if the present proprietor would not make him a money offer, to initiate a process of restitution in his own favour ; but statutes of limitation may make all such attempts hopeless. There can be no doubt that in Caithness itself legitimate relatives of the Earl, greatly nearer of kin than the Stevensons, could be easily found. The question is whether Earl Alexander had the right to give his lands as he pleased, even if there may have been debts upon them to the Stevensons or others. The earldom, which included the property of the earls, went to the nearest male heir by express State enactments, under the Great Seal of the kingdom.

P. 201 (b).—The Ratter family were very poor when they succeeded to the earldom, William being objected to by the previous earl Alexander as not having had a gentleman's education. A letter which recently appeared in an Inverness paper from one of his ancestors, John, in prison for a debt of £1400 from 1700 to 1709, explains ; but of this in "The Second Contest for the Earldom."

P. 201 (c).—Hogg's son was tutor to the family of Mr William Innes of Sandside, and he and Mr Innes accompanied Bishop Pococke, the traveller, from Sandside to Thurso, when he was in Caithness in 1760. See the Pococke MSS. in the British Museum.

P. 204.—Rev. Alexander Pope entered in the Reay parish register the date of baptism (which was then considered more important than the birth two or three days before) of John Swanson, son of John in Achayullan, as February, 1736. This was written from memory, because the roll of baptisms began to be properly kept only in 1745. Achayullan was blamed for the murder, near Georgemas, of Mr Nicolson, scripture-reader. When an officer in America, he had among others a Reay soldier of the Royal army prisoner, whom he surprised by familiar questions and good treatment. He was ultimately executed, it is said, confessing the justice of his fate, and characteristically mourning that he only got a fourpenny piece and a penknife on Mr Nicolson. The man who whipped Achayullan was a Sinclair, and so enraged were the Sinclairs at the disgrace of one of the kin accepting such an office, that he was ever afterwards boycotted. The Tullochs say that his wife even never dared enter the door of a Sinclair again.

P. 209.—Dunbeath's powers as a swordsman made a foreign expert call on him one day for a bout, which he got till he cried halt. Bishop Forbes was jealous of him as a Methodist or Baptist and lay-preacher ;

but the following, from the journal edited by Rev. J. B. Craven of Kirkwall, may be given as indicative of an original character, ready with deeds and words:—" I came to Keiss at six, the seat of Sir William Sinclair of Dunbeath, the preaching knight, a wrong-headed man confessedly by all who know him best, for he has taken up that odd way of strolling about and preaching, without commission or appointment of any man or any sect of men whatsoever, and vents the wildest and most extravagant notions that ever were hatched in the most disordered brain. It was upon account of his lady, a sister of Sir William Dunbar of Hempriggs, and one of Mr Taylor's (of Thurso) little flock, that I called here. She, poor lady! was confined to bed, and had been long in an ailing way, with the distress of her husband's unaccountable ways of doing, a shocking narrative of which I had from Mr Sutherland of Wester, and then from Sir William Dunbar, besides some general strong hints I had got from others, before I could see them. I drank tea at Keiss, and made my visit as short as possible, the knight being at home. The good lady would needs have me to taste something at her bedside, and a dram having been called for, her ladyship desired to have a grace, at saying of which the knight kept his seat. This I remarked afterwards to Sir William Dunbar and his lady, and Wester, who joined in saying it was a pity I did not keep my seat, for then he would have been sure to have started up, as he seldom fails to do things by the rule of contratries." Forbes was bishop of Ross and Caithness from 1762 till 1775.

P. 210.—In the *Scots Magazine* this occurs:—" November 29th, 1779, at Edinburgh, after a tedious illness, William, Earl of Caithness." On Feb. 19th, 1783, his son, Major John, Earl of Caithness, was made lieutenant-colonel. In the same magazine is a notice of his death:—" April 8th, 1789, at London, the Right Honourable, John, Earl of Caithness. The earl possessed the rank of lieutenant-colonel in the army, and served in the last war in America with distinguished honour. At the siege of Charleston, while reconnoitering with Sir Henry Clinton, he received a musket shot in the groin." He was the last of the Ratters, his brother having died before him.—" At New York, of a fever and flux, which was occasioned by his lying for several days with the army in the fields, the Hon. Lieutenant William Sinclair, second son of the Earl Caithness." The most remarkable Caithnessian, and one of the greatest men of the revolutionary period in America, was Arthur Sinclair, born at Thurso in 1736, the son of William Sinclair, merchant there. The title-page of his biography is: "The St. Clair Papers: The Life and Public Services of Arthur St. Clair, Soldier in the Revolutionary War, President of the Continental Congress, and Governor of the North-Western Territory; with his Correspondence and other Papers, arranged and annotated by Hon. Wm. Henry Smith of Chicago; 2 vols. 8vo., with two portraits and a map, 30s.; published by Robert Clarke & Co., Cincinnati, Ohio, 1881." General St. Clair's portrait is in a public building at Washington as one of the Commanders-in-Chief of the United States Army. He was the bosom friend of General and President Washington, who took his plan at Princeton battle, which won the Republic. His evacuation of Ticonderoga, it is now admitted, saved the colonists from suppression. He was especially great in civil administration, and corresponded in French as well as in English with the greatest men of his time. His life is as pathetic as it is romantic, ending at eighty in poverty, but honour. Henderson made him one of the Asserys, and his name, Arthur, with other circumstances, points to the Inneses of Isauld, who were married into the Asserys.

P. 212.—The warlike spirit aroused in the county by Sir John Sinclair of Ulbster and Sir Benjamin Dunbar of Hempriggs had a curious test in 1807. On 1st January there was news of a French privateer of 16 guns at Flota. Lieut.-Colonel Sinclair, of the third battalion of Caithness Volunteers, assembled two Thurso companies on four fishing smacks. He was joined by Captain Mason and thirty privates of the regulars. Captain James Henderson, of the Clyth company, was chosen surgeon. When they reached Flota the vessel was gone, and they did not get their blow at Bonaparte and the French. How they were to conquer the privateer it is difficult to imagine, though there can be no doubt of the courage of their *bona fide* endeavour.

P. 216.—Much has been printed recently of Bishop Abernethy. His son William was minister of Thurso, and married to Henrietta of the Ulbster family. One of the incidents in his life was being seized by an enemy while crossing the river at Brawl Castle on horseback, and held down in the water till nearly drowned. He was himself of a violent turn, for he compelled his wife to sign papers giving him power over the property of Carsgo. Of all the Caithness clergy there are abundant notices in Hew Scott's " Fasti Eccl. Scot."

P. 219 (a).—Bishop Murray is one of the saints in Butler's work, where he is said to have been bishop over Caithness for 20 years, and died 1st April, 1240. The Aberdeen Breviary writes of him, and Keith in his "Lists" gives 1140 as the date of St. Gilbert's death, St. Magnus or Mans being his contemporary in Orkney. Beside Westfield House (the home of the Hon. Francis Sinclair, brother of Lord Hemer, and afterwards of Captain Thomas Dunbar, married to a Miss Sinclair of Scotscalder, the parents of the founder of the Thurso Hospital) there was the chapel of St. Drostan. In its churchyard wall is the font, which, with the love of miracle dear to Romanism, was said never to dry. The date of the chapel is limited backwards by St. Drostan, abbot of the Saint Columba rule and a prince of royal blood, having died in 809, his remains being deposited in a stone coffin at Aberdeen. Such inquiries could be pursued with regard to most of the ruined chapels. The chapel of Lybster, Reay, is of great antiquarian architectural interest from its two chambers and sloping door. See Aberdeen and others.

P. 220.—A great deal is known of the Ponts besides what Hew Scott gives so plentifully. In a tack which he gives of the teinds of Bower and Watten, dated 5th July, 1610, Zachary is Archdeacon of Caithness. His wife's sister married Welsh, an Ayrshire minister, from whom Mrs Carlyle traced her descent. The father, Robert Pont, who had a small patrimony on the Forth, near Alloa, was a very busy man in his time. He appears on the " allegit Commissar of Moray " in the attempt of Beatrix Gordon, sister of the Earl of Sutherland, and first married to Alexander Innes of Cromarty, to repudiate her marriage with William Sinclair of Dunbeath, and so recover her estates. In the " Register of the Privy Council " there is a sederunt at Holyrood of date 27th May, 1574, dealing with this peculiar case. The lady denounces Pont's jurisdiction as an imposture, and describes the possession for "seven years by-past" of all her property by William, which has put her to "such utter wrack" that if she "were not supported she had been able to perish, being put to such miserable case." The rents of Fischerne were appointed to her by the Lords of Council till the marriage cause should be settled by the head Commissariet, that of Edinburgh. Pont evidently sided with Dunbeath. It would appear he was Church Commissioner rather than Commissary of Moray. His son Timothy has tributes to his genius in note to P. 1.

It is good fortune to be able to give an ancient document, the original of which has been just favoured by James Grant Duncan, Wick, in which places, names, and other particulars of historical importance occur. The writing is in the contracted legal Latin and special caligraphy of the period, but the inquisition and its translation into English, now first published, may be accepted as substantially accurate:—

"Hæc inquisitio facta fuit in curia vicecomitatus de Caithness, in pretorio burgi de Weick, per honorabilem virum, Dominum Jacobum Sinclair, militem de Murkill, ultimo vero die mensis Septembris, Anno Domini millesimo sexcentesimo tragesimo quarto, coram, Alexandro Sutherland de Fors, cancellario hujus inquisitionis electo, Davide Sinclair de Dune, Alexandro Innes de Borrowstoune, Johanne Murray de Pennieland, Alexandro Bruce, portionario de Holland, Gavino Bruce, portionario de Lythe, Johanne Groitt, portionario de Dungasbey, Malcolmo Groitt de Warres, Gulielmo Murray de Clairden, Patricio Mowatt de Syistetter, Donaldo Budge de Toftingall, Alexandro Cogill de eodem, Carolo Caldell de Lynagar, Alexandro Sutherland in Oustrisdaill, et Gulielmo Sutherland, portionario de Bannaskirk: qui jurati dicunt quod quondam Magnus Mowatt de Balquhollie, maritus Isobellæ Cheyne, obiit vestitus et sasitus, ut de feodo ad fidem et pacem supremi domini nostri regis, in re totius, omnium et singularium villarum et terrarum, cum domibus et edificiis, de Owkingill, Milnetonne de Freswick, Tostes, Astruea, Bleaberriequayes, Sousequy, Fittisquy, et Stroubster, cum earundem partibus et pendiculis et pertinentibus, jacentibus in parochia de Cannesbey et infra vicecomitatus de Caithness; et quod dicta Isabella Cheyne, relicta presentim, fuit quondam spousa dicti quondam Magni Mowatt; et quod deseruit dictam Isabellam, ejus relictam, in rationabile tertia parte solari omnium et singularium villarum et terrarum, cum domibus et edificiis, de Oukingill, Milnetowne de Freswick, Tostis, Astruea, Bleaberriequyes, Souesquy, Fittisquy, et Stroubster, cum earundem partibus et pendiculis jacentibus ut supra; et, post deliberationem, ipsa lacuta est et solarem partem humiliter requisivit; et judices ipsam cognoscerent, et intrarent ad dictam suam tertiam omnium et singularium predictarum terrarum aliarumque suprascriptarum, qui ita facere promiserunt in cujus rei testimonium. Extractum ex libris vicecomitatus Cathanensis per me, Gulielmum Pattoune, notarium publicum hujus scribæ ac clericum deputatum ejusdem, teste mea manu propria et subscriptione, die, mense, et anno supra.

"W. PATTOUNE, Clericus Curiæ."

"This inquisition was made in the Sheriff Court of Caithness, in the tolbooth of the burgh of Wick, by an honourable man, Sir James Sinclair, knight of Murkle, on the last day of the month of September, A.D. 1634, in the presence of Alexander Sutherland of Forse, elected

X

chancellor of this inquisition; David Sinclair of Dun; Alexander Innes of B)rrowston; John Murray of Pennyland; Alexander Bruce, portioner of Holland; Gavin Bruce, portioner of Lyth; John Groat, portioner of Duncansbay; Malcolm Groat of Wares; William Murray of Clairden; Patrick Mowat of Scister; Donald Budge of Toftingal; Alexander Coghill of Cogle; Charles Calder of Lynegar; Alexander Sutherland in Oustrisdale; and William Sutherland, portioner of Banniskirk; who, being sworn, say that the deceased Magnus Mowat of Bucholly, husband of Isabella Cheyne, died vested and possessed, as of a property held on the faith and sanction of our supreme lord the king, in the matter of the whole and all and singular of the town- ships and lands, with the houses and buildings, of Oukingill, Milton of Freswick, Tostes, Astruea, Blæberryquoys, Souesquoy, Fittisquoy, and Strupster, together with the parts, pendicles, and belongings of the same, lying in the parish of Canisbay, and within the sheriffdom of Caithness; and that the said Isabella Cheyne, now his widow, was formerly the wife of the said deceased Magnus Mowat; and that he served the said Isabella, his widow, in the reasonable third part of all and singular of the townships and lands, with the houses and buildings, of Oukingill, Milton of Freswick, Tostes, Astruea, Blaeberryquoys, Souesquoy, Fittisquoy, and Strupster, together with the parts and pendicles lying as above; and, after deliberation, she spoke, and humbly desired the southern part; and the judges recognised her, and entered her to the said third part of all and singular the aforesaid lands and other things above-written, who, in testimony of this busi- ness, promised to act thus. Extracted from the books of the sheriffdom of Caithness by me, William Patton, notary-public of this document and deputed clerk of the same, witness my own hand and subscription, day, month, and year as above.

"W. PATTON, Clerk of Court."

The original endorsement is illegible, but a later one is as follows:— "Retour of Service to her Tierce of Isobel Cheyne, relict of Magnus Mowat of Bucholly, Sep., 1634."

These Notes would not be complete without some reference to Dr. Smiles's "Robert Dick: Baker of Thurso, Geologist and Botanist," in which there is much that is of scientific and general county interest. The biographic sketch which the book contains of Charles Peach of Wick, geologist, gives it further local value.

With direct and renewed study of the historic materials in the libraries and State record offices of London and Edinburgh, these illustrative notes could be multiplied and perfected to an extent not easily realisable to readers who do not consult MSS. as well as books. If it is shown that the field has not been nearly reaped, one purpose has been gained by a handling for many reasons slighter than could be wished. The publication of the names of the proprietors on com- mission of supply, committees of war, &c., in the county, which are mentioned with dates in the "Acta Parliamentorum," would of itself be a great enlightenment; and many printed and written pieces lie buried either in untouched places or in expensive books which only a few can consult. The county history is most deficient during the century or so before the local newspapers began. Fortunately there is a printed account of two great legal contests : one of date 1719 till 1723, by Alexander, Earl of Caithness, for the recovery of Ormly and several other properties from the second Earl of Breadalbane, Sir James Sinclair of Dunbeath, and John Sinclair of Ulbster ; and the other a House of Lords appeal, of date 1767 to 12th Feb., 1770, by Katherine Sinclair and James Sinclair of Duran, her trustee, Henrietta, Janet, Emilia, and Margaret Sinclair, infants, and James Sinclair of Harpsdale, their father and administrator at law, against David Thriepland Sinclair, an infant, and Stewart Thriepland, his father and administrator at law. In both these causes the pleadings of the lawyers are historical from distant periods, and nothing could better fill up what is confessedly a barren chapter of the county's past. But it is impossible to do more now than mention subjects with so large a burden of facts, and to congratulate those who have interest in extraordinary money, bond, and estate affairs that there is such a home feast safely preserved for them, whosoever may be the dispensor. With help of the writings of Sir John of Ulbster and of his daughter Catherine, and more especially the former's biography and "Distant Times and Places," both works by his nephew, Archdeacon Sinclair of Middlesex, not to mention the "Life" of Sir George, by James Grant, editor of the *Morning Advertiser*, London, brother of the late Mrs Duncan, Pulteneytown, the last century's history might be made full and readable. If any one has facts or documents on county affairs, "Press Club, London," is a continuous address ; and they will be used with gratitude, and to all the purpose ability can allow.

THOMAS SINCLAIR.

VILLA DU PALMIER, ALGIERS, 1887.

EARLY NOTICE OF CAITHNESS.—The earliest notice we have of Caithness is to be found in the Life of Ambrosius Merlin, who flourished in the fifth century ; but although the "strange prophecies" of this author are looked upon by many as being of an apocryphal character, yet it may interest not a few in Caithness to know who were the inhabitants of the county in the first century. Merlin says that Marius, son of Arviragus was "crowned king (of Britain) in the yeare of our blessed Saviour threescore and fourteene, a wise and just man, and flourished in great prosperity and wealth ; in whose time one *Loudricus* (whom some writers call *Rodicus*), with a mighty Army of *Picts* or *Scythians*, whom some call also *Goths*, and *Huns*, landed in a part of *Scotland*, wasting and spoyling wheresoever he came with Iron and Fire, whom *Marius* met in Battaile and gave him a great overthrow, in which their Duke *Loudricus* was slaine ; in remembrance of which victory in *Stanismore*, a place of *Westmaria* or *Westmoreland*, where this battaile was fought, he caused a great stone or pillar to be erected, upon which was inscribed in capitall Letters *Marii victoria*. The remnant of the Army that survived the battaile humbly besought the King to allow them some place under his dominions in which to inhabite, who commiserating their case granted them a place in *Scotland Cathnese*, to whom the *Britaines*, disdaining to give their daughters in marriage, they allyed themselves with the *Irish*, and were afterwards called *Pictavians*."

A SKETCH OF THE HILL OF WICK CASE.

IN the minds of many of the present generation much misconception prevails with respect to the extent of the rights possessed by the feuars of the burgh, and the liberties enjoyed by its inhabitants in the common known as the Hill of Wick. These rights were not of a proprietory nature—merely servitudal, and held by the feuars in virtue of a provision in the titles to their respective properties within the burgh ; and, as shall be shown, but few of those claiming this right could produce titles to substantiate their claims.

This common, situated about half a mile northward of the royal burgh of Wick, was surrounded by the cultivated land occupied by the tenants of the Hempriggs estate. Its limits, as defined by one who knew them in 1746,* were as follows :—"Bounded by the following lands, viz., the lands of Wick, Gallowhill, Smallquoys, Gillock, Whiterashes, Kilminster, Ackergill, West Noss, Quoystain, Staxigoe, Dam of Papigoe, and the lands of Papigoe." On the tract of land thus surrounded, the tenants on the estates of Hempriggs and Hopville (now Sibster), and the feuars of Wick and their tenants from time immemorial pastured their cattle and sheep, cast feal and divot, and prepared clay for building purposes. The witness quoted above states that about the year mentioned "the feuars of Wick and their tenants had upwards of 80 head of cattle and 300 to 400 sheep pasturing on the said commonty."

The liberties thus enjoyed by the townspeople were neither restricted nor encroached upon until the beginning of the present century, when one of the tenants of Sir Benjamin Dunbar (afterwards Lord Duffus), proprietor of the Hempriggs estate, began cutting a ditch at Blackbridge so as to enclose a considerable portion of the common where the feuars had hitherto exercised their rights of pasturage.

The Magistrates and Town Council, considering themselves "the natural guardians" of the rights now encroached upon, met and instructed a "Protest and Interruption," and afterwards an interdict. A deputation from the Town Council visited Sir Benjamin on the subject, and it was only after considerable delay on his part, and being hard pressed by the action of the Town Council that he would condescend to give a definite reply to their remonstrances or come to terms with them so as to have an amicable settlement of the subject in dispute. Several years after the action taken by the Magistrates and Town Council, Sir Benjamin did condescend to approach that body, and this he did in a pompous and magniloquent "Representation," wherein he says, "it must be a very desirable circumstance that all bounding property, servitudes, and claims of both parties should be ascertained and fixed, for while they remain unsettled the rapacious attempts of individuals will, under the mask of public exertions, appropriate to their present advantage everything they can filch from both parties ; and the proprietor of the estate of Hempriggs finds himself in this manner hindered from dealing on that liberal footing with the inhabitants of the burgh that he would be inclined to do, or giving them those accommodations he otherwise wished to do. Sir Benjamin Dunbar therefore proposes to enter into

* See William Swanson's evidence in proof led in 1818.

a submission upon the broadest basis of all claims competent to each party against the other party in which their interests may clash."

A submission or plan of arbitration was drawn up by the Town Council, and concurred in by sundry heritors and feuars—between Sir Benjamin and the provost, bailies, and council—for having the rights of the superior, feuars, and other inhabitants of the town to the Hill of Wick and the Mosses of Hayland and Bronzie ascertained, and to have the same divided according to the rights of the respective parties. Following upon this submission, an action was raised in the Court of Session at the instance of Sir Benjamin Dunbar, Mr William Macleay (residing magistrate of the burgh), Mr James Horne (Writer to the Signet, Edinburgh), Mr John Macleay (of Rosebank, Wick), and Mr Harry Bain (merchant, Wick), against the feuars of the burgh, to "exhibit and produce their several rights and titles whereby they claim right to the said commonty and mosses, or to the rights of servitude thereon." The summons is dated and signeted the 1st February, 1813. Proceedings had gone on for some years in the case, when the baronet appears to have got some legal enlightenment on the position he should take in the action, which resulted in his presenting a petition to the Court of Session craving to be sisted from being a pursuer in the case to that of a defender. The Lord Ordinary decided against him ; but, on a reclaiming petition to the First Division of the Court, their lordships "alter the interlocutor of the Lord Ordinary reclaimed against, allow the name of the petitioner to be withdrawn from this process as a pursuer, and to sist himself a defender therein." Accordingly, Sir Benjamin lodged his defences, which resolve into the statement that the whole tract of land sought to be divided was his property. By an interlocutor of 3rd July, 1818, Lord Alloway "sustains the defences for Sir Benjamin Dunbar, assoilzies him from the conclusions of the libel, and decerns." Litigation, notwithstanding, continued ; but this reverse decision was doubtless a severe blow to the pursuers—their co-litigant, the leading pursuer in the case, and upon whose support they chiefly relied, thus to assume a decidedly hostile attitude towards their cause, and to have had legal sanction for his action, must have had a very depressing effect upon the Town Council and feuars, who had hitherto displayed the utmost energy and determination in prosecuting their cause.

But before this interlocutor was pronounced, and while Sir Benjamin appeared as a pursuer in the action, a commission was granted to Mr Henderson, Sheriff-Substitute of Caithness, and proof to a certain extent taken. After this, proceedings were suspended until 1824, when a remit was made to Sheriff Traill as judicial referee ; but this appears to have fallen by the tacit consent of all parties. Six years after there was " a wakening of the process which had fallen asleep." In June, 1830, Lord Newton renewed the commission at the instance of all parties—pursuers and defenders, or either of them—to the Sheriff-Depute or Substitute of Caithness to take the proof, with the powers and in the terms specified in former interlocutors.

Mr Gregg, Sheriff-Substitute, accepted the commission, held his court at Wick, where all parties having interest were cited to appear. At the first diet fixed for proof, Mr Stuart, Edinburgh, and Mr Rose, town clerk, appeared for the superior of the burgh and Magistrates, as representing the community, and for Mr Horne of Langwell, and others. Mr George Lewis Sinclair, W.S., Edinburgh, appeared for

Lord Duffus, who gave in a Representation and Protest from his lordship, wherein it was stated "that by an Act of Parliament, when a royal burgh and an entailed property are concerned, no division of commonty can take place except by a special act obtained for that purpose. That the burgh, or pretended burgh of Wick, has no land or feudal investment or burgage tenure. Therefore that in the present case no claim from them can be admitted nor any proceedings take place whilst they assert a title." This reference to the Act of 1695 clearly indicates the cause of that sudden and inexplicable change of action manifested by Lord Duffus in presenting the petition to the Lord Ordinary to sist him from being a pursuer to a defender in the case. By this statute, commonties belonging to the sovereign and royal burghs are expressly excluded from division.

Sheriff Gregg, after leading a full and voluminous proof, gave in a most elaborate and exhaustive report on the evidence adduced, wherein he states, in considering the case for the magistrates as representing the burgh, "I have great doubts whether a claim, such as is urged by the burgh, can be at all legally sustained . . . on one point. Murray's case (a case previously quoted) is not without value; it shows that it is inconsistent with the nature of servitudes of this kind, that any party not in possession of the dominant tenement should have the benefit thereof in claiming. Consistently with this principle, if a whole burgh were feued out, the magistrates, for the community, could not claim as well as the individual feuars. At best they claim only for what the feuars do not claim for; but in this case where is the line of distinction to be drawn? On what proof does the burgh found, except the proof adduced in evidence of individual right?"

The commissioner shows indisputably that the rights possessed by the feuars of the burgh were merely of a servitudal character, and in no degree proprietory; and after a careful examination of titles produced with the evidence led, he could admit only the rights of ten feuars, with respect to whose claims he reports:—"I sustain the following for right of servitude of pasturage and divots, each for one cow." There were fifty-eight feuars in the burgh. Of these, twenty claimed, but neither proved nor produced titles; nineteen produced titles, but did not bring proof to support their claims; nine claims were defective in proof, and were not sustained. From this it will be seen that on investigation the rights of the feuars and inhabitants to the Hill of Wick were limited to that of ten of the former, and that to the extent of pasture for one cow, and to cut divot for house purposes.

Notwithstanding the sound legal opinion expressed by the commissioner in his report, the magistrates still looked upon themselves as the "natural guardians" of the people's rights, and persisted in the action, with the result as shown in Lord Fullerton's interlocutor of 11th July, 1833:—"The Lord Ordinary having heard parties' procurators, and considered the cases together with the proofs, finds that the parties now appearing as pursuers have not a title to insist in the present action; therefore refuses the representation given against Lord Alloway's interlocutor of the 3rd July, 1818 years; sustains the defences for Lord Duffus, and assoilzies him from the conclusions of the libel, but finds no expenses due, and decerns."

Although costs were not given against the magistrates, yet the expenses incurred amounted to £580, being paid by them out of the burgh funds. The council proposed to bear the one-half thereof, and to apportion the other amongst the feuars. But few of those for whom the magistrates "fought and bled" paid their share of the expense allocated upon them. In the annual balance-sheet of the burgh the claim against the feuars for expenses incurred in the Hill of Wick process stood as an asset until 1877, when it was wiped off the council's books as irrecoverable. This case cost the Town Council fully £500.

Had the ten feuars whose claims were sustained continued to send their cattle to the common, it is not in the least degree probable that they would have been prevented, but failing to do so for the past fifty years, their right has doubtless lapsed.

The Hill of Wick at the beginning of the century was a large tract of uncultivated land, but has for the last thirty years been all under cultivation, and yields excellent crops. The road formed in 1847 to Nosshead Lighthouse runs through it, having about a fourth of its extent to the east of the road.

PRICE OF FARM PRODUCE IN CAITHNESS
FROM 1750 TO 1810 INCLUSIVE.

	1750.			1790.			1798.			1810.		
A cow with calf cost	£0	15	0	£3	10	0	£5	5	0	£7	0	0
Do. without	0	12	0	2	8	0	4	0	0	5	10	0
A horse or garron for the plough	1	10	0	3	7	0	7	0	0	12	0	0
A three-year-old wedder in season	0	2	6	0	7	6	0	12	0	1	5	0
A lamb	0	0	6	0	2	6	0	4	0	0	10	0
A sow or hog	0	2	6	0	10	6	0	15	0	1	10	0
A goose in September	0	0	6½	0	1	2	0	1	8	0	2	6
A hen	0	0	2	0	0	4	0	0	6	0	1	0
18 eggs in 1750 for a dozen,12 now	0	0	1	0	0	1½	0	0	2	0	0	3
A stone of butter (24 lbs.)	0	5	0	0	15	0	0	18	0	1	2	0
A stone of cheese (24 lbs.)	0	2	6	0	4	0	0	6	0	0	8	0
1 lb. beef or mutton, by the qr.	0	0	1¼	0	0	2½	0	0	4½	0	0	6

LIVINGS OF CAITHNESS CLERGY.—In answers to the Agent of the Committee of Mid-Lothian anent the livings of the Caithness clergy about the middle of last century, it is stated that "The conversion of bear and meal at six shillings eleven and a third of a penny sterling per boll is now and has been at least for forty years back the rate universally admitted in Caithness in the sale of lands, and though this may be true that in cheap years ministers have sold their victual stipend at five shillings and fourpence per boll (as the minister of Watten in particular says he did his) yet as true it is that he did sell, or at least might have sold, his victual for double the price in some other years."

In one of the answers, it is stated, "There is no county in Scotland where vivers in general are sold cheaper than in Caithness. Good beef sells, from the beginning of the season till about Christmas, from three shillings to four shillings per quarter, salted beef is sold for five shillings or five-and-sixpence per quarter, good mutton from six pence to a shilling per quarter, according to size, and as the county happened to be well stocked with sheep or otherwise, pork from three farthings to a penny farthing a pound. A goose for sixpence, a hen for twopence halfpenny, a cock for threepence, a dozen of eggs for a penny, a good cod for a penny or three halfpence at most, a dozen haddocks or twenty whitings for a penny, good butter three halfpence a pound, cheese at three halfpence."

COPY OF THE CHARTER

OF THE

ERECTION OF THE BURGH OF WICK INTO A FREE ROYAL BURGH, 1589.

JAMES, by the grace of God, King of the Scots, to all true men of his whole land, clergy and laity, greeting: Know ye that we, understanding that not only are the annual revenues or income of our crown increased by the industry and increase of free burghs within our kingdom, but also that the lieges of the same are very greatly enriched by the foreign commerce and trade of the burgesses and free inhabitants of the said burghs; and, also, considering that there is no free burgh within the limits or bounds of Caithness, and that the town of Wick, lying within our sheriffdom of Inverness, is situated on the sea-coast in a place very suitable and fit for navigation: so that, if the said town of Wick were erected into a free royal burgh, and the ordinary magistrates of the same were elected, with the advice of our trusty cousin, George Earl of Caithness, his heirs, and successors, not only would our said annual revenues be increased by the customs and taxes of the said burgh, and those living within the said bounds of Caithness be enriched by the frequent access of merchants and foreign traders and rendered more civilized, but also thefts, rapines, murders, and other oppressions committed amongst the said inhabitants, would be repressed through fear of punishment. Therefore, and for various other reasons and considerations us moving, from certain knowledge and of our own accord, after our perfect and legitimate age of twenty-one years completed, declared in our Parliament and our general revocation made in the same, we have made, constituted, created, erected, and incorporated, and in terms of these presents do make, constitute, create, erect, and incorporate the whole and entire aforesaid town of Wick with all and sundry houses, buildings, tenements, waste places, yards, orchards, tofts and crofts lying within the territory of the same, into one free royal burgh, with a free harbour, to be called the burgh of Wick in all time coming: with special and plenary power to the free inhabitants and burgesses of the said burgh and their successors in the future, with the express advice and consent of our said cousin, George Earl of Caithness, his heirs and successors, and not otherwise or in other manner of making, electing, constituting, and creating a provost and four bailies, indwellers or inhabitants of the said burgh, together with a treasurer, dean of guild, councillors, burgesses, serjeants, and other officers necessary within the said burgh for the government of the same, and those as often as shall be deemed expedient for reasonable causes, of depositing one-half part of the monies paid by the said burgesses in respect of their freedom in our said burgh for our said cousin and his successors in future, and the other moiety of the same monies to be applied for the public good of the said burgh. With free, also and special, power to the said burgesses and free inhabitants duly elected, received and admitted to the freedom of the said burgh, through the present and future councillors and dean of guild of the same, of buying and selling within the said burgh and freedom of the same (lie) pakpeil and wine, ale, cloth, as well linen as woollen, narrow, long, and broad, and other kinds of commerce and goods (*lie*), those called stapill guidis (*lie*), taip. And also with power to the said provost, bailies, and councillors of the aforesaid burgh and their successors of admitting and receiving within the same burgh bakers, tinsmiths, butchers, fishers, dealers in fish and flesh, tailors, blacksmiths, weavers, fullers, carpenters, and all other necessary artificers and operatives pertaining and relating to the freedom of a free burgh, with power also to the said craftsmen of using and exercising their aforesaid trades as freely as they are used and exercised in any royal burgh within our said kingdom. And likewise with power to the said provost, bailies, councillors, burgesses, and their successors of building one public prison or more within the said burgh, and a market cross; and of holding a market every week on Friday, together with three free fairs thrice in the year, viz., on the Feast of All Saints, on the Lord's Day for Palm Branches, and on the Nativity of John the Baptist, which are popularly called Allhallowmas, Palm Sunday, and Midsummer, and these for the space of four days each; and of charging, levying, receiving, and collecting the customs and dues of the same, and of applying them for the public good of the said burgh; also of charging, levying, receiving, and collecting all and sundry petty customs of the aforesaid harbour of the aforesaid burgh, as well by land as by sea, and of applying them to the aforewritten use. And also with power to the said bailies and their successors of receiving resignations of all and sundry lands, tenements, annual rents, yards, tofts, crofts, and others lying within the said burgh and freedom of the same, and of handing over and disposing of the same to any person or persons, with infeftments, charters, sasines, and other necessary evidents; of appointing, fixing, beginning, confirming, holding, and, as often as need be, of adjourning burgh courts within the said burgh and freedom of the same twice in the week, viz., on Tuesday and Saturday; of making, creating, and appointing clerks, sergeants, bailiffs, and all other officers and necessary members of court; of punishing transgressors according to the form of law; of levying and applying to their peculiar uses the forfeitures and fines of the said courts, and, if necessary, of seizing and distraining for the same; of making and ordaining acts, laws, and statutes within the said burgh and freedom of the same, for the keeping and observance of good order; of apprehending, arresting, imprisoning, punishing, and, according to the laws of our kingdom, beheading and hanging all transgressors and delinquents with pit, gallows, in fang thief, out fang thief, and generally of using and exercising all, any, and sundry, with all privileges, immunities, and liberties whatsoever, as freely, in all respects, as any other free royal burgh within our said kingdom. To hold and have the whole and entire aforesaid burgh of Wick, with all and sundry houses, buildings, tenements, waste places, yards, tofts, crofts, and others whatsoever lying within the territory of the same, together with the harbour aforesaid, anchorages and customs of the same; and with all and sundry liberties and immunities and privileges aforewritten of the said burgh to the aforesaid provost, bailies, councillors, burgesses, and free inhabitants of the same, and their successors, of us and our successors, in free burgage in perpetuity, by all their righteous ancient meathes and divisions, according as they lie in length and breadth, in houses, buildings, bounds, grazings, fields, tofts, moors, marshes, ways, paths, waters, pools, streams, meadows, pasturages, mills, multures, and their sequels, fowlings, huntings, fishings, peats divots, coals, coal-pits, rabbits, rabbit-warrens, pigeons, pigeon- cots, forges, malt-kilns, and breweries, woods, forests, thickets, beams, and timber, quarries of stone and lime, with courts and their ishes bloodwits, and with all and sundry liberties, commodities, profits, assythments, and their proper pertinents whatsoever, as well those not named as those named, as well those under the earth as those above the earth, far and near, belonging or seeming in any manner whatever justly to belong to the said burgh, harbour, and others particularly mentioned before, with their pertinents, in all time coming, freely, quietly, fully, entirely, honourably, well, and in peace, and without revocation, contradiction, hindrance, or obstacle in any way. The said provost, bailies, councillors, burgesses, and free inhabitants, and their successors, to render therefor annually to us and our successors the sum of ten merks of the money of this our realm, on the Feast of Pentecost, in name of *alba firma* only, together with the due and accustomed burghal service only.

In testimony of which we have commanded our seal to be put to this our present charter in presence of our much-loved cousins and advisers, John Lord Hamilton, commendator of our monastery of Aberbrothock, Archiband Earl Angus, Lords Douglas, Dalkeith, and Abernethy, our very reverend and venerable Fathers in Christ Patrick Archbishop of St Andrews, Walter Prior of Blantyre, keeper of our Privy Seal; our chosen privy councillors, Alexander Hay of Easter Kennet, clerk of the register and council of our rolls; Lewis Bellenden of Auchnoull, knight, clerk of our justiciary; and Mr Robert Scott, director of our chancery. At Edinburgh, the twenty-fifth day of the month of September, in the year of our Lord, one thousand five hundred and eighty-nine, and the twenty-third of our reign.

Extracted from the registers in the archives, kept under the Parliament House on this and the two preceding pages, by Mr Thomas Gibsone, one of the principal clerks of council and session, having power to this effect from the Lord Clerk of the Register.

(Signed)   THO. GIBSONE.

King James VI., who granted the charter, was born on the 19th June, 1566, and was crowned on the 29th July, 1567, when he was about thirteen months old.

It may be interesting to know that this charter was granted after two devastating raids into Caithness by Alexander Earl of Sutherland —the first in 1588, when, in virtue of a Commission from the Privy Council, he entered the county at the head of all the forces he could command, burnt the town of Wick, besieged the Earl of Caithness in Girnigoe Castle for twelve days, killed several of the inhabitants, and returned to Sutherlandshire with a great spoil of cattle.

The second marauding exploit took place in the following year, and but a few months (Whitsunday 1589) prior to the date of the charter, when Earl Alexander sent Alexander Gordon of Kilcalmekill, with three hundred chosen men, into Caithness, who struck terror into the inhabitants, ranged the county at large, spoiled and wasted freely all the country before them, filled many places with ruin and desolation, and pursued their enemies with a bloody execution as long as their fury lasted, and slew a number of the inhabitants.

Earl George and the victims of the Earl of Sutherland's cruelty resident in the town, doubtless considered that having the town erected into a free burgh, under the King's seal, would prevent the recurrence of such like depredations in future, ensure the protection of the lives and property of the inhabitants from fierce and furious freebooters, and, in the words of the charter, "thefts, rapines, murders, and other oppressions committed amongst the said inhabitants would be repressed through fear of punishment."

THE "SWELCHIE" OF STROMA.

LITHGOW mentions a curious custom, probably sacrificial in its original meaning, as being practised in his time. "This dreadful firth," he says, "is in breadth between the continent of Caithness and the isle of South Ronaldshaw, in Orkney, twelve miles, and I denote this credibly, in a part of the north-west end of this gulf, there is a certain place of sea where these distracted tides make their rencountering rendezvous, that whirleth ever about, cutting in the middle circle a sloping hole, with which, if either ship or boat shall happen to encroach, they must quickly either throw over something into it, as a barrel, a piece of timber, and such like, or that fatal euripus shall then suddenly become their swallowing sepulchre : a custom which those inhabiting Caithness and Orkneys have ever heretofore observed."—"Travels," p. 400.

But the most interesting association of the "Swelchie" is the story of its origin, which is given in old Norse legend. The "Younger Edda" contains a famous ballad, known as the "Grotta-songr," *i.e.* the "Mill Song," grotta being the Norse for mill or quern. The poem is preceded by a prose introduction, headed "Fenja and Menja," which is thus translated by Mr Rasmus B. Anderson in his "Younger Edda" :—

"Odin had a son by name Skjold, from whom the Skjoldungs. He had his throne and ruled in the lands that are now called Denmark, but were then called Gotland. Skjold had a son by name Fridleif, who ruled the lands after him. Fridleif's son was Frode. He took the kingdom after his father, at the time when the Emperor Augustus established peace in all the earth, and Christ was born. But Frode, being the mightiest king in the Northlands, this peace was attributed to him by all who spake the Danish tongue, and the Norsemen called it the Peace of Frode. No man injured the other, even though he might meet, loose or in chains, his father's or brother's bane (murderer). There was no thief or robber, so that a gold ring would lie a long time on Jalanger's heath. King Frode sent messengers to Svithjod, to the king whose name was Fjolner, and bought there two maid-servants, whose names were Fenja and Menja. They were large and strong. About this time were found in Denmark two millstones so large that no one had the strength to turn them. But the nature belonged to these millstones that they ground whatever was demanded of them by the miller. The name of this mill was Grotte. But the man to whom

King Frode gave the mill was called Hengckjapt. King Frode had
the maid-servants led to the mill, and requested them to grind for him
gold and peace and Frode's happiness. Then he gave them no longer
time to rest or sleep than while the cuckoo was silent or while they
sang a song. It is said they sang the song called the "Grotte-song,"
and before they ended it they ground out a host against Frode, so that
on the same night there came the sea-king whose name was Mysing,
and slew Frode, and took a large amount of booty. Mysing took with
him Grotte, and also Fenja and Menja, and bade them grind salt, and
in the middle of the night they asked Mysing whether he did not have
salt enough. He bade them grind more. They ground only a short
time longer before the ship sank. But in the ocean arose a whirlpool
(maelstrom, mill-stream) in the place where the sea runs into the
mill-eye."

This narrative connects together two separate and independent
legends—that of Frode and the quern of peace and gold, and that of
Mysing and the salt-mill, the latter of which is a version of the folk-
tale which is found among so many nations of the world, "How the
sea became salt." The "Grotta-songr" itself contains no reference to
the latter legend, but breaks off with the threat on the part of the
giant maidens that they would grind out war instead of peace in
punishment of Frode's avarice and oppression. But Norse tradition
makes the avenger come in the person of the Viking (or Wicking, *i.e.*
Man of *the Wick*, the bay, viz., the Skage-rack, the great centre of
the Wickings) Mysing, and it localises the foundering of his ship and
the loss of the Grotte in the Pentland Firth, at a place said to be called
Mysinghole, which is probably to be identified with the Swelchie of
Stroma. That whirlpool is, according to this legend, created by the
sea rushing through the hole of Mysing's Grotte, the quern, which is
still grinding on for ever, and keeping the sea salt.

CASTLES SINCLAIR AND GIRNIGOE, AND MEY.

BRAND states that when he visited Castles Sinclair and Girnigoe in 1698
he found the year of grace upon the lintel of a window in the former
to be 1607, but that both castles had been then, by "a righteous God,
turned into a ruinous heap" on account of "much sin" that was
alleged to have been committed within their walls. He is fond of
moralising over the fortunes of the Caithness family, which were then
at an exceptionally low ebb. Their estates had gone to Lord Breadalbane, and the heir to the title had, he says, lived entirely on "an
aliment allowed him by Glenorchy during his life." But he adds—
"The heir having died about a year ago, the heiress, his sister,
succeeds to the honours, and is in a very mean condition, living in
a place where the former earls used to keep their hawks. So to
this ancient and honourable family of the Earls of Caithness there
is almost put in holy providence a period and close ; they who had
four great houses in this country like palaces for pleasure and
convenience and castles for strength, now in their heirs enjoy none
of them ; three are ruinous and one possessed by a stranger." One
of the ruinous castles he refers to was Thurso East, of which he
states that "an honest countryman, observing the many great sins

that had been committed about that house, is said to have predicted
to one of the late earls its ruin and desolation, saying 'That the cup
of sin was filling and this house would shortly become a den of
dragons (using the scripture phrase), and seeing there are no such
creatures among us, it shall be of foxes;' and accordingly it was
observed that a fox haunted it when ruinous a few years after, which
stayed there till about nine or ten years ago, when a part of the house
was repaired."

The present seat of the Earls of Caithness is Barrogill Castle, Mey,
on the shore of the Pentland Firth and the following description of
this castle as it was in A.D., 1628, is given in verse by William Lithgow in his "Travels through Europe, Asia, and Africa:"—" And now
being arrived at Maji (Mey) to embark for Orkney, sight, time and
duty command me to celebrate these following lines, to gratify the
kindness of that noble Lord, George Earl of Caithness, with his
honourable cousin and first accadent of his house, the right worshipful
Sir William Sinclair of Cathell, knight, laird of Maji:—

> Sir! sighting now thyself and palace fair,
> I find a novelty and that most rare;
> The time though cold and stormy, sharper sun
> And far to summer, scarce the spring begun;
> Yet with good luck, in Februar, Saturn's prey,
> Have I not sought and found out fruitful May,
> Plank'd with the marine coast, prospective stands,
> Right opposite to the Orcade isles and lands:
> Where I for flowers, ingorg'd strong grapes of Spain
> And liquor'd French, both red and white amain.
> Which palace doth contain two four-squar'd courts
> Graft with brave works, where th' art-drawn pencil sports
> On walls, high chambers, galleries, office bowers,
> Cells, rooms, and turrets, platforms, stately towers;
> Where green-fac'd gardens, set at Flora's feet,
> Make nature's beauty quick Apelles greet,
> All which survey'd, at last the midmost gate
> Design'd to me the arms of that great 'state,
> The Earls of Caithness; to whose praise imbaged
> Thy muse must mount, and here's my pen incadg'd;
> First then their arms; a cross did me produce
> Limb'd like a scallet, trac'd with flour du luce;
> The lion, red and rag'd, two times divided
> From coin to coin as heralds have decided;
> The third join'd stance denotes to me a galley,
> That on their sea-wrapt foes dare make a sally;
> The fourth a gallant ship, puft with taunt sail
> 'Gainst them their ocean dare, or coast assail:
> On whose bent crest a pelican doth sit—
> An emblem for like love, drawn wondrous fit:
> Who as she feeds her young with her heart blood,
> Denotes these lords, to theirs, like kind, like good:
> Whose best supporters guard both sea and land
> Two stern-drawn griffins, in their strength do stand:
> Their dictum bears this verdict, for heaven's ode
> Ascrib'd this clause, *Commit thy work to God.*
> O sacred motto! Bishop Sinclair's strain
> Who turn'd Fyfe's lord on Scotland's foes again.
> Lo! here's the arms of Caithness, here's the stock!
> On which branched boughs rely as on a rock.

But further in I found like arms more patent ;
To kind Sir William and his line as latent :
The premier accade of that noble race,
Who for his virtue may reclaim the place ;
Whose arms, with tongue and buckle, now they make
Fast cross sign ty'd, for a fair Lesly's sake.
The lion hunts o'er land ; the ship, the sea ;
The ragged cross can scale high walls ; we see
The wing-laid galley, with her factious oars,
Both heavens and floods command, and circling shores ;
The feather'd griffin flees, O, grim-limb'd beast !
That winging sea and land, upholds thy crest ;
But for the pelican's life-sprung kind story
Makes honour sing, *Virtute et amore.**
Nay, not by blood as she herself can do,
But by her pattern, feeding younglings too ;
For which this patron's crescent stands so stay,
That neither spite nor tempest can shake May ;
Whose scutcheons cleave so fast, to top and side,
Portends to me his arms shall ever bide.
So Murckle's arms are so, except the rose
Spread on the cross, which Bothwell's arms disclose ;
Whose uterine blood he is, and present brother
To Caithness Lord, all three sprung from one mother ;
Bothwell's prime heretrix, plight to Hepburn's race,
From whom religious Murckle's rose I trace,
This country's instant shrieve ; whose virtue rais'd
His honour'd worth ; his godly life more prais'd.
But now to rouse their roots and how they sprung.
See how antiquity time's triumph sung.
This scallet, worth them blanch'd, for endeavour
And service done to England's conqueror ;
With whom from France they first to Britain came,
Sprung from a town, St. Clair, now turn'd their name.
Whose predecessor, by their val'rous hand,
Won endless fame, twice in the Holy Land ;
Where in that Christian war, their blood been lost,
They loath'd of Gaul, and sought our Albion coast.
Themselves to Scotland came in Canmoire's reign
With good Queen Marg'ret and her English train.
The ship from Orkney sail'd, now rul'd by Charles,
Whereof they Sinclairs long time had been earls.
Whose lord, then William, was, by Scotland's king
(Call'd Robert Second ; First, whence Stewarts spring)
Sent with his second son to France, cross'd James,
Who eighteen years liv'd captivate at Thames.
This prisoner last turn'd king, call'd *James the First,*
Who Sinclair's credit kept in honour's thirst.
The galley was the badge of Caithness lords,
As Malcom Canmoire's reign at length records
Which was to Magnus given for service done
Against Macbeath, usurper of his crown.
The lion came, by an heretrix to pass,
By marriage ; whose sire was sirnam'd *Douglas.*
Where, after him, the Sinclair now record
Was Sheriff of Dumfries and Nithsdale's lor

* Sir William Sinclair's motto,

Whose wife was niece to good King James the Third ;
Who for exchange 'twixt Wick and Southern Nidde,
Did lands excambiate; whence this Caithness soil
Stands fast for them ; the rest their friends recoil
Then circle-bounded Caithness, Sinclair's ground,
Which Pentland Firth environs, Orkney's sound ;
Whose top is Dunkane's bay, the root the Ord,
Long may it long stand fast for their true lord ;
And as long, too, heavens grant what I require,
The race of Maji may in that stock aspire,
Till any age may last, time's glass be run,
For earth's last dark eclipse, of no more sun.

DR. MORRISON OF CANISBAY.

In the memoir of Dr. Morrison (p. 235), the author of some of our best paraphrases, it is regretted that no memorial stone " indicates the spot where reposes the dust of one of the best poets of the Church of Scotland." A monument to his memory has now been erected in the churchyard of Canisbay, and bears the following inscription :—

TO

THE MEMORY OF

THE REV. JOHN MORRISON, D.D.,

MINISTER OF CANISBAY

FOR EIGHTEEN YEARS.

Died 12th June, 1796,
Aged 49 Years.

Joint Author with Dr. Logan
Of the 27th and 28th Metrical Paraphrases,
And sole Author of the
19th, 21st, 29th, 30th, and 35th.

Archdeacon Barbour, in his poem " The Life and Times of King Robert the Bruce," written about the close of the fourteenth century, when describing the action of Edward, King of England, after he had adjudged the Scottish crown to Baliol, to overawe the followers of Bruce, thus incidentally mentions Wick :—

When Sir Edward the King
Had thus done his liking
Of John the Baliol, that so soon
Was all defaulted and undone,
To Scotland went he then in by
And all the land did occupy
So haill, that both castle and town
Were into his possession
From Weik, anent the Orkney,
To Mulesnuke in Galloway
With Englishman.

AN OLD WICK CHARTER.

THE following is a copy of what is believed to be the oldest charter extant in the burgh of Wick.   The tenement referred to is that now known as the Temperance Hall Park :—

To all who shall see or hear this charter, we, Andrew, by the Divine mercy, Bishop of Caithness, in the Lord, greeting everlasting : Know ye that we, with the assent and consent of our chapter, have given, confirmed, assigned, and in feu farm disponed, and by this our present charter have confirmed, and also do give, grant, assign, and in feu farm dispone ; and by this our present charter confirm to our beloved and faithful Alexr. Byrsbane our tenement lying in the town of Wick, in Caithness, on the south side of the same between the lands of Gilbert —on the west side on the one part, and the lands of ———— Gardener on the south side, on the other part : To hold and to have all and whole the said tenement, according to its bounds, by the said Alexander, his heirs and assignees, of us and our successors, Bishops of Caithness, in feu farm and heritage for ever, according as it lies with all its right marches, present, old, and divided in length and breadth in earth, wood, stone, and lime ; also with all and sundry liberties, commodities, and easements, and its righteous pertinents whatsoever, as well not named as named, as well under the earth as above the earth, with the pertinents belonging to the said tenement, or that righteously shall be known to belong thereto in any manner of way in future, freely, equally, everywhere, honourably, well, and in peace, without any retainment or obstacle whatever ; moreover, as freely, ———— ———— fully, everywhere, and honourably as any tenement whatever within the kingdom of Scotland, in feu farm of any church, is given, granted, assigned, or possessed, with liberty of the church lands, and all necessary accompaniments, for the use of the said Alexr. Byrsbane and his heirs and assignees ————, with common pasturage for one horse and two cows, with free ingress and egress to the houses and pertinents as use is ; paying therefor annually the said Alex. Byrsbane and his heirs and assignees to us and our successors in (the said Bishopric of) Caithness two shillings of the usual money of Scotland annually, payable at two terms in the year, one at at Whitsunday and the other at Marts. by equal portions, and attending three suits and our three head courts at the foresaid town of Wick with all arms ; and that for all service and ———— custom and exaction or demand from the said tenement and pertinents that can be exacted or required ; and we, the said Bishop Andrew, bind ourselfs and our successors to warrant the said Alexr. Byrsbane and his heirs and assignees in every way and manner in all and whole the foresaid tenement, with the pertinents, as said is, against all mortals : In witness whereof our seal (the round one), and the seal of our chapter (a heart) are under affixed to this our present chapter at our (cathedral church) of Dornoch, the 14th day of the month of Feby., 1503.

ANDREAS EPUS. CATHANENSIS.

JOHN O'GROAT'S HOUSE.

THE silence of travellers before Morrison's time respecting the interesting tradition, first reported by him, of the octagonal house erected by John O'Groat is indeed very remarkable, and, on the supposition of its truth, very puzzling. Pennant's silence is mentioned in the text; but before his day, John O'Groat's House was visited by various other writers who have published accounts of their travels. The famous William Lithgow, who lived in Caithness part of the winter of 1628-9, crossed over to Orkney from Duncansbay in the spring, but in his "Travels through Europe, Asia, and Africa for Nineteen Years," he makes no manner of mention of John O'Groat or his house, though he describes with considerable detail the "nine contrarious tides" of the Pentland Firth, and dwells with great unction upon the jovial hospitality by which the Caithness people had made February to be "fruitful May" for him. Their country was more fertile than he expected; and as for themselves, they were "all of them the best and most bountiful Christmas keepers (the Greeks excepted) that ever I saw in the Christian world, whose continual incorporate feasting, one with another, beginning at St. Andrew's Day, never end till Shrovetide, which ravished me to behold such great and daily cheer, familiar fellowship, and jovial cheerfulness, that methought the whole winter time seemed to me but the jubilee of one day." He mentions the story about the barnacle geese of Orkney, which were alleged to grow from the fir trees in the spring, and expresses his disbelief in it; and it cannot but be considered at least singular that he abstains from the smallest reference to a tradition of scarcely less interest.

It is doubtful whether Richard Franc Re, Philanthropus (as he styled himself), was ever at John O'Groat's, though he would apparently have his readers believe so, and was certainly on the borders of Caithness. His "Northern Memoirs" were published in 1658, and after describing Caithness and Strathnaver generally as places where the people were "as barbarous as cannibals," because, when they killed a beast, they "boiled him in his hide (once the common practice in all Scotland, indeed), made a caldron of his skin, browis of his bowels, drink of his blood, and bread and meat of his carcase," he goes on to say, "More north, in an angle of Caithness, lives John a Groat, upon an isthmus of land that faceth the pleasant isles of Orkney," the isles, he proceeds, where grow the barnacle or wooden geese, in which he has a firm belief. Franc Re seems to be so fond of recounting any story likely to entertain, that he would be the last to omit the tradition of the octagon, had he heard of it.

The silence of the Rev. John Brand, Commissioner of the General Assembly, is more singular still, for he not only visited John O'Groat's, but he lived over night in the famous house itself in 1698, and he actually speaks of its celebrity, but only for being the northernmost house in Scotland. It was then an inn, and kept by a person of the name of John Grot; and the author went, as modern tourists still go, searching for groatie buckies on the seashore, and was struck to find, as he had been told by the innkeeper he should, that though they seemed so like, there was really not one of them but differed from the other. Yet while mentioning all this in a leisurely way, he has not a word about the octagonal building. The landing-place, he says, was called "John Grott's House, the northernmost house in Scotland; the man who now liveth in it and keepeth an inn there is called John Grot, who saith this house hath been in the possession of his predecessors of that name for some hundreds of years; which name of Grot is frequent in Caithness. Upon the sand by John Grot's house are found many small pleasant buckies and shells, beautified with diverse colours, which some use to put upon a string as beads, and account much of for their rarity. It is also observed of these shells that not one can be found altogether like another, and upon the review of the parcel I had I discovered some difference among them, which variety renders them the more beautiful."—Brand, in "Pinkerton's Voyages," iii. 801.

In 1769, a "Tour through Great Britain" was published, which was begun by Daniel Defoe, and continued by Richardson, the novelist, and various other hands. The writer who does Caithness for this work seems to have visited the district, and mentions that the people were "extremely well furnished with provisions," "very good bread, as well oat bread as wheat," venison in great plenty and at all seasons (for they were allowed to kill game without restraint) salmon in incredible abundance, no want of cows and sheep, and cheese of excellent taste made in Stroma; but he has only a passing reference to "the famous house called John O'Groat's." Whether the fame belonged to the shape and origin of the house or merely to its northernmost situation he does not say.

Mr Robert Mackay's suggestion of the derivation of the name of "Groat" from the coin the ferryman is supposed to have charged for passage-money is very wide of the mark. A groat would have been no remuneration even centuries ago for a passage of twelve miles over such stormy and difficult water. The actual fare, in the seventeenth century, at all events, was four pounds Scots, as we learn from a "Journal from Kirkwall to Edinburgh," printed along with the "Acts and Statutes of the Lawting, Sheriff, and Justice Courts of Orkney and Shetland, 1602-1644."

BOTANY (p. 3).—The following are some of the rarer species of phanerogams, which are characteristic of the *flora* of the county, and which have been discovered since this History was first written :—Nuphar pumila, Sm., Cochlearia alpina ; Viola Curtisii, Forster, var. Mackaii, Spergularia neglecta, Syme, Oxytropis Halleri, Bunge, Alchemilla alpina, L., Rosa mollissima, Willd., Callitriche autumnalis, L., Ligusticum scoticum, L., Hieracium iricum, Fries., H. crocatum and corymbosum ; Loiseleuria procumbens, Desv., Lamium intermedium, Fries, Ajuga pyramidalis, L., Mertensia maritima, Don, Oxyria reniformis, Hook., Salix pentandra, L., S. phylicifolia, "Linn;" S. ambigua, Ehrh., S. herbacea, L., Potamogeton praelongus, Wulf., P. filiformis, Nolte, Orchis incarnata, L., Scillaverna, Huds., Scirpus uniglumis, Link., Carex incurva, Lightf., Carex Watsoni. The following three species occur in Caithness, but in no other county in Britain :—Hierochloe borealis, R. and S., Carex salina, Wahl., var. Kattegatensis, Fries., and Calamagrostis strigosa, Hartm. Little, or nothing, has been done in the examination of the cryptogams of the county, except the ferns.

DISTINGUISHED VISITORS. — Their Highnesses the Prince and Princess of Wales, accompanied by Prince John of Glucksburg and the Duke and Duchess of Sutherland, visited the county in October, 1876. They received addresses of welcome at Wick and Thurso amidst great demonstrations of loyalty by the people. The autograph of the Princess in the visitors' book at John O'Groat Hotel commemorates the visit of royalty to that historic spot. In July, 1863, the Duke of Edinburgh arrived late one evening in Wick bay on board H.M.S. Racoon, of which he was an officer; and in January, 1882, he, as inspecting officer of the naval reserve forces, landed at Wick per H.M.S. Lively. The corporation presented him with a burgess ticket, and the same evening the town was illuminated in honour of the Sailor Prince.—General Grant and Mrs Grant, accompanied by General Badeau, visited Caithness in September, 1877. At Thurso the magistrates presented him with an address; at Wick he received the freedom of the burgh, and everywhere he was greeted with a demonstrative welcome. Caithness felt proud of him as a descendant of Scotch ancestors, and honoured him for his bravery on the battlefield in the cause of freedom, and for his abilities as a statesman, which were recognised by his countrymen twice electing him President of the great American nation, and the first President elected by a wholly free people.—In Sept. 1863, Elihu Burrit, the eminent American writer, and often referred to as the learned blacksmith, visited Wick on his walking tour from Land's End to John O'Groat's, and on his return lectured in the old Free Church here on "The Benevolent Associations of the Day; their Philosophy and Power." The late Rev. Charles Thomson presided, and in conveying a vote of thanks to the lecturer, which was seconded by the late Rev. Andrew Key, said he had never listened in Wick or anywhere else to a more eloquent address or one more characterised by noble Christian sentiment. The following are his own remarks taken from the Album kept at John O'Groat's Hotel :—" Elihu Burrit of New Britain, Connecticut, U.S. America, on a walk from Land's End to John O'Groat's, arrived at Huna Inn, upon Monday, September 28th, 1863. He visited the site of that famous domicile so celebrated in world-wide legend for its ingenious construction to promote domestic happiness, and fully realised all he had anticipated in standing on a spot so rich with historical associations and surrounded with such grand and beautiful scenery. He desired also to record his testimony to the hospitality and comfort of this cosy little sea-side inn, where he was pleasantly housed for the night, and of which he will ever cherish an interesting remembrance."— The Right Honourable John Bright spent a few days in Caithness in 1874. A movement for giving public expression to the general feelings of esteem and regard with which the great orator and politician is held in the north, was abandoned in deference to the state of his health.—The Right Hon. Robert Lowe, Chancellor of the Exchequer, now known under the title of Lord Sherbrook, was made a burgess of Wick in August, 1872.—Mr John Pender, who represented the Northern Burghs in Parliament from 1872 to 1885, is the youngest honorary burgess of Wick. This honour was conferred on him in August, 1884, in recognition of his services to the burgh, especially in connection with harbour affairs. Mr Pender holds a world-wide reputation as chairman of several cable companies which bind the nations of the world together by telegraphy. During his visit to Wick on that occasion he was accompanied by the Hon. A. S. Hewitt, a member of the United States Congress.—In the same year another American—Mr Henry George—a man of distinguished literary and oratorical abilities, and well known as the author of "Progress and Poverty," made a tour through the county, and delivered several lectures on social science. Curiously enough, two years afterwards Hewitt and George were two of three candidates for the mayoralty of New York, when the former was elected. —In September, 1885, Sir Thomas Brassey's yacht, the "Sunbeam," with the Right Hon. W. E. Gladstone, M.P., Mrs and Miss Gladstone, Sir Thomas and Lady Brassey, and Mr Arnold Morley, M.P., arrived off Wick Bay on their return cruise from Norway. A deputation from Wick proceeded out to the yacht, and bade the veteran politician and his friends welcome to the Caithness coast. Mr Gladstone did not come on shore, but Sir Thomas and Lady Brassey and Miss Gladstone visited the town for a few hours.

MEMBERS OF PARLIAMENT.—The following are the names of those who represented the county of Caithness and Wick Burghs in Parliament since 1796 :—*County.*—1796, Hon. Frederick Stuart ; 1805-11, Sir John Sinclair ; 1812, George Sinclair ; 1814-18, Sir John Marjoribanks ; 1819-20, George Sinclair ; 1823-25, Lord James Stuart ; 1826-30, Hon. J. Sinclair ; 1831, Right Hon. Sir William Rae, Bart. ; 1832-42, George Sinclair ; 1842-71, George Traill ; 1872-84, Sir J. G. T. Sinclair ; 1885-87, Dr. Clark. —*Burgh.*—1796, William Dundas ; 1805, Right Hon. J. C. Villiers ; 1806, James Macdonald ; 1808, Brigadier-General Mackenzie ; 1809-12, W. H. Freemantle ; 1814-18, Hugh Innes ; 1819-30, Sir Hugh Innes ; 1831-52, James Loch ; 1852-57, Samuel Laing ; 1858-59, Lord John Hay ; 1860, Samuel Laing ; 1861-64, Right Hon. Viscount Bury ; 1865-68, Samuel Laing ; 1868-71, George Loch ; 1872-85, John Pender ; 1885-87, J. Macdonald Cameron.

PROVOSTS OF WICK.—In 1790, Sir John Sinclair of Ulbster ; 1811, George Sinclair, yr. of Ulbster ; 1814, William Macleay ; 1818, George Sinclair, yr. of Ulbster ; 1820, George Macpherson Grant of Ballindalloch and Invershie, M.P. ; 1822, Right Hon. Lord Francis Leveson Gower, M.P. ; 1831, James Loch, M.P. ; 1833, John Kirk ; 1836, William Bruce ; 1838, Josiah Rhind ; 1839, William Bruce ; 1843, Josiah Rhind ; February, 1858, William Waters ; November, 1858, Alexander Bruce ; 1863, James Louttit ; 1870, Alexander Adam of Lynegar ; 1871, Alexander Corner ; 1874, William Rae ; 1886, James Reiach.

THE VOLUNTEERS.—The author notices (p. 45 and 211) the patriotism of Sir John Sinclair and Sir Benjamin Dunbar of Hempriggs in raising fencible regiments in past troublous times, and the loyalty shown in Caithness when the patriotic feeling which produced the present volunteer army first spread over the country. At the present time there are eight volunteer companies in Caithness—two in Wick, two in Thurso, and one each in Halkirk, Castletown, Watten, and Mey, four being artillery and four rifles. Each of them will average about 100 volunteers, and at the periodical inspections are always complimented for their efficiency. The Wick Artillery Company, or, as it was for long known, the 1st Caithness, was one of the earliest organised of the Caithness corps. Those who first joined were mostly all men in the prime of life, and showed their genuine enthusiasm in the movement by providing their own uniforms, which cost them several pounds. So eager were they also to perfect themselves in their duties that it was not uncommon to see them hard at drill on the Bleaching Green between six and seven o'clock in the morning. This company has always been characterised by much *esprit de corps*. On the occasion of the first grand Scottish Volunteer Review by the Queen at Edinburgh .in 1860, the 1st Caithness sent up a crack detachment. As they arrived by steamer some days before the review came off, and were also the last volunteers to leave, their marching to and from drill in the Queen's Park to their place of rendezvous in Edinburgh brought them special and favourable notice in the papers. At a volunteer entertainment in the Temperance Hall the Company was, in its early years, presented with a silver bugle, and on this occasion Lieutenant Maclean read a poem by the late Mr Grant, teacher, Canisbay, on the volunteer movement, in which the incident of the 1st Caithness detachment being the first to arrive to take part in the review and the last to depart, is thus referred to :—

> " And none would sooner stand to arms,
>   For glory all athirst,
> Nor meet their foes with stouter blows,
>   Than the gallant Caithness 1st.

> " The first and last upon the field
>   In Scotia's grand review,
> The first and last, in Britain's need,
>   They'd be to dare and do."

Besides the creditable land force of volunteers which the county possesses, it is the head-quarters of a splendid naval battery, its members being well drilled and of a fine *physique*. The total number of men enrolled for the year 1886-7 are—1st class, 53 ; 2nd class, 895 ; total, 948. There has been a large increase during the last four years. The men come from all parts of Scotland, and are generally employed in the fishing trade. There is a permanent gunner's mate attached to the battery, who holds the appointment for five years. During the drill season, which commences on 1st October and ends on 1st April, there are 8 instructors sent up from H.M.S. " Excellent " at Portsmouth, viz., 2 gunners' mates, and 6 seamen gunners. The present battery and drill shed, which stand at the south Head of Wick Bay, are not large enough for the number of men drilled, and require additions. The Hon. Walter Hylton-Jolliffe is the divisional officer in command.

INDUSTRIAL AND ART EXHIBITIONS.—Several of these exhibitions have been held in the county. It is now over forty years since the first one was held in Wick, which was chiefly due to the public spirit of the late Bailie Waters, and the profits of which were devoted to building part of the dyke enclosing the Bleaching Green. Four others have been held in Caithness. The first of these was an industrial one at Wick, to which Her Majesty sent a bust of the late Prince Consort executed by the Princess Royal. This exhibition was opened by Provost Louttit on 3rd March, 1868, in the Temperance Hall. There was a large number of articles of local manufacture, etc., shown, and medals were awarded to the best exhibits.   The next was also held at Wick, and was a Fine Art Exhibition.   Her Majesty was one of the patrons, which also included the county families and influential persons connected with the north.   It was opened by the Duke of Sutherland, who was accompanied by the Duchess, on 15th Oct., 1874.   This exhibition contained a large collection of splendid paintings in oil and water colours, oleographs, photographs, engravings, antiquities, curiosities, etc., many of the articles being of great value, and some of them coming from places as far away as America and New Zealand.   The next exhibition was an industrial one held at Thurso in October, 1876.   From the fact of the Thurso one having been opened by the Prince of Wales, accompanied by the Princess and a numerous suite, it created special interest.   Thousands of persons from all parts of the county gathered in Thurso on the occasion, which, in honour of the Royal visit, was gorgeously decorated and in the evening brilliantly illuminated.   The Thurso Exhibition also contained a large and choice display of industrial and fine art objects, and awards were given to exhibitors.   The last exhibition was an industrial one in connection with the Wick Band of Hope, which was got up to develop a taste among juveniles for making useful and ornamental articles, and was very successful.   It had for patron the Duchess of Westminster, was heartily encouraged by Sir Tollemache Sinclair, and opened by Sheriff Spittal in May, 1883.   These exhibitions have no doubt helped to forward the laudable object their promoters had in view—the cultivation of a more general taste for the industrial and fine arts in the county of Caithness.   In inaugurating and carrying through the exhibitions held in Wick no small credit is due to the committee of the Wick and Pulteneytown Total Abstinence Society, a body which has often shown itself willing to further objects for the benefit of the community.

CAITHNESS ASSOCIATIONS.--The noble examples of the patriotism of Caithnessmen in forming themselves into associations in the large towns of the south is referred to at p. 44.   It may here be remarked that these associations continue to prosper, and have proved specially useful in affording assistance to fellow-countrymen in misfortune.   Their annual social meetings have been invariably successful, and testify to their native clannishness and love of the mother county.   The Glasgow Association, which is the oldest one of them, having been founded in 1836, held its jubilee last year in a grand gathering in the largest hall in the city, when upwards of 1800 people were present, including the three surviving original members.

THE ORNITHOLOGY OF CAITHNESS (p. 31).—The catalogue of birds found in Caithness is surpassed by but few counties within the three kingdoms.   Previous to 1840, the late Dr Sinclair of Wick had collected and prepared with his own hands 191.   This list has been added to and the ornithology of the county advanced by the observations on the subject published in the local and other papers by the late Mr Robert Innes Shearer, Thrumster, and the late Mr Henry Osborne, Wick.   A list of birds found in Caithness, published by Mr Shearer in 1860, numbered 203.

CAITHNESS IN 1887.

Since the second edition of this work was prepared for the press by its author, who died in 1864, many social and material changes have taken place in the county. During this period telegraph and railway communication have been extended to Caithness; a large expenditure of money has been made in attempted harbour extension; Wick and Thurso have been much extended by new buildings; and improvement has also taken place in the houses of our smaller farmers and cottars. Some of the following brief details bring down to date subjects referred to in the body of the work :—

The Telegraph.—This very important benefit to trade was extended to Caithness in September, 1868, after security had been given by a number of local business men guaranteeing the Telegraph Company from loss; but the experience of a few months showed the business at the Wick office to be so large that the Company soon gave up the security. Since the telegraph came under the management of the Government in 1870, and the rate of messages was reduced, the business at the Wick and other offices in Caithness has largely increased, that done at the Wick office being equalled by few towns of the same size. In securing these important advantages to the north, and especially in urging on harbour improvement, no small credit is accorded to the late Mr John Mackie, editor of the *Northern Ensign*.

The Railway.—The extension of the railway to Caithness in 1874, connecting Wick, Thurso, and the county generally with the southern markets, was a much-needed boon, and gave additional impetus to trade in the north. A fortnight previous to the line being opened for public traffic, the Duke of Sutherland, accompanied by a few friends, gave the first practical announcement that through communication was effected, by travelling in a saloon carriage, drawn by his beautiful little engine, the "Dunrobin," from Dunrobin to Wick and Thurso. The visit was unexpected, and the authorities in these towns, though they had no time to organise a public demonstration adequate to the occasion, met the ducal party at the respective stations, and expressed the congratulations of their fellow-citizens. The staple trade of fishing, however, has not received that benefit from railway extension which was expected from it, arising from the high rates charged for carrying fresh fish to the English markets. It is earnestly to be hoped, in the interests of the fishing industry of the north and the population of the large towns, that railway directors will soon adopt a more reasonable tariff. The Wick station, which is of considerable extent, has several sidings for loading long lines of fish trucks.

Harbour Extension.—It has long been realised by those connected with our fishing interest that if Wick was to hold its position as a leading fishing station, harbour extension was an absolute necessity. The directors of the British Fisheries Society, as trustees of the harbour, attempted to provide this on a large and liberal scale, but, unfortunately, their efforts only resulted in failure. In 1857, they applied for an Act to construct a harbour to cost about £45,000. To this the Admiralty refused its consent, on the ground that while it might meet local requirements, it would not provide a refuge for the passing trade, or a place for coaling war ships. They proposed an alternative scheme, but although the scheme was approved of by a committee of the House of Commons in 1857, and a Royal Commission in 1859, and was also approved of by Sir John Coode, who estimated its cost at £250,000, it was not carried out. In 1862, a modified harbour, of which Messrs D. & T. Stevenson, Edinburgh, were the engineers, was adopted. In October, 1863, the foundation-stone of this ill-starred work was laid with much rejoicing. The building, superintended by its energetic contractors, Messrs A. & K. Macdonald of Lynedale, made satisfactory progress for a couple of years, when a storm occurred which threw down a part of the work. The breach was made good, and the pier again extended. Successive years, however, brought similar calamities, until 1873, when the fabric was damaged to such an extent that the work was abandoned. Upwards of £132,000 was spent on this undertaking, which with interest amounted to over £150,000. Of this sum, £41,000 was paid out of harbour dues, £54,000 by the British Fisheries Society, and the balance, given on loan by the Government, is still unpaid.—*Lybster Harbour.*—The sum of £16,000 was expended, in 1883, by the Duke of Portland, in improvements on this harbour, from a plan by R. E. Cooper, C.E.

THE HARBOUR TRUST.—In 1879 an Act was passed by which the British Fisheries Society ceased to be trustees, and the management of the harbour was handed over to a local trust of nineteen members. A Provisional Order, passed in 1883, authorised the extension of the south pier of Pulteney harbour, the re-facing the existing harbours with concrete walls, a bridge for traffic across the river of Wick, etc. To carry out these improvements on a plan proposed by Mr James Barron, C.E., a loan of £50,000 was granted by Government, and this sum will be supplemented by the harbour revenue. The south pier has been extended a hundred and thirty-two feet, and the inside wall of this pier has been re-faced and the quay widened. The deepening of the harbour basin is now being proceeded with, and promises to be a most valuable aid to the prosecution of our fishing industry.

BURGH EXTENSION.—A partial extension of Wick burgh took place in 1883, when the royalty was extended to include Louisburgh and Boathaven on to the limits of the parliamentary burgh, and on the south side of the river to include Bankhead, Janetstown, and East and West Banks.

WATER SUPPLY.—The introduction of an abundant supply of excellent water, in the year 1882, was the greatest improvement which has taken place in the royalty of Wick. It was taken through iron pipes from the loch of Yarrows, eight miles inland, and is filtered through a reservoir at Toftcarle, on its way to the town.

HERRING FISHING.—During the last twenty years a marked change has taken place in the manner of prosecuting the herring fishing. In 1862 over 1100 boats fished at Wick, and though the numbers have almost yearly decreased till they are now only about one-half, yet the total catch of fish for the season remains about the same. This is accounted for by the progressive improvements in the size and seaworthiness of the boats which have been built of late years. About twenty-five years ago their sizes ranged from twenty-eight to thirty-six feet of keel. There are few now even of the latter size. Those now used will vary from forty to about sixty feet, are full-decked, well found, and carry double the length of netting, and of course are more than double the tonnage. About the time the number of boats was highest one could be built under £100. One of the largest boats will now cost about £300, and the value of the drift of nets carried has risen in an equal degree. The class of boats built by the Caithness boatbuilders are not excelled for speed, gracefulness of model, and general fitness for fishing purposes. Crews now go much further to sea to fish, and in summer often remain out for days until success is met with. Of late years a winter herring and cod fishing has been gradually rising in importance, and only needs remunerative markets to rival in extent our summer fishing. A large number of Caithness boats go to the important West Highland fishing in summer, and a few to the Yarmouth winter fishing. While the bulk of the summer catch at Wick continues to be cured for export to the Baltic ports, a large proportion of the herrings caught in winter is sent in a fresh state or kippered to the English markets. There are now about twenty kippering places here. Another change which has been introduced in the trade of late years is the manner of selling the fish. The herrings, cod, and other fish, caught at the winter fishing are mostly sold by auction, but this arrangement has only been adopted as yet to a very limited extent at the summer fishing.

MANUFACTURES.—Barrel making, a necessary adjunct to the staple industry of the town, gives employment to a greater number of tradesmen than that of any other class of skilled labour. Boat building is another important but variable local trade. After a profitable fishing season, when from thirty to fifty boats will be built, carpenters, ropemakers, and blacksmiths are kept busily employed. This trade is at present very dull. At one time when herring nets were made from hemp twine, nearly all the nets were manufactured by hand in the locality. On the introduction of cotton, which is now universally used in netting, machinery superseded hand power. There are three net factories in town, but the greater part of the nets used is imported. The cabinet works and wood yard of A. M'Ewen & Sons are very extensive, and employ a greater number of skilled artizans than any works of a similar kind north of Dundee. The Distillery and Meal Mills of James Henderson & Co. are not less important. The inland and export trade of this firm, in their celebrated "Pulteney Whisky," had increased to such an extent that in 1885 they were obliged to make considerable additions to their building, accommodation, and plant. In Halkirk, too, the manufacture of whisky is again to be tried. Although the old Gerston distillery as a going concern has been dead for a number of years, the reputation it had for the superior quality of its whisky still lives ; and a new distillery, of large proportions, has been erected near the site of the former by a London company. Cloth manufacture, on a comparatively large scale, is successfully carried on in the building known as the Flax Mill, Pulteneytown, and at the Wool Mills, Stirkoke. The quarrying, manufacture, and export of pavement, although characterised by dulness of late years, is still a very important business in Thurso, Castletown, and other places in the west end of the county.

LOCAL TAXATION.—With the privileges of modern civilisation come taxes, and these now amount to a goodly array. The following show the rates at present (1886-87) assessed on tenants in the burgh of Wick, as also that of Pulteneytown and Thurso :—

By the Parochial Board—

Poor Assessment, . . . per £,	1s	0d
Registration of Births, &c., Act, ,,	0s	0¼d
Registration of Voters Act, . ,,	0s	0½d
Public Health Act, . . . ,,	0s	0½d
Burial Grounds Act, . . ,,	0s	0¾d
Education Act, . . . ,,	0s	9d
		———— 1s 11d

By Town Council as Police Commissioners—

Water Rate, ... per £,	1s	6d
Police Rate, ... ,,	1s	6d
		———— 3s 0d

By Town Council as Road Trustees—

For Roads, &c., . . . per £,	0s	1d
		———— 5s 0d

Tenants in Pulteneytown—

Parochial and Road Assessments, as above, ... per £,	2s	0d
Police, &c., ... ,,	1s	3d
Public Health, ... ,,	0s	1d
		———— 3s 4d

Thurso Assessments.—

By the Parochial Board—

Poor Assessments, . . . per £,	0s	8d
Education Act, . . . ,,	0s	3d
Burial Ground, . . . ,,	0s	0½d
		————0s 11½d

By Commissioners of Police—

Water Rate, ... per £,	1s	5d
Cleansing, Lighting, Improving, ,,	1s	1d
Public Library, . . . ,,	0s	1d
		———— 2s 7d

By Commissioners of Supply—

Police, ... per £,	0s	3¼d
General, ... ,,	0s	1d
		———— 0s 4¼d

By Road Trustees—

For Roads, ... per £,	0s	3d
		———— 4s 1¾d

With the exception of water and police rates, which are only payable by occupiers, proprietors pay assessments on their rentals at the same rates as those stated above.

NEW BUILDINGS.—During the last quarter of a century many new buildings have been erected in the county, more especially in Wick and Thurso. One of the most substantial and useful is the new bridge of Wick. Built on the site of the old one, it spans the river to the breadth of 220 feet, is 40 feet wide, and has three arches, the centre arch having a span of 60 feet, and its roadway is level. It was erected at a cost of £4000. On the centre of the bridge is an iron plate with the following inscription :—"This bridge, opened on the 6th July, 1877, was, when in course of construction, crossed by their Royal Highnesses the Prince and Princess of Wales, Prince John of Glucks-burg, the Duke and Duchess of Sutherland, and a distinguished party, on the occasion of a visit by their Royal Highnesses to Wick on 6th Oct., 1876. W. Rae, Provost; Charles Bruce, James Reiach, and Alex. Malcolm, Bailies; George Simpson, Dean of Guild; Thomas Adam, Treasurer; William Miller, Town Clerk; Daniel Miller, Con-tractor; Murdoch Paterson, Inverness, Engineer." During the con-struction of this building, a wooden service bridge with stone pillars was erected nearer the mouth of the river, connecting Williamson Street, Pulteneytown, with the burgh wharf, and has been found a great convenience. Whole streets of new houses have been erected in Pulteneytown, and numerous villas of substantial size, ornamental and varied in style, have been planted on the outskirts of the town on both sides of the river. The Wick Free Church, completed in 1864, is an ornament to Bridge Street, while its handsome spire can be seen from a considerable distance outside of the town. The Congregational Church, opened for worship in 1884, in High Street, though less in size, is equally elegant in style. The United Presbyterian Church, in Francis Street, a splendid building of imposing appearance, was built in 1882. It and the neat little Episcopal Church in Moray Street, consecrated in 1870, adorn the west end of Pulteneytown. The Baptist Church, in Union Street, is a small but compact building. Union Street has now been built up to the bridge, the large new build-ings nearest it being called Ebenezer Place, and principally occupied as shops, offices, and as a temperance hotel. A little down the same street are the handsome houses built by Bailie Dunnet, and in which are the large and well-fitted up Telegraph Office, Reading-room, etc. The Court-house, with offices for the law officers of the crown, built in 1866, and the New Hotel buildings, add dignity to Bridge Street. Further north in the same street is the Town and County Bank, a magnificent building of much architectural beauty; and immediately opposite is the fine new building erected by the late Mr D. Gunn, and in which is the Post-Office. The North of Scotland Bank, in High Street, at present in course of being finished, is a splendid building in the Grecian style, is unique as a building in Caithness, its massive front being built of Aberdeen granite. The south end and east side of the well-known park at the back of the Temperance Hall has been all built with large and fine-looking houses and shops. The fine block auction-room and cattle sale-ring, erected off Bridge Street by Mr Sinclair, is a commodious, extensive and well-designed erection, and supplies a much needed want. Buildings are also in course of erection in Sinclair Terrace, Smith Terrace, West Park, and other places in town. It is very satisfactory to have to record, too, that on many estates in the county the houses of the small farmers and crofters have of late years undergone great improvement.

BEQUESTS.—Mr John Kirk, merchant, Wick, who died in March, 1863, provided that £10 per annum shall be divided among the various schemes of the Free Church, £2 10s. to the Free Church teacher of Wick, and a small donation to the Royal Infirmary, Edinburgh. He also provided that on the Friday before New Year's-day, the Free Church minister of Wick shall give away, among eighty deserving individuals, as many half-crowns, and the Free Church minister of Bower twenty half-crowns among as many of a like character, the same to be known as "John Kirk's New Year's Gift." The interest of a sum of about £9000 was to be applied as follows:—One half for the benefit of decayed labourers and aged females in Wick who had seen better days and are not in receipt of parochial relief; the other half to be devoted to educational purposes in Wick and Bower, and to the parish of Canisbay also, should the amount exceed a certain stipulated sum. The trustees are the Sheriff-Substitute of Caithness, the Provost and Bailies of Wick, etc.—Mr Henry Rhind, whose father, Mr Josiah Rhind, had been for some years Provost of Wick, bequeathed the sum of £7000 to found an institution for training orphan girls in all the branches of domestic service. A building, with grounds enclosed, at East Banks, acquired by the trustees, has been enlarged, and made suitable for the purpose.— A number of years ago, Mrs Malcolm, Pulteneytown, left £200 for the education of children in that place. Mr Rhind, banker, first admini- stered the fund, and his son left it in charge of the Town Council, by whom its mangement has been given to the Burgh School Board.— Bailie Wares, who for many years acted as agent for the Wick branch of the Union Bank, and died in April, 1886, left a bequest of £7800, the interest of the money to be divided amongst the necessitous poor of the burgh, and the Magistrates of Wick to be trustees.

THE NEW CEMETERY.—Owing to the crowded and ill-kept condition of the Old Churchyard, a desire had grown up in the public mind some years ago that a new place of interment should be provided. The movement met with some opposition for a time; but the Parochial Board considered it their duty to provide a new cemetery, and secured 6½ acres of ground for the purpose in what is known as Harrow Park in the outskirts of Pulteney. It was enclosed, drained, and laid out from the plans of Mr M'Kelvie, Dundee, and has now a fine appear- ance. Besides a carriage drive all round, there are walks intersecting the borders and plots, and young trees have been planted along the walls. The cemetery was opened in June, 1872, and there have now been erected in it a number of beautiful monumental stones. A pleas- ing feature, too, in connection with it is the taste which has been shown in keeping the grave plots well-trimmed and planted with flowers. The cemetery cost £3000, of which sum £2500 was got on loan from Government, repayable in twenty years, at five per cent. of interest.

THURSO.—This town, the principal centre of export for the cele- brated Caithness pavement, has made great progress in house-building and other improvements during the last quarter of a century. Its population in 1881 was 4026. The Town Hall, an elegant Gothic structure, built in 1870 at a cost of £2500, contains a large hall, a courtroom, a public library, and a museum. An excellent supply of good water has been brought into the town, through iron pipes, from the Loch of Calder. An esplanade, 300 yards long, built in 1882, greatly improved the town, and may be said to be a monument to the public spirit and patriotism of the ladies of Thurso. A finely gravelled walk, eight feet wide, with neatly coped fence and turf border, has now been formed from the west end of Esplanade along the cliffs to the Bishop's Palace, where it joins the county road to Scrabster, a distance of fully 1¼ mile. This footway is undoubtedly one of the finest promenades in the north of Scotland, commanding, as it does, a magnificent view of sea and rock scenery. The footway has been tastefully carried out, following the natural curves around the various promontories, and will, doubtless, form an additional attraction to visitors, and a source of enjoyment to the inhabitants. A small public garden in the centre of the town, presented to Thurso in 1876 by Sir Tollemache Sinclair, has been enclosed with an ornamental railing, and the ground artistically laid out at an expense of £213. The West Free Church built in 1860 is a handsome building, and its spire is the highest in the county. The neat Congregational Church was erected in 1876 at a cost of £1100. The Artillery and Rifle Volunteer halls are spacious and ornamental buildings. The Dunbar Hospital, palatial in size and beauty, was built from funds left for the purpose by Mr Alexander Dunbar, Scrabster, who died in 1859. The foundation stone of this imposing institution was laid by the Duke of Edinburgh in 1882. Whole blocks of houses have been erected on both sides of Traill Street, and a number of stylish villas adorn the west end of the town. A substantial new bridge of three arches, now nearly completed at a cost of £4000, spans the river on the site of the old bridge. A lofty monument in the new and well-laid-out cemetery commemorates Robert Dick, the scientific baker, who was eminent as a botanist and geologist, and whose memory has been immortalized by Dr Smiles' "Life of Robert Dick." Thurso has one newspaper—the *Caithness Courier*—which was established in 1866. From its picturesque situation, beauty, and cleanliness, its splendid beach and bathing facilities, Thurso has become a popular resort for tourists.— A public hall and reading-room, a munificent gift from the late Miss Margaret Traill to the people of Olrig, was opened with appropriate ceremony on New Year's-day, 1867, in the village of Castletown. The length of the building is 80 feet, the breadth 28, and it has a beautiful and large oriel window. The building is a boon and ornament to the locality.

EDUCATION.—The education of the county received a great impetus by the passing of the Education (Scotland) Act of 1872, which authorised the formation of school boards for every parish and district, and made education compulsory. In Caithness, Government loans for building purposes were largely taken advantage of, so that existing school-houses were enlarged and new schools erected in the towns and outlying districts suitable for the requirements and convenience of the population. The school boards of Caithness have been careful in the selection of teachers holding Government certificates, and who are otherwise capable and efficient, and pay them fair salaries. Fees for the standards have been made very reasonable, and where the compulsory clause has been firmly put in practice, school attendances have greatly improved. It is something to be proud of and thankful for to know there are now no children growing up altogether uneducated, and this happy change will doubtless bear good fruit in due season.

LIFE SAVING APPLIANCES.—Caithness is often visited with violent easterly gales, on which occasions shipwrecks are but too common on its coasts. Under these circumstances it is satisfactory to know that at various places along its shores there are now means of rendering aid to shipwrecked crews. The Wick Harbours Trust keeps up an efficient lifeboat, and within the last twelve months this boat has rescued the crews of two vessels wrecked in Wick bay. There is also a Board of Trade rocket apparatus at the same place, with a well-drilled staff, which has shown great promptness and efficiency on several occasions. The National Lifeboat Institution a few years ago placed a lifeboat at Sinclair's Bay, which lies a little to the north of Wick bay, a place where one was much needed. The fishing and seafaring communities of the district were deeply grateful to this noble institution for making Sinclair's Bay one of its stations. This is almost the only place on the east coast of Caithness to which boats can run, when overtaken with a south-east gale, with any hope of riding it out ; and a fishing season seldom passes without many of them being forced to run to it for shelter. It is also often the scene of shipwrecks. The placing of a lifeboat at this place was hastened by the sad loss of life attending the wreck of the German schooner "Emilie," of Wolgast, on 23rd December, 1876, when several persons were drowned in attempting to rescue the crew. No lifeboat being nearer than Wick, nine brave fellows manned a salmon coble and pulled out through a heavy surf to the wreck, which they reached safely. Taking on board three of the crew, they made for the shore, but the coble swamped when within twenty yards of it, and four of the rescue crew and three of the crew of the "Emilie" were drowned almost within the reach of hundreds of spectators. After the lifeboat for this station had reached Wick by rail, the occasion of taking it out to its scene of action was held as a holiday, and a trade's procession, with banners, accompanied the boat to the sands of Reiss, where, after prayer by the Rev. Mr Clark, it was launched. This boat has several times given aid in cases of distress. There are also National Lifeboat Stations at Scrabster Roads and Mey. The Scrabster Roads' boat has often rendered important aid to vessels. There is, too, a Board of Trade rocket station at Scrabster and another at Scarf-skerry.

SOCIAL INFLUENCES.—Of late years various organisations have come into existence in the towns, villages, and landward districts of the county having for their object the material, social, and religious benefit of the community. The names of a few of the more important of these may be here given, and their objects very briefly noticed :—
Farm Servants' Benefit Societies.—The aim of these societies, which have been formed in several parishes, is to raise by all proper means the social condition of farm workers as a class, and by means of a periodical payment by members to provide a little means for sickness, want of work, and old age.—*The Fishermen's Association.*—This association looks after and discusses, with much intelligence and practical wisdom, matters bearing upon the fishing interest, and promises to be useful to themselves as well as to the public generally.—*The Workmen's Union.*—This body, which has been organised in Wick for

the commendable purpose, among others, of providing a reading-room and library for its members, has shown during its short existence sympathy with local and national movements for the public good.— *Co-Operative Stores.*—These have been successfully conducted for years in the east and west ends of the county ; and the most creditable management of them by working men have been productive of good to the members and the community.—*Templar Lodges.*—The main objects of these are to secure personal abstinence, cultivate brotherly feeling among members, and further temperance principles in the public mind.—*Salvation Army.*—This well-known organisation has for some time had Caithness within its sphere of action, and meetings are held in Wick and Thurso daily. While opinion differs as to the appropriateness of some of its forms of religious service, its well-attended meetings testify to the large public sympathy with the objects of the army.—*Band of Hope and Boys' Brigade.*—These are most promising juvenile societies for the spread of temperance principles, and, generally, for cultivating the habit of "learning to do well."—*Public Cafés.*—Places where strangers and others may be supplied promptly with well-cooked and cheap food and non-intoxicating refreshments, have been introduced of late. In connection with them there are also reading-rooms and places for recreation. They have been well patronised in Thurso and Wick since their introduction.

AREA, POPULATION, AND RENTAL OF CAITHNESS.—*Bower*—Water, 231 acres ; land, 19,908 do.; population in 1881, 1608 ; rental in 1887, £9750 3s.—*Canisbay*—Water, 101 acres ; foreshore, 605 do.; tidal water, 8 do.; land, 26,958 do.; population, 2626 ; rental, £5712 5s.—*Dunnet*—Water, 519 acres ; foreshore, 388 do. ; tidal water, 6 do. ; land, 17,758 do.; population, 1607 ; rental, £6380 18s.—*Halkirk*—Water, 2300 acres ; land, 98,063 do. ; population, 2705 ; rental, £18,998 15s.—*Latheron*—Water, 618 acres ; foreshore, 207 do.; tidal water, 2 do.: land, 120,367 do. ; population, 6675 ; rental, £19,845 16s.—*Olrig*—Water, 25 acres ; foreshore, 289 do. ; tidal water, 7 do. ; land, 10,336 do. ; population, 2002 ; rental, £8887 15s.—*Reay* (Caithness part of)—Water, 1086 acres ; foreshore, 327 do.; tidal water, 8 do.; land, 46,326 do.; population, 1197 ; rental, £8738 16s.—*Thurso*—Detached, 6860 acres ; water, 368 do. ; foreshore, 329 do. ; tidal water, 20 do. ; land, 28,767 do. ; population, 6217 ; rental (including burgh), £26,057 14s.—*Watten*—Water, 1172 acres; land, 31,751 do.; population, 1406 ; rental, £9025 19s.—*Wick*—Water, 715 acres ; foreshore, 570 do. ; tidal water, 78 do. ; land, 48,627 do.; population, 12,822 ; rental (including burgh), £51,796 10s.—*Summary*—Land, 438,877 acres ; water, 7139 do. ; foreshore, 2717 do. ; tidal water, 131 do.—total, 448,866 acres ; total population, 38,865 ; total rental (including Wick burgh), £166,194 11s.

AGRICULTURE.—Caithness, notwithstanding climatic disadvantages, has been keeping abreast of the times as an agricultural county. That this is so is due scarcely less to the scientific than to the practical knowledge of its farmers, added to their native shrewdness. They are quick to perceive and avail themselves of the advantages of the most improved agricultural implements ; and it is the exception now to find a farm of any size without its reaping machine, threshing mill, and other labour-saving machines. Great attention is paid to the breed and rearing of stock ; and Caithness beef, mutton, and wool fetches high prices in the southern and local markets. Indications, however, are not wanting to show that the agricultural distress so prevalent over the country is also being felt in Caithness, and tenants entering on farms of late have done so in many cases at a considerable reduction of rent. This is shown also by the reduced rental of Caithness for 1886–87, which was £139,418, exclusive of Wick, that of the latter being £26,775. In the previous year the county had reached its maximum rental of £141,557. In 1855 it was £93,907 ; in 1861, £113,845 ; in 1867, £125,127 ; in 1872, £136,885. The numerous crofters of the county are anxiously looking forward to the visit of the Crofter Commission, which will shortly take place. Over five hundred applications have been lodged for fair rent, etc.

CAITHNESS FIARS' PRICES.

		1865.	1875.	1885.
Oats,	per qr.,	£1 2 6	... £1 3 5	... £0 17 11
Bere,	,, qr.,	1 5 10½	... 1 7 7¾	... 1 0 8½
Barley,	,, qr.,	1 7 1	... 1 8 6¼	... 1 1 3½
Oatmeal,	,, boll,	0 17 2¼	... 0 18 8¼	... 0 14 11¼

ROADS. — The roads of Caithness, which are not excelled by those of any other county in Scotland, intersect the county, exclusive of private roads, to a length of 287¾ miles. Tolls were abolished in 1874, and the roads are maintained by an assessment which, for the current year, amounts to 9d. per pound. The amount expended for the year 1885-6 in ordinary repairs, extra work, and improvement, was £4085 16s. 9d., and this sum is an average annual expenditure. The roads within the burgh of Wick are under the management of the Town Council. The average annual expenditure is about £150. A few years ago the Council had a surplus from the assessments that enabled them to forego imposing the assessment for a year. The present assessment is 2d. per £, one-half of which is payable by the tenant.

THE END.